# The Mutual Housing Experiment

In the series ***Urban Life, Landscape, and Policy***,
edited by Zane L. Miller, David Stradling, and Larry Bennett

Also in this series:

Kathryn Wilson, *Ethnic Renewal in Philadelphia's Chinatown: Space, Place, and Struggle*

Robert B. Fairbanks, *The War on Slums in the Southwest: Public Housing and Slum Clearance in Texas, Arizona, and New Mexico, 1936–1965*

Carlton Wade Basmajian, *Atlanta Unbound: Enabling Sprawl through Policy and Planning*

Scott Larson, *"Building Like Moses with Jacobs in Mind": Contemporary Planning in New York City*

Gary Rivlin, *Fire on the Prairie: Harold Washington, Chicago Politics, and the Roots of the Obama Presidency*

William Issel, *Church and State in the City: Catholics and Politics in Twentieth-Century San Francisco*

Julia L. Foulkes, *To the City: Urban Photographs of the New Deal*

William Issel, *For Both Cross and Flag: Catholic Action, Anti-Catholicism, and National Security Politics in World War II San Francisco*

Lisa Hoffman, *Patriotic Professionalism in Urban China: Fostering Talent*

John D. Fairfield, *The Public and Its Possibilities: Triumphs and Tragedies in the American City*

Andrew Hurley, *Beyond Preservation: Using Public History to Revitalize Inner Cities*

KRISTIN M. SZYLVIAN

# The Mutual Housing Experiment

*New Deal Communities for the Urban Middle Class*

TEMPLE UNIVERSITY PRESS
*Philadelphia • Rome • Tokyo*

TEMPLE UNIVERSITY PRESS
Philadelphia, Pennsylvania 19122
*www.temple.edu/tempress*


Cloth edition published 2015
Paperback edition published 2016

Library of Congress Cataloging-in-Publication Data
Szylvian, Kristin M.
The mutual housing experiment : New Deal communities for the urban middle class / Kristin M. Szylvian.
pages cm. — (Urban life, landscape, and policy)
Includes bibliographical references and index.
ISBN 978-1-4399-1205-8 (hardback) — ISBN 978-1-4399-1207-2 (e-book)
1. Housing, Cooperative—United States—History—20th century. 2. Housing policy—United States—History—20th century. 3. Urban policy—United States—History—20th century. 4. Community development—United States—History—20th century. I. Title.
HD7287.72.U6S99 2015
334′.1097309043—dc23

2014047599

ISBN 978-1-4399-1206-5 (paper : alk. paper)

Printed in the United States of America

082916P

# Contents

# Acknowledgments

My work on mutual and cooperative housing began in the 1980s, when I was in graduate school at Carnegie Mellon University and was fortunate to have the late Eugene Levy as my dissertation director. It is my hope that the remaining members of my committee, Lizabeth Cohen (now at Harvard University) and Joe William Trotter, will find this study barely recognizable as the original study I completed in late 1988. During those days, archivist Aloha P. South at the National Archives guided me in the use of the record groups containing items pertaining to the construction and sale of defense public housing.

Work on this book has extended across time and place. I am grateful to the University of North Carolina at Wilmington's College of Arts and Sciences for a 1990 Summer Stipend and to my former colleagues, Kathleen C. Berkeley, the late Andrew F. Clark, Bruce Kinzer (now at Kenyon College), and Susan P. McCaffray, for their encouragement and assistance. I kept the Randall Library Inter-Library Loan librarians busy, and they were always cheerful in filling my many requests. Student Thomas L. Schumacher provided valuable research assistance and support. At Western Michigan University where I taught from 1996 to 2010, James M. Ferreira, Cheryl Lyon-Jenness, Jose A. Brandao, James Palmitessa, Robert Berkhofer, the late Nora Faires, and the late Catherine Julien, were among the colleagues who offered assistance and encouragement. A small stipend was awarded by the Burnham-MacMillan Fund for research in Washington, D.C. April D. Bryan, Joshua Cochran, Ashley Emerson, Matthew A. Schuld, and LaDale C. Winling, all students, provided valuable research help. Jason Glatz of the Map Library staff produced a map for the book. Since coming to St. John's University in January 2011, Fran Balla in the Department of History has been of assistance to me many times. I appreciate the research assistance of graduate students Elizabeth Bencke and Lisa Borten.

Over the years I have received grants for travel to collections and other small stipends from the President Harry Truman Library Foundation, the North Caroliniana Society, the New Jersey Historical Commission, and the National Endowment for the Humanities. Ellen Kuniyuki Brown, archivist at the Texas Historical Collection at Carroll Library at Baylor University, and Thomas Charlton, the collection's director (now at Texas Christian University), patiently assisted me with Lawrence Westbrook's papers. Assistance with the papers of Richard and Dione Neutra was provided by Simon Elliot of the Special Collections Library at the University of California at Los Angeles. Elizabeth Clemens from the Walter P. Reuther Library and Archives at Wayne State University also offered kind assistance.

Colleagues from the Urban History Association, the Society for American City and Regional Planning History, and the Vernacular Architecture Forum offered critiques and suggestions that helped me improve my work. At a key turning point in the preparation of this manuscript, Alexander von Hoffman provided a careful and thorough reading, and I greatly benefited from his numerous ideas for revision. I am grateful to Roger Biles, John F. Bauman, Howard Gillette Jr., Robert Fairbanks, and Gail Radford for commenting on earlier drafts of this work. Arnold Alanen, Robert Fishman, David Goldfield, Brad Hunt, Roger Lotchin, Edward "Ted" Muller, Janet Ore, Mark Rose, Joel A. Tarr, and the late Raymond Mohl unselfishly shared their advice and expertise over the years. Robert J. Robertson cheerfully helped me find research resources pertaining to the Roosevelt years in Texas.

Years ago Gail Radford suggested that I share my work with Zane Miller of the University of Cincinnati, whose Urban History series was at one time sponsored by Ohio State University Press. I am so glad I took her advice. Zane not only spent countless hours editing my manuscript but also taught me how to be a better writer and historian. I also wish to thank Temple University Press *Urban Life, Landscape, and Policy* series co-editors David Stradling and Larry Bennett, staff members Aaron M. Javsicas, Micah Kleit, Sara Jo Cohen, and Gary Kramer, and the manuscript referees, including Andrew Hurley (who identified himself). In the end, however, responsibility for errors and oversights is mine.

A discussion about Audubon Park, New Jersey, that took place at the January 1995 meeting of the American Historical Association in Chicago ultimately led to my first date with my husband, Michael J. Chiarappa (now at Quinnipiac University), and our sixteen-year stint as colleagues at Western Michigan University. He has supported my work and this project in countless ways.

I visited and corresponded with dozens of people who either live, manage, represent, or are otherwise involved with mutually owned communities today or were in the past. Mutual home owners from Texas to New Jersey invited me into their homes, answered my questions, and allowed me to photograph them.

Past or present mutual housing association managers and board members, such as Susan Shuffler and the late Romie Stewart and from Avion Village, Pat Levins and Barbara Schade from Bellmawr Park, Gary Mastroddi and Denise Balderama of Audubon Park, and Dennis Clawson from Overlook Homes, answered dozens of questions and helped me gain perspective on their communities. Alice H. Minyon and John A. Green, the daughter and son of labor leader John Green; Professor Jay Westbrook, grandson of Lawrence Westbrook; Margaret Brown, Westbrook's stepdaughter; and Dr. Raymond Neutra, son of architect Richard J. Neutra, enriched and encouraged the research process. Pittsburgh attorney J. Craig Kuhn answered many questions about the mutual housing associations he admirably represented for so many years. Matthew Weismantel of Rutgers University, who has both written about mutual housing and enjoyed an insider's view (his late grandparents were among Winfield Park's "pioneer families"), was a source of inspiration and insight. All of these individuals and the residents of the thirty-five mutual housing associations I have identified, helped the Mutual Plan become a "living legacy [of] the New Deal" capable of inspiring public policy innovation—just as Walter Reuther of the United Automobile Workers Union had predicted.

# Acronyms and Abbreviations

| | |
|---|---|
| AFL | American Federation of Labor |
| CIO | Congress of Industrial Organizations |
| Cooperative Corporation | National Mortgage Corporation for Housing Cooperatives |
| DHD | Defense Housing Division |
| DSH | Division of Subsistence Homesteads |
| EFC | Emergency Fleet Corporation |
| FERA | Federal Emergency Relief Administration |
| FHA | Federal Housing Administration |
| FPHA | Federal Public Housing Authority |
| FSA | Farm Security Administration |
| FWA | Federal Works Agency |
| HHFA | Housing and Home Finance Agency |
| HUD | Department of Housing and Urban Development |
| Mutual Division | Mutual Ownership Defense Housing Division |
| Mutual Plan | Mutual Home Ownership Plan |
| NHA | National Housing Agency |
| PHA | Public Housing Administration |
| PWA | Public Works Administration |
| RA | Resettlement Administration |
| Shipbuilding Workers | Industrial Union of Marine and Shipbuilding Workers of America |
| USHA | United States Housing Authority |
| USHC | United States Housing Corporation |
| WPA | Works Progress Administration |

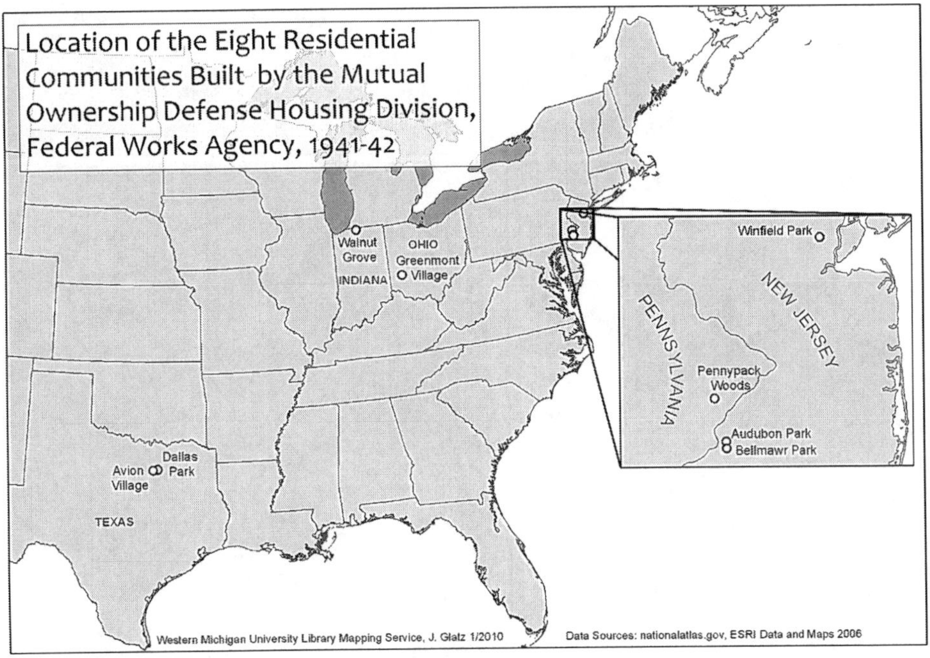


Locations of the eight communities built by the U.S. Federal Works Agency, Mutual Ownership Defense Housing Division, between 1940 and 1942. Map by Jason Glatz, Western Michigan University Map Library.

# The Mutual Housing Experiment

# Introduction

In June 1985, as a graduate assistant at Carnegie Mellon University, I visited Electric Heights, a housing development in Turtle Creek, Pennsylvania, located on a hillside overlooking Westinghouse Electric Corporation's East Pittsburgh plant. My professors were drawn to Electric Heights because its vibrancy stood in contrast to many working-class neighborhoods in the region, where the economic despair and social dislocation brought about by plant closures and relocations could be measured in the number of dwellings listed for sale. The networks of surveillance and mutual assistance—the "eyes on the street," as described by author Jane Jacobs, functioned effectively.[1] Unemployed electrical and steel workers busied themselves on home maintenance or improvement projects or repaired their own or each other's cars and lawnmowers. Playing children ran from one house to another. Elderly residents positioned themselves so they could watch the television and the activity outside at the same time. Electric Heights seemed a world away from the rest of Turtle Creek, the Monongahela Valley, and the larger "Rustbelt," which was then engulfed in yet another wave of plant closures and shutdowns.[2]

Surprised and impressed by what I saw at Electric Heights, I asked Eugene Levy, the history professor who became my dissertation director, about it. No, Electric Heights was not former military housing as I had guessed, but was one among hundreds of similar housing developments constructed nationwide by the federal government during World War II for the civilian employees of important defense contractors. It stood, Levy argued, as evidence of the wartime influence of labor unions, particularly the Congress of Industrial Organizations (CIO). But Electric Heights differed from most defense housing developments, Levy said, because at the war's end the federal government sold it to residents, who had formed a not-for-profit corporation (called a mutual housing association) that would own and manage the new community. When I asked for more information about when and how Electric Heights was purchased from the federal government, Professor Levy suggested that I try to find out. So I did, and in my dissertation I explained that Electric Heights ranked among roughly a dozen such communities in the region sold to mutual housing associations between 1947 and 1958 as part of the huge postwar disposition program that involved nearly a million units of temporary and permanent housing nationwide. The Federal Works Agency created the mutual housing program in consultation with organized labor for the benefit of the "middle-income" worker employed in the defense industry who could not afford to buy a house but did not economically qualify for federally subsidized, low-income public housing.

I found that in the 1950s U.S. Department of Labor cooperative expert Florence Parker and her fellow researchers closely monitored the mutual housing associations that had formed to buy government property—including two Greenbelt towns, a subsistence homestead community, a federally funded community in Puerto Rico, and defense housing projects "scattered throughout the country." They regarded the mutual housing associations as a "special group" of what was known in housing circles at that time as "all-the-way" or "sales" housing cooperatives.[3]

Electric Heights and about fifty other former defense housing developments were sold to residents on a cooperative or "mutual" basis under the Mutual Home Ownership Plan (hereafter Mutual Plan) created by Lawrence Westbrook of the Federal Works Agency (FWA). Under this plan residents jointly owned and managed their own communities. Had the war and the postwar housing situation unfolded the way Westbrook envisioned in 1940–1941, federal housing officials would have hired leading modernist architects to design residential communities earmarked for sale to their residents under the Mutual Plan wherever there was an ongoing need for affordable housing. Westbrook and the FWA would have collaborated with workers represented by the United Automobile Workers Union (UAW) and modernist architects in the design and construction of a mutually owned city for 10,000 people, and postwar developers like William Levitt would have built hundreds of architect-designed planned communities like Electric Heights.[4] That did not happen, of course, and this book examines the origins of Westbrook's Mutual Plan and its application at eight pilot projects: three in New Jersey, two in Texas, and one each in Ohio, Pennsylvania, and Indiana. It also explains why the President Franklin D. Roosevelt administration abandoned the Mutual Plan and prepared for postwar commercial market growth that would place fee-simple home ownership within the economic grasp of most wage earners.

During the late 1940s and early 1950s with the backing of President Harry S. Truman, Congress created economic incentives to entice wage earners to pursue home ownership through a commercial market mortgage. At the same time, there was sufficient interest in mutual and cooperative housing in 1950 for a group of influential members of Congress to try to establish a public-private corporation to provide seed money for middle-income cooperative housing development, but their effort failed. Since then, policy makers have seldom looked back and asked whether home ownership for almost all is in the nation's best economic and social interests. The home mortgage crisis that began in 2008 raised many questions about why banks granted mortgages to applicants with limited financial resources, but it did not precipitate serious debate over Congress's unquestioned commitment to sustaining the profitability of the commercial real estate market. In a 2012 *New York Times* editorial, Jeanne Gang and Greg Lindsay suggested that "some of the nearly 250,000 foreclosed houses acquired by Fannie Mae, Freddie Mac and the Federal Housing Administration" ought to be placed in a "national trust or a series of local trusts," but U.S. lawmakers have yet to embrace this idea and allocate greater resources to noncommercial market options such as housing cooperatives, land trusts, and other joint ownership ventures.[5]

During the first half of the twentieth century, public aid was used to strengthen the nonprofit housing market in times of national crisis, beginning with World War I. Federal funds were used to construct several widely admired war workers' communities, but Congress and President Warren G. Harding refused to follow the precedent set by England and sell them to residents on a cooperative or joint-ownership basis. President Franklin D. Roosevelt responded to the Great Depression with a much studied program of federal intervention in areas such as housing and community planning that had hitherto been the domain of private or local interests. When faced with a choice either to "follow Hoover's lead and seek measures to stimulate private home building and individual home ownership" or to "get behind proposals from congressional liberals like Robert Wagner for large-scale, European-style public housing programs," as David M. Kennedy, a leading Roosevelt scholar, explained, the President "essentially adopted—and significantly advanced"—the approach of his predecessor.[6]

Under Roosevelt's New Deal program, nonprofit housing opportunities were nonetheless made available to a small number of low- and middle-income families in new rural and suburban communities built by the Department of the Interior's Division of Subsistence Homesteads, the Federal Emergency Relief Administration, the Resettlement Administration, and the Farm Security Administration, which employed leading architects and planners. Resettlement Administration officials optimistically expected its three suburban Greenbelt towns to "open a new road for America's builders and money-lending institutions," and offer "invaluable examples" that would guide them in future residential development.[7]

The urban housing programs administered by the Public Works Administration and the U.S. Housing Authority sought to advance a concept called "modern housing" developed by reformer Catherine Bauer in the 1933 book of the same title, and known as "community modernism" by more recent scholars. Had the modern housing program succeeded, it would have made a "publicly supported, broadly targeted, noncommercial housing sector the centerpiece of federal housing policy," contends Gail Radford, a close student of the subject. But it did not succeed. Roosevelt administration officials responded to the defense housing emergency in 1940 by assigning the noncommercial housing sector a supporting role of compensating for the commercial market's deficiencies, filling in gaps, and helping those who fell through the cracks. Among those slipping through the cracks were defense workers, many of whom were organized and politically influential.[8]

Nonetheless, and from a slightly different perspective, the 1940s may be seen as a "crucial decade in the formation both of a new urban vision and of a political coalition emboldened to carry it out" that has too often been overlooked by historians and other scholars of cities and public policy.[9] The consequences of wartime housing policy decisions, both intended and unintended, "long outlasted the war."[10] When the decade began, housing and urban development policy making remained in the hands of New Dealers seeking to revitalize community life by replacing substandard dwellings and neighborhoods built by speculative builders with new neighborhoods that featured bright and easy-to-maintain dwellings; safe streets and play areas; and nearby civic, educational, recreational, and commercial facilities and amenities. Reform-minded New Dealers who enjoyed the support of labor responded to mobilization by devoting special attention to middle-income defense workers caught in the "'no-man's land' of housing."[11] The FWA's Westbrook took the lead by reaching out to John Green, the president and founder of the CIO's Industrial Union of Marine and Shipbuilding Workers of America (hereafter Shipbuilding Workers), whose dramatic Capitol Hill testimony helped persuade Congress to address the critical shortage of housing in centers of defense production by passing a housing and community facilities bill known as the Lanham Act.

In late 1940 Westbrook started working with Green's Shipbuilding Workers and other CIO unions to test the practicality of the Mutual Plan at eight federally funded pilot projects. Each project featured modern architecture and planning features designed by leading architects, including Richard J. Neutra, George Howe, Albert Mayer, Louis I. Kahn, and Oscar Stonorov. Dwelling units were grouped together in clusters serviced by cul-de-sac roads. The front doors of most residences faced a large interior park or green that served as an extended living room and fostered resident interaction. Pedestrian paths linked groups of houses with the community center and, depending on the size and location of the community, an elementary school and a shopping center.

In February 1942, before the completion of all eight of Westbrook's Mutual Plan projects, President Roosevelt ordered the reorganization of the federal housing bureaucracy under the National Housing Agency (NHA). Under Executive Order 9070 the programs created for low-income households and defense workers were consolidated under the NHA's Federal Public Housing Authority. The newly appointed head of the NHA, John B. Blandford, cultivated his alliances with builders, bankers, and real estate developers more carefully than he did his ties to New Deal communitarian reformers. Westbrook, dismayed with the Roosevelt administration's political turn to the right and the shift in emphasis in housing and community development away from reform, went into the U.S. Army and served overseas. Meanwhile, Blandford relocated administrative responsibility for the eight communities from NHA headquarters in Washington, D.C., to agency field offices, an action convincing many that residents would never get a chance to become joint or mutual owners as promised.

In 1945, after the war ended, Westbrook returned to Washington D.C., where he found little interest in communitarian housing reform among housing and urban policy makers in President Harry S. Truman's administration. The eight pilot projects and the other communities built under the New Deal as models were now regarded as the antithesis of what postwar developers claimed that the homecoming veteran wanted—a detached house and yard situated in a neighborhood and community of like houses and like people, where individualistic goals and aims could be pursued.[12]

The mutual housing program entered a second phase after World War II, when federal housing officials faced a congressional mandate to dispose of defense and wartime housing built with federal funds. Fearing displacement in the midst of the widely publicized postwar housing shortage, residents of the 167,700 units of permanent defense housing made available for disposition on December 31, 1945, sought an opportunity to buy their government-owned dwellings under a modified version of the Mutual Plan.[13] Facing Congressional pressure to liquidate the nation's stockpile of defense workers' housing, federal housing officials responded to these requests with a cumbersome process that presented many stumbling blocks for newly formed mutual housing associations.

Infant associations that secured the assistance of a labor union leader, veterans' advocate, or attorney were most successful in complying with the labyrinth of rules, regulations, and procedures imposed by the Federal Public Housing Authority and its 1947 successor agency, the Public Housing Administration (PHA). Congressional intervention and the outbreak of the war in Korea delayed the disposition process, and today thirty-seven mutual housing associations, including Electric Heights, are still in existence (see the Appendix).

Advocates of cooperative housing aid were encouraged by the passage of the Housing Act of 1949, which established the national goal of a "decent home and living environment" for every American family and called for resumption of the construction of low-income public housing and for funds for urban revitalization.[14] In that context, Senators Burnett R. Maybank (D-SC) and John Sparkman (D-AL) and Congressman Brent Spence (D-KY) introduced in 1950 companion bills calling for the creation of the National Mortgage Corporation for Housing Cooperatives. This public-private entity was to serve as the financial center of the nonprofit middle-income market by providing direct loans or loan guarantees and to advance the standing of cooperative housing as the FHA did for the for-profit market.

A positive, unintended consequence of the pitched battle over the proposed National Mortgage Corporation for Housing Cooperatives was that the Housing Act of 1950 marked a significant turn in the road for federal support of cooperatives.[15] As it became clear that most middle-income people would pursue traditional housing on the commercial market, supporters of cooperative housing no longer felt compelled to tout it as an emergency or experimental program but won acceptance for it as a "normal" part of the broad package of housing and community development programs and funds available to cities and towns. To be sure, new federal legislation did not offer direct incentives, but in one administration after another Congress adopted legislation that strengthened the ability of the Federal Housing Administration (FHA) to insure commercial market mortgages granted for the sale or construction of middle-income cooperative housing. President John F. Kennedy, for example, gave his support to the Housing Act of 1961, which made it possible for qualified nonprofit or limited-dividend corporations to obtain special loan guarantees from the FHA for the construction of such housing. And during the administration of President Richard M. Nixon, George Romney, secretary of the Department of Housing and Urban Affairs (HUD), created Operation Breakthrough and paired modular or manufactured housing producers with locally controlled nonprofit corporations to develop a series of mixed-income, cooperative communities on the outskirts of Seattle, Washington, Macon, Georgia, Kalamazoo, Michigan, and a handful of other cities.[16]

Examined from a global perspective, the postwar growth of cooperative housing in the United States was insignificant compared to that in other nations. A recent comparative study of the United States, Sweden, and India concluded that state involvement and support were key factors in determining the postwar growth of cooperative housing. In the United States (with the important exception of New York State and New York City), there was no "cooperative-state relationship" to speak of.[17] Despite increasing federal involvement with cooperative home ownership, the postwar increase in cooperative housing bills in Congress, the provision of FHA mortgage insurance for housing cooperatives, the postwar rise of consumer interest in cooperatives, and the activities of advocacy organizations, the history of cooperative housing in the United States remains oddly "hidden."[18] The eight Mutual Plan communities were relegated to the policy sidelines to protect the profitability of the middle-income commercial housing market and maintain the top-down structure of the low-income public housing program. They faded into obscurity while millions of moderate-income families took advantage of federal home ownership incentives. Electric Heights and the other Lanham-financed properties that contributed to the growth of cooperative housing in the United States became part of a forgotten chapter in U.S. housing policy.

Defense housing developments like Electric Heights were sold to mutual housing associations at a time when ownership of a detached house in a culturally homogenous suburban or suburban-like urban neighborhood was presented as the fulfillment of the American Dream. According to the Pennypack Woods Home Ownership Association, its residents jointly purchased their community "so we could have our homes here . . . [and] raise our children in pleasant surroundings." Their goal was to keep the cost of living down and "get more of the better things in life." It did not matter if "those better things in life meant a new car, or a television set, a vacation, or the possibility of a college education for our children, or even an extra case of beer for Pop on Saturday night." The important thing was that the "purchase of this property cooperatively has meant something to all of us."[19] Whatever that something was, Pennypack Woods residents knew that the six-year campaign to purchase the community under the Mutual Plan was just the beginning and not the end of their struggles. Despite "amazing progress," they knew that the mutual association would survive only if every community member was willing to "pitch in and help."[20]

The mutual housing associations that purchased Pennypack Woods, Electric Heights, and other defense housing communities were organized by ordinary wage earners with the help of labor and other workers' organizations. Hundreds of hours were devoted to meetings with each other and with local and federal government officials, bankers, realtors, and attorneys. People with limited formal education who may never have held title to a piece of real estate in their lives pored over contracts and other legal documents and correspondence written in "governmentese" in an effort to figure out how to comply with the regulations imposed on them by federal housing officials. Those who built the tanks, planes, and ships in support of the war were astonished to find members of Congress not only unsupportive of their efforts but willing to undermine them by requiring mutual housing associations to seek commercial-sector financing. Mutual housing advocates faced resistance from real estate and banking interests from outside the community and opposition from within as residents clashed not only over the sale of a project under the Mutual Plan but also over how to democratically run the community once it was theirs.

Mutual home owners took advantage of their ability to regulate membership and control the purchase of shares in the nonprofit corporation to maintain their original, federally assigned racial designation, just as white home owners used every means at their disposal—including violence and intimidation—to retain residential class and color lines. Only one African American defense housing community and three biracial developments sold under the Mutual Plan remain today. It was not until the 1970s and 1980s that local, state, and federal courts and agencies began to require mutual and cooperative housing associations to uphold fair housing laws and court rulings. And yet they remain overwhelmingly segregated.

Electric Heights and its mutually owned sister communities represent a road not taken in federal housing policy. Roosevelt-era policy makers had confidence in the ability of wage earners to purchase and manage democratic, jointly owned communities of affordable housing. The eight pilot communities and other publicly financed developments sold by the federal government to their residents during the late 1940s and 1950s are forgotten legacies of an era in policy making when there was growing recognition of the need for a noncommercial housing market to serve low- and middle-income families whose commercial market choices were few. A look at the mutual housing experiment and how its participants fared is not only well overdue but timely in an era of economic stagnation, growing income inequality, and a shrinking middle class.

In January 2015 President Barrack Obama spoke of his intention to emphasize "middle-class economics" and help "working families feel more secure in a world of constant change." In recognition of the importance of home ownership in achieving that goal, he supports measures to make it easier to purchase a house.[21] If, however, there are any lessons to be learned from the 2008 mortgage crisis, one is that a healthy housing market offers consumers housing options—options that fit their budgetary and other household needs. The story of how and why mutual home ownership was offered—and ultimately rejected—as a mainstream economic and social alternative to traditional home ownership will hopefully ignite interest in the Roosevelt administration's Mutual Plan and inspire the development and testing of the next-generation model.

# 1

# The New Deal Origins of Mutual Housing

In October 1934, the *New York Times* excitedly announced that the Museum of Modern Art had opened a housing exhibit of "such importance and such urgent timeliness" that "every man, woman and child in this problem-haunted metropolis" should attend. The exhibit coincided with the publication of a seventy-eight page booklet, with the "desperately challenging title" *America Can't Have Housing*, which featured leading housing experts and urban reformers explaining that the United States could have an adequate supply of affordable family dwellings if local, state, and federal governments accepted responsibility for the inadequacies of the private commercial market. Noncommercial housing opportunities, they argued, would remain practically nonexistent in most U.S. cities as long the nonprofit market was dependent on uncoordinated philanthropic, union, and charitable investment. In contrast, the noncommercial sector in Northern and Western Europe benefited handsomely from a post–World War I infusion of funds and expertise from government bodies, labor unions, and other reform organizations that backed the construction of modern housing communities designed by leading architects.[1]

In 1936 the Museum of Modern Art opened an "enormously stimulating" exhibit to show that U.S. housing conditions were improving as a result of President Franklin D. Roosevelt's New Deal. Entitled "Architecture in Government Housing," the exhibit featured limited-dividend housing corporations that, aided by the Housing Division of the Federal Emergency Administration of Public Works, known as the Public Works Administration (PWA), hired renowned American and European émigré architects to build new residential enclaves that integrated well with their larger neighborhoods. It included the PWA-sponsored Carl Mackley Houses in Philadelphia and Langston Hughes Terrace in Washington, D.C., which had "garden areas, community laundries, playgrounds, swimming pools, and other services to help create a suitable environment for living." These developments were regarded by reformers, labor union leaders, and other activists as worthy models for public and private investment that would both strengthen the noncommercial housing market and increase its stature in American society. The exhibit offered a "convincing argument" for the Wagner-Ellenbogen Bill then being debated in Congress and ignored critics disturbed by the PWA's left-leaning program. Along with several other exhibits sponsored by the museum in the years prior to 1945, it "both underscored and catalyzed commitment among architects and planners to apply modern housing design to the American house."[2]

The PWA was among a handful of agencies created by President Roosevelt and his advisers during his first administration to aid the economically distressed noncommercial real estate market. Relief, recovery, and reform for the commercial market were provided by the Home Owners' Loan Corporation, which refinanced roughly 1 million home mortgages; the Federal Housing Administration (FHA), which offered loan guarantees to qualified home buyers; the Federal Home Loan Bank Board, which purchased home mortgages from banks to make more capital available for investment; and other agencies. During the early 1930s, Roosevelt was convinced that making noncommercial housing options available to those unable or unwilling to undertake a mortgage and the other demands associated with home ownership would not harm the for-profit market but lend it much needed stability. He rejected the arguments of realtors, land developers, and bankers that helping the noncommercial sector would harm the commercial residential market and jeopardize the American dream of owning one's home.[3]

In 1932, when Roosevelt was the Democratic presidential candidate, he met with Columbia University economist Rexford G. Tugwell, who later served as undersecretary of agriculture, and Milburn L. Wilson, an agricultural economist from Montana State Agricultural College, to discuss the use of public funds to build a series of communities for unemployed city workers who wanted to return to the subsistence lifestyle they had recently left behind for wage labor and consumerism. After a victorious election, Roosevelt and his aides incorporated the subsistence homestead idea into Section 208 of Title II of the National Industrial Recovery Act of 1933 and Congress made an initial $25 million available for demonstration projects administered by Wilson.[4]

In early 1934, shortly after Wilson began building what would ultimately be thirty-four subsistence homestead communities, Lawrence Westbrook, head of the Division of Rural Rehabilitation of the Federal Emergency Relief Administration (FERA), commenced work on a series of twenty-eight residential communities to cooperatively resettle relief recipients who had lost their jobs as a result of technological change or the unsuitability of their land for agriculture.[5] However, Roosevelt's critics opposed his subsistence homesteads and Westbrook's rural resettlement communities because they promoted noncommercial options for householders unable to afford a house with a commercial mortgage.

Similarly, the Greenbelt Town program created by the Resettlement Administration (RA) in 1936 was the subject of public and congressional criticism because its target audience was not rural relief recipients considered broken in health and spirit but middle- or moderate-income office and clerical workers seeking a second chance in the suburbs. These developments, Westbrook's study of the effects of the Great Depression and drought on the housing market, and his stint as assistant administrator of the Works Progress Administration (WPA) in 1935–1936 convinced him that noncommercial housing options were needed to help low- and moderate-income households negotiate the vicissitudes of the commercial housing market.[6]

Westbrook and other New Dealers thought that public housing should not only provide decent, affordable residential communities but also, as a respected historian put it, make "better citizens" by providing them with a physical and social environment that would encourage the cultivation of social and civic responsibility.[7] As the 1930s unfolded, Westbrook became increasingly focused on middle-income households whose hold on traditional home ownership remained tenuous even after the creation of the FHA and other programs that helped safeguard them, home builders, and home mortgage providers. Between 1932 and 1940, he directed the development of a series of publicly and privately funded residential communities whose purpose was to elevate wage earners by giving them the opportunity to own and govern their own communities. Some of these communities offered an opportunity for gradual ownership of dwellings and others anticipated joint ownership.

## Westbrook's New Deal Roots

Born in Belton, Texas, on August 23, 1889, Lawrence Westbrook learned his first lessons in rural economics and sociology on his family's Brazos River Valley cotton farm. During his youth, populist candidates vied for the support of East Texas cotton planters by promoting self-help and other collective efforts.[8] Westbrook served in France with the U.S. Army Signal Corps as a lieutenant colonel in World War I and, after his discharge, returned to McLennan County to study civil engineering at the University of Texas at Austin in 1923. He left college before completing his degree and was elected to the Texas State Legislature in 1928, serving as chairman of the Committee on Agriculture until 1932.[9]

A founding member of the Texas Cotton Cooperative Association, Westbrook was also involved in the establishment of the American Cotton Cooperative Association, which was created in 1933 to coordinate the activities of state and regional cotton cooperatives.[10] His firsthand knowledge of the plight of families who sought to return to the land to avoid the indignity of living in the city on relief expanded dramatically when he was selected by Texas governor Miriam "Ma" A. Ferguson to head the Texas Rehabilitation and Relief Commission. Also in 1933 he accepted a concurrent appointment from national relief administrator Harry Hopkins to serve as civil works administrator for the state of Texas.

During his time as commissioner of rehabilitation and relief in drought-stricken Texas, Westbrook witnessed the desperate plight of thousands. He reviewed the results of the physical exams given to male relief recipients in East Texas to verify their inability to pick cotton so they could continue to receive benefits. The state's Board of Welfare and Employment found that some of those denied relief and sent to the fields in Westbrook's native McLennan County were not hale and hearty but half-starved, many of them "slowly dying of disease."[11]

Westbrook thought it possible for unemployed wage earners to return to the countryside, achieve self-sufficiency, and enjoy decent living standards if they were organized in producer and consumer cooperatives. He tested his ideas in 1933 after obtaining a FERA loan for Texas Rural Communities, Inc., to purchase and complete construction of Woodlake, a farm community located in Trinity County that began as a private philanthropic venture for farm families that had migrated to Houston during the 1920s and 1930s and now wished to return to the countryside. A not-for-profit corporation, Texas Rural Communities held the land and improvements on behalf of residents, who would either one day become cooperative shareholders or purchase their homestead outright. The cooperative farms, livestock, machinery, and other improvements and major capital investments would eventually become the collective property of all.[12] Woodlake, as one observer noted, "possessed some characteristics of a European village, with its outlying fields, or of a Russian co-operative farm, with its individual subsistence plots and its collectively operated fields."[13]

In the fall of 1933, Westbrook hired architect David R. Williams, who had been working for the U.S. Department of the Interior's Historic American Building Survey, to design the dwellings, barns, and other improvements planned for Woodlake. Combining traditional values of rugged individualism and cooperation, Westbrook and Williams developed a plan that featured 101 prefabricated dwellings, a school, a meetinghouse, a store, a bathhouse, and two 600-acre farms. The entire community was situated around a 225-acre interior park built by laborers employed by the Civil Works Administration. Each family farmed its own three-acre subsistence plot and contributed labor to the cultivation and processing of crops grown in the community's collective fields. Westbrook promoted Woodlake as a model for other communities built with relief funds by making it the subject of an eleven-minute documentary motion picture called "The New Frontier."[14]

As a publicly funded community development project with a cooperative social and economic agenda, Woodlake represented an alternative to the typical route of residential development and was an unwelcome reminder of the politics of relief. Concerns about expenditures at the planned community were only part of why in 1933 opponents of "Ma" Ferguson in the legislature charged the State Senate with investigating Westbrook and the Rehabilitation and Relief Commission.[15] The probe revealed the difficulties Westbrook faced in creating an honest, efficient bureaucratic system to distribute relief funds on a local level throughout Texas in a three-week period. Asked to reply to a series of detailed questions regarding county-level expenditures Westbrook employed the tactic of burying his political opponents in paper. His response to the Senate's questions came in at 1,100 pages, which was "a considerable bit more than the senate wanted to hear, or to read," a staff member recalled.[16] In February 1934, shortly after testifying that he was aware "that in some instances outright fraud has been committed, forgeries, [and] misapplication of funds," Westbrook resigned.[17]

The investigation and his resignation from the Texas Rehabilitation and Relief Commission did not taint Westbrook for long. He soon capitalized on his state-level experience and began community development on a national scale. In February 1934, the same year that Harry Hopkins invited Westbrook to Washington to discuss creation of a program for rehabilitation of rural communities, The *New Republic* reported that Hopkins looked favorably on Woodlake and Westbrook's larger "plan for setting up a series of cooperative communities for dispossessed small planters and sharecroppers." Westbrook held a series of meetings in early 1934 to discuss the issues involved in relocating farmers and others who lived on exhausted or infertile land.[18] Shortly after, Hopkins announced that Westbrook would head FERA's new Division of Rural Rehabilitation and Stranded Populations with a mandate "to rehabilitate farm families by assisting them to become self-supporting."[19] The *Washington Post* reported that Westbrook's main focus was to be the "problem of the farmers on sub-marginal lands or . . . rural groups that are underprivileged."[20] As depicted in Figure 1.1, Westbrook and Hopkins became close personal friends.

## Rehabilitation FERA Style

During his FERA tenure, Westbrook helped Hopkins develop and implement a national system for the distribution of relief and drought assistance. During the summer of 1934, he traveled across the Western United States to assess the human and economic cost of the Depression and drought conditions, reporting his findings directly to President Roosevelt. These and other assignments earned the "quiet, dignified and likeable" Westbrook a place among New Deal insiders.[21] For his part, Westbrook cultivated the persona of one who knows how to get things done, the level-headed civil engineer and alter ego of his friend Hopkins, the former social worker.[22] Westbrook's can-do image was reinforced by the *Washington Post* when it reported his "credo": "Sometimes the man needs only a mule, sometimes a cow, sometimes chickens or other farm equipment" to get back on his feet economically.[23]

Westbrook believed that the best way to address the poverty of people living on marginal and drought-stricken land was through state-chartered rural rehabilitation corporations that could be granted or lent federal, state, or private funds. He encouraged the directors of state rural rehabilitation corporations

**Figure 1.1** Lawrence Westbrook and Martha Collings were married in Hot Springs, Arkansas, in March 1937. Westbrook worked closely with his best man, Harry Hopkins, during the early days of the New Deal. Courtesy of the Library of Congress, LC-USZ62-139565.

to consider using at least a portion of their allocated FERA funds to seed the growth of a new economy by planning and building communities on productive land where holders of marginal or exhausted land could relocate, take up subsistence farming, and participate in consumer and producer cooperatives. Relying heavily on the ideas of architect David R. Williams, who was now FERA chief of planning, Westbrook also called for the construction of a few rural-industrial communities to demonstrate how collectivist agricultural and industrial manufacturing might be effectively merged to achieve greater economic stability and environmental sustainability than the sharecropping system could.[24]

The difficulties Westbrook faced in extending the benefits of cooperative enterprise to rural dwellers were vividly chronicled in *Forty Acres and Steel Mules*, by Herman Clarence Nixon, head of the Louisiana Rural Rehabilitation Corporation. Nixon concluded that, because of their poverty and lack of education, "neither black nor white southern tenant farmers" could be expected to "easily take an interest in cooperative activities and societies that have remade many rural communities." As an example, he pointed to FERA's Dyess Colony in Arkansas, where every household head was suffering from hookworm, malaria, or other "energy-sapping diseases."[25]

Westbrook did not want rural resettlement communities to become "Federal islands," and he planned for their disposition on the noncommercial market under a plan that had certain similarities to those proposed by reformers for the sale of publicly funded housing for war workers in 1919–1920.[26] These communities would be sold to not-for-profit corporations, governed by boards of directors made up of local, state, and federal representatives, that would hold the property in trust on behalf of the residents. The purchase price would be negotiated and the trust would make installment payments over a fixed period of time. Roads, bridges, parks, and other improvements would be deeded over to local governing bodies, and individual homesteads would be leased or eventually sold to residents. Westbrook recommended that FERA homesteaders first complete a five-year trial lease and then exercise an option to purchase their homes from the trust, which would require a 15 percent down payment with the remaining sum to be paid over a forty-year period at 3 percent interest.[27]

Acting on the advice of George Creel, chairman of the controversial World War I–era Committee on Public Information, Westbrook took pains to familiarize the public with the goals, methods, and accomplishments of the Division of Rural Rehabilitation, using radio addresses, newspaper reports, motion pictures, and *Rural Rehabilitation*, a "profusely illustrated" magazine.[28] In 1935 he reported that FERA was planning to help impoverished Americans establish a subsistence lifestyle by building 150 cooperative communities, each consisting of about a thousand inhabitants. Most of the twenty-eight rural resettlement communities already built were occupied by white relief recipients.[29] FERA had built a small number of biracial communities such as Virginia's Roanoke Farms, but maintained segregated sections within them.[30]

From the outset, a great deal of publicity surrounded the FERA-funded colony in the Matanuska Valley of the Alaska Territory established in 1935 by the Alaska Rural Rehabilitation Corporation (ARRC). Recruits for the Matanuska Colony, found among relief recipients residing in the cut-over logging regions of northern Michigan, Wisconsin, and Minnesota, agreed to accept the credit necessary to transport themselves and a limited number of pounds of belongings to Alaska and start a subsistence homestead. The original 200 families also pledged to eventually purchase their house and farm acreage from the ARRC over a thirty-year period at 3 percent interest and to participate in consumer and producer cooperatives.[31]

The Matanuska Colony featured prefabricated housing designed by David R. Williams for assembly by homesteaders with little construction experience. Williams wanted FERA staff and contractors to teach the homesteaders how to use power tools and other labor-saving devices so they "may be able to profit from the economies and speed which the machine will afford." He hoped that they would "have the leisure to learn to do well with their own hands such work as will give joy in its doing and add beauty to their homes and the things with which they live."[32]

Residing in tents while they waited for building materials the Matanuska colonists grew dismayed with the financial arrangements and the living conditions in the valley. Some turned to their elected representatives back home for help. Newspapers such as the *Chicago Tribune* that were politically at odds with Roosevelt and the New Deal printed the letters and telegrams from disgruntled colonists, who were now heavily in debt to the ARRC. In June 1935 Senators Arthur H. Vandenberg of Michigan, Robert LaFollette of Wisconsin, and Homer Shipstead of Minnesota sponsored a tripartisan (Republican, Progressive, and Farmer-Labor) resolution calling on federal relief administrator Harry Hopkins to investigate allegations of mismanagement, including a lack of medical supplies.[33]

Hopkins defended Westbrook, assuring both Congress and the public that neither disease nor starvation faced the FERA colonists in the "Land of the Midnight Sun," and a complete investigation revealed that, although Westbrook and other FERA officials had made a few planning and logistical errors and miscalculations, living conditions in the Matanuska Colony were generally satisfactory. Indeed, the architect-designed prefabricated dwellings the colonists erected with the help of FERA laborers were far superior to the houses most had lived in back home. Arville Schaleben, who was sent by *American Magazine* to accompany the colonists, was grateful for the "privilege of participating in one of the greatest dramas of modern times"; he observed the Matanuska colonists as they "fought not only with raw nature, but with raw politics, inefficiency, and themselves."[34]

## Lessons Learned from the Division of Subsistence Homesteads

Westbrook and Wilson worked independently to strengthen the noncommercial housing market through cooperative home ownership. Wilson put his ideas into an international context when he observed that the back-to-the-land movement was being embraced throughout the industrial world. He noted that the United States was not alone in seeking to "realize a new security by re-establishing contact with the soil," and found lessons for the work of the Division of Subsistence Homesteads (DSH) in nineteenth-century collectivist communities such as Oneida in New York, Amana in Iowa, and Brook Farm in Massachusetts, and in twentieth-century communities such as the Llano Cooperative Colony of Louisiana, the European immigrant communities founded in eastern North Carolina by Hugh MacRae, and the Durham and Delphi colonies in California. Wilson believed that DSH-sponsored communities would succeed where those based on "some religious or philosophic[al] ideal" had failed. They would be "cast in a different mold from most past ventures"[35] and be free of dominating religious or political beliefs or ideologies.

For Wilson, the key to success for the subsistence homestead communities was local initiative and control; any top-down decision making from Washington would doom them to failure. And he was convinced that "if the homestead projects were to become real communities," they had to be "wanted, planned, and managed by the people within the locality where they were to be constructed."[36] In accordance with these views, the DSH lent funds to locally owned and controlled corporations to improve existing communities or develop new ones organized around producer or consumer cooperatives or both. These included the Dayton, Ohio, community called Liberty Homestead founded by Ralph Borsodi, and Penderlea, the Cape Fear, North Carolina, community planned by landscape architect John Nolen for Hugh MacRae. First Lady Eleanor Roosevelt took a special interest in the DSH's Arthurdale, a new community built outside of Morgantown, West Virginia, for "stranded" bituminous coal miners. In the Arthurdale and Westmoreland Homestead communities, homesteaders combined cooperative agricultural and industrial production. Located in the countryside within a few hours drive from Pittsburgh and the small cities of Weirton and Morgantown, these communities were considered places that were likely to attract industry after recovery took place.[37] For secretary of the interior Harold Ickes, the purpose of the subsistence homesteads was to demonstrate the "benefits of a sound community life based on a combination of part time industrial employment and small-scale farming." He called the "experimental" subsistence homesteads program a "new venture in the field of social endeavor."[38]

Milburn Wilson's interest in the way a subsistence homestead could operate as a "social endeavor" was seen in his support for hiring architects Louis I. Kahn and Alfred Katsner to test the appeal of modern design among Jewish workers from the needle trades and other industries at Jersey Homesteads in Monmouth County, New Jersey. This project, which included 200 dwellings, a school, a community center, and a clothing factory, was described as Kahn's "first attempt (in an actual context) to implement the principles of modern architecture on a large scale." The simple, flat-roofed, concrete-block dwellings were thoughtfully arranged in a "park-like landscape, adjacent to a circular village street" and were quickly assembled using mass-production construction methods.[39]

According to DSH staff member Bruce L. Melvin, the agency sought to test a "completely new plan of construction involving the most modern designs and materials." Like Williams, Melvin saw the relationship between a house and its "physical environment" as the key to successful community development. Both favored "the indigenous architecture of the region" and maintained that "houses should be part of the landscape and at the same time have a harmonious relation to each other" and to the cooperative farm and garment factory as well.[40]

The DSH's experimentation in architecture, planning, and construction did not extend to challenging the status quo of residential segregation. The subsistence homestead communities sought by and promised to African American leaders were slow to materialize. In mid-1935, while construction was under way on thirty-one projects for white families, none of the fifteen promised to African Americans had yet been started. In November 1936 the first subsistence homestead for African American families, Aberdeen Gardens, was dedicated near Newport News, Virginia. This 159-unit community was completed with the aid of faculty and students from the nearby Hampton Institute. White opposition ended DSH plans to develop biracial subsistence homestead communities near Dayton and Indianapolis. As historian Paul K. Conkin observed in his now classic study of the New Deal community program, when it came to race, the "contemplated new society" would "remain very much like the old society."[41]

Acting with the consent of President Roosevelt, in May 1934 Harold Ickes federalized the DSH program, taking control, through the Federal Subsistence Homestead Corporation, of the stock of all local development corporations. Opposed to this centralization effort, Wilson terminated his community development work and took a post in the Department of Agriculture. Ickes's decision to federalize the program put in limbo the skeletal plans Wilson and the DSH staff had made for the sale of subsistence homesteads to residents through low-interest, long-term loans.[42]

According to Lawrence Westbrook, federalization of the DSH program allowed tighter control over the expenditure of public funds, but he questioned whether the benefit justified the reduction in local control needed for a project to be successful. He remained favorably inclined toward state and local redevelopment corporations that operated under federal supervision until they were capable of surviving the termination of federal financial and administrative support and functioning independently. These corporations had the ability to help the noncommercial housing sector become stronger and more economically resilient.[43]

## New Deal Innovation in Mass-Assembly and Prefabricated Housing

At the same time that Westbrook and Wilson were experimenting with prefabricated housing in their respective agencies, Louis Grandgent, chief of the Tennessee Valley Authority (TVA) Architectural Section, was completing plans for prefabricated dwellings to house workers assigned to remote dam, power plant, and other construction sites. TVA workers built sections of two styles of dwelling in a workshop and trucked the roof and wall components to prepared building sites, where assembly was completed. The dwellings were designed so that when the agency's housing needs changed they could be disassembled and shipped by flatbed truck for reassembly elsewhere.[44] In 1937 the Farm Security Administration (FSA) "emerged with many fresh approaches to construction."[45] It made the production of affordable housing for rural dwellers "a kind of sideline" by erecting prefabricated dwellings in Missouri, Georgia, South Carolina, and Alabama.[46] In 1938 relief recipients employed by the WPA worked in assembly-line fashion to fabricate plywood panels used to build small detached houses on leased lots. The much publicized Fort Wayne Plan was backed by the FHA, the Fort Wayne Realty Board, and the Lincoln National Life Insurance Company, but housing reformers saw little promise that it could solve the long-term need for affordable housing nationwide.[47]

The research into and experimentation with prefabricated housing undertaken by FERA, DSH, TVA, and other federal agencies lacked any centralized organization or planning; each agency developed its own research agenda, competed for funding, conducted its own investigations of the prefabricated dwellings available on the commercial market, and disseminated its own findings. A periodical established in 1930, the *Federal Architect*, briefly functioned as an informal clearinghouse for information on prefabrication research and mass-production building methods in publicly funded building projects. Taken together, these investigations suggested both the potential and the limitations of prefabrication in commercial housing and contributed to growing consumer expectations for its future.[48]

As an industry, prefabricated housing remained in its infancy during the 1930s despite impressive public and private investment. In July 1938 architect William Lescaze expressed admiration for the privately funded prefabricated dwellings designed and built by Walter Gropius, Marcel Breuer, and other architects, but he was convinced that prefabrication "as a solution to the housing problem is too far away," by his estimate "20 years distant."[49] In 1940, a conference on prefabricated housing at Texas A&M University convinced Richard Neutra and his wife Dione that prefabricated housing could become commercially viable only with "state subsidies." Dione observed that because the United States invested so much of its resources in "armaments" the poor remained in their "miserable hovels" and that the idea of good, affordable prefabricated housing remained "utopian."[50]

## Westbrook and the Westacres Suburban Community

In April 1935 the first phase of the New Deal community program came to an end when President Roosevelt transferred the communities built or funded by the DSH under Wilson to the newly created Resettlement Administration (RA) and named as the RA's director Rexford G. Tugwell, an agricultural economist full of ideas on reforming American life.[51] Two months later, the administration shifted the operations of Westbrook's Division of Rural Rehabilitation to the RA. Tugwell offered Westbrook a position as one of four assistant administrators. Convinced that he would not be allowed a "free hand in running his program," Westbrook declined Tugwell's offer, but watched the RA's development programs with interest.[52]

Westbrook's influence in New Deal community development declined with the creation of the RA and Tugwell's appointment, especially after the Greenbelt

Town program was unveiled. This project produced three suburban planned communities, Greenbelt, Maryland, near Washington, D.C., Greendale, Wisconsin, outside of Milwaukee, and Greenhills, Ohio, near Cincinnati. Like the residential communities developed by the DSH and the Division of Rural Rehabilitation, these towns were regarded by federal officials as prototypes to encourage and guide future suburban development. But they did not target low income rural dwellers; instead, they aimed to attract middle-income urbanites seeking a "family and community life which will be better than they now enjoy," in communities both free of city congestion and the haphazardness of unregulated suburban growth.[53]

Westbrook identified at least two shortcomings in the Greenbelt Town program. First, Tugwell had failed to adequately plan for the eventual ownership of the towns by residents or a land trust, and as a result, they remained under federal ownership until after World War II. When the program was first inaugurated, the RA's stated goal was that the Greenbelt Towns be "held in one ownership, preferably a local agency."[54] Second, the Greenbelt Town program came under intense criticism even before construction began because the RA had failed to pave the way with advance publicity explaining the nature and goals of the program. This oversight contributed to negative publicity and helped derail plans to start several other demonstration communities at suburban sites in various parts of the country.[55]

Westbrook was also closely attuned to the controversy that emerged in March 1935 in Sunnyside Gardens in Queens, New York. Residents of the widely admired planned community developed by a limited-dividend corporation called the City Homes Corporation, went on strike to protest the unwillingness of the Home Owners' Loan Corporation to restructure their mortgage debt. The Sunnyside Gardens mortgage crisis underscored the importance of long-term, low-interests loans for wage earners to safely pursue home ownership.[56] In Manhattan's Lower East Side, Arthur C. Holden, an architect and city planner described as a "tireless, articulate propagandist . . . well connected with corporatist planning circles" was trying to find backing for "the pooling of tenement properties as a basis for districtwide rehabilitation."[57]

In July 1935 Westbrook accepted a position with the WPA as one of four assistant administrators in charge of "Colonies and the Information Service."[58] A partnership with U.S. Senator James Couzens, a Michigan Republican, gave him a new field of operations and the chance to coalesce his ideas about planned communities and housing development. Couzens was a wealthy banking and Ford Motor Company executive who held a number of posts in Detroit, then the nation's fourth largest city, including police commissioner, transit commissioner, and mayor, before turning to national politics and philanthropic work. Like many Republicans, he disliked the New Deal's social welfare programs, especially public housing, which he regarded as paternalistic. He also criticized the PWA's public housing program on the grounds that it subsidized employers who underpaid their workers, compelling them to live in substandard dwellings.

But Couzens admired the New Deal's rural homestead efforts as an encouragement of self-sufficiency and wanted to apply that approach in locations on the urban periphery—not isolated rural hamlets—where wage earners could raise their own food and still be in proximity to job opportunities. Indeed, Couzens and Henry Ford had once seriously considered creating a homestead community for workers, "back in the days of the five-dollar plan," but they never followed through on the idea.[59]

Couzens now approached Westbrook in search of a way to start a suburban community development project along homestead lines. Westbrook responded by offering Couzens a community plan he had formulated that involved "rental ownership under which the occupants of homes in a given community lease the premises which they occupy from a company owned by the occupants themselves." Eventually this nonprofit company would make it possible for residents to own their dwellings by offering a low-interest, long-term loan. Couzens took up the idea, created a fund of $550,000 of his own money, and gave it to the WPA to create a nonprofit corporation to build a planned community for autoworkers called Westacres in the Detroit metropolitan area. Westbrook combined Couzens's donation with a $300,000 grant from the Federal Emergency Relief Administration so that Oakland Housing, Inc., a nonprofit corporation chartered in 1935, could function as the real estate developer and marketing agent for Westacres.[60]

Oakland Housing used its funds to obtain an 874-acre parcel of wooded land twenty-four miles from Detroit and nine miles outside of Pontiac, where it built 150 low-cost housing units for workers whose annual income ranged from $1,200 to $1,800. Plans for Westacres called for houses on one-acre lots—enough land to accommodate a "thrift garden" that could provide most of the family's fruits and vegetables during layoffs and produce for sale during full employment times. Oakland Housing provided loans to residents to start them toward home ownership; these funds also served as seed money for various enterprises and services such as a greenhouse, a credit union, a weekly newspaper, and recreational facilities to assist residents in the "sound and satisfying development of their communal life."[61]

Oakland Housing, Inc., broke ground in September 1935 and Westbrook supervised the laying out of this social experiment, as Couzens called it.[62] He brought in FERA architect Barton Jenks, a Harvard University graduate who had attended the Ecole de Beaux Arts, to lay out the initial 150 dwellings, which offered several variations of the same basic style. Landscape architect Genevieve Gillette, a student of Jens Jensen, who was a leading proponent of naturalized landscape, was selected to ensure the preservation of the site's rustic, wooded character and to make the streets, housing lots, and "thrift gardens" as graceful and aesthetically pleasing as possible. As the years went by, as shown in Figure 1.2, most of the original dwellings were enlarged and embellished.[63]

Westacres led Westbrook to recognize the need for "broadening the field of rental housing" and fostering a "new conception of the landlord-tenant

**Figure 1.2** Only a small number of the dwellings at Westacres near Pontiac, Michigan, suggest their original appearance. Most of the houses have been enlarged and, in some cases, extensively remodeled. Photograph by the author.

relationship."[64] Wage earners, he now believed, particularly those in trades or industries subject to unemployment or underemployment, had to be especially cautious when obligating themselves to pay for shelter. Westacres allowed Westbrook to test "new procedures in community planning, in construction, [and] in financing" that could be applied in rural, suburban, or urban settings. In July 1936, shortly after the Westacres project got under way, he resigned his post as assistant administrator of the WPA to pursue privately funded cooperative housing development. He was convinced that he could obtain sufficient private or public financial backing, and his optimism was likely reinforced by continued interest in consumer cooperatives. In October 1936 the Cooperative League of the United States called for Congress to create an "agency similar to the Farm Credit Administration for the purpose of assisting consumers' cooperative housing through the provision of low-priced credit."[65]

## The Influence of Neutra and the Park Living Colony

Westbrook began his short-lived career as a private residential real estate developer in 1936 when he resigned from the WPA. Convinced that sufficient economic recovery had taken place, he hired Richard J. Neutra, the internationally renowned Austrian architect who had re-established himself in California in the 1920s, to design the Park Living Colony for a site in Duval County, Florida, near Jacksonville. Neutra's Park Living design called for a long finger of land with up to a thousand units scattered in clusters around small parks or open spaces, an arrangement that promoted the extension of living space into the outdoors. At Sunnyside, Radburn, and elsewhere, Neutra's contemporaries Clarence Stein, Henry Wright, and others used similar community planning concepts involving superblocks that broke with the tradition of imposing a grid upon the city, to achieve similar ends.[66]

The *Architectural Forum* took note of the plans for the Park Living development as a result of Neutra's stature and Westbrook's growing acquaintance with publisher Howard Meyer. Operating in the development phase as a nonprofit venture similar to Westacres, Westbrook worked with local government officials to secure federal funds for relief workers to install utility lines and make certain public infrastructure improvements. The appraised value of these improvements would be "capitalized as private stock to be distributed among families buying houses, thereby avoiding any need to plunk down the customary first payment."[67]

Westbrook's decision to combine cooperative development and modern architecture and to hire Neutra was likely influenced by a mutual friend, David R. Williams. Neutra saw architecture "as a sort of a preventative medicine for mental health and happiness."[68] He joined with Westbrook to create the Park Living Plan because the "psychological significance of this *mutually insured and conditioned ownership* with control and enjoyment of community facilities—day nursery, shops, pools, playgrounds—filled us with enthusiasm."[69] The Park Living plan featured the "simple hierarchy of open spaces" that appeared in Neutra's drawings for his 1920s prototype automobile city, Rush City Reformed.[70] Westbrook and Neutra had to abandon the Duval County project in 1937, "when private enterprise failed to ante the $271,200 in mortgage proceeds required for the initial 111-house section of five cul-de-sacs."[71]

During the time he worked on the Park Living Colony with Neutra, Westbrook served as chairman of the WPA's National Advisory Board and persuaded the Senate's Temporary National Economic Committee to review the housing plan he implemented at Westacres. His effort went nowhere because the committee had "buried it under heaps of testimony pointing to the need for some such solution to the housing problem."[72] By the time committee made its report, congressional patience with publicly funded experiments in cooperative community building had all but evaporated. One of the most vocal senate critics of the New Deal community program was influential Virginia Democrat Harry Flood Byrd, who claimed that the expenditures for projects at Greenbelt, Maryland, Hightstown, New Jersey, and Newport News, Virginia, were "approaching a national scandal."[73]

## Westbrook Turns to Defense Housing

Westbrook's New Deal work, his private sector experience with the Park Living Colony project, and the tepid response his mutual housing ideas received from the Temporary National Economic Committee underscored his political difficulties in gaining—and sustaining—support for public aid for noncommercial community development during the 1930s. Toward the end of the decade he had come to realize that securing the support of organized labor for federal sponsorship was crucial. But Westbrook also felt he needed some way to cultivate the backing of business and commercial interests that blocked federal intervention in the noncommercial housing sector and at the same time demanded direct and indirect aid to ensure commercial market growth or stability.[74]

The Congressional elections of 1940 were a further indication of a political shift to the right, with an increase of only five Democrats in the House of Representatives and a loss of three in the Senate. By that time, the onset of World War II in Europe had intensified American national defense expenditures for arms and other war materials. In that context, federal housing officials shifted their focus from the "nation one-third ill-housed" to the residential needs of moderate and middle-income workers in defense industries.[75]

Westbrook saw the growing demand for housing aid for civilian employees of defense contractors as an opportunity to firmly link cooperative home ownership with the middle-income or moderate wage earner who neither qualified for low-income public housing nor could afford a home mortgage. In October 1940 he was once again employed by the WPA and immediately assigned to the Federal Works Agency (FWA). Westbrook's agenda was to apply the lessons in residential development learned under the New Deal and in the private sector to the "National Defense Housing Program," authorized by Congress under the Lanham Act. On October 7, 1940, shortly before the president signed the bill into law, Westbrook sent WPA acting commissioner Howard O. Hunter a set of "Suggested General Policies" to guide the administration's response to the growing shortage of housing in centers of industrial production and military activity.[76]

Westbrook proposed to Hunter that defense workers become shareholders in not-for-profit mutual housing corporations that would gradually acquire ownership of publicly funded residential developments. "Management of community affairs, including relationships with local governments," he suggested, would be placed in the "hands of the householders" operating under federal supervision and guidance. He favored the construction of "modern and attractive" dwellings that were as "individual in design as possible" so they could be "easily and naturally assimilated into the noraml [*sic*] scheme of the locality."[77] Convinced that the public housing program created under the U.S. Housing Act of 1937 was flawed because it offered no way for low-income residents to gain equity in their homes, Westbrook recommended testing his mutual housing plan as an alternative route to federal housing aid for middle-income households. He regretted that Congress had created a "narrow program aimed at sheltering the very poor and clearing the slums" instead of doing what was needed—providing a "broad-based program to house a majority of the population in small planned communities."[78]

Hunter sent Westbrook's "Suggested General Policies" to his supervisor, John M. Carmody, head of the Federal Works Agency (FWA) who had recently been entrusted by Congress with oversight of the expenditure of Lanham housing funds. In his earlier service as administrator of the Rural Electrification Administration, Carmody used cooperative enterprises to provide affordable electricity to rural dwellers. He now appointed Westbrook as his special assistant, assigning him the task of turning his mutual housing proposal into a more comprehensive plan that could be administered with defense housing funds provided under the Lanham Act. Carmody also asked Westbrook to meet with John Green, the president and founder of the Industrial Union of Marine and Shipbuilding Workers of America (IUMSWA; hereafter Shipbuilding Workers), who had recently appealed to him for funds to build cooperative housing for shipyard workers employed on defense projects.[79]

Although little is known of the meetings between Westbrook and Green, the outcome was clear. With Green's advice and assistance, Westbrook modified the Mutual Home Ownership Plan (hereafter Mutual Plan) and adjusted it to suit the needs of defense workers and the requirements of the Lanham Act. The two now joined as supporters of mutual housing, which they lobbied for as the best means for wage earners to secure the economic and social benefits of the American Dream of home ownership without all of the risks. And their approach to defense housing policy not only benefited war workers but also helped carry the New Deal's communitarian spirit into the 1940s as an aspect of federal housing policy during and immediately after the war.

# 2

# Mutual Housing

## *"Contingency-Proof" Home Ownership for Labor*

Mobilization brought economic recovery to home building. Chairman of the Federal Home Loan Bank Board John H. Fahey reported that 1940 was the "best year of residential construction since 1928," with 545,000 new family units started in nonfarm areas—a 16 percent increase over 1939. The home-building boom paved the way for a successful year for the "thrift and home-financing industry" with a 22 percent increase in new loans during 1940. "Lower interest rates, smaller down payments, and long amortization periods together," Fahey said, "operated to make homes available at easier terms than ever before in the history of American mortgage finance."[1]

Labor leaders and housing reformers looked with skepticism at the expansion in home ownership opportunities for defense workers "at easier terms than ever before." The National Committee on the Housing Emergency expressed concern that the "temporary increase in incomes of many workers in defense industries, coupled with a shortage of houses to rent" would result in the workers "being persuaded to make extravagant or unwise commitment for homeownership which may lead to future foreclosures and distress." Labor leaders did not want their members to owe more on their houses than what they were worth or to be unable to sell their houses when war contracts were canceled and many would be out of work.[2]

Convinced that defense workers and other wage earners needed to approach home ownership with great caution, Lawrence Westbrook sought an alternative housing solution that would make it possible for them steer clear of speculative builders and unscrupulous bankers. He applied what he had learned from administering housing programs for rural dwellers for the Federal Emergency Relief Administration (FERA) and those for urban workers when he worked for the Works Progress Administration (WPA). Westbrook took the lease-to-own plan he devised for Westacres, the community he had developed in Michigan in 1935–1936 with the approval of the United Automobile Workers Union of America (UAW), and altered it to suit the housing needs of highly mobile middle- or moderate-income defense workers who neither qualified for low-income public housing nor could afford a commercial market mortgage and the other costs associated with home ownership.

Westbrook altered the Westacres plan in consultation with John Green, the founder and president of the CIO-affiliated Industrial Union of Marine and Shipbuilding Workers of America (IUMSWA; hereafter Shipbuilding Workers). Green had arrived in Philadelphia after serving a shipbuilding apprenticeship in his native Scotland during World War I. Steeped in socialist politics and tenant militancy, he shifted his political allegiance in the early 1930s to the Democratic Party. Seeking to help his shipbuilding workers secure decent and safe homes without indebting themselves to exploitative landlords and bankers, Green sought cooperative housing aid from the Roosevelt administration.

Green made his request at a time when attitudes toward federal intervention in the housing market were hardening and many Congress members were coming to believe that defense workers should rely on the commercial market to supply their housing needs. Green pressed defense housing officials for aid, aware that the scarcity of rental housing prompted shipbuilding workers to obtain a mortgage to buy one of the newly built houses in subdivisions located "strategically close" to the shipyard of the New York Shipbuilding Corporation (hereafter New York Ship). When Congress authorized the FHA to create the Title VI program, the developer of a subdivision called "Runnemede Ridge" was able to reduce down payments from $370 to $170, prompting the Shipbuilding Workers to urge its members to think ahead to the day when war contracts would be canceled and unemployment might be widespread. The union maintained that cooperative home ownership was a safer bet for the wage earner who needed to be geographically mobile.[3]

## The Origins of Labor Involvement in Federal Housing Policy

The American Federation of Labor (AFL) tried to convince Congress to remedy the shortcomings of the commercial housing market in 1914, when it endorsed a proposal calling for public loans for "municipal and private ownership of sanitary houses" for low-income families. Congress refused to appropriate funds to increase the supply of affordable dwellings until 1917 when shipbuilders, munitions producers, and other war contractors convinced its members that housing was partly to blame for the alarming rates of employee turnover.[4] The U.S. Shipping Board's Emergency Fleet Corporation (EFC) financed the private construction of thirty-one housing developments for shipbuilding and other maritime workers, and the U.S. Department of Labor's U.S. Housing Corporation (USHC) brought twenty-two residential communities to completion on behalf of munitions and other war workers. Both of these wartime programs benefited from the advice and assistance of Electus Litchfield, John Nolen, Walter H. Kilham, and other nationally prominent architects and planners. Influenced by the popular garden city approach to community planning, Union Park Gardens in Wilmington, Delaware and Atlantic Heights in Portsmouth, New Hampshire were two communities that offered war workers many of the attributes found in more affluent communities such as the widely admired Forest Hills Gardens in Queens, New York This was a philanthropic venture backed by the Russell Sage Foundation.[5]

After the war, labor leaders and reform-minded architects and planners urged President Warren G. Harding and Congress to remain involved in housing and expand the noncommercial options open to wage earners by selling the war workers' towns and villages to cooperatives or limited-dividend or nonprofit corporations formed by or on behalf of residents. But instead of allowing the residential communities to form the "nucleus of a noncommercial housing sector" whose economic and social importance would expand in time, the war workers' villages were subdivided and sold on the private market.[6]

Among those who regarded the 1921 sale of Camden's widely admired Yorkship Village as a lost opportunity for shipbuilding workers was John Green, the newly arrived Scottish immigrant with skills in shipbuilding, sheet metal fabrication, and, as time would soon reveal, labor organization. During the early 1930s, Green took on Camden's landlords as part of the larger struggle to unite the nation's skilled and unskilled shipbuilding and maritime workers in a single organization and win recognition from the biggest and most powerful firms in the industry, beginning with New York Ship. With the support of Green's Shipbuilding Workers, two public housing communities called Westfield Acres and Branch Village had been built in Camden. In September 1940 Green was selected by the CIO to go to Capitol Hill and urge Congress to appropriate funds for the construction of housing for civilian employees of defense contractors and the armed forces. The resulting Lanham Act was signed into law by President Roosevelt on October 14, 1940.[7]

As soon as the Lanham Act was passed, Green appealed to the Roosevelt administration to earmark funds for defense housing for shipbuilding workers in Camden and other coastal cities. Recalling the 1921 sale of Camden's Yorkship Village and the ensuing displacement of shipbuilding and other industrial workers, he called for guarantees that residents of new defense housing would have the chance to acquire an economic interest or stake before a community was placed on the auction block. He also asked Federal Works Administration (FWA) head John M. Carmody for his backing to use the newly appropriated funds to build cooperative housing for shipyard workers employed in national defense. Carmody responded by putting Lawrence Westbrook, his new special assistant, and "Green and his [housing] committee together." As he later recalled, they "did the rest."[8]

When Westbrook and Green joined forces to tweak the Mutual Plan and inaugurate its pilot projects, a turning point in federal-labor collaboration was reached and community development, at least temporarily, became a participatory process. Government officials working with labor representatives and private home builders joined together to produce models or patterns for postwar residential construction.

## John Green: From "Red Clyde" to "America's Clyde"

As a former member of the National Labor Relations Board, John Carmody could provide Westbrook with a sense of what to expect from John Green and the Shipbuilding Workers. Green was born in 1894 in Clydebank, the heart of the Scottish shipbuilding region known as "the Clyde." He attended school for about five years before becoming an apprentice in sheet metal work. As he was coming of age, improvement in housing conditions for wage earners was a leading political issue. Reformers, including some aligned with the Labour Party and some tied to the Socialists, backed various collective and cooperative workers' housing programs.[9] Green, like other shipbuilding apprentices, found that labor was in demand when the United Kingdom went to war in 1914, but workers' wages failed to keep pace with the increase in prices in everyday necessities, particularly housing. The Glasgow rent strike organized by trade unionists and Socialists was being described as "one of the most important rent strikes in urban history." The famous uprising might well have been in the back of Green's mind when he warned the House Committee on Public Buildings and Grounds that if Congress did not immediately offer workers housing aid, they were "not going to keep on 'taking it.'"[10]

Imbued with trade union militancy, Green organized a strike of his fellow apprentices in 1916 in violation of British law prohibiting strikes in vital defense industries during wartime, and he stood trial for violating the Defense of the Realm Act. Described as a "victim" of the postwar shipbuilding slump and the "blight" of industrial decline in the United Kingdom, Green emigrated to the United States. He arrived in Philadelphia on July 4, 1921, hoping he had left the pattern of "soaring peaks and Yawning valleys of ship production" behind him. Green's skills help land him a job at Cramp's shipyard in Philadelphia, but there he was soon reminded that there was no escape from the "economic dislocation, social waste, and disaster created by industrial capitalism" when the yard closed.[11]

Around the time of John Green's arrival in Philadelphia, the Fairview Realty Company, a wartime subsidiary of New York Ship, defaulted on the loan it had been given by the Emergency Fleet Corporation to build Yorkship Village. The company's decision to walk away from Yorkship (an action duplicated by shipbuilders and defense contactors nationwide) was taken with total disregard for residents and the city of Camden. Reform-minded architects and planners in the United States and abroad wanted residents to be given an opportunity to obtain collective ownership and keep Yorkship Village free from the corroding effects of real estate speculation. Yorkship's architect, Electus Litchfield, argued that if Congress forced the development's sale on the commercial market, it would be guilty of "throw[ing] away a great opportunity to show the country what an industrial community should be."[12]

On December 10, 1921, the first day of the Yorkship Village auction, prominent New York City realtor and auctioneer Joseph Day took the unusual step of personally urging the workers to buy their homes, but he stopped short of offering any advice or assistance on how they could comfortably afford them.[13] According to the *New York Times*, the auction of the 1,578 dwellings brought in "nearly 5,000 prospective buyers." The building selected for the auction could not accommodate everyone, and "windows were broken in the scramble to get within hearing distance of the auctioneers." Dwellings that might have cost up to $5,000 to build were sold "in the first hour and a half at prices ranging from $1,800 [to] $2,600." The *Times* report observed that "many speculators were present."[14]

The auction recouped about 30 percent of the construction costs of Yorkship Village, subsequently known as Fairview, for the federal treasury. Residents who could not afford the purchase price or an increase in rent following the sale moved voluntarily or were evicted.[15] The 1921 sale of Yorkship Village became deeply embedded in the collective memory of local shipbuilding workers. Twenty years later, Henry J. Andreas of the Local No. 1 Housing Committee was speaking of Yorkship when he said that the union wanted to "prevent a reoccurrence of the evils which followed the last war" when the homes of shipbuilding workers were "placed on the auction block without regard to the welfare of the people living in them." Local shipyard workers vowed that they would never again be "evicted, thrown into the clutches of the mortgage sharks, or exploited by speculators who bought up the World War homes for a song and then drew high rentals from them for years while letting the home go to rack and ruin."[16]

## A New Deal for Shipbuilding Workers

The international decline in shipbuilding that followed World War I was felt in the shipyards of the "American Clyde"—the Delaware River waterfronts of Camden and Philadelphia. The symbol of the dramatic postwar downward slide of the region's shipbuilding industry was Hog Island, where the fifty shipways built during World War I now sat idle and began slowly sinking into the marshland. Green returned to Scotland in1923 to escort his wife Annie and daughter Jesse to their new home in the Philadelphia area. Unable to find work in shipbuilding, he worked in local manufacturing plants, including Atwater Kent, the Philadelphia-based producer of radios.[17]

During the late 1920s and early 1930s, when Green was living in the Kensington section of Philadelphia and working in various factories around the city, he met and mingled with numerous socialists, communists, and other labor and social activists. He befriended Philip Van Gelder, an organizer for the Amalgamated Clothing Workers of America, and Moshe H. Goldstein, a labor attorney. Both would later become employees of the Shipbuilding Workers. In this context Green "put his knowledge and gifts [for labor organizing] . . . at the service of" striking workers at Philco and other nearby plants.[18]

In November 1931 Green was hired by New York Ship in Camden as part of a workforce expansion made possible by U.S. Navy contracts. If company officials knew of his leftist leanings, they elected to overlook them because of their need for skilled and experienced workers. New York Ship had been "at the heart of the United States naval construction program and military-industrial complex for over a half a century" and was not about to miss out on the biggest naval expansion program in years.[19]

Green's "talents as a leader, a tactician, and a negotiator" were soon revealed. In 1933 the tin shop at New York Ship became the "delivery room" for Local No. 1 of the Shipbuilding Workers—giving birth to the nucleus around which Green and his closest advisers built an industry-wide union that aspired to represent and improve the lives of workers employed in shipping and shipbuilding on the Atlantic, Pacific, and Gulf coasts and the Great Lakes. The June 1933 passage of the National Industrial Recovery Act, whose Section 7a recognized the right of workers to engage in collective bargaining, gave them hope that they could build one big union to unite all who worked on the docks and the shipyards in the United States.[20]

The Shipbuilding Workers' 1933 organizing drive at New York Ship benefited from a number of factors, including the company's labor-management policies, previous union organizing of certain crafts and trades under the AFL, the quality and style of union leadership, and a changing political climate that brought federal oversight to labor-management relations.[21] The Philadelphia-Camden region was by this time a well-established hub of activity for the left wing of the AFL, whose members were tied to the Socialist Party of America. When New York Ship started cutting wages in the early 1930s, dissatisfaction with both the company's union and the AFL helped pave the way for acceptance of the industry-wide negotiating approach advocated by Green.[22]

The militancy of the Shipbuilding Workers was quickly established in 1934, the "busiest year in a decade," at New York Ship. Acting union president Green and his right-hand man, Thomas Gallagher, a locally born, Irish Catholic with long-standing ties to labor unions and mainstream Democratic Party politics, convinced a majority of the 2,704 production workers to vote to strike. With the support of local residents and city government and without a single arrest or violent incident, in March 1934 the Shipbuilding Workers forced the company to the bargaining table. Green's tactics of mass action involving picketing by thousands of workers and their families resulted in a union contract, but they failed to garner full recognition of the union as the exclusive bargaining agent for the production workforce.[23]

## Housing and Industrial Democracy

During the time he was seeking recognition for the Shipbuilding Workers of New York Ship, Green realigned himself politically, shifting away from the Socialists and strengthening his ties to the Democratic Party. He regarded the New Deal programs created under the National Industrial Recovery Act as a way of helping labor to help itself. Green looked to Philadelphia for inspiration and guidance for his plans for Camden. He knew, for example, that the city had been recognized as a national leader in progressive housing reform as a result of the work of Octavia Hill, John Ihlder, and other reformers. And he observed how activist Catherine Bauer, architects Oscar Stonorov and Alfred Katsner, and union leader John Edelman of the American Federation of Full-Fashioned Hosiery Workers helped this union form a limited-dividend housing corporation, Juniata Park Housing, and obtain a loan from the PWA to build a housing development on a union-owned parcel of land in North Philadelphia. Named for a hosiery worker killed during a strike, the Carl Mackley Houses was designed by Stonorov and Katsner and was well received by workers and architectural critics alike.[24]

Green admired the Carl Mackley development for its sleek International Style appearance, its swimming pool, club rooms, laundry, and other facilities, and for the way it fit snugly into the fabric of the existing neighborhood. He wanted PWA funds to build a similar residential community in Camden for low-income shipbuilding and other workers. However, he saw PWA's policy of accepting a neighborhood's "prevailing" social and economic patterns as the basis for designating a project as "white," "colored," or "mixed" as both incongruous with industrial unionism and a threat to social democracy. The Shipbuilding Workers welcomed all production workers in shipbuilding and shipping into its ranks, but Green apparently felt its limited organizational and financial resources were insufficient to challenge public and private occupational and residential segregation.[25]

Charles F. Hollopeter, a member of Camden's Local No. 322 of the Plumbers and Steamfitters Union, provided insight into the difficulties that Green and other labor advocates faced in obtaining federal public housing aid for Camden. Hollopeter served on the city's Committee on Housing, formed by the mayor, which was dominated by local real estate and banking interests determined to keep the PWA out of the local housing market and maintain the status quo of segregation by color and class. After defecting from the committee in 1933, Hollopeter helped set up the Labor Housing Committee, Inc., to negotiate with the PWA for a loan to build a limited-dividend housing development for Camden.[26]

The zeal and effectiveness of Camden's labor housing advocates impressed Catherine Bauer, who by this time was executive secretary of the Labor Housing Conference, an AFL-affiliated group she had helped to establish in 1934 to build union support for the kind of federal housing aid that had resulted in the Carl Mackley Houses. Bauer was "astounded . . . [by the] general comprehension and enthusiasm" for housing reform in Camden. The Labor Housing Conference wanted the PWA to provide a loan for a development to be called Westfield Acres. They also wanted it to promise to consult with potential residents "in matters of design and management." Bauer endorsed the housing committee's emphasis on "democratic self-determination in how housing would come into existence and also how it would be run."[27]

Camden's Labor Housing Committee applied for a PWA loan amid rising labor tensions. Seeking union recognition, 15 percent wage increases, and the abolition of piecework, the Shipbuilding Workers went on strike again in May 1935 with an appeal to the Department of Labor, the U.S. Navy, and the City of Camden for support. In July, ten weeks into the strike, New York Ship's management rejected an offer of arbitration from secretary of labor Frances Perkins because it would "spell" the company's "ruination," and attempted to reopen the shipyard.[28] According to the *New York Times*, about a hundred police officers were assigned to "watch the 3,000 pickets and perhaps 2,000 other spectators, including many women," who marched to the shipyard on the morning of July 23. Those assembled outside the gates "alternately cheered and booed the early morning developments," which included an appearance by Camden mayor Frederick Van Nieda and a "minor clash between a striker and a plant official."[29]

One of the strikers involved in the scuffle was none other than John Green himself, who entered the yard while a "conference" was taking place at the shipyard gates between Mayor Van Nieda and New York Ship executive vice president Carl M. Kaltwasser. A scuffle ensued, with Green complaining to the police that Kaltwasser "pushed" him from the yard and "swung at him." Kaltwasser was charged with assault and battery. As accounts of the incident traveled around the city and to other shipbuilding centers, the crowd outside the shipyard gates grew. Reports began to circulate that New York Ship had sent men to the homes of new employees to pressure them to cross the "half mile long" union picket line and return to work in the morning to save their jobs. There were also allegations that the company was sneaking strikebreakers into the shipyard.[30]

Shipbuilding workers and those sympathetic to the union responded to the company's actions by taking to the streets on July 24 in Camden and nearby Collingswood. A seventeen-year-old apprentice was assaulted after trying to report for work, and a small number of cars were vandalized. The company sought a temporary restraining order to force Shipbuilding Workers' Local No. 1 to curtail its picketing, but was denied. When it stopped production the following day, Green predicted that management would soon come to terms with the Shipyard Workers. The union, he said, was forced to fight the shipbuilding giant on "economic grounds. . . . They have taken away our bread and butter and we must take away theirs."[31]

Within days of the Green-Kaltwasser incident, New York Ship legal counsel Henry F. Holthusen went on the offensive, alleging that there was no need for the company to recognize the Shipbuilding Workers as the exclusive collective bargaining agent because "only a small percentage" of the 3,702 production workers employed by New York Ship were union members. The strike lacked popular support, Holthusen contended, and stemmed from "communistic agitation on the part of a mugwump union." He also claimed that the workers had no right to hold up work on existing Navy contracts and prevent the company from pursuing more, warning that the "radical element at Camden is a bad influence."[32]

Shortly after, John Metten, president of New York Ship, attempted to discredit Green and the Shipbuilding Workers on the national stage in testimony before the House Labor Subcommittee. According to the *New York Times*, Metten claimed that the Shipbuilding Workers were responsible for the trouble and that Green had called the strike for purposes of "advancing communism." Most of the men wanted to return to work, Metten argued, but were intimidated by "threats of violence from the communist minority with the aid of imported professional strikers." Shipbuilding Workers executive secretary Van Gelder dismissed Metten's "streak of lies" and assured the subcommittee that Green was not and never had been a communist. In a statement issued immediately after the hearing, Green said, "If Metten wants to break our union the red herring won't do the trick."[33]

## The Limits of New Deal Housing Reform in Camden

Through all the confrontations and strikes that were necessary to bring industrial unionism to New York Ship, Green and the Housing Committee continued to seek PWA aid for Camden. Much to their disappointment, in May 1934 Harold Ickes, Roosevelt's secretary of the interior, announced the termination of the limited-dividend program before reaching a decision on their loan application. However, he kept hopes for housing for Camden alive by assigning the Federal Emergency Housing Corporation the task of reviewing applications for pending limited-dividend program funds with an eye toward directing federal construction of low-income residential communities that would remain in the public domain indefinitely.[34]

In 1935 Camden was selected as one of thirty-seven U.S. cities where the Federal Emergency Housing Corporation would undertake construction of fifty low-rent housing developments consisting of a total of 21,600 units.[35] A contract was awarded to the Associated Architects of Camden, a collaborative that included Oscar Stonorov, to design the 514-unit Westfield Acres. The project's $3 million budget frustrated reformers' efforts to provide workers access to housing that was designed for their needs and that offered a "new appearance, expressing an entirely new meaning of life."[36] One of the project's few "frills" was a lobby mural completed by PWA artists, including Marion Greenwood, who was recruited by Stonorov. Greenwood painted a shipbuilding worker's wife and child watching him depart for work from the doorway of a nondescript, clapboard-covered dwelling—the type that Westfield Acres replaced. She depicted the Shipbuilding Workers' 1934 picket line as a confrontation necessary for shipyard workers to escape slum housing conditions.[37]

Labor praised the PWA for its work in raising the stature of the noncommercial housing market. The AFL noted that even though the agency was "hampered by inadequate funds and court litigation," it produced "a number of outstanding projects which demonstrated conclusively the advantages of slum-clearance and low-rent modern housing under the supervision of the federal government."[38] At its annual meeting in October 1935, the AFL endorsed the work of the Labor Housing Conference. In 1935 Catherine Bauer and members of both the Labor Housing Conference and the National Public Housing Conference began working with Senator Robert Wagner (D-NY) and Congressman Henry Ellenbogen (D-PA) to draft a bill that would eventually become the U.S. Housing Act of 1937. In its original form, the bill allowed public and private organizations, including housing authorities, cooperatives, and limited-dividend and nonprofit corporations to become recipients of federal housing aid. Bauer told the Senate Committee on Education and Labor in 1935 that "if a great many new dwellings are to be produced without the stimulus of the profit motive, some other spark must be provided in its place."[39]

Labor advocates hoped that a bill that distributed federal housing assistance through a "variety of mechanisms," both public and private, would not provoke an attack from real estate and development interests, but they were wrong. Determined to keep the growth of the noncommercial market in check, the Public Housing Committee of the U.S. Building and Loan League favored elimination of provisions allowing nongovernmental participation by "consumers' housing societies" and "limited-profit housing agencies." Later, in the final version of the 1937 act, the U.S. Housing Authority (USHA) was authorized to lend funds for housing construction only to qualified public housing authorities for razing substandard "slum" housing and constructing the equivalent number of new units. Bauer and her allies backed the bill, popularly known as the Wagner-Steagall Act, erroneously believing they would later be able to restore loans to limited-dividend and nonprofit housing corporations.[40]

Housing activists in Camden wasted no time in laying the political groundwork in Trenton needed to take advantage of USHA housing funds. In 1938 John Green was one of five members of the Municipal Housing League, a group appointed by the Camden City Council to help secure passage of state legislation necessary for the city to establish a housing authority and receive federal subsidies from the USHA. Shortly after the New Jersey State Assembly passed the enabling legislation, the Camden City Council authorized the creation of the Camden Housing Authority and Green was appointed to its first board of directors. The Federal Emergency Housing Corporation conveyed Westfield Acres to the Camden Housing Authority, and the board applied for USHA approval for a housing development for African Americans to be named the Clement T. Branch Village.[41]

The construction of Branch Village was delayed by a scandal in the newly created housing authority over real estate deals made prior to any announcement of site selection. To preserve the board's credibility, USHA administrator Nathan Straus demanded the resignation of all board members, including Green and others who had not been implicated in the scandal, and he ordered the selection of a new site for the proposed Branch Village. By December 1940 the board of the Camden Housing Authority had been legally reconstituted and Wilbert F. Dobbins had begun serving as labor's representative. A contract was awarded to the architectural partnership of Joseph N. Hettel and Oscar Stonorov to design a 279-unit community on a parcel of land on the Delaware River bordered by Second, Fourth, and Milton streets. By the time Branch Village was dedicated in September 1941, its budget had been subjected to stringent cost cutting by USHA over the objections of the Housing Advisory Committee, a watchdog organization created by Camden's Central Labor Union.[42]

Green became familiar with the shortcomings of USHA's congressional charge to couple slum clearance with public housing construction when the heavily publicized Red Hook development in Brooklyn, New York, displaced many members of the Shipbuilding Workers. "Great hardship" faced those displaced because their "earnings disqualified them from obtaining homes in the splendid new development, yet were inadequate to find satisfactory accommodations elsewhere." The Red Hook experience helped convince Green that shipbuilding workers who made too much money to qualify for public housing but could not afford to purchase a house should have opportunities for cooperative home ownership. He quickly discovered what other unions had found in the past—obtaining funds for cooperative housing development was not going to be easy.[43]

## Green Helps Labor Secure Defense Housing Aid

Labor's pivotal role in the creation of the low-income public housing program was matched by an equally determined campaign to force Congress to appropriate funds for the construction of housing for defense workers. The AFL and CIO spoke with a single voice in rejecting the notion that the private sector would provide an adequate supply of safe, affordable dwellings suitable for families. They agreed that any defense housing funds appropriated by Congress had to be used to build residential communities that would stand the test of time and improve the quality of life for workers and their families—there would be no barracks or other temporary structures for defense workers to appease real estate interests. As Figure 2.1 depicts, under union pressure the FWA expanded affordable housing opportunities in the small industrial cities and towns located outside of major defense production centers such as Pittsburgh.

Despite the demands of responding to the housing crisis, union leaders did not ignore or forget about the hard-won low-income housing program. Harry Bates of the AFL agreed with USHA administrator Nathan Straus in 1941 that

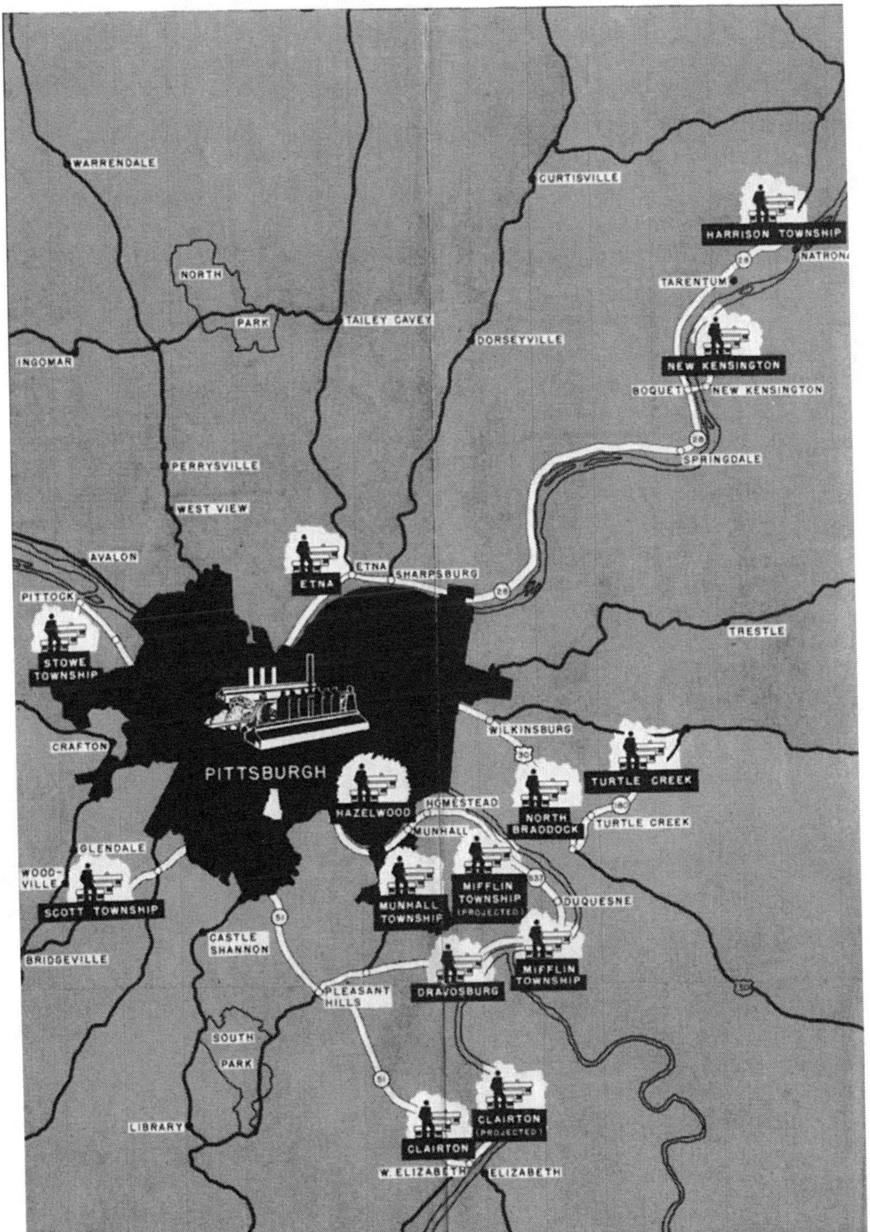


**Figure 2.1** At the insistence of organized labor, the Federal Works Agency dramatically increased the supply of affordable housing in the heavily industrialized mill towns of Greater Pittsburgh. Most of the communities depicted here were sold under the Mutual Plan in the 1950s. Courtesy of the State Library of Pennsylvania.

the United States had the resources to continue razing slums and building low-income housing, *and* launch a new program for defense workers. Labor insisted on the construction of publicly funded defense housing by labor-friendly agencies such as USHA to keep workers from being forced into buying houses they did not need or would not be able to afford when defense employment ended.

Under pressure from the AFL and the CIO for immediate action to address the shortage of housing in centers of defense production and military activity, in June 1940 Congress authorized the War Department, the Navy Department, and USHA to use their existing appropriations to build housing in designated areas for civilian employees of defense contractors and the armed forces. Local public housing authorities, operating under agreement with USHA, built the 200-unit Moreno Court in Pensacola, Florida, in eighty-seven days, and the 424-unit Riverside Heights Addition in Montgomery, Alabama, in ninety-six days.[44]

Labor applauded President Roosevelt's decision to create the Office (changed to Division on January 11, 1941) of Defense Housing Coordination (DDHC) under the auspices of the Council of National Defense. On July 21, 1940, Charles F. Palmer, a realtor who backed the construction of Atlanta's PWA-sponsored Techwood and University Homes, was appointed to the post of DDHC coordinator.[45] When John Green visited Palmer before the House Building and Grounds Committee vote on the Lanham Bill, he emphasized that mobilization had brought a new twist to old housing problems. Shipbuilding workers in the region now enjoyed steady work and bigger paychecks, but decent, affordable rental housing was scarce on both sides of the Delaware River. On the New Jersey side, enterprising builders had erected new homes a short drive from New York Ship and advertised them in union and local newspapers, but most workers either could not afford them or lacked the employment security needed to undertake a mortgage.[46]

Noting changes in the housing market precipitated by mobilization, in March Green wrote to Anthony Wayne Smith, the CIO's assistant general counsel, for assistance in obtaining financing for cooperative housing from the Reconstruction Finance Corporation (RFA) or other federal agencies. The union leader explained his support for cooperative home ownership by noting that when shipyard workers, "by dint of the greatest privation" bought a house, they often found the cost "either above their means, or altogether impossible to meet because of the vicissitudes in their employment."[47]

In May Green assured readers of the nationally circulating *CIO News* that he and other union leaders were working with officials from the Roosevelt administration to solve the housing problems that accompanied mobilization. They recognized that most defense workers lacked the employment security needed to purchase one of the "glittering bungalows which fill the real-estate pages of the daily newspaper." The "very ones who produce the wealth of the nation," Green observed with irony, "are those who are disregarded, at least when it comes to housing, in sharing that wealth."[48]

According to Green, the Shipbuilding Workers had found a way for workers to enjoy lasting benefit from defense employment and obtain "decent, up-to-date, and attractive homes" without taking on the economic risk involved in traditional home ownership. Cooperative home ownership would make it possible for a worker to enjoy "modern kitchen appliances, tiled bathroom and shower, an oil burner or coal stoker to fire his furnace, and numerous other conveniences that will free him and his wife from many of the chores of housekeeping." Such dwellings hardly constituted "extravagant desires" but were the types of dwellings defense workers and their families needed and deserved.[49]

In the absence of a flexible program of federal housing aid, Green saw that labor would have to find private funds to help it build communities of "decent, up-to-date and attractive" cooperatively owned houses. Despite the attention the noncommercial housing sector had received from the Roosevelt administration, affordable housing remained "a problem for the labor movement. The government is not answering it. We must do it ourselves."[50] During the Summer of 1940, Green lobbied for housing funds for defense workers by sending delegations of shipbuilding workers to Washington "at least once a week" to request federal aid. Both CIO and AFL unions backed Texas Democratic representative Frederick "Fritz" G. Lanham's bill calling for funds to build housing for civilian employees of the armed forces and defense contractors. During the late-summer debate over the bill, Green avoided any reference to cooperative housing, likely out of concern that it might detract attention from the main issue—the inability of the private market to meet the demand for affordable housing in centers of defense production.

On September 2, 1940, Green captured the attention of members of the House Committee on Public Buildings and Grounds with his gripping description of the plight of defense workers caught in the "no-man's land of housing" whose income was too high for them to qualify for public housing but too low or uncertain for them to buy a house.[51] Lanham's bill would help defense workers like those in the Camden shipyards who were preyed on by unscrupulous real estate investors using "threats of eviction or rent increases" to compel them to "buy homes which they don't want or [for] which they can't afford to pay."[52]

The members of Shipbuilding Workers Local No. 16 who worked for the Federal Shipbuilding Corporation (hereafter Federal Ship) in Kearney, New Jersey, similarly found that defense mobilization magnified their housing problems. Housing was so scarce that many lived in "cold-water flats in Jersey City that can only be classified as slums." Green reminded the members of the Buildings and Grounds Committee that New York Ship, Federal Ship, and other defense contractors were given generous financial incentives to convert to wartime production. In contrast, the Shipbuilding Workers had "sought neither subsidies nor guarantees, but only the things that we as workers must have to be able to do the job the government and the people want us to do."[53] In the days preceding his House testimony, Green and members of the Shipbuilding Workers Local No. 1 Housing Committee met with John Carmody, Sidney Hillman of the National Defense Advisory Committee, and DDHC head Charles Palmer to impress on them the need for quick action to solve the housing shortage in Camden and other centers of defense production.[54]

R. J. Thomas, president of the United Automobile Workers of America (UAW) and a member of the CIO's Housing Committee, regarded Green's testimony as the "climax of the campaign" labor had waged for defense housing aid. Until Green and other labor activists organized for housing reform, Camden's workers had lived in "old homes in varying states of disrepair," with the poorest residing on the Delaware riverfront in an area known as the Line, where shacks were "scattered pell-mell all over the place. A solitary faucet, from which water flows with a sluggish gurgle, is the sole source of water."[55]

Thomas enumerated the steps Green and the Shipbuilding Workers had taken to get decisive action from Congress and the White House. Green had directed Shipbuilding Workers attorney M. H. Goldstein to make sure that the union took "advantage of every possible opening in its attempt to get more and better homes in Camden" and that "all legal angles were handled." Green had also cultivated contacts with architects such as Stonorov who were known to be "labor minded" and solicited their advice and counsel on housing and planning matters.[56] Union workers sent to Washington to lobby for housing aid or to meet with housing officials were compensated for their expenses and lost working time. As a consequence of these efforts, said UAW activist and architect Alan Mather, Green, the Shipbuilding Workers, and Camden "seemed to be shooting ahead of what Philadelphia is doing."[57]

The appropriation of defense housing funds under the Lanham Act had "scarcely been made" when Green and the Shipbuilding Workers made a return visit to Carmody's office. Aware that Congress had just charged Carmody with oversight of defense housing funds, Green and members of the union's executive council asked to "be allowed to participate in planning and building a housing project in Camden" that the residents would "acquire over a period of years out of rentals adjusted for that purpose." The union wanted residential development for its workers to take place "on new land just outside the city" to symbolize their break from the hold of Camden's exploitive landlords. The union sought total control of the project and did not want "AF of L craft unionists building our houses for us. We can build houses too, as well as we build ships, and we want the privilege of doing so."[58]

Carmody was impressed with the Shipbuilding Workers' proposal. He told Lawrence Westbrook that the cooperative ownership aspects of Green's offer were "neither new nor strange" to him and "had all the elements I had seen succeed in rural electrification." The Shipbuilding Workers already had "a committee working on housing in the Camden area" that had gathered data on the city's housing needs and "talked to architects and others interested in building."[59]

At Carmody's request, Westbrook wrote to Green and briefly outlined his mutual housing ideas. He suggested that they meet because Green's ideas "with respect to management by householders . . . [about] the necessity for a decent environment . . . appear to coincide with the views I have submitted to Mr. Carmody and which he has approved."[60]

Labor justifiably took credit for the legislative campaign for defense housing assistance that concluded on October 18, 1940, when President Roosevelt signed Lanham's defense housing bill into law.[61] The Lanham Act stipulated that funds appropriated under the law could be used to build housing only in those places where the president, working through DDHC coordinator Charles F. Palmer, certified a need. Once a project won executive authorization, FWA administrator John Carmody, who controlled the funds appropriated by the bill, would assign responsibility for the construction of specific housing projects to constituent agencies within the FWA or other federal departments and agencies. The situation warranted a "housing czar," but Roosevelt provided a "traffic cop" instead. The administrative setup of the defense housing program not only did little to help advance mutual housing; it would later be manipulated by Palmer to undermine it.[62]

## The Mutual Plan Emerges

John Carmody's background and upbringing likely contributed to his decision to allow Lawrence Westbrook to test the mutual home ownership plan among defense workers. The son of Irish immigrants who had settled in western Pennsylvania, Carmody was educated at a number of business schools before attending Columbia University. He spent his early career in the coal-mining industry, where he became acquainted with working-class activists from the United Kingdom whose belief in social and economic class militancy brought them into the labor movement. Now Carmody acted on these principles by creating the Mutual Ownership Defense Housing Division (hereafter Mutual Division) and giving Westbrook, with the strong support of organized labor, the chance to use defense funds to launch his own cooperative community development program.

In meetings and correspondence exchanged during late 1940 and the early months of 1941, Westbrook worked out the details of what became known as the Mutual Home Ownership Plan (hereafter Mutual Plan) with Green, the members of the union's executive council and legal counsel, and the members of the Local No. 1 Housing Committee.[63] Henry Andreas later recalled that the union's plan was "presented to the Government officials in Washington. Jointly, we worked out what became known at that time as the 'Camden Plan.'" The Shipbuilding Workers "put forth the best interests of all the members of our organization," and the Mutual Division agreed to almost everything, including the creation of reserve funds for specific purposes such as maintenance and upkeep or for unemployed, ill, or injured shareholders.[64]

Westbrook recalled that before passage of the Lanham Act and the creation of the Mutual Division, "for more than two years a [Shipbuilding Workers] housing committee had endeavored, without success," to secure aid for a mutual ownership and management housing program. He remembered that "Mr. Green and his committee worked constantly with Government officials" and that many of the union's suggestions were "embodied in the plans and procedures as they have been carried out." However, nothing is known about the procedures used to gain input from workers on what they needed or wanted in a dwelling and a new community.[65]

The single-family houses most workers presumably would have preferred for maximum private or individualized space could not be provided under the strict cost ceilings imposed by the Lanham Act. As a result, semidetached units became the predominant housing type in the Mutual Plan pilot projects.[66]

Thanks to Westbrook and Green, labor finally had its own housing program. According to Marvin M. Miniard, a Dayton electrical worker and labor activist who made a career change after discovering mutual housing, the mutual home ownership plan was "The Workingman's Housing Plan"; he expressed the hope that out of the "horror" of the war "patterns would be developed and experiences gained" that could be put to use to guide peacetime development.[67]

The Mutual Plan called for the creation of legally chartered, nonprofit corporations, called mutual housing associations, that would lease and later purchase residential communities built by or financed by the federal government. Before he began collaborating with Green, Westbrook decided to substitute "mutual" for "cooperative" because he wanted to signify a break with cooperative housing's former shaky financial footing and ideologically fueled past. He also claimed that it was appropriate to use "mutual" because he had borrowed certain practices from the mutual insurance companies familiar to many householders. Pointing to the success of housing cooperatives in Sweden, Denmark, and Holland, Westbrook said, "We have here at home something that very nearly approaches the idea, although it has had a different application. I refer to our mutual insurance companies, which have been so successful." Because consumers purchased insurance "to make certain of the provision of shelter for their families," it stood to reason "that a means can be developed whereby the same insurance companies could provide both housing and insurance."[68]

Under the terms of the Mutual Plan, residents bought equal shares in a nonprofit corporation, called a mutual ownership housing association, that leased and later, with the shareholders' consent, purchased the entire community, including land, homes, and community buildings, from the federal government with a government-provided thirty-three-year mortgage at 3 (later 4) percent interest. No down payment was required, and the sale price was determined according to fair market value, not the price of actual construction. Once the sale was completed, the mutual ownership housing association held the fee simple or land title. In exchange for the purchase of shares in the association, residents were issued perpetual occupancy agreements for their dwelling units. They had to pay a monthly fee to cover amortization of the mortgage, mortgage interest, depreciation, repairs, insurance, vacancy losses, operating expenses, taxes, and a reserve account. Once the mortgage was retired, the residents would see a lower monthly fee.[69]

The mission of Westbrook's Mutual Division was to demonstrate the practicality of the Mutual Plan and determine if it was "economically sound and desired by the general public."[70] Looking ahead to the end of the defense crisis, Westbrook hoped that the Mutual Plan would "provide a pattern of housing, for use by private capital as well as by Government, which might overcome some of the more serious defects inherent in home-ownership housing on the one hand and rental housing on the other."[71]

## Westbrook and Green Make "Housing History"

Once war mobilization got under way and congressional support for New Deal programs waned, real estate developers, home builders, and home finance providers hoped they had seen the last of publicly funded programs for middle- or moderate-income householders seeking cooperative home ownership or other noncommercial market options.[72] Much to their dismay, however, as soon as Congress appropriated funds for defense housing under the Lanham Act, Westbrook quickly teamed up with John Green, the militant up-and-coming CIO leader. Westbrook's Mutual Division was neither the first nor the only Roosevelt administration community development agency that encouraged union workers to seek noncommercial market options. But it was the best planned and most securely funded initiative to help wage earners escape unscrupulous landlords, greedy home builders, merciless mortgage bankers, and other commercial market hazards and find economic and social refuge in the nonprofit housing sector. Initially, it was unclear just how many Lanham projects John Carmody would assign to Westbrook to develop under the Mutual Plan. At one point, as many as thirty might have been contemplated, but that number was eventually reduced to eight.[73]

Carmody supported the selection of Camden as the site of the first Mutual Division project because the "whole arrangement [then] seemed to me to be made to order for a successful defense housing experiment." Camden was considered "one of the bad spots from the point of view of rent rises and accompanying disturbed morale among vital shipbuilders," and the need for defense housing funds there was well established. Carmody explained that the FWA was going to "build houses in any event. We would restrict tenants to families of certified defense workers. We would dispose of them 'in the public interest'"[74] as required under the Lanham Act.

Westbrook worked with Green in developing the Mutual Plan and laying plans for its implementation with the knowledge that Texas congressman Fritz G. Lanham, sponsor of the defense housing bill, had "unofficially recommended . . . [that] limited experiments . . . be conducted for the purpose of developing principles and procedures with respect to housing financing, tenure, and construction."[75] Westbrook later stated that Lanham had "persuaded"

Carmody to authorize "a series of projects, beginning with Audubon Village, on the outskirts of Camden, for the purpose of testing out mutual home ownership principles as applied to housing for medium income families." Such housing could be "adapted to private use after the end of the emergency."[76]

Regardless of whether Lanham had actually given a behind-the-scenes blessing to the use of defense housing funds to test mutual housing, Carmody was willing to give the Mutual Plan a trial application. Westbrook and Green sought to relieve the defense housing shortage in Camden and elsewhere using methods and approaches developed and successfully implemented by earlier New Deal agencies such as the Rural Electrification Administration. The Mutual Plan was even referred to as the "REA plan for housing."[77] Carmody thought that mutual housing offered a "high degree of protection for the Government's investment by reason of the occupants' direct, selfish interest in the home he occupies." Selected on the basis of "probable permanent employment," residents would not be those who "flooded the real estate market" at war's end but would provide economic and social stability for communities in transition. The feasibility of the Mutual Plan would be demonstrated by a "carefully selected group of stable citizens who will have a permanent stake in the community."[78]

Carmody believed that the Mutual Plan would economically appeal to defense workers because it offered greater housing security than a lease or a home mortgage. Residents of mutual housing communities would establish a reserve fund "during the period of full employment which may be drawn upon in time of need." It would be used as necessary to halt "individual foreclosures, thus inhibiting neighborhood blighting and depreciation of values, making possible low-cost maintenance and repairs, and provide opportunities for large-scale refinancing and more effective means of investment protection."[79] Carmody, who early in his career frequented the bleak coal patch towns of Pennsylvania, praised the Mutual Division for showing that "poor people have the right to beauty."[80]

Kathryn R. Murphy of the Department of Labor's Bureau of Labor Statistics supported the Mutual Plan and called it good for defense workers. Recalling the days before the Great Depression, when balloon mortgages were common, Murphy said that wage earners needed a housing plan that allowed them to make a small fixed payment each month without enduring "serious financial losses" if circumstances forced them to move. She emphasized the plan's no-down-payment provision, which was especially important to workers who had to drain their savings to cover the costs of migrating to defense production areas and seeking employment and housing.[81]

Westbrook and Green agreed that shipbuilding and other defense workers caught in the "no man's land of housing" were ideal for testing the Mutual Plan. They sought to make "housing history" by developing an "easy and what might be called contingency-proof" form of home ownership for middle-income wage earners frustrated with their limited commercial market options. The plan they developed would have won the acclaim of reformers and architects like Electus

Litchfield who had sought to transform World War I villages into the cooperative property of their residents.

Westbrook and Green established a new level of federal-labor collaboration when working together to modify the Mutual Plan. Westbrook learned that union workers were not of one mind when it came to community design and planning. They expected to be consulted and involved in decision making and were not adverse to innovation in architecture and design. Green learned that no matter how amicable Westbrook and Carmody might be to workers' requests and interests, the congressionally imposed limit on per-dwelling spending constricted policy choices.

In 1920, the American Labor Party had proposed a plan to directly involve workers and unions in the development and implementation of housing policy. The plan had called for worker representatives to help oversee the operation of nonprofit organizations charged by states or municipalities with constructing affordable housing, and workers were to be given opportunities to learn the basics of home building and repair so they could gain sweat equity in their dwellings. The party had announced its housing plan following months of economic turmoil and social turbulence that included violent and divisive strikes, civil uprisings, and riots. But by the mid-1920s, when the growth of the real estate market was being propelled by speculative investment, this proposal seemed all but forgotten. Two decades later, when Westbrook and Green were collaborating on mutual housing, neither man ever mentioned the American Labor Party, but, however unwittingly, they were advancing its vision of collaboration between government, labor, architects, and home builders on behalf of affordable housing for workers.[82]

# 3

# Mutually Compatible?

## *Mutual Housing and Modern Architecture*

In 1927 when the Amalgamated Clothing Workers Union built its first cooperative apartment complex in the Bronx, it selected a site plan that allowed the new Tudor Revival–style buildings to fit seamlessly into the larger cityscape, ignoring the modern trends in residential development embraced by European municipal and trade union building councils. Abraham Kazan, the founder and president of Amalgamated Housing, believed that cooperative home owners could, and perhaps should, have dwellings that looked conventional.[1] Thirteen years later, when Lawrence Westbrook and John Green considered the architecture and site planning for the federal government's inaugural mutual housing projects, despite their admiration for Kazan as a labor leader, they broke from his precedent and the prevailing patterns of urban development and design.

Westbrook and Green thought they could win support for the Mutual Plan by creating a new social and physical environment, one influenced by "community modernism" as an approach to architecture and planning in which the amount of physical space, financial resources, and attention allotted to individual dwelling units—private space—was secondary to that allotted to the public space enjoyed by all. Fascinated by modern architecture and prefabricated home building, Westbrook enthusiastically brokered the marriage of mutual home ownership and modern architecture. But, as with every such arrangement, there were unintended consequences that would forever influence the Mutual Plan.[2]

### Audubon Village: The "Prefabricated Guinea Pig"

When Westbrook and Green began working together on the Mutual Plan, architects Joseph Hettel and Oscar Stonorov were already employed as "technical advisers" by the Shipbuilding Workers union. On November 28, 1940, after securing presidential approval for 500 units of defense housing in the Camden area through Division of Defense Housing Coordination (DDHC) head Charles F. Palmer, Westbrook and Green met with Hettel and Stonorov in Washington, D.C., to discuss the proposed project.[3] One month later, Hettel and Stonorov's firm was awarded a contract to design the Mutual Division's inaugural community, Audubon Village. The site selected for the new project consisted of "100 acres of moderately rolling land bounded by two highways and an overgrown creek" that was "a hefty stone's throw" from the World War I–built Yorkship Village.[4]

In early January 1941, when Westbrook met with Audubon Borough officials, he promised to build "very attractive housing" set in "beautiful surroundings." Audubon Village, they were assured, would be a "credit to the community."[5] Westbrook arranged for the employment of WPA workers to do the rough grading and install drainage, water, and sewer lines. Site preparation work commenced on January 6, 1941, in unseasonably cold weather. The WPA site superintendent divided the 400 relief workers into two seven-hour daily shifts and "pushed the job vigorously," defying the stereotype of government inefficiency. Workmen used power tools and earthmoving equipment, including "12 cu. yd. carrying scrapers, tractors, bulldozers, and trench diggers."[6]

Westbrook's use of WPA workers to operate heavy construction equipment for preparing the Audubon building site antagonized local AFL leaders. Labor tensions intensified when he refused to accept a bid from the American Homes Company on the Audubon Village contract because the firm had employed only AFL workers at its Kearny, New Jersey, prefabricated housing plant. Instead, the contract for the prefabricated dwellings went to the Day Housing Company, which set up shop in a nearby vacant building and hired CIO-affiliated workers to do the job.[7] When the AFL threatened to picket the site, John Carmody brokered an agreement. The result was that twenty-eight dwellings would be built by AFL workers using "conventional hammer-and-saw in the field." The *Architectural Forum* predicted that the AFL tradesmen would build the twenty-eight houses like "expensive furniture" so that they would easily "outshine their prefabricated neighbors."[8]

Housing analysts closely monitored the FWA-CIO foray into the prefabricated market. One observed that Day Housing Company employees "entered an empty factory at Gloucester, N.J., on March 15 to begin to set up a plant for the manufacture of the houses" and delivered the first of them in just a month despite the fact that the firm had never before produced a single unit of prefabricated housing.[9] The company founder, Joseph P. Day, was a New York City–based businessman and former American Homes Company employee who was not unknown to Camden-area residents; he was the "leather-lunged and dramatic" real estate auctioneer who had presided over the sale of Yorkship Village in 1921. A father of six children who neither drank nor smoked, Day claimed that working was his hobby.[10]

Day's crew quickly converted 110,000 square feet of leased factory space into a plant capable of turning out wall and roof sections for twenty houses a day.[11] The 8 million feet of lumber consumed in the production of the houses arrived at the plant by rail. It was graded and stored in special racks until workers used "six, 14-inch circular swing saws, each manned by an operator and helper" to cut it to size. Each worker had a specific task he was expected to perform. One crew member "picked up the precut, keyed members, [and] dropped them in their keyed places on the jig tables." A second worker "walked along the table nailing the members together, while the first crew dropped the window and door frames in place, covered the tables with 12-inch sheathing boards precut to fit the lengths of the exterior walls and roof sections." A third crew member "lifted the finished sections from the tables and loaded them on trucks."[12] The *Architectural Forum* reported that Day's crews framed 102 houses in five days of work.[13]

With a waste rate of "less than half of one percent of the lumber used," Day was justifiably proud of his record of accomplishment on the Audubon Village job. In December 1941 he boasted to President Roosevelt that if he ran three shifts a day, his firm could produce prefabricated houses at the rate of one every nine and a half minutes or one hundred and fifty every twenty-four hours. Eager to secure another prefabricated housing contract, Day told the president, "We now have a well equipped plant and an efficient technically trained organization, a large stock of materials on hand ready to produce immediately—where do we go next?"[14]

The president provided no definitive answer, but FWA technical consultant and architect Burns Roensch pointed out that the Audubon Village job offered some important lessons for union leaders and building contractors. He explained that complete "readiness" was needed to achieve the "rate of twenty or more family units per day" and praised the "shop fabrication method . . . [because it] permitted efficient employment of unskilled labor and thus lowered cost of production."[15] The *Architectural Forum* noted approvingly that "private architects have had a hand" in the Audubon Village project and made it possible for prefabrication "to show its stuff."[16]

Officials from the Wheeling Engineering Company, the general contractor, praised the FWA and its subcontractors, suppliers, and workers for joining together as "a smooth functioning team to set a national speed record on this Defense Housing Project."[17] Key to the "smooth functioning team" was construction superintendent John Weigel, who organized a "labor force that at its peak numbered 2500 . . . into a harmonious working team."[18] According to reports, Weigel fostered such intense competition between construction crews that "foremen were swiping lumber from each other to get their jobs done faster, and as the job neared completion, their [workers'] cry was, 'Boss, where do we go next?'"[19]

Weigel's crews transformed a site that featured "nothing above ground" on April 9, 1941, to one that welcomed the arrival of residents two months later. In 26 working days—208 working hours—they erected 499 houses (see Figures 3.1

**Figure 3.1** The architects Joseph Hettel and Oscar Stonorov designed one- and two-story dwellings for Audubon Village, New Jersey. This drawing, one of a series of four produced by the architects in 1940, hangs on the wall of the Audubon Park Mutual Housing Association's administrative offices. Courtesy of the Audubon Park Mutual Housing Association.

and 3.2). The remarkable pace of production was achieved despite a jurisdictional strike, "mud and ice and frost two feet thick, and temperatures ranging from 10 above zero to 106." The Camden *Courier-Post* reported that the "large red, white, and blue sign atop the field office of the Wheeler Engineering Company" that read "Defense workers, the eyes of the world are upon us—let us do a first-class job," had in fact, been honored.[20]

Like Day, Weigel gained confidence in prefabricated housing's potential as a result of the Audubon Village project. Eager to see further use of prefabrication in defense building, his firm sought contracts that would allow him to shift his smoothly functioning team to another site to assemble more prefabricated defense housing. In December 1941 Weigel told the *Courier-Post* that his work crews "ought to be staking out houses right now."[21]

In July 1941, the *Engineering News-Record* identified Audubon Village as part of the FWA's larger effort to "make a practical study of the workability of the 'Camden Plan' for financing large-scale housing developments."[22] The FWA wanted to "demonstrate a method of financing housing, based on mutual insurance principles, which will prove attractive to private capital."[23] By November of the same year, the *Engineering News-Record* declared that the completion of the first three Mutual Plan pilot projects was the "biggest news thus far in the defense-housing program." With Audubon Village and her sister developments, the FWA introduced a "new form of financing for large-scale housing by means of a mutual insurance plan" and offered a "vivid demonstration of the possibility of mass production methods applied to wood frame house construction."[24]

**Figure 3.2** Many of the two-story dwellings at Audubon Village are located on short cul-de-sacs. This resident has kept the same type of fencing that originally enclosed each yard. Photograph by Michael J. Chiarappa.

The *American Builder* also approved of the defense-housing program as a platform for experimenting with new ideas in housing. At Audubon Village the FWA was "trying out both an experimental construction method and an experimental mutual home ownership plan known as 'The Camden Plan.'" If it proved successful, its implementation would likely be expanded.[25] *The Real Estate Record and Builders Guide* also took the view that a "new method of home purchasing" [mutual ownership] was about be "tested" at Audubon Village.[26]

## The Camden *Courier-Post* Celebrates Audubon Village

In December 1941 the Camden *Courier-Post* published a sixteen-page supplement commemorating Audubon Village's completion; it consisted largely of "news" features culled from press releases, photographs supplied by the FWA, congratulatory advertisements from contractors, subcontractors, and supply houses, and a small number of maps and diagrams illustrating the importance of the metropolitan region to the defense effort. Described as "distinctive and trail-blazing" Audubon Village was a worthy model for such initiatives. The "first of [its] kind," it was "a signpost of what can be accomplished in housing when it is considered in terms of town planning and not just individual shelter." The Mutual Division was said to be "Break[ing] New Ground" in "Layout,

Construction, Facilities [and] Financing" in readiness for postwar changes in residential development.[27]

Audubon Village was distinguished by low density and other amenities. It contained "five houses per acre, whereas most U.S.H.A. projects have 15 to 25 to the acre," and 56 percent of the houses had five rooms, the "largest room ratio of any defense project or any public housing project." Attached garages and full-size utility rooms (as opposed to closets) were unmatched in public housing. Plastered walls, hardwood floors, copper tubing, and "standard sanitary plumbing" were provided despite growing scarcities of these materials.[28] Working within the $3,500 per-unit construction limit imposed by the Lanham Act, Hettel and Stonorov designed six types of dwellings for the community, including one-story side-by-side duplexes and two-story buildings containing two or more dwelling units each. The pitched-roofed dwellings had white asbestos shingle siding and abundant windows that were trimmed in one of several contrasting colors. White picket fences enclosed each yard.

In contrast to neighborhoods in the Camden area developed by real estate speculators, there would be "no cramping for space" at Audubon Village because the "wide dispersal of the units allows plenty of fresh air, [and] emphasizes the park-like development." The caption of a drawing of the street layout of the streets was "Safe for Children."[29] On the cover of the special supplement was a drawing of Audubon Village. Beneath an unfurled American flag, a table, two chairs, and an umbrella awaited the worker's arrival home. The implication was that when the war was won there would be leisure time for shipyard laborers among family and friends in a bucolic setting that was worlds away from the shipyard's noise and grit.[30]

Audubon Village's greatest asset was an inspired site plan developed by Roensch. At Westbrook's request, Roensch adapted Neutra's Park Living Colony design in a plan that promoted community interaction through shared green spaces and recreational and commercial facilities. The work of David R. Williams, who had prepared the Greenway Park plan for a Dallas neighborhood nearly two decades earlier, may also have influenced Roensch. At Greenway Parks, dwellings faced a "residential commons" and provided automobile access to each dwelling from a rear service drive.[31]

In Roensch's scheme, three roadways were linked to form the crescent-shaped green space in the middle of Audubon Village. Most of the dwellings faced the interior park and backed up to their access roads—twenty-six cul-de-sacs named for birds drawn by the famous wildlife artist John James Audubon. A series of pedestrian pathways connected the homes, the central green space, and the communal buildings, which eventually included a community center and an elementary school. A fire station was later added facing New Jersey Route 168, the busy thoroughfare known locally as the Black Horse Pike.[32]

Audubon Village joined the defense housing developments on the west bank of the Delaware River in Philadelphia, forming "laboratories for an emergent urban-suburban lifestyle, nourishing all the aspirations for a more affluent postwar society."[33] John Green certainly regarded his shipbuilding workers as well poised to make the transition from Camden to blue-collar suburbs. Those who applied to live at Audubon Village generally had "English or Scottish roots, and most of them are shipbuilders. The heads of households average thirty years old and earn an average of $2500 per year." Among the selected applicants were "John and Mary D. Fence," who had moved "six times in eleven years" because John, a riveter at New York Ship, was often unemployed. When John was out of work the couple and their two sons "doubled up" with Mary's parents to keep the family out of debt. As soon as the shipyard workers were called back to work, the family rented their own apartment. They regarded Audubon Park and the opportunity for mutual home ownership as a step toward housing security and away from the cycle of renting, doubling-up, and renting again. Shipbuilding and defense workers like Fence welcomed the "new twist" in housing offered by the Mutual Plan.[34]

According to one observer, "everyone laughed" in early 1941 when the FWA began construction of the $2.3 million Audubon Village on a "mud flat." But the laughter subsided as Audubon Village became "a garden spot marked by curved driveways, white cottages, tulips by the wide-paved paths, [and] fir trees by the doorways," earmarked for mutual home ownership by its residents.[35] Among those who took up residence were Shipbuilding Workers president John Green and his family. A three-bedroom unit (which the Green family qualified for by virtue of its size and gender composition) on Whippoorwill Drive became a permanent home for the man who, in a twenty-year period, had gone from shipyard laborer to founding president of an industrial union who was consulted on matters of national defense in Washington and had gained recognition for the Shipbuilding Workers from some of the country's largest shipbuilders. As *Commonweal* would later observe in 1942, it was characteristic of "Johnny Green" to live among the workers he represented.[36]

## The Mutual Division Brings Community Modernism to the Mid-Atlantic

In December 1941, the Camden *Courier-Post* described the cities of Philadelphia and Camden jointly as a "U.S. Workshop" suffering from "the nation's greatest housing shortage." An estimated 12,000 defense workers desperately needed homes in the Delaware and Schuylkill valleys because "more than ten percent of all national defense contracts, for a total of $1,250,000,000" were held by firms in the Philadelphia-Camden metropolitan region.[37]

To help provide the 12,000 units deemed necessary for the metropolitan region, Carmody assigned Westbrook responsibility for building two additional developments in the lower Delaware Valley. He authorized a fourth Mutual Division development, Winfield Park, for northern New Jersey to serve workers employed in the shipyards in and around New York City, including Federal Ship in Kearney, New Jersey.

In May 1941 Westbrook announced plans for the construction of a 500-unit development, to be named Bellmawr Park, on a 133-acre site several miles away from Audubon Village. The cost was $2.1 million, and the construction contract ran for 100 calendar days, from October 23, 1941, to May 30, 1942. The Mutual Division hired the architectural firm of Mayer & Whittlesey, with Joseph N. Hettel working as consulting architect. In an interview, the architects told the *Architectural Forum* that before landing the commission "we had argued for, and thought about, and hoped for a community to plan." Mayer & Whittlesey, along with Hettel, wanted to a project where "inches of land didn't count, where even feet didn't count violently if one did not go hog-wild, where land was thought of in acres, not in price per sq. ft., where there was ROOM, within and around."[38]

The architects believed that "civilized, spirited living demands not only good floor plans and good plumbing, the right number and location of playgrounds, and safety from traffic, it also requires a lot more which has only very rarely been achieved in the large Government projects." They hoped to accomplish "a lot more" than previous public housing architects had by striking a balance between a community that is "recognizable as such but not at odds with what's around it." The community plan they proposed offered visual surprises of different groupings of dwellings, including two-story brick veneer and one-story asbestos siding structures, arranged around Bellmawr Park's focal points and "community symbols": the elementary school and the community building. To avoid monotony, hip-roofed dwellings of two or four units alternated with flat-roof dwellings.[39]

To make Bellmawr Park look like a "real community," the community building featured a clock tower sheathed in cypress wood selected for its grainy appearance and treated to preserve its natural color. The clock tower provided Bellmawr Park with a symbolic link to other communities developed specifically for workers, including company towns where early industrialists used clock towers to instill punctuality in their workers. Writing in January 1943, Mayer, Whittlesey, and Hettel acknowledged that if they could go back they would change the location of certain roads and buildings in Bellmawr Park, but by and large they were pleased with the results.[40]

Across the Delaware River in Philadelphia's Northeast section, Westbrook built the Mutual Division's largest community, Pennypack Woods, for workers employed by the Philadelphia Navy Yard and other defense contractors in the area. The 1,000 dwelling units and the community building were designed by architects Oscar Stonorov and Albert Kahn. Developed on a 120-acre tract in the northeast section of the city, the community was large enough to allow deviation from the city grid with a curving road partially skirting the perimeter. Many of the flat-roofed dwelling units faced an interior green space and

**Figure 3.3** In the "Park Living Plan" implemented at Pennypack Woods in northeast Philadelphia, the dwelling units were designed to face the large central green space, which was connected to the shopping center, community building, and swimming pool (a postwar addition) by a series of pedestrian pathways. Photograph by Michael J. Chiarappa.

backed up either to cul-de-sacs or short access roads (see Figure 3.3). Modernism and the vernacular met in the community building, which featured a wall of local fieldstone. According to scholar Andrew M. Shanken, projects such as Pennypack Woods were an opportunity for Stonorov, Kahn, and other communitarian architects to show how planning "transcended narrow professional or technical definitions"[41] (see Figure 3.4).

The *Philadelphia Record* reported in May 1942 that the $4.2 million community was the result of an FWA plan to conduct "tests" in cooperative housing to demonstrate how to solve an "old problem"—the lack of affordable housing. At a program sponsored by Philadelphia's CIO Housing Committee, defense workers learned about the opportunity to become mutual home owners at Pennypack Woods. Pamphlets such as "Pennypack Woods, A Defense Home Plan" and "Pennypack Woods Homes for War Workers" were distributed at the Navy Yard and other defense job sites.[42]

Attorney M. Herbert Syme observed that applicants for Pennypack Woods had frustrated home ownership aspirations. He described them as "*people who normally would not have been able to own their own homes*. Most of them never had their own homes. Some of them had their own homes and lost them.

**Figure 3.4** A centrally located shopping center and community building were constructed by the FWA to serve residents of the 1,000 dwelling units at Pennypack Woods in northeast Philadelphia. Today the shopping center includes a retail store, professional services, and the administrative offices of the Pennypack Woods Home Ownership Association. Photograph by Michael J. Chiarappa.

Pennypack to them has meant the fulfillment of a hope."[43] The *Pennypack Chit Chat*, the community newspaper, confirmed that the chance of mutual home ownership attracted many residents to the development, noting, "From the very beginning there was strong interest here at Pennypack for the government's own plan to sell Pennypack to the residents."[44]

In June 1941 the *Shipyard Worker*, the weekly published by the Shipbuilding Workers union, informed readers that, thanks to the efforts of Local No. 16, North Jersey shipbuilding workers employed at Federal Ship would also have a chance to become mutual home owners in another new project named Winfield Park,[45] which the paper described as a "beautiful suburban site" next to the scenic Rahway River and nearby parkland that offered "unusual possibilities" for community recreation.[46]

The Housing Committee of Shipbuilding Workers Local No. 16 was optimistic that Winfield Park would mark a new day in housing for shipbuilding workers. The development would be "revolutionary in design for this part of the country . . . contain[ing,] in addition to homes, such community facilities as a swimming pool, tennis courts, riding paths, baseball fields, gymnasium, social hall; [*sic*] clinic, and many other cooperative enterprises to benefit the people living there."[47]

John Rowland, an architect who worked out of Jersey City, won the contract for the design of Winfield Park in April 1941. One month later, he submitted preliminary drawings for 700 flat-roofed dwellings, including 454 with two bedrooms, 106 with one bedroom, and 140 with three-bedrooms. The dwellings were to be distributed around an interior park according to a site plan prepared by the architectural firm of Clark & Rapuano as subcontractor to Rowland (see Figure 3.5).[48] John Carmody, Lawrence Westbrook, and John Green attended the June 1941 ceremony marking the start of construction amid rising tensions between the Shipbuilding Workers and Federal Ship over contract negotiations.[49]

As later revealed by the Senate defense contracts investigative committee, known as the Truman Committee, the Local No. 16 Housing Committee had considerable input into the design of Winfield Park's houses. General contractor Clifford MacEvoy told chief counsel Hugh A. Fulton that as the houses were nearing completion, a "business representative of the CIO union of the Kearney Shipyard" named Thompson and two other members of a "shipyard workers designated" delegation arrived at the worksite accompanied by a group of women—presumably shipyard workers' wives—who took it upon themselves "to mill in and out of the buildings and look them over." During the visit, when

**Figure 3.5** Winfield Park's two-story dwelling units have either two or three bedrooms. Residents enjoy convenient pedestrian access to the community building and the elementary school. The New Jersey State Legislature retaliated against the Roosevelt administration for building the community by forcing it to become its own borough. Photograph by Michael J. Chiarappa.

Thompson told MacEvoy that "the tenants wanted washtubs in the cellars," MacEvoy told him that the basements were "not designed for washtubs. The sewer outlet is too high." Dissatisfied with both MacEvoy's response and the laundry tubs in the kitchens, the union took its case to Westbrook, who apparently complied with their request. Fulton sought to both discredit Westbrook and put an end to what he saw as the administration's pandering to the CIO when he indignantly observed how a "grievance committee of the union" had gone to Washington to "tell the Government how to build a house."[50]

Regarding Winfield Park as union turf, Peter Flynn, president of Local No. 16, and James E. Thompson, chairman of the local's housing committee, were on hand in late 1941 to welcome over a hundred "pioneer families" to their new homes.[51] Among the first of the eager arrivals were William and Leona Burke, whose enthusiasm was only slightly dampened when they discovered that their new home was not yet finished and an extension cord was their only source of electricity.[52] Federal Ship worker Joseph Wright Sr. and his family also moved into an uncompleted home and had to use a garden hose for about two months. The Burkes, the Wrights, and other "first families" waded through mud when it rained, endured clouds of dust when it was dry, and faced temporary hazards, hardships, and even tragedy. An outbreak of infantile paralysis (polio) claimed the lives of three children in a three-week period and resulted in a quarantine in September 1942. People in nearby communities resented the newcomers.[53]

## Avion Village: Prefabrication's "Finest Hour"

Real estate developers, bankers, and home builders operating in the Dallas area, like those in metropolitan Philadelphia and New York City, consistently argued that the private sector could provide all the housing needed for aircraft and other defense workers. They saw the construction of defense housing for workers at North American Aviation's Grand Prairie assembly plant and at the nearby naval air station as a threat both to real estate values and to the maintenance of established patterns of residential segregation by class and color. The members of the Defense Housing Committee created by the Dallas Chamber of Commerce favored "only such action from the Federal authorities as will best serve our community" and expressed alarm at Westbrook's early 1941 announcement of plans for the construction of the 300-unit Avion Village in Grand Prairie and, a short time later, the 300-unit Dallas Park in the city of Dallas. Even though Westbrook's Mutual Division furthered existing patterns of racial segregation by reserving both communities for white occupancy, concerns about the impact of mutual housing development on the commercial market remained.[54]

Westbrook turned to his talented and trusted friends, Mutual Division staff architect David Williams and Richard Neutra, his collaborator on the failed Park Living Colony, for help on the Grand Prairie project. They joined with Roscoe DeWitt, who was one of a "number of young Texan architects devoted to contemporary design of housing," to design Avion Village's dwellings and community center.[55] Avion Village captured national attention on May 16, 1941, when Carmody, Westbrook, other federal, state, and local officials, and representatives of the Navy and North American Aviation gathered in Grand Prairie to eat lunch while watching two teams of fifty workers compete to assemble a prefabricated house in less than one hour. When the winning crew was done, Mr. and Mrs. Charles Swore immediately moved into their new home. *Life* and newspaper photographers from across the nation captured Mrs. Swore cooking dinner in the kitchen, Mr. Swore busy with a Fuller Brush salesman, and model Veneta Perry discreetly bathing in the bathtub.[56] Avion Village was considered an "excellent example of cooperation between architect and contractor in developing designs suitable to extensive prefabrication."[57]

Prior to the construction of Avion Village, both Williams and Neutra had been involved with the design and construction of prefabricated housing elsewhere. Early in his career, Williams designed prefabricated housing for workers employed by oil companies in Mexico.[58] Neutra's previous experience convinced him that prefabrication could make it possible for ordinary wage earners to afford "convenient and efficient homes."[59] He hoped that while wartime restrictions on consumer goods were in effect Americans would "learn how to appreciate smaller dwellings and design efficiency and get over the idea that bigger is better."[60]

Both Williams and Neutra were directors of the Housing Producers Cooperative, Inc., a private organization that likely involved Westbrook behind the scenes. In August 1940 the cooperative tried to secure an agreement with Maryland's Greenbelt Homeowners Cooperative to develop a series of prefabricated, one-and-a-half-story Cape Cod–style dwellings on lots originally set aside by the Resettlement Administration (RA) for future development. Although their plans were not realized, Neutra thought that the proposed addition of prefabricated houses to Greenbelt was consistent with his conviction that such housing ought to be "properly fitted into different localities whether demountable, prefabricated or conventional in construction."[61]

The May 1941 contest at Avion Village came off without a hitch largely because a few weeks earlier Williams, at the request of President Roosevelt, had agreed to forgo a much needed spring vacation in Mexico. Williams was called in because a lack of experience with prefabricated housing on the part of both DeWitt and the project's general contractor, Henry C. Beck of the Central Construction Company was holding up the project. To get it "off dead center," Williams met with DeWitt and Beck to plan the construction process and put an end to the "confusion and indecision as to design and method of construction."[62] Working in two shifts, carpenters built the prefabricated wall and roof sections for Avion Village's 300 homes in 100 days in an on-site workshop under three giant circus tents. Specially trained crews handled and installed the panels to minimize damage and increase efficiency.[63]

In May of 1941 Beck reported to Williams that the "Prefabricating Shop is working splendidly. We are working two shifts, and have a jig for every panel in the job now, including the roof panels." The contractor acknowledged his initial reluctance to embrace Williams's prefabricated system, but said it was now "working out 'slick.' The panels are going together nicely, and I am strong for Prefabrication now."[64] Despite Beck's satisfaction with the system, there were innumerable snafus that needed resolution. Just days before the May 16 contest, workers discovered that some prefabricated roof panels had warped because the lumber had not been allowed to season long enough.[65]

Avion Village offered the wartime prefabrication program its "finest hour," but its construction was not free of dispute. Dallas trade unions affiliated with the AFL objected to Westbrook's use of WPA labor on roadwork and rough landscaping. Despite assurances that the union would not make trouble, a strike took place at Avion Village on July 23, 1941. Westbrook instructed Beck to immediately resolve the issue and resume construction. "It is not the policy of the government to work these things out with the unions," he told Beck. "It is our policy to see that such important projects are completed on schedule."[66]

Avion Village featured twenty-one two-story buildings containing four one-bedroom apartments. They were located on the western edge of the community and formed a "hard-edged buffer between the one-story units and a planned major thoroughfare."[67] Among the more notable architectural features were the three-bedroom units, in which the walls of the smallest bedroom were constructed of Masonite panels fit into tracks that allowed them to be folded away to increase the size of the living room.[68] Ray Holder, who later became manager and general counsel of the Avion Village Mutual Housing Corporation, recalled the inspiration for the innovative design, attributing it to Williams, the "globe-trotting architect," who drew on his observations of Japanese dwellings. With "an absolute minimum of space with which to work," Williams "conceived the idea of turning two rooms into one, or one room into two, by means of sliding panels." Holder reported that the houses "do not seem stuffy or crowded, but they are homey and very livable." More important, the "occupants of these houses admire them very much, and the fact that they were so carefully thought out and designed has made for a happy occupancy throughout the history of these projects."[69]

Williams looked to the region's vernacular structures for inspiration when seeking ways to help Avion Village residents keep their homes warm in the winter and cool in the summer. The small porches on the two-story dwellings, celebrated as a "staple of Central Texas residential architecture," were situated to "to take advantage of the prevailing southwest breezes."[70] Williams regarded the community's homes as "the most modern of their type ever constructed in the southwest."[71]

Neutra's Park Living concept was an organizing principle in devising the site plan for Avion Village.[72] Promoted as a "Permanent Park Community," most of the dwelling units faced a central park or common that provided play areas and informal meeting spaces.[73] Additional groups of dwelling units backed up to lanes lined with carports and parking areas. Footpaths traversed the park, making it possible for residents to reach the school and community center without crossing roads. An automobile access road was located on the community's outer perimeter. Architect Willis Winter credited the Mutual Division with producing a site plan "graciously balancing suburban density and a pervasive rural character."[74]

Located at the widest end of the teardrop-shaped site was the community center, housing the Avion Village administrative office, where prospective residents could obtain information about eligibility, vacancies, and the functioning of the Mutual Plan. A promotional pamphlet promised aviation workers and their families "unrestricted enjoyment of community social and recreational facilities," sponsored by a community council offering activities that contributed to the residents' educational development and personal enrichment. Serving as the hub of Avion Village social life, the sprawling, flat-roofed community building contained, along with the administrative offices, a nursery school, a library, an assembly hall, a kitchen, and several multipurpose meeting rooms.[75]

The community center boasted a stone terrace on the western end of the building situated to maximize sunset views over the Texas prairie. A source of community pride, according to Ray Holder, it "evoked much comment from thousands of visitors" who admired it "from a utility and an artistic point of view." The "many enjoyable events . . . held on this terrace during the balmy evenings of the spring and summer, under the Texas sky" helped residents form the social bonds that gave them the confidence to join together and economically endure as mutual home owners.[76]

Architect Albert Mayer included a photograph of Avion Village in his September 1941 *New York Times Magazine* article on defense housing as an example of "what can be done with careful thought and reliance on past experience." He commended the FWA for hiring architects whose "previous work and known outlook indicated their deep interest in and their ability to make a constructive contribution to housing and planning."[77] Tom Treanor, a critic for the *Los Angeles Times* similarly regarded the community as setting new standards for the future. He liked how the architects drew from both modern precepts and the vernacular, which he believed meant that Avion Village would likely "still be providing good homes for its 300 families long after Hitler is an unpleasant memory and the aircraft plant is either empty or doing something besides build [*sic*] bombers."[78] Dallas-area realtors called Avion Village "a model for future defense housing in this area" mainly because, after its sale to the residents, the mutual housing association would pay property taxes.[79]

Avion Village won praise despite the fact that behind the scenes, serious problems were lurking. In mid-1941 as the political tide turned against the use of defense housing funds for experimentation in New Deal-inspired communitarian housing, Westbrook's Mutual Division appears to have lapsed in its administrative oversight. Architect Arch Swank wrote to Richard Neutra to alert him that after he left the Avion Village job site and returned to California to begin the Channel Heights project, DeWitt and Williams were "eased out of the picture." As a result of "very bad supervision by government inspectors" Central Contracting Company officials did "just what they pleased." The final details were so "awful," Swank advised Neutra to professionally distance himself from the Avion project and encourage Westbrook to "find out what happened here." It was a "shame" that a "project with such possibilities" and such "wonderful preliminary work" should have been "so buggered completely in execution."[80]

## Dallas Park: Modern Texas Vernacular for Aircraft Workers

Lawrence Westbrook's arrival in Dallas in May 1941 for a meeting with local government and defense industry leaders fueled rumors that plans were in the making for a sister development to Avion Village. "Heated arguments" erupted as members of the "recently organized Building and Housing Association at the Chamber of Commerce," debated the potential impact of more mutual housing on the commercial real estate market. Reporters descended on Westbrook at the landmark Hotel Adolphus in hopes of determining whether the Mutual Division intended to develop another community slated for mutual home ownership in the Dallas area.[81] Speculation came to an end on July 10, 1941, when the Mutual Division awarded a 120-day contract to the Central Construction Company, the same firm that built Avion Village, for the construction of Dallas Park. According to the *Dallas Times Herald*, the production method Williams devised for Avion Village would be replicated at the new development.[82] The *Architectural Record* reported that exterior walls and roof trusses prefabricated under the circus tent were loaded onto trucks, driven to the site, and installed by specialized crews.[83] The installation of water and sewer lines constituted the City of Dallas's contribution to the $972,166 project.[84]

Burns Roensch, an architect who had been on the Mutual Division staff, left the employment of the Federal Works Agency in mid-1941, took a job with Beck's Central Contracting Company, and obtained the contract to design Dallas Park. His design for the 300 one-, two-, and three-bedroom units and community center included elements of both modernism and vernacular tradition. Eighty-four one-bedroom apartments were located in two-story frame buildings with four dwelling units each. There were 68 two-bedroom duplex dwellings and 112 two-bedroom detached units. The 36 three-bedroom detached dwellings lacked the movable panels found at Avion Village but, as the *Architectural Record* noted with approval, they were on average some fifty square feet larger. They were, however, built with the "same machinery" and the "same jigs."[85]

The Dallas Park project gave Roensch an opportunity to carry out the "long dreamed idea of building a house that was livable and modern, along typical Texas lines." He designed the dwellings "to be as livable as moderate homes can be . . . [and to] please the eye of the Texan and make him happy with the external appearance of his home." As a result, "instead of having flat roofs, the Dallas Park homes have peaked roofs with a fairly low pitch." Roensch designed "every house in Dallas Park so that every bedroom in every house and every apartment would have a southern exposure and a cross draft to permit the passage of the southerly winds across the face of the sleeper and to give cross ventilation in a positive manner." Another observer who was not as enamored with Roensch and his work said that the "Early Texas Architectural details," including "pitched roofs and double hung windows" were "added for charm."[86]

The community building at Dallas Park resembled a large ranch house. Roensch put the administrative offices and assembly hall (complete with a wood-burning fireplace) on the east side of the breezeway. On the west side was a nursery school later converted into a clubroom. The building also contained a kitchen, a library, and a multipurpose meeting room. As in Avion Village, the community center had an outdoor terrace and fireplace.[87]

Avion Village and Dallas Park showed that mutual housing offered workers an opportunity to live in affordable homes designed for busy households of multiple wage earners in a community with ready access to educational, civic, commercial, and recreational services. Neutra, Williams, DeWitt, and Roensch created communities that were different from the neighborhoods in which most wage earners resided but vaguely reminiscent of them because of the incorporation of vernacular idioms.

Working in a more familiar political setting allowed Westbrook to cultivate support from defense contractors and other business interests and gain their acceptance for his projects. Leading business groups including the Chamber of Commerce took advantage of the attractive, low-cost meeting space available in the Avion Village community center, helping to integrate it into the larger civic life of Grand Prairie and metropolitan Dallas. At the same time, however, they remained concerned that mutual housing might gain a foothold in the postwar residential market in the Dallas area and elsewhere.[88]

## By Request: CIO Workers Bring Mutual Housing to Dayton and South Bend

As the Mutual Division completed work on the four Mid-Atlantic and two Dallas projects, Westbrook and his staff were addressing the defense housing needs of two Midwestern cities struggling to accommodate an influx of defense workers. Dayton, Ohio, had suffered from a scarcity of affordable housing even before the 1940 increase in employment at Wright Patterson Air Base, General Motors, and other local defense contractors.[89] At a July 1941 meeting called by the Dayton League for Progressive Action, local elected officials and civic leaders acknowledged that the lack of decent, affordable housing was creating or exacerbating social problems, including vice and public health issues such as contagious disease. The consensus was that the lack of housing contributed to the dissolution of families and to the startling discovery that the city's divorce rate was the "worst in the U.S. next to Hollywood."[90]

CIO-affiliated unions, including the UAW, the United Electrical, Radio, and Machine Workers of America (UE), and the United Steel Workers Organizing Committee (SWOC) actively sought Lanham funds for housing. UE president Albert J. Fitzgerald complained that defense workers were forced to reside in unsafe or unsanitary conditions, including "junked trolley cars."[91] Werner Laging, a power plant engineer employed by the War Department at Wright Field, paid $60 per month so he, his wife, and son could live in an apartment that was "half heated, no hot water, [and] no service utilities whatever." The family shared an apartment that consisted of "one bedroom, a small living room, a kitchenette, and a totally unsatisfactory bathroom" and was "blocks away from a school or shopping center."[92]

The growth of the mutual housing movement among unionists in Dayton was in large measure the result of efforts by Marvin M. Miniard, a former electroplater at Frigidaire, who had found his forte in community organizing. As chairman of Dayton's CIO Housing Committee, he helped establish the Montgomery County Industrial Union Housing Council in 1940, which formed a defense housing committee to gather statistics on housing vacancies and overcrowding; interview defense workers and their families on housing conditions, expenditures, and needs; and lobby for defense housing in the city. Volunteers took photographs of the places where defense workers lived and their children played and documented the steps realtors, bankers, and developers took to block federal intervention in Dayton's critically stressed housing market.[93]

Dayton's defense workers eagerly embraced mutual housing as a new economic option. Greenmont Village manager Charles McGuerin later recalled that as soon the Defense Housing Committee "heard that a plan, then known as the Camden plan, was being sponsored by the FWA . . . [representatives of] various labor groups in Dayton came to Washington to get information." A delegation of workers visited Audubon Village, met John Green, and learned what their fraternal brethren thought about working with Lawrence Westbrook and the Mutual Division. After several meetings, federal housing officials "granted permission for the building of what is now known as Greenmont Village." In February 1942 the Dayton *Journal-Herald* announced that a "new village . . . [was] rising" and that the city's "Camden Plan project" was moving forward.[94]

According to the *Greenmont Forum*, the local newsletter, the community's layout was "modeled after the Camden project with the streets having their only outlet on a central circle." Plans for the dwelling units were studied by the Defense Housing Committee and finally accepted only when architects took to heart some "worthwhile advice" from the wives of shipbuilding workers who wanted "large, convenient kitchens rather than the dining alcove and kitchenette combination that had been a part of the original design."[95]

Dayton's CIO Housing Committee sponsored the 500-unit Greenmont Village and supported its construction by AFL-affiliated craftsmen. Architect Ellasson Smith and engineers from the F. H. McGraw Company, the general contractor, developed a "system of prefabricating the homes right there on the grounds." The team shipped huge quantities of lumber by rail to the prefabrication site, where it was "cut and planed to exact dimensions in a little planning [*sic*] mill, and built into sections which are then hauled bodily by truck to the foundations." Company officials estimated that "one-third to one-fourth of the cost of a house is saved by these mass production methods."[96]

The housing committee of the Montgomery County Industrial Union Council observed that Greenmont Village came into being "despite the opposition of the local real estate board, chamber of commerce, and building and loan associations."[97] Those who resented the federal government and the CIO for Greenmont Village called it a "mud village" and its modernist dwellings "cracker barrel houses" (see Figure 3.6). But Lew Carr of the Dayton *Journal-Herald* admired the community for its "quite beautiful 'park living plan.' With the streets radiating out from a central circle or park, and with ample ground supplied for recreational purposes." He saw Greenmont Village as a model for new communities all across the country.[98]

At roughly the same time that Miniard and other CIO housing activists in Dayton were asking for defense housing under the Mutual Plan, Westbrook received a similar request from UAW workers in South Bend,

**Figure 3.6** The flat-roofed dwellings at Greenmont Village give the Kettering, Ohio, community a distinctively modernist look. Today most of the dwellings have vinyl siding, and leaking flat roofs have been replaced by pitched roofs. Photograph by the author.

Indiana, whose critical shortage of housing prompted the UAW to join with other "progressive elements in town" in the South Bend Civic Housing Council to secure federal housing aid. The council faced opposition from allied home building, real estate, and business interests, which succeeded in preventing the creation of a municipal housing authority until January 1941. Prior to that time, South Bend had been identified as one of Indiana's three "critical problem areas."[99]

South Bend mayor Jesse I. Pavey expressed confidence that the South Bend-Mishawaka Real Estate Board would "appreciate [its] responsibility to the city as a whole . . . [and] play a major role in providing the needed housing rather than make it necessary to have it provided from other sources entirely."[100] He was counting on local business interests to build housing for defense workers and low-income families before federal officials imposed public housing from above that might potentially alter or challenge the city's segregated residential patterns. Despite Pavey's efforts to stimulate action among private home builders, however, UAW and city housing activists continued to pressure housing officials in Washington until it was announced that Lanham funds would be used to construct the 350-unit Southmore Heights for Studebaker workers and the 150-unit Beacon Heights for Bendix workers.[101]

In May 1941 authorization of an additional 250-unit development was announced for either South Bend or nearby Mishawaka, even though Fay M. Paul of the Mishawaka Chamber of Commerce insisted that another "defense housing project was not needed."[102] Speaking in his capacity as chairman of the CIO Housing Committee, R. J. Thomas explained that the president had authorized an additional 250 units for the South Bend area because the UAW's representatives in Washington had "*kept after various Government officials until they got some promise of action*." The union's visit, he said, "put South Bend on the map with the federal officials who count as far as defense housing, rent control, and consumer prices are concerned." Following the Dayton unionists' precedent, a South Bend UAW delegation visited Green and the Shipbuilding Workers in Camden. "*While in the East*," Thomas reported, "*the boys took in some outstanding housing and slum clearance projects in Camden, New Jersey and in Philadelphia and got a better picture of what actually can be done*." Their visit helped convince the UAW that the new 250-unit development ought to be built under the Mutual Plan.[103]

On June 13, 1941, after complaining that "the government was determined arbitrarily to give Mishawaka something it does not want," local building interests discovered that the Mutual Division planned to locate its new defense housing development in South Bend.[104] Clarence E. Keller of the South Bend Housing Authority, who was also a member of Studebaker Local No. 5, had "long been active in labor committees battling the low-rent housing problem." He was determined to secure the best site possible for the city's mutual housing experiment and acquired an option on a piece of desirable property with the intention of turning it over to federal housing authorities.[105]

The tract favored by UAW-affiliated interests was an undeveloped wooded parcel on the corner of 26th Street and fashionable East Jefferson Boulevard. Nearby property owners organized in opposition, arguing that they had "invested many thousands of dollars . . . [in their] permanent [homes] . . . expecting to live the rest of their lives in those homes." Property values would decrease when the neighborhood became inhabited by transient, traffic-creating "factory, store, and other business employees . . . [who were] compelled to own an automobile" to keep their employment.[106]

The *South Bend Tribune* confirmed the selection of the disputed site in June 1941 and tried to smooth the ruffled feathers of long-time city residents, reminding them that *Time* and the *Architectural Forum* had recently reported favorably on the architectural and planning accomplishments of the Mutual Division. Westbrook announced plans to come to the city on July 3 to meet with concerned property owners on East Jefferson about the development, to be known as Walnut Grove, and personally assure them that it would be an asset to their neighborhood.[107]

In July the Mutual Division contracted three architects, N. Roy Schambleau, Karl R. Schwarz, and Roy A. Worden, to design Walnut Grove. As a local contribution, site engineering was to be carried out by the City of South Bend under the supervision of Clyde E. Williams, the city engineer. In mid-July, while consulting with local officials, Mutual Division architect David Williams promised that Walnut Grove would be a "'beautiful development' with many modern recreational facilities." He expected that "85 per cent of the 250 units authorized more than a month ago will be single family buildings."[108]

The architects were given three weeks to complete their plans for the community, which by July 21 were on their way to Washington for Westbrook and his staff to review.[109] In the meantime, WPA workers laid utility lines and prepared road beds. The Mutual Division agreed to build a cross street at Colfax Avenue to connect with 26th Street, as requested by the City Plan Commission, but otherwise it ignored South Bend's "criss-cross plan of building in favor of the oval scheme of layout." Williams stated that the nucleus of Walnut Grove would be "a park and general recreation plot which will be available to the public."[110]

As plans for Walnut Grove moved forward, residents of the East Jefferson Boulevard neighborhood fought on. Fearful that the project would be completed "whether or not they like it," they established communication with a "high public [borough] official" in Audubon, New Jersey, who told them that the Mutual Division had built "500 small low-cost homes . . . entirely segregated from the rest of the town in a section consisting of farm land." The official claimed that Mutual Division officials had refused to make their contractors adhere to local building codes and, most egregiously, had not yet specified how much money the federal government would give to the borough in lieu of taxes, raising fear that the deal would impose an "unjust burden on our tax payers."[111]

The unidentified Audubon Borough official also told opponents of Walnut Grove that he understood their position but did not think they could do anything about it. The Borough of Audubon, he said, had "gone to great extremes to avoid" Audubon Village's construction but had been unable to succeed. Those who wanted to stop the project, he added, were now trying to obtain the political backing needed to persuade the state legislature to make Audubon Village a separate borough.[112]

Despite the controversy over the South Bend project site, the Mutual Division awarded a contract to the Henke Construction Company, a Chicago-based firm, for the construction of Walnut Grove, to begin on October 11, 1941, and end on April 1, 1942. Groundbreaking for the houses, designed "with an eye to simplicity and economy of construction," took place on October 13.[113] The 71 one- and two-bedroom units on the street that ringed the periphery of the community were reserved for couples without children or with infants. Families with older children were typically assigned to the 179 dwelling units located on the cul-de-sacs. The placement of these units allowed access to "a green local play area from the living room of each dwelling unit, which . . . extends into the central free area with no interference from roads or utilities" (see Figure 3.7). The first of the simple flat-roofed dwellings to reach completion were occupied in April 1942.[114]

Walnut Grove's one- and two-bedroom units offered a living room, kitchen, and dining alcove on the ground level. A short staircase provided access to the finished basement, and a half-flight of stairs gained access to the bedroom/bath area. Deep overhangs (approximately 24 inches wide) protected the large windows with southern exposure and kept the dwellings as cool as possible in the summer while allowing the winter sun to penetrate the interior. In the bedrooms, the windows were placed high on the walls to allow cross-ventilation without interfering with the placement of the furniture. "Interior convenience with maximum living space including basements was given precedence over considerations of exterior appearance," according to local real estate appraiser Richard A. Meussel, to accommodate the UAW housing committee, which reviewed the architects' preliminary plans.[115]

In December 1941 G. Gresham Griggs, chief of the Mutual Division's management section, visited the South Bend site to inspect the progress of the general contractor. According to a press report, Griggs stated that the residents would be "hand-picked with an eye to the possibilities of permanency, credit stability, and reputation as neighbors." Resident selection was critical, he said, because some would directly participate in community governance through a board of trustees that included "four owner-tenants, four public-spirited persons and a representative of the government." In February 1942, as soon as the first units were completed, families began to take up residence.[116]

Completed in 1943 and situated near a carefully preserved grove of black walnut trees, the Walnut Grove community building housed a nursery school, cooperative grocery store, assembly hall, kitchen, administrative offices, and meeting room. "Neighborliness and community spirit" arose as a result of "this type of living," said Harold B. Schultz, president of the Walnut Grove Mutual Housing Corporation. "Everyone is the better for it, children and adults alike."[117]

**Figure 3.7** Walnut trees grow on the common green at Walnut Grove in South Bend, Indiana. Most of the two-story dwelling units are located in cul-de-sacs in the community's interior. One-story dwellings are on the service road that runs parallel to the periphery. Photograph by the author.

Frank J. Moore and his wife Violet were among the first families to move into Walnut Grove. Moore, who had been hired by the Studebaker Corporation to build aircraft engines, recalled that the dwellings weren't finished when they were allowed to move into their apartment. Rejected for military service because of polio, Moore regarded the Mutual Plan as a "nice deal." He appreciated not having to come up with a down payment and "you could just pay rent like you were renting an apartment." Both Frank and Violet acknowledged that at that time they did not know much about mutual home ownership. What they learned convinced them that it was especially beneficial to "youngsters like us who were just married and needed a place to live."[118]

## The Shipbuilding Workers Fight Mortgage Interest Payments

One of the first official indications that the Shipbuilding Workers were dissatisfied with both Audubon Village and the terms of the Mutual Plan came in May 1941 when the union's general counsel, M. H. Goldstein, asked FWA administrator John Carmody to waive interest payments on the Audubon Village mortgage for five years after the war ended. Goldstein's request was based on the

CIO's assertion that its unions should be offered the same benefits and advantages as defense contractors, which were not charged rent while they occupied plants newly built or refurbished at the public's expense. Ignoring growing political dissatisfaction with the CIO and its demands for social and economic equity, Goldstein argued that shipbuilding workers were as "entitled, at the least, to be considered in no less favorable light by the Government than the machines for the housing of which plants are presently being supplied gratis by the Government to its contractors." The workers regarded themselves as "essential in the production of armaments for defense as these machines. Hence, if the Government is willing to assume the cost of providing plants to house machines, it should be no less willing to assume the cost of providing the dwellings for the workers who will operate the machines."[119]

Goldstein pointed out that since September 1939 $10.5 million in public funds had been spent improving the shipyard owned by New York Ship. When the war ended the shipbuilding giant would not be expected to pay interest on the public funds expended on its behalf, but would be "permitted to pay the principle out of profits earned from Government work exclusively." When union workers discovered that the "Government grants such largess to their multi-million dollar employer but treats them in a diametrically opposed fashion," would they be as ready and willing to make sacrifices as they had been?[120]

In his carefully worded reply of June 14, 1941, Carmody acknowledged as "an expression of basic democratic principle that the Government should not discriminate against labor in favor of capital." But he argued that even if such discrimination existed, it could not be rectified "through special concessions in housing accommodations to the relatively small percentage of defense workers who will occupy defense housing projects constructed under the Lanham Act." Rather, "the basic conception of the 'Camden Plan' was for Government to develop a pattern which could be substantially so followed by private capital." He expected that alterations to the Mutual Plan would be made over time, but the "omission of interest . . . would in my opinion, destroy the plan for pattern purposes and definitely bring about its rejection not only by private capital but also, it is very likely, by Congress itself."[121]

Carmody tried to convince the union to withdraw its request by emphasizing that the Roosevelt administration regarded labor as a full partner in defense production. He hinted that if the Shipbuilding Workers continued to make an issue of interest payments its action could potentially diminish the "inestimable value of the services rendered" by the Housing Committee, Green, and the work of union attorney Goldstein in the "development of this experiment." Carmody looked forward to the future when "the legal documents necessary to put the 'Camden Plan' into effect as prepared by your attorney, Mr. H.M. Goldstein, with the advice and approval of the legal staff of this Agency, will take their place along with the first charters of the great labor unions in historical significance." Carmody was mindful "that the work of all of you was not done for personal gain or glory, but for the benefit of workers everywhere like yourselves."[122]

The Shipbuilding Workers' Executive Council likely appreciated Carmody's prediction that in the future the Camden Plan would take its place alongside other historical union documents, but it was not deterred from what it saw as its duty to gain parity for workers with defense contractors. The council passed Resolution No. 27 condemning the FWA for seeking interest payments from the workers who organized the Audubon Village Mutual Housing Corporation to lease and later purchase the community under the Camden Plan.[123]

Goldstein conceded that Local 1 had made its exemption request in part out of concern for Audubon Park's survival in the postwar housing market. The Philadelphia-based lawyer underscored the extent to which labor support for mutual home ownership was more economically than ideologically motivated, explaining that defense workers who had purchased dwellings built by private developers "by force of necessity" and "by means of making heavy mortgage loans" were now fearful that when the war ended and wages and real estate values fell, wartime housing would be "thrown upon the market at very low value prices." Goldstein also thought Carmody might waive the interest if reminded just how disappointed the Shipbuilding Workers union was in the quality of Audubon Village. The houses built for defense workers by speculative builders were "built on traditional lines and out of traditional materials," but those at Audubon Village were "not so built."[124] Given that the "American workman is traditionally devoted to the idea of owning his own piece of ground, and that the Camden worker traditionally prefers red brick on that ground," what was to keep workers from abandoning Audubon Village and purchasing "the red brick house when they are thrown upon the market at low prices"? According to Goldstein, "[a] good percentage of the residents of Audubon Park will not have been educated to complete abandonment of their traditions during the few years of the emergency. It is, therefore, quite possible that a substantial number of them will desire to [undertake traditional home ownership]."[125] In other words, as soon as Audubon Village residents could afford to do so, they would buy a house and leave mutual home ownership behind them.

Carmody consulted with Lawrence Westbrook regarding the Shipbuilding Workers' request, and the two agreed that granting an interest waiver might place the Camden Plan "at odds with some groups from other industries." Westbrook reminded Carmody of his determination to "establish a 'Camden Plan' which will serve all Unions," not just the Shipbuilding Workers.[126] The union's request was an indication that Green now believed that he had been too quick to agree to the terms offered by Westbrook. Even if Carmody and Westbrook had been willing to grant an interest waiver or reduce payments on the mortgage that was to be extended to the Audubon Park Mutual Housing Association, the timing of the union's request mitigated against it. By late 1941 an antilabor backlash had arisen in Washington and administration critics were seeking evidence that the industrial unions had been allowed to gain too much power. In addition, the Shipbuilding Workers were seeking concessions from the FWA during a time when the agency was facing "vicious opposition from [DDHC head Charles] Palmer and other sources." Goldstein's larger question—what would happen to mutual home ownership once workers could afford traditional ownership—was not addressed.[127]

Attendees at the Shipbuilding Workers' seventh national conference in November 1941 expressed dissatisfaction with Audubon Village and the Mutual Division. Union officials were "disappointed in the low quality of the construction . . . [and] the absence of certain facilities, such as garages, cellars, and community recreational and shopping centers," essential to the successful functioning of the new community.[128] Ignoring the fact that some of the dwelling units had garages, that the community center was under construction, and that plans were in place for a new elementary school, *Business Week*, taking advantage of the situation to criticize the Roosevelt administration for intervening in the housing market on behalf of the noncommercial sector, spread news of union leaders' "bitter disappointment" with what it called "union shanties": "[The] boys of Local 1 think privately that plaster walls and ceilings would stay put, that exterior paint would still be fresh looking if Uncle Sam had given their idea a better break by granting a larger building appropriation."[129]

Refusing to acknowledge that local financial interests felt threatened by the Shipbuilding Workers' involvement in publicly funded, noncommercial residential development, *Business Week* emphasized the Borough of Audubon's aesthetic objections, quoting an unidentified borough commissioner: "We were led to believe it was to be a nice place. It looks like a lot of shanties and garages. It would never pass our building laws." The borough refused to acknowledge that federal agencies were not required to uphold local building codes and, against the advice of its legal counsel, levied a $100 fine for code violations against a plumbing contractor working for the federal government. The three-member board of commissioners, all of whom were Republicans, denied the FWA access to the borough's sewage disposal system, but quickly backed down when Westbrook announced his immediate intention to seek a federal injunction against them.[130]

The *Chicago Daily Tribune* praised Audubon, the "south Jersey borough of 8,500 inhabitants" for fighting back against the government by billing the FWA $150,000 for expenses incurred as a result of the construction of Audubon Village. Borough solicitor J. Claud Simon argued that the $36,000 offered as a payment in lieu of taxes was insufficient to cover what was needed to accommodate 500 new households, citing "[a] new school, more teachers, a new sewage disposal plant costing $100,000, three additional policemen, and a 20 percent hike in the cost of garbage collection and street maintenance." He said Audubon Borough residents were victims of federal willingness to "saddle on to a group of small American homes a burden which would almost double their present tax burden" and charged that the FWA's disregard of local building codes and zoning ordinances jeopardized the value of all the real estate in the borough.[131]

Regarding the development of nonprofit housing in the borough as an unwarranted federal intrusion into local affairs, the borough's commissioners attempted to politically "sever the project from Audubon," reasoning that if Audubon Village were an independent political entity, its residents, presumably mostly Democrats, would be unable to challenge local Republican domination. The mutual housing movement could be nipped in the bud when the responsibility for borough government was placed on the unprepared residents and the Mutual Division. According to this reasoning, the combined legal and financial obligations of political independence would be so great that the mutual housing initiative would fail and the community would be sold on the commercial market.[132]

The New Jersey State Legislature responded to the Mutual Division's announcement of plans to develop a residential community for the members of Shipbuilding Workers' Local No. 16 and other North Jersey defense workers with a clear indication that it viewed mutual housing and federal investment in noncommercial housing as a challenge to the commercial market. On July 28, 1941, overriding the veto of Governor Charles Edison, a Democrat, the legislature created the Borough of Winfield Park, creating a federal island out of portions of largely undeveloped and sparsely populated Linden and Clark townships. As the legislature intended, the bill's impact was felt most deeply in Washington, where Westbrook was forced to stretch his meager staff and budgetary resources for the creation of a mutual housing association for Winfield Park to cover the costs of establishing a borough government.[133] New Jersey Republicans would have to wait until October 1947, when, after a referendum vote in Audubon, the legislature incorporated the Borough of Audubon Park.[134]

## Modernism and Mutual Housing

The decision by Westbrook and Green to combine mutual housing, modern architecture, and mass-production construction helped to mend the strained relationship between the federal government and private-sector architects frustrated by their lack of collective influence in the defense construction boom.[135] In May 1941 the *Architectural Forum* credited Westbrook with putting the design of publicly financed housing and communities back into the hands of private-sector architects, where it belonged, but complained that with the exception of the projects assigned to Westbrook most of the drawings for the 128 Lanham-financed housing developments then under construction were produced in the federal "Public Buildings Administration's 'design factory'" by federal architects and engineers. Westbrook's Mutual Division, according to the magazine, was "blessed" to have Hettel and Stonorov design its inaugural project, Audubon Village.[136]

Westbrook's Mutual Division revealed that if prefabricated housing was going to play a key role in the defense program, federal housing officials would have to devote more attention to manufacturers and producers, reviewing their plans and building materials before they began production. To address this issue, in November 1940 Carmody appointed an "alter-ego," Clark Foreman, director of the Power Division of the PWA, as his special assistant.[137] Shortly before, Foreman and Joan Raushenbush had published a book, *Total Defense*, arguing that New Deal social reform and defense preparedness were not incompatible.[138] As director of the Division of Defense Housing (DDH), Foreman was "in charge of all defense housing clearing through FWA." Interested in improving the design and appearance of prefabricated housing for workers, he set out to determine "if the best architects of the country could not come up with some better solutions." Relying on his own judgment and operating with "no system for selection," he hired Walter Gropius, Marcel Breuer, Frank Lloyd Wright, William Wilson Wurster, and other architects whose work was "sufficiently creative to justify giving them free scope within the limitations imposed by Congress." Foreman did not work with any of the architects who designed dwellings for Westbrook's Mutual Division, including Neutra, who "tried hard to be included" but, for reasons Foreman left unspecified, was not.[139]

The modern designs produced by Westbrook's and Foreman's architects baffled many defense workers. At Aluminum City Terrace and the eight Mutual Division projects, residents initially questioned the placement of dwelling units to face the woods or a green space instead of the street. Mrs. L. J. Murphy's living room in Aluminum City Terrace overlooked the "garden area," which was the only place for her to hang the wash. She told a reporter, "I didn't want to move in and I still don't like the looks of the outside," but conceded that the community was "swell for the children and the inside's wonderful."[140]

By October 1941 $359 million in Lanham Act funds had made possible construction of 342 defense housing projects nationwide, including 61 assigned to the DDH and ten assigned to the Mutual Division.[141] Two months later, in anticipation of the funding of more defense housing, Foreman brought the DDH staff together with architects and manufacturers of prefabricated housing in an effort to improve its design and durability. At a December 1941 "prefabricators' pep talk," he encouraged representatives of twenty-one firms to hire leading architects to improve prefabricated housing's "livability."[142]

Foreman counted on prominent architects and experienced practitioners such as architect William Wilson Wurster, husband of Catherine Bauer and dean of the College of Architecture at the University of California at Berkeley, to mentor professional colleagues who knew little of prefabrication and even less about designing public housing. Architects were strongly encouraged by Foreman and others to keep their designs simple and to diversify the exteriors to avoid a monotonous appearance. At Carquinez Heights, a DDH canyon-top development in Vallejo, California, Wurster used a bold color scheme to distinguish the various portions of the community, an effort that brought mixed results.[143]

During the roughly seven-month existence of the DDH, public housing architecture reached its zenith. Foreman brought in "clear-visioned, far-seeing, and broad minded" modernists such as Gropius and others who had taken up the challenge of prefabrication and the industrialization of house construction.[144] As *Time* observed, star architects helped transform prefabricated housing, which it called "the unwanted and long-ailing stepchild of the housing industry." The industry had been adopted by "[its] Uncle Sam and handed a fattening diet of government funds ($135,789,730 in orders since January)," and now the "infant is . . . one of the lustiest war babies . . . [and] may grow so big on war profits that it will be able to go on thriving after the war."[145] Bauer later recalled that some "crazy things" came out of the "Carmody-Foreman epoch," but there was no disputing that it had broken the "architectural stodginess of the past wide open" and raised standards in prefabricated and mass-assembly housing.[146] Ironically, Carmody and his two special assistants, Westbrook and Foreman, have seldom been given any credit—or blame—for busting open public housing's stodginess and helping to shape its postwar direction.[147]

## Modern Architecture and Prefabrication Prove Costly to Mutual Housing

Lawrence Westbrook and John Green were already convinced of the merits of community modernism before they began collaborating on the Mutual Plan. They regarded the clustering of dwellings facing a community green or park as more conducive to the long-term success of a mutual ownership association than detached dwellings scattered along a road. The public places and spaces found in the eight pilot projects would, they believed, foster community identity and belonging, making it possible for residents to cope with the anxiety accompanying their transition from leaseholders to mutual owners.

The Mutual Division tried to secure workers' acceptance of mutual home ownership and modern architecture by involving them in the planning process. Henry Andreas of the Shipbuilding Workers Local No. 1 Housing Committee recalled that before construction of Audubon Village began, Westbrook, Green, and the project architects agreed that "the prospective occupants of the dwell[ings] were to be consulted, and their constructive criticisms and suggestions incorporated with the housing program." This was important because the workers "know something about how [the developments] should be laid out."[148]

The CIO Housing Committee praised the Mutual Division for its efforts to suit the project to local conditions and for recognizing that in order to "secure the valuable collaboration of the workers it is necessary that their representatives take part in the initial planning." The result was that the "entire physical layout of a project intended for mutual home-ownership" was "basically different from the P.B.A. or U.S.H.A. conceptions."[149] The UAW maintained that because the architects listened to prospective residents the result was "houses which are not only inexpensive but highly livable. In the long run that means that the government will come out of the deal in the blue." In contrast, "PBA projects were designed by architects and then the people had to fit in them. Mutual Home Ownership plan houses are designed for living—then they are built."[150]

The architects and planners Westbrook selected designed communities that were inspired by the garden city concept introduced at the turn of the twentieth century by Ebenezer Howard in the famous book *Garden Cites of Tomorrow.* The heart of each Mutual Division pilot project was a generous interior green that served as the community's informal civic plaza and extended living room. Unlike a true garden city, however, the projects lacked the outer rims of industrial, agricultural, or conservation land use. The clustered dwelling units, pedestrian walkways, and civic and commercial spaces strongly resembled those created by the Greenbelt town architects and planners to foster economic and social bonds among residents.

Westbrook later wrote that "some very valuable lessons were learned" from the Mutual Division's experimentation with modern design and mass-production construction. At Audubon Village and Avion Village, he dealt with labor union conflict over the use of WPA relief labor and prefabricated construction. Avion Village nonetheless most effectively demonstrated Westbrook's skill in bringing architects, planners, and general contractors together for efficient assembly of prefabricated housing. At Walnut Grove, the Mutual Division showed that modern, mass-produced houses could sit comfortably side by side with conventionally built ones; they did not ruin the neighborhood aesthetically or economically.

The avant garde design and method of construction used by the Mutual Division in many of the other 167,700 dwelling units intended to be permanent additions to the local community housing stock sent a clear message of impending change to housing consumers and producers. Taken together, the pilot projects suggested that when the end of the war would bring changes in the way housing was designed, planned, built, and financed that might overtake the wasteful, exploitive patterns of urban and suburban development promoted by speculative builders. Wage earners who could not afford to own a house and often took a financial battering in the commercial market would have an opportunity to help plan and eventually mutually own a community of affordable, easily maintained dwellings.[151]

In the end, the coupling of mutual housing and community modernism brought more detractors than friends. Westbrook's commitment to a physical layout unlike that of most other residential developments made it easy for local realtors and bankers to brand the new communities a threat to real estate values and private control of the middle-income housing market. Modern architecture and mass-produced housing provided ammunition for its critics and detracted from Westbrook's ability to win a broad base of support for mutual housing.[152]

# 4

# Mutual Housing Offers a "New Day in Housing"

From Camden, New Jersey, to San Pedro, California, defense workers greeted mutual housing with enthusiasm. In April 1941 CIO president Philip Murray told President Roosevelt that support for the Mutual Plan had "spread throughout the country, and unions in many sections have addressed inquiries or sent delegations to Washington to urge that it be used in conjunction with their local defense housing needs." Murray wanted federal housing officials to make it possible for the residents of all Lanham-funded housing developments to have a chance to buy their homes on a mutual basis.[1]

Union backing for expanded application of the Mutual Plan came to a crescendo in September 1941, when Walter P. Reuther, an up-and-coming UAW Executive Council member, asked President Roosevelt to authorize the use of Lanham funds to build an entire mutually owned city for 10,000 Detroit-area bomber workers.[2] Five months later, local, state, and federal housing and planning officials; architects and planners; and representatives of 136 AFL and 96 CIO locals met at the February 15, 1942, War Workers' Housing Conference in Los Angeles. Labor's representatives put aside their differences and united behind a call for expanded application of the Mutual Plan. Modern housing appeared to be taking root.[3]

## Reformers Back the Mutual Plan

When first developing the Mutual Plan Westbrook, who was described as a "one-man building agency," did not consult with the members of formally and informally organized groups that promoted communitarian reform, such as the Regional Planning Association of America and the National Public Housing Conference. But once the plan's implementation began, he actively sought—and gained—their support and approval. In January 1941 Westbrook assured members of the National Public Housing Conference that mutual housing could fill the "housing gap" that existed for families whose income was "between $1000 and $2000 annually"—too little to safely purchase and maintain a house and too much to qualify for low-income public housing. He sought to convince them that mutual housing was the "shaft of light through the clouds . . . [that would reveal a] new day in housing for many thousands of medium-income families."[4]

Westbrook's Mutual Plan received backing from Dorothy Rosenman, president of the National Committee on the Housing Emergency and the wife of presidential adviser Samuel I. Rosenman. She believed that the Mutual Plan brought together "the satisfaction of home ownership with the mobility of rental housing which is so important to workers."[5] From July to October 1941 the National Committee on the Housing Emergency's board of directors, whose members included Charles Abrams, Catherine Bauer, Edith Elmer Wood, and other leading activists, gave "intensive" study to the Mutual Plan. After offering Westbrook a few suggestions for improvement and clarification, the board resolved to call on the Roosevelt administration to expand the mutual housing program. Rosenman regarded the housing developments constructed by the Mutual Division as some of the best of those built under the Lanham Act. "Planned for a continuing population and in the way that people today wish to live," she said, the communities would "continue to be attractive neighborhoods after this war is over." In response to critics of the use of Lanham funds for housing experimentation, Rosenman contended that defense housing officials were "justified in this use and "ought to try out every device and experiment with every method in order to gain knowledge and experience in a field that is vital to the core of living."[6]

Westbrook's Mutual Plan won endorsements from planning advocates alarmed by the explosion of real estate development in portions of California in the wake of mobilization. The California Housing and Planning Association stated that the Mutual Plan offered what "Americans long divided fifty-fifty between owning and renting, have been looking for—a system with the advantages of both and the drawbacks of neither." It was "one of the most significant developments in American housing, perhaps also a significant development in American culture."[7]

The California Housing and Planning Association was outspoken in its support for the Mutual Plan, in part because of the involvement of Catherine Bauer. She regarded the Mutual Plan as potentially "the most important thing that happened to housing during the war"[8] and saw labor's "nation-wide spontaneous interest" in the Camden Plan as "extremely important."[9] For Bauer, the Mutual Plan was an opportunity to compensate for one of the major flaws in the Housing Act of 1937—the provision limiting government aid to public housing bodies and thereby preventing civic, labor, and other nonprofit organizations from assisting their members. It did not matter whether "the scheme has been effectively worked out as yet. Whenever such experiments are sound, they should certainly be encouraged." If a successful formula for true cooperatives could be found, it might help undo the "lingo and atmosphere of paternalistic reform [that] was necessary to get the public housing business started in this county."[10]

Bauer believed that, although the Mutual Plan was "one tiny chapter" in the history of war housing, it might have the most far-reaching implications. One reason was the nationwide support of unions, which "represented a spontaneous effort of workers to get housing for themselves, on a cooperative basis." Westbrook's eight pilot communities could "stimulate a vigorous and important new chapter in American housing."[11]

In broadening and diversifying his base of political support beyond labor and housing and planning advocacy groups, Lawrence Westbrook sought the assistance of Ray Holder, who after studying law at the University of Texas and serving in the Texas State Legislature with Westbrook, came to regard mutual home ownership as "a second religion." Together, the two worked to win converts to mutual housing among manufacturers, bankers, and other business leaders, who opposed public housing generally, by emphasizing that the Mutual Plan required no operating subsidies and would become private, tax-generating property. Because they would be joint owners, residents had an economic incentive to take care of their dwellings and community property and keep utility and maintenance costs low.[12]

Westbrook enjoyed only modest success in securing endorsements for mutual housing in business and commercial circles. One supporter was Alpheus Winter, executive secretary of the Bridgeport, Connecticut, chapter of the National Association of Manufacturers. He praised the Mutual Plan, convinced that mutual housing opportunities would attract the type of workers that Bridgeport's manufacturers wanted—those with the skills and work habits who wanted to be permanent residents of Bridgeport and could make their mortgage payments. Defense housing developments built under the Mutual Plan, Winter said, were "in no way to be confused with the re-settlement of slum clearance projects" built by the USHA.[13]

Not surprisingly, Westbrook was most effective in strengthening and diversifying mutual housing's base of support in his home state of Texas. He used his local, state, and national Democratic Party connections to gain cooperation and support for Avion Village and Dallas Park from public officials, defense contractors, and allied business interests. With Holder's assistance, he recruited a group of "high caliber" businessmen and civic leaders, including a leading Texas industrialist, a former president of the Dallas Real Estate Board, a bank president, and the mayor of Grand Prairie, to guide Avion Village in its evolution from public to private ownership by the Avion Village Mutual Housing Association.[14] Westbrook's task was made easier by the fact that in Dallas and other southwestern cities, business leaders and civic boosters were far more likely to play an active role in obtaining federal funds for public housing than in northeastern or upper midwestern cities, where labor and coalitions of liberal reformers took the lead.[15]

John Carmody understood how important it was to obtain backing for the Mutual Plan from respected business and industrial leaders and, after leaving the FWA, continued to help Westbrook win friends for mutual housing. In February 1942, as head of the U.S. Maritime Commission, Carmody encouraged industrialist and shipbuilder Henry Kaiser to contact Westbrook, believing that Kaiser was seriously interested in mutual housing because it was "along the lines of his own thinking and planning as applied to insurance and a good many other human relations problems." Aware of the prominent defense contractor's interest in prefabricated construction, Carmody likely also told Kaiser that Westbrook had combined prefabricated home construction with mutual ownership. Kaiser's involvement in prefabricated housing would grow, but he did not pair it with mutual or cooperative home ownership. Like most defense contractors, he was leery of the Mutual Plan if for no other reason than that it commanded the interest of both labor leaders and housing reformers, who agreed that it ought to be applied to all suitable defense housing developments.[16]

## Mutual Housing: "One of the New Deal's Highest Cards"

The architectural profession rewarded Westbrook for arranging the marriage of mutual housing and modern architecture with endorsements for the Mutual Plan. Architect Albert Mayer called the Camden Plan a "significant contribution in human terms" and regarded it as a turning point in federal housing policy. He believed mutual housing to be the solution to the defense housing problem because it offered workers both the stability of traditional home ownership and the flexibility of renting. Wage earners could escape from the "deadly millstone" of a home mortgage and enjoy a chance to live where they would have an "active share in all civic affairs, whether economic, managerial, spiritual or social." The Mutual Plan offered defense housing officials a chance to strike a balance between what Mayer described as the "urgent primary need [for housing] with a thoughtful, long-range social objective." His laudatory *New York Times Magazine* article featured a picture of Avion Village to illustrate "what can be done with careful thought and reliance on past experience."[17]

Architect Edmund N. Bacon, who later achieved recognition for his postwar role in the redevelopment of Philadelphia's Society Hill neighborhood, shared Mayer's interest in the work of the Mutual Division. He briefly served as an apprentice under architect Oscar Stonorov and, when mobilization for war began, "campaigned hard to alert Philadelphia officials to the critical link between housing and defense production." Bacon called the Mutual Plan an "important channel of release for the initiative and enterprise of the average American family seeking a home for itself."[18]

The architectural profession's most ringing endorsement of the Camden Plan came in June 1941, when the *Architectural Forum* called Audubon Village "trail-blazing" and praised the Mutual Division for setting new standards in site planning and experimenting with prefabricated housing. More important, according to the *Forum*, Westbrook and his staff made it possible for wage earners to enjoy the advantages of both renting and home ownership, including: "1) no cash down payment, 2) low monthly charges, 3) accumulation of equity, 4) incentive to maintain the property in good physical condition, 5) participation in management, 6) provision for moving readily from one size dwelling unit to another with changes in income and family size, [and] 7) ability to move at will."[19]

The *Architectural Forum* encouraged architects and builders to regard the Mutual Division's approach to residential development as a model. The clustering of homes around community facilities and green spaces was an alternative to the style of development favored by speculative builders, where block after block of detached dwellings were erected in undeveloped portions of the city or on the urban periphery. Audubon Village, Avion Village, and their sister developments challenged architects, planners, and builders to ask how they might independently or in conjunction with labor, civic, or other organizations, profitably engage in urban development that was less land- and resource-consuming than the automobile-oriented suburban development of the pre–Depression years. Could they lower construction costs by applying the Mutual Division's lessons in prefabrication and standardization? If mutual home ownership among middle-income families proved to be "as significant and revolutionary as some authorities believe," it could break the deadlock between renting and buying.[20]

In the *Architectural Forum* article, the Mutual Plan was presented as a potential tool to ease the economy back to peacetime production. If an ambitious public works program was necessary to create jobs and stimulate home building, the now-tested Mutual Plan could be implemented on a wider scale. Publicly funded dwellings that would not remain in the public domain, and thus not require operations subsidies, were far more likely to secure bipartisan support than those that remained in the public domain. The self-liquidating nature of the Mutual Plan made it possible to "at least partially relieve Government, and in turn the taxpayers, of much of their costly public housing program." The Mutual Division's continued use of relief labor was endorsed as a means of holding down site development costs and "might well prove to be a more profitable use of relief activity than leaf-raking and its ilk."[21]

Once the Camden Plan was further analyzed, "private enterprise may deem it smart to kidnap the plan bodily or at least some of its most important and adaptable features."[22] If the mutual housing plan was to provide a structure for private interests to profit from investment in large-scale, low-cost, government-supervised housing developments, it could be "one of the New Deal's highest cards, which if played right, may prove to be one of its most significant contributions. Coming from sources outside of the Government, these convictions would indicate that the Camden Plan is much bigger than even inventor Westbrook claims."[23]

Endorsement of the Mutual Plan by the *Architectural Forum* as "one of the New Deal's highest cards" was followed by a wave of favorable press coverage. On October 29, 1941, the *Christian Science Monitor* reported that 500 families had "taken it upon themselves to prove a new idea in housing" on the outskirts of Camden that could "revolutionize the way millions of Americans buy their homes." A short time later, the *New York Times* concluded that the success of the mutual home buying as implemented by the Mutual Division in Camden could "revolutionize real estate practices."[24]

Lew Carr of the Dayton *Journal-Herald* wrote that Dayton's Greenmont Village "may (or may not) revolutionize several things in the housing world." But until the Mutual Division entered the local market, Dayton, like hundreds of other cities and towns across America, had had no noncommercial housing options for wage earners. Carr thought it was a good thing that the Mutual Plan was "having considerable tests and trials which seem to indicate its workability and soundness," and he was confident that further application would likely be supported by reformers and business interests alike.[25]

Camden's *Courier-Post* similarly emphasized the far-reaching impact of the Mutual Division's pilot projects, declaring that "comment on the now famous Camden Plan, used in the construction of Audubon Village, has been widespread." To impress on its readers the national importance of this new housing development in their midst, the paper emphasized the interest expressed in the Camden Plan and how it worked by *Time* and other prominent news outlets.[26]

*Business Week*, *Time*, and other national news and trade magazines provided evidence that Westbrook had successfully distanced mutual housing from New Deal concerns with the working poor, rebranding it for middle- or moderate-income households. If the Mutual Plan proved to be workable at Audubon Village and was applied at other defense housing developments not originally built by the Mutual Division, it could, according to *Business Week*, "change the whole trend of defense labor housing."[27]

Audubon Village was described by *Time* as a "Government housing project the likes of which the U.S. has never seen before." The "ingenious Colonel Lawrence Westbrook" had found a way to provide quality, affordable housing for the "48% of all non-farm families which pay $20–$40 a month [in] housing costs . . . [and] can ill afford to risk home-ownership." The magazine encouraged readers to read the June 1941 issue of the *Architectural Forum*, also published by Time-Life, for more details. Much to Westbrook's satisfaction, *Time* reiterated the suggestion that investors might find in the Mutual Plan a possible avenue for postwar private investment. In that case, "private capital would have a new investment outlet, the building industry would gain a stable market and the U.S. would get badly needed housing."[28] Given the attention devoted to the Mutual Plan, it seemed almost certain that it would be included in the "Public Work Reserve" that Carmody created in June 1941. This "national shelf of work projects" was placed in readiness for local, state, and federal agencies to use for economic "pump-priming" when the national defense crisis was over.[29]

## Defense City: Community Modernism for Bomber Workers

The most compelling expression of support for Westbrook's Mutual Plan emerged from the Detroit headquarters of the UAW. On June 13, 1941, as work progressed on the huge, publicly funded B-24 Liberator bomber plant on Ford Motor Company property in rural Washtenaw County, UAW president R. J. Thomas called on Division of Defense Housing Coordination (DDHC) head Charles Palmer to immediately seek executive authorization for the construction of 10,000 units of housing for defense workers.[30] Siding with Ford Motor Company officials and allied real estate interests, neither of which wanted workers' housing built near the plant, Palmer argued that he could not request the president's authorization for the construction of Lanham housing in the vicinity of the plant until further study of Ford employment projections was completed. Investigative reporters and health and social service officials joined labor in condemning Palmer's unwillingness to take action to improve living conditions in the Willow Run area. Later, when Agnes Meyer visited Willow Run on behalf of the *Washington Post* in March 1943, she found conditions defying "the dignity of man" and ample evidence to show that private interests were not adequately addressing the demand as Palmer, industrialist Henry Ford, and allied interests maintained. One dwelling devoid of running water and sewer service was occupied by a large number of related and unrelated aviation workers, including five men who lived in the basement, a family of five residing on the first floor, and four men sharing the second floor. Nine defense workers resided in the garage. The number of workers who took shelter in the four trailers parked in the yard was unknown.[31]

Labor organized to demand defense housing for metropolitan Detroit, starting in July 1941, with the creation of the Metropolitan Detroit UAW-CIO City-Wide Housing Committee, established to give labor a "voice and authority in all phases of the defense [housing] program." A Housing Department was established within the CIO's War Policy Division, and a full-time representative was assigned to Washington to lobby federal officials, members of Congress, and the Roosevelt administration on housing matters.[32]

In August, the Detroit-based architect and planner Alan Mather argued for what he called the "one good solution" to the problem of housing for workers (up to 60,000) expected to be employed at Ford's bomber plant roughly twenty four miles from Detroit. That solution, he said, was to "have the U.S. Housing Authority build a garden city nearby." Mather thought garden cities for workers should be built outside of Los Angeles, New York, and other cities where major aircraft manufacturing facilities were located or under construction. He regarded the Hartford Housing Authority's 1,000-unit garden village then under construction for defense workers at United Aircraft as a model for Detroit and other cities where the influx of aviation production workers worsened housing conditions. The 135-acre site in West Hartford was bisected by a river and included a community center, a nursery school, and a shopping center that were linked by paths and secondary roads to "duplex and row houses arranged in courtyards around dead-end streets." Mather's loyalty to USHA director Nathan Straus, who resented competing with Westbrook and others for Lanham housing assignments and experienced staff, likely prevented him from suggesting that the proposed garden cities be sold to the residents under the Mutual Plan.[33]

Mather's call for garden cities outside of Detroit and other industrial cities was greeted with a lukewarm response from the UAW, probably because the union was busy preparing its own home-building and finance organization. The UAW warned its members that speculative developers and real estate investors saw them "as a large and fertile field to exploit" and were "looking with great anticipation toward the post-war period to repeat their profits of former boom years."[34] On July 11, 1941, R. J. Thomas and several other union representatives visited Palmer's "sumptuous offices" seeking his support for the union's effort to extend the "principle of collective bargaining to secure decent homes for auto workers." They agreed to undertake a new experiment in which the union would create a revolving fund to help its members realize the American Dream of home ownership of a single-family dwelling without placing themselves and their families at too much economic risk.

One UAW local at a time, monies from the revolving fund would be used by a "Mutual Housing Corporation" to hire an architect, a general contractor, and a real estate attorney. The corporation would sell $50 shares of stock to prospective residents and "find private financing that qualified under the Title VI FHA program." The UAW envisioned the construction of detached dwellings featuring "phenol plywood" panels prefabricated by CIO factory workers. The dwellings would be located in planned communities, with no through traffic and a "ten-acre park." Once the housing was sold and the funds returned to the UAW revolving fund, another local could begin a project.[35]

The mutual housing corporation created by UAW Local 174 on Detroit's West Side was selected to be the first recipient of a UAW revolving fund loan. Its plan was to develop a community of single-family dwellings designed by union architectural consultant Otis Winn for a site in Lincoln Park, Michigan, that would be sold to the residents over a fixed period. The plan won Palmer's endorsement and was reported to have received backing from a Detroit bank and the FHA. Aware that its members saw their economic and social interests as best served by ownership of a detached house with a small plot of land, UAW leaders abandoned the European concept of modern housing advocated by Bauer and others, replacing multidwelling units and the superblock with small, single-family homes situated on individual lots on cul-de-sacs and other secondary roads. Despite these preparations, it appears that the community was never built.

In *Housing for Defense*, UAW leader R. J. Thomas emphasized that the revolving fund was one potential source of funding for union-sponsored cooperative housing; the Lanham Act was another. He said that John Green's

Shipbuilding Workers Union "insisted on and was given the right to be represented in the actual community planning by the architects," which Thomas saw as a major accomplishment that other unions needed to duplicate it in their negotiations.[36]

On September 26, a few days after the UAW's release of *Homes for Workers*, while Carmody was in the Virgin Islands recovering from "accumulated fatigue" and Westbrook was on his own to contend with Palmer, Walter Reuther sent President Roosevelt a proposal to resolve the Willow Run housing situation.[37] Acting on architect Oscar Stonorov's ideas, he asked the president to immediately authorize the construction of an entire "Defense City" of 10,000 homes for Willow Run workers with funding appropriated under the Lanham Act. He proposed that Defense City be "mutual in character" and modeled on Audubon Village and the defense housing developments "sponsored by shipyard workers in Camden and Kearney, and built by John Carmody through Lawrence Westbrook, [of the] Division of Mutual Ownership Defense Housing." Conceived as a model for urban redevelopment, the proposed community was to be self-contained with educational, recreational, and commercial facilities. The architect-designed prefabricated houses and public buildings would be assembled by CIO workers.[38]

Reuther asked the president to order that the job begin immediately and to assign its supervision to the UAW's "friend," FWA administrator John Carmody, who would delegate the task to Westbrook.[39] The automobile workers had confidence in the two men, he told the president, and could successfully work with them in selecting architects and jointly planning the project. Reuther also wanted Carmody and Westbrook because they had already proved friendly to the CIO's efforts to gain a foothold in the home-building industry through prefabricated housing. A strong showing for prefabricated housing at Defense City would put the CIO in a stronger position to demand a role for itself in the anticipated post–defense development boom.[40]

Reuther based his call for Defense City on research conducted by local, state, and federal agencies and the union showing that, although the population of Detroit and its industrial suburbs had increased greatly since mobilization, the supply of affordable housing had not. He regarded the low-income public housing program initiated under the New Deal excellent but not adequate to solve the housing problems faced by workers whose incomes had risen as a result of defense employment. The private home-building industry in metropolitan Detroit produced too few rental units or houses affordable for purchase by these workers. Palmer had tried to appease labor by allowing a "few hundred housing units to dribble out here and there," but the need was for some "really *big* projects that the whole country will hear about."[41]

Reuther warned that unless a massive federal undertaking was immediately initiated, a production bottleneck would paralyze the Detroit area, the "most strategic center of mass production industry" in the United States.[42] Roosevelt had to act because his DDHC chief (Palmer) sided with Henry Ford, an opponent of publicly funded residential development near the Willow Run plant. When the UAW had volunteered its organizational expertise and manpower to help Palmer gather the data necessary to estimate how much public housing was needed for Willow Run, Palmer "brushed aside" the offer, dismissing the findings of the UAW Housing Committee as though the union were incompetent or too partisan to provide accurate, reliable information on industrial workers' housing needs.[43]

Palmer's downplaying of the need for defense housing in metropolitan Detroit and his appeasement of local business and political interests with financial ties to the real estate market and Ford prompted Reuther to conclude that Palmer cared little about the "poor devil" who worked on the defense production line. He was "perfectly willing to permit overcrowding and scarcity to exist so that local rent racketeers" could take advantage of defense workers in need of housing. Palmer's "reluctance and niggardliness" had discredited the Roosevelt administration, according to Reuther, who urged the president to make *"a big and decisive gesture,"* bypass Palmer and authorize Carmody to proceed with the construction of Defense City.[44]

Reuther tried to persuade President Roosevelt to give the immediate go-ahead to his proposal by arguing it was not only essential for defense but also politically prudent. He projected that by the close of 1942, UAW membership would swell to over 600,000, surpassing the nation's largest union, the United Mine Workers. By building Defense City, the Roosevelt administration could retain the political loyalty of the "organized and militantly conscious" automobile and aircraft workers. Such a gesture would show the UAW rank and file that the administration had *"ceased appeasing real estate interests and is determined to do an all-out job to build the morale that full and sustained production requires."*[45] Reuther also reminded the president that if unemployment and "industrial stagnation" returned after the defense crisis ended and a new public works program was necessary to promote economic stabilization, Defense City could be ready as a guide to urban renewal.[46]

Reuther tried to convince the president to build Defense City as a way to shape his legacy. Long after his administration was over, Defense City would remain as a "conspicuous symbol of the New Deal" to be regarded by future generations as the "human counterpart to the TVA" and the culmination of the goals of relief, recovery, and reform.[47] Defense City would be viewed as representative of "our national belief in Democracy as a way of life" and would typify the administration's success in directing a "vast job of production while at the same time advancing the ideals which inspire the whole defense effort."[48] As a symbol of its time, the project would be "a beacon pointing the way toward the development of an America in which all workers, are enabled by their government and by their union to lead a decent life in modern, model surroundings."[49]

Reuther conceived of Defense City as "complete in every respect," an enlarged version of the Mutual Division's pilot projects. It would be designed by a team of modernists consisting of "12–15 of the best and most experienced housing architects and engineers of the country" that would work with labor representatives to build a community to serve as a model for those built with either public or private funds as part of the larger process of community revitalization and offer a "lasting pattern of diversified expression."[50]

To ensure that Defense City was designed with the social and economic needs of working people in mind, Reuther proposed that an advisory committee be appointed to work with Carmody and Westbrook. The members would include Reuther, UAW education director Richard Deverall, labor economist Isador Lubin, planner and social critic Lewis Mumford, Columbia University sociologist Robert Lynd, United Textile Workers Union official and housing advocate John Edelman, and at least one representative drawn from the UAW membership at large.[51] Worker participation in the planning and construction of Defense City was essential to "assure complete acceptance of and support for the project." More important, Reuther argued, it would "morally bind the future citizens to the task of making life in the Defense City rich and significant."[52]

Reuther presented Defense City as the beginning of a much larger process of urban rebuilding that would be necessary when the war was over. He had witnessed the impact of decentralization of Detroit's industrial, commercial, and residential development and the shift in investment to the urban fringe, especially in the vicinity of the new Ford Freeway (later U.S. Route 94). Located outside Detroit near the new highway, Defense City would serve as a "laboratory for post-war housing and life" and as a measure of the success of mutual housing and industrial unionism. Defense City would be the first to initiate urban renewal and rebuilding from the outside—the urban fringe—moving inward toward Detroit's decaying core neighborhoods and downtown business district.[53]

Reuther's Defense City proposal was a combination automobile-age garden city plan and urban and economic revitalization program. After the emergency was over, the United States could turn its manufacturing might, technological expertise, and finely tuned industrial workforce to replacing gritty old commercial and industrial cities and slum housing with planned communities mutually owned by the residents. Houses, stores, schools, offices, hospitals, factories, and other buildings would be constructed by CIO workers from building components or modules assembled in safe, clean, and efficient prefabrication plants Convinced that residential and commercial real estate development would grow in economic and political importance when the crisis had passed, Reuther sought to realize a goal set forth years earlier by Catherine Bauer with the backing of other communitarian reformers—"housing for, of and by workers."[54] Defense City was a means of claiming a place for the CIO in a postwar economy predicated largely on suburban development and urban redevelopment.

The UAW described and promoted Reuther's Defense City proposal in both its newspaper and in *The Distributor*, its weekly magazine. Readers were assured that the idea was not "picked out of a hat by a couple of starry-eyed auto and aircraft workers," but was the "culmination of the thought of auto and aircraft workers who realized that you can't have good production without good homes." Defense City would be a "laboratory for post-war housing and life" because it represented "the best thought of government and the best thought of auto and aircraft workers." Members of democratically elected committees would work with Westbrook and his staff in planning the new community. The result would be the first publicly funded city in the U.S. designed, built, run, and cooperatively owned by industrial workers.[55]

According to *The Distributor*, the union wanted to work with the "brilliant Colonel Lawrence Westbrook," because he understood how "most homes for workers today are built by men who want to make a lot of money in a short time." Defense City would provide workers with houses designed to be livable on "winding streets" with "parks, a community center and all [the] best features which go to make a model city." At the same time the houses would be built at a minimum cost in contrast to the "barracks-type of dwellings erected by so many federal housing agencies" such as the PBA.[56]

The UAW emphasized that Defense City would become the property of a mutual housing association that would pay back the government, pay its own taxes "[and] not rely upon government handouts, or any sort of subsidy."[57] In this aspect it was the antithesis of the FHA's Title VI program, created to help speculative home builders take economic advantage of house-seeking defense workers. Such developers often got "all of their money from the government" and profited handsomely without putting anything in. The houses they built, although typically high-priced, would not "stand the wear of the years." Often haphazardly constructed, they were "designed for profit, not for community living."[58]

## Palmer Responds to the Camden Plan

Allied real estate, banking, and home-building interests were alarmed by Reuther's Defense City proposal and by those made by other CIO unions to expand application of the Mutual Plan. They were determined to keep middle-income families dependent solely on commercial market housing options, but they had to be careful not to appear unpatriotic and insensitive to the needs of defense workers and contractors. Real estate developers and investors looked to DDHC head Charles Palmer for assistance in keeping the Mutual Plan a small, relatively obscure offshoot of the larger defense housing program. They remained firmly in Palmer's corner even when he felt he had to fight fire with fire and directed his staff to develop a privately funded cooperative housing plan for urban defense workers to compete with the publicly funded Mutual Plan.

Westbrook ran afoul of Palmer early on when he arranged for WPA work crews to clear the Audubon Village site, complete the rough grading, and install utility lines. For Palmer and his staff, the use of WPA labor was "unrealistic to the solution of the Mutual Housing Program," which made "any data, or experience gained unrealistic for application elsewhere."[59]

In March 1941, as construction of Audubon Village was rapidly progressing, Palmer accused Westbrook of misusing Lanham funds by giving preference to applicants who planned to remain in the area at the war's end. He declared that so-called in-migrants who had recently arrived for defense work deserved first consideration over workers from the area, even though the Lanham Act drew no such distinctions. Westbrook argued that the Mutual Division had to give preference to applicants who planned to remain in the area to ensure the future success of the Mutual Housing Plan.[60]

Concerned about the tenant selection issue, Westbrook apparently expressed his apprehensions to John Green, who took the matter up with the CIO Housing Committee. On April 14, 1941, the committee sent a memorandum to Palmer voicing support for Westbrook and for giving preference to applicants from the local area who wished to remain as permanent residents. It was not right that "newly employed workers who may remain in the locality only during the current emergency should have priority over permanent residents who may be expected to stay on and purchase the houses occupied from the government. The houses vacated by them will be available to the more transient workers."[61]

Disregarding the CIO Housing Committee, Palmer refused to let the issue drop. On April 30, 1941, he met with the President Roosevelt and informed him that John Carmody was allowing Westbrook to violate the Lanham Act by letting the Mutual Division pass over recently arrived defense workers who had no intention of staying in the area.[62] The president's specific reaction to Palmer's accusation is not known, but the emergence of friction between Palmer and Carmody, which, according to *Time*, "took the form of a cat & dog fight," could hardly have been surprising to him.[63] Roosevelt had created a bureaucratic setup that divided responsibility for the defense housing program between the two administrators. He expected those involved in the turf battles and personality clashes that resulted from his practice of making overlapping or vague assignments to settle their differences privately, without his intervention. Mindful of how much Roosevelt disliked being cast in the role of Solomon, Carmody made no direct appeal to him.[64]

The tenant selection policy was still simmering when Carmody told Westbrook that Palmer was now seeking legal counsel to determine whether the Lanham Act made it possible for the FWA to "sell houses and allow the purchasers to acquire and withdraw an actual cash equity when the Government has written off part of the cost for certain items such as site improvement and utilities charge." Concerned that the matter was getting out of hand, Carmody agreed that Westbrook needed to meet with Palmer to hash out their differences.[65]

On May 25, 1941, after a final early-morning consultation with Carmody, Westbrook and Clark Foreman, director of the Division of Defense Housing, set forth to meet with Palmer. On arrival at Palmer's office they were informed that the coordinator had been "suddenly called to New York." The pair met with assistant coordinator Jacob Crane but, not surprisingly, made little progress in settling the disputed issues.[66] Palmer continued to accuse Carmody of allowing Westbrook to improperly use Lanham Act funds by permitting the Mutual

Division to give preference to defense workers who were already established in the community over new arrivals.[67]

Carmody undertook a second major effort to smooth over the differences between the FWA and the DDHC. Hoping that the favorable publicity around Audubon Village and the pilot projects would prompt Palmer to back off, Carmody sent him a letter acknowledging that he "had no idea when we undertook the so-called Camden Plan that interest in it would spread so rapidly or so intensively as it has in a wide variety of quarters." He expressed the hope that "nothing will be done to interfere" with the completion of Audubon Village and her sister developments "while questions about the wisdom of the plan may be in the process of being cleared up in the minds of those who may fear the spread of such a plan of management or ownership."[68]

Carmody evidently failed to gauge the extent to which Palmer and his supporters in real estate, banking, and home building did in fact "fear the spread" of support for mutual and cooperative home ownership among the middle-income households so important to the commercial market's profitability. Palmer refused to overlook the tenant policy even though, as Carmody noted, the "whole business represents so small an experiment in a major defense program that is already absorbing so much of the time of our major executives." Carmody also told Palmer that if he had further challenges to the Mutual Plan he ought to present them "early and sharply" and state his specific objections."[69]

By late July 1941 Palmer was so determined to stop Audubon Village from being filled with Green's militant shipbuilding workers that he again complained to President Roosevelt, alleging that conflict with Carmody had become "so bad that the entire program of Defense Housing Coordination is threatened unless prompt action is taken."[70] Several days later Palmer offered Roosevelt fresh evidence of Carmody's unwillingness to follow his directives when the Audubon Village Tenant Selection Committee turned down the application of a Navy inspector assigned to New York Ship in favor of an applicant who wished to remain indefinitely. Palmer, who resented the involvement of Green and the Local No. 1 Housing Committee in the tenant selection process, knew that Carmody and Westbrook were not violating the Lanham Act, but he felt compelled to protest their breach of "definite understandings."[71]

On July 30 Carmody tried to appease Palmer by drawing a distinction between the tenant selection processes at the different pilot projects. Westbrook would be allowed to proceed with the selection of residents for Audubon Village, Avion Village, and Winfield Park, which made up the Mutual Division's original 1,500-unit assignment. With regard to the other Mutual Division communities, "no commitments have been made as to tenant selection or other management procedures on any other projects assigned to Colonel Westbrook for construction." Although Carmody appeared to be leaving the door open to negotiation on the other Mutual Division projects, he wished to "make it entirely clear that I do not agree with your contention that occupancy of dwelling units constructed under the Lanham Act is intended primarily for 'migrant population caused by the defense program.' I do not intend to apply this principle to tenant selection to any of the projects coming under my jurisdiction." He closed by reminding Palmer that he "[did] not believe that 'recommendations' which you are authorized under executive order to make and which I have always cooperatively received and considered, have the effect of orders from the president."[72]

"Suggested General Principles Governing the Execution and Operation of Mutual Home Ownership Projects," released by the FWA in October 1941, underscored that the best candidates for mutual ownership of the pilot projects were middle-income defense workers who hoped for long-term community residence. The FWA explained: "Insofar as possible applicants selected shall be from among those who may be expected to continue to live and work in the locality concerned after the expiration of the defense emergency." Palmer wanted to force the Mutual Division to accept any qualified applicant regardless or how long he or she intended to remain in the area as a way to diminish the mutual association's ability to purchase the community.[73]

Carmody later defended the Mutual Division's tenant selection policy, explaining that the Mutual Plan was developed "for defense workers in plants which are regarded as [a] permanent part of the industrial life of the communities in which they are located. The objective is not only to meet emergency needs but to fit long-term community plans."[74] Westbrook believed that the tenant selection policy was followed so that "post-war disposal would be greatly simplified and the government's property would be much better taken care of if the workers permanently living in the community were permitted to occupy the new houses and especially so if they should be given an option to buy at the end of the emergency."[75]

The California Housing and Planning Association monitored the dispute over resident selection for the Mutual Plan projects, concluding that Palmer was a major impediment to housing betterment. Regarding the Mutual Plan as "the best development to emerge from the confusion of defense housing," association members were surprised that more projects were not under construction. There would have been more if Palmer had not "thrown his weight with the real estate boys" in opposing the Camden Plan.[76]

When asked for a response to the *Architectural Forum*'s prediction that the near future would see the expansion of mutual housing, Palmer stated that Congressman Lanham and the members of the Committee on Public Buildings and Grounds were confused by the mutual housing experiment and wondered why it was a part of the defense housing program. Determined to give substance to his contention that Lanham Act funds were being used inappropriately, he argued that Westbrook could do a "great service indeed" if he saw to it that the Mutual Plan was altered, amended, or "so clarified that it will do the defense job under the terms of the legislation which provides the money." Only then could it "blaze the way in this field for workers other than those engaged in defense."[77]

## Imitation as the Most Sincere Form of Flattery: Palmer's Rival Cooperative Housing Plan

Charles Palmer's awkward response to the California Housing and Planning Association came at the time when he was plotting to do just what the *Architectural Forum* had suggested—"kidnap" the Mutual Plan and develop a copycat version adapted for private funding. Palmer hoped to ride the wave of interest in cooperative housing and broker deals between defense contractors, private investors, unions, and home builders qualified under the FHA's Title VI. In July 1941, while Palmer was formulating his privately funded cooperative housing plan, he was advised by his staff that it was "of paramount importance whether the cooperative housing societies created by the defense program become a success or a failure." A successful wartime experiment with mutual or cooperative housing, it was said, could "contribute greatly to a rapid increase in the cooperative movement." If it failed, the entire movement for community modernism "and especially cooperative housing, will be seriously checked for a long time to come."[78]

USHA economist Warren J. Vinton agreed that the wartime showing of the Mutual Plan would help determine the level of interest in postwar cooperative housing. Referring to the plan, he observed that it was "most unfortunate to compromise the long-term possibilities of this device by attempting to utilize it in the solution of the complex and difficult problems of housing for defense workers." Cooperative home ownership, he astutely noted, was "difficult to promote in this country even under the most auspicious circumstances." The CIO's involvement in policy making, the use of mass-produced housing, and the embrace of modern design and planning complicated the task of explaining and gaining acceptance for the Mutual Plan.[79]

Palmer promoted his rival cooperative housing plan to undercut Westbrook and reduce the appeal of the publicly funded Mutual Plan. There is no evidence that he ever considered joining forces with Westbrook to determine what changes or modifications were needed for the plan to effectively function with either public or private funds. Instead, he used the human and financial resources at his command—including staff borrowed from the Rural Electrification Administration (REA)—to divert attention and support away from Westbrook and the Mutual Division.

The DDHC's cooperative housing plan proved to be no match for the Mutual Plan in the eyes of labor, its target audience. The UAW-backed Wichita Citizen's Housing Committee was not impressed and vowed to continue its fight for "4,000 to 6,000 government houses built on the Camden Plan," for the city's growing number of aviation workers.[80] The committee favored the Mutual Plan over Palmer's plan because of its full government financing and the participation of prospective residents in planning and design. Moreover, workers could "buy these homes without any down payment . . . without any government dictator raising . . . rents."[81]

Wichita's UAW Local No. 935 Housing Committee endorsed the construction of 4,000 units of Camden Plan housing. Union leaders regarded the city and its industrial workforce as well suited for mutual home ownership considering the city's growing preeminence in aircraft manufacturing and the demand for housing of all kinds. They argued that "this 4000 unit housing expense will be a good investment for the government and we [union members] will pay its way over a period of years" and that the use of Lanham funds to increase mutual housing opportunities would help local industries recruit and retain the best workers. Mindful that many people lacked significant exposure to industrial work and urban life, the union also saw the mutual housing associations as agents of acculturation. Using language then in common use to describe the transformative powers of traditional home ownership, supporters of mutual home ownership presented it as just as capable of developing within workers "an attitude of self-respect that can come only through the pride of possession of a home where American people can continue to dwell in peace" without the federal government as their landlord.[82]

Palmer's proposal failed to capture the support of mutual housing advocates who admired the work of the Mutual Division. Syndicated newspaper columnists like Dorothy Thompson, who described the Mutual Plan as a "model for further housing activities after the war emergency has passed," believed that Audubon Park and its sister developments would "pave the way for grandiose slum clearance and re-housing projects in the future, in which both private and public credit and capital might be engaged."[83] Once the emergency was over, she said, Westbrook's plan for mutual housing would likely prove capable of attracting private investment. Conservative elements would be pleased by the fact that the Mutual Plan was based primarily on "the mutual insurance idea and is excellent investment capitalism." And unlike low-income public housing, no federal subsidies were required for operational costs. At the same time, however, the plan was "thoroughly social" and garnered the support of liberals because it provided workers with affordable housing they could mutually own and democratically control.[84]

According to the FWA, the Mutual Plan offered more than just a "method of disposing of the projects to the residents after the war." It was an "experiment in group home-buying [for] families of modest incomes who as individuals have not usually been able to provide the margin of financial security generally necessary to obtain good new homes." This blueprint for the future of home building suggested a route toward "a sense of security and permanent living not possible in most war centers."[85]

In December 1941, as rumors circulated that the president would soon put an end to the turf war between the DDHC and the FWA by announcing a reorganization of the entire federal housing bureaucracy, Palmer grew quiet on his cooperative proposal. The DDHC's lack of further action left the cooperative housing plans of labor unions in La Porte, Indiana, and Dayton, Ohio, and public housing authorities in Chicago, Pittsburgh, and Dallas in limbo. Not one unit of privately funded housing was built as a result of the DDHC-UWA agreement or the DDHC's cooperative housing plan.[86]

## The Closing Days of the New Deal in Housing

Reuther and the UAW anxiously awaited the president's response to the Defense City proposal. Their anxiety grew amid speculation that Carmody would not be returning to the FWA. Rumors of his resignation were rampant, but the White House denied them, according to Oscar Stonorov, who believed it to be urgent that UAW president R. J. Thomas contact the president to prevent Carmody's resignation. Stonorov understood, seemingly before anyone else, that if Carmody stepped down, not only was the Defense City proposal at risk; mutual housing would likely see diminished or curtailed federal support.[87] On October 19, 1941, Richard Deverall, UAW education director, told an anxious Stonorov that there was still no word from anyone on the Defense City proposal and he was eager for news of any positive developments or evidence that the "entire plan [was] washed up."[88]

On October 21, 1941, the *Washington Post* reported that Carmody was "rumored to have resigned in what apparently presages a general shake-up of Federal housing agencies." It was understood that once the "faithful New Dealer" regained his health he would have his choice of jobs at any number of agencies that needed his strong administrative hand. The U.S. Maritime Commission was accurately predicted as the most likely. On November 19, Brigadier General Philip B. Fleming, a "hard-hitting Army engineer," took over as acting FWA administrator, but was unable to do the job for reasons of health. In late December 1941, FWA second in command Baird Snyder III was appointed, retaining the title of assistant administrator.[89]

Catherine Bauer reflected on Carmody's departure, noting that he had been "admirably bold in tackling prefabrication, hiring modern architects, initiating the 'Camden Plan' for Mutual Home Ownership and fighting the good fight with Coordinator Palmer." However, she found fault with him because he had "neglected and alienated the local officials and citizens who alone could have saved him when the showdown came."[90] Even so, if Bauer regarded Carmody as too assertive of federal power and unwilling to accommodate local interests, it was these very traits and qualities that racial leaders admired and respected. Carmody quietly and persistently chipped away at the national mountain of official racism and discrimination in employment and at the same time extended segregated housing.

In his "National Grapevine" column in the *Chicago Defender*, Charley Cherokee reported that "Good old Papa Ickes" had been a friend to African Americans but Carmody had gone a step further and taken action to make it possible for "Negro contractors to be given an opportunity to get defense housing contracts." He had "awarded a contract to a Negro architect on a defense housing project . . . appointed a Negro lawyer on his legal staff . . . [and given] a certain contractor hell for refusing to hire Negro carpenters on a defense housing job." Wishing to give credit where it was due, Cherokee said, "Take a bow brother Carmody."[91]

The *Chicago Defender* saw the departure of New Dealers like Carmody as evidence of a disturbing trend in which "liberal white administrators . . . [were] being forced out, one by one, by a clique of prejudiced congressmen determined to curtail benefits Negroes have received under liberalized interpretations of laws recently enacted."[92] Carmody's illness and October departure from the FWA was both a setback in the battle for civil rights and harbinger of the difficult times ahead for mutual housing.

In October 1941 UAW officials reported a breakthrough when Sidney Hillman of the Office of Production Management agreed to discuss Reuther's Defense City proposal with the president.[93] Thomas and Reuther considered Hillman the ideal person to present the case for Defense City because he already had Roosevelt's ear regarding defense matters and understood cooperative housing as a result of his long years of involvement with the Amalgamated Clothing Workers Union. Hillman's new assignment was to convince President Roosevelt to bypass Palmer and existing DDHC procedures and order work to commence on Defense City immediately. Stonorov suggested that Hillman tell the president that "no better means could be found at the present time to emphasize mutual confidence between the Federal Government and the Worker on the production line." The project would boost national morale and stand as a "realization of an American Community as a sample of things to come."[94]

Stonorov thought the president might be persuaded to order construction of Defense City if its proponents could capture his imagination with a big drawing of the proposed community prepared by him, George Howe, and Louis I. Kahn. The architects built a model instead. Stonorov planned for the climax of the CIO's November 1941 annual convention to be a message from Roosevelt broadcast on the public address system accompanied by the unveiling of the model. This "panoramic visualization" would, Stonorov predicted, electrify the Detroit conventioneers and give them a tangible example of what the CIO sought to achieve through industrial unionism. The occasion could also be used to announce the appointment of an administrative liaison to work with the UAW on the Defense City project, one who was cognizant of the project's potential to serve as an urban renewal template with "vast potential meaning for the future."[95]

Convinced that Hillman would secure the executive action needed for the project to move forward without Palmer's blessing, Stonorov could hardly contain his exuberance. He wrote to Reuther: "I am quite excited about the whole thing and we will work our heads off."[96] Stonorov might have felt it necessary to reassure Reuther of his commitment, having caught wind of the fact that, unlike Reuther, not all of those influential in labor circles were enamored of Stonorov and his talents. Later, in December 1941, Michael Harris of Philadelphia's Steel Workers' Organizing Committee (SWOC), who backed the construction of Pennypack Woods, sent a letter to Roy Reuther, Walter's brother, regarding Stonorov. Harris was convinced that the architect had hitched his wagon to labor less out of personal conviction than out of a desire to secure lucrative commissions.[97]

Stonorov, who thought he knew "what the typical union member thought was the ideal home," tried to make himself indispensable first to Green and then to Reuther as an adviser in matters relating to architecture, planning, and housing policy.[98] Anticipating the commissions and fame that would likely arise from successful completion of Defense City, he was constantly on guard for any sign or indication that the UAW was unwilling to expend its limited political capital and human resources on making the project a reality. By early November, fearful that other UAW priorities such as contract negotiations were beginning to taking precedence, Stonorov encouraged Reuther to remain in Washington to make sure that Hillman took the Defense City issue to President Roosevelt. Only by staying in the nation's capital could Reuther obtain a "clearing" of both the Defense City proposal and the stalled Center Line, Michigan, project designed by the Saarinens.[99]

Stonorov worked tirelessly to build support for the Defense City proposal. He drafted a memo to Judge Samuel Rosenman, Roosevelt's adviser and speechwriter, arguing that too many defense housing developments had been designed by "the regular run of private architects [who had] actually set back the cause of sound community planning and public housing and have diminished enthusiasm for the defense-housing program itself." Autoworkers had "nicknamed the Public Buildings Administration the 'Public Barracks Administration' to describe their antipathy to the type of housing provided."[100]

For Stonorov it was essential that the architects who had done "the few outstanding jobs in the defense housing program" be hired for Defense City. "Richly diversified designs of individual housing units can be achieved within the frame work of a fine city planned for modern living," he maintained.[101] In prose strikingly similar to what appeared in Reuther's proposal, Stonorov appealed for Rosenman's support by arguing that Defense City could become one of the administration's most admirable legacies. Camden's Yorkship Village, the garden community built by the Wilson administration, Stonorov noted, was now regarded as one of America's "most outstanding example[s] of community planning," and the Roosevelt administration had a chance to build "even finer and more efficient projects" as evidence that America was "confident in the triumph of Democracy [and the] Democratic way of life." The proposed Defense City would constitute as "conspicuous [a] symbol of the New Deal in the United States as the TVA itself."[102]

At Stonorov's request, Joel W. Schenker of M. Shapiro & Son, the general contractor for the 1,000-unit Pennypack Woods development, wrote to the White House in September 1941 that the Defense City project merited executive intervention because it would "serve as an indication to the men employed in the [defense] plants, of the sort of America that they may expect to live in." This "new American Way of Life, so often spoken of," would, he claimed, be "physically demonstrated by giving these men the opportunity to live in a model community that they own themselves in truly democratic fashion."[103]

President Roosevelt met with Reuther and Thomas in the fall of 1941 regarding the Defense City proposal and agreed to write a letter endorsing the project, but he stopped short of issuing an order for construction to commence. The November 6, 1941, draft of the letter to Sidney Hillman, co-director of the Office of Production Management, recommended the construction of Defense City under the "plan now well developed on some eight projects by [the] Mutual Ownership [Defense Housing] Division of the Federal Works Agency." The mutual housing plan should be applied at Defense City, Roosevelt said, because it was "strongly urged and widely supported by Organized Labor and especially the CIO."[104]

On November 12, 1941, portions of the letter President Roosevelt sent to Hillman were reworked into a new version and released to the press two days later. UAW members should "be assured of my interest in making this housing proposal a reality" the president wrote, stating that a "city of homes, well planned designed and owned by defense workers should be a symbol of the America we are defending and the America we are rebuilding for the future." This was an indication that the chief executive understood the CIO goal of setting the stage for postwar urban renewal through Defense City.[105]

As Stonorov had suggested, news of President Roosevelt's letter of endorsement was announced at the CIO convention as the architectural model was dramatically unveiled. In a telegram released to the press from the convention, Thomas expressed his appreciation to President Roosevelt for recognizing that Detroit, as the "center of strategic defense production," was the appropriate place to build a template of the kind of community workers could enjoy after the war. He predicted that "Detroit defense workers and this union in particular will regard Defense City as a symbol of the greatest coordinated drive in history to destroy tyranny while at the same time building our future for anticipated victory." Thomas hoped that the president would recognize the necessity to cut through the red tape and order work to commence immediately on a project that had "already captured the imagination of every rank and file member of the UAW-CIO."[106]

Roosevelt's unwillingness to circumvent his own administrative procedure and order the construction of Defense City was one of a number of factors that contributed to the project's doom. Content to let the process take the usual channel through Palmer's office, in his November 14 letter the president offered assurance that he would soon be "instructing the responsible Federal housing agencies to survey the possibilities of 'Defense City' and submit the results of their findings [by the] earliest possible date."[107]

On November 19 the cost of the UAW's efforts to convince the president to order the construction of Defense City became apparent. Palmer informed

Roosevelt's budget director, Harold Smith, that he had examined the proposal and found it to be "relatively obscure as to important detail." He also wanted assurance that, unlike Audubon Village and the other Mutual Division projects, Defense City would be inhabited only by newcomers to Metropolitan Detroit.[108] Palmer justified his delay in reviewing the request by arguing that the DDHC staff needed to consider whether Lanham funds might be more effectively spent on a series of smaller defense housing projects scattered over a broad area, allowing for the use of existing utility lines and social services. He further maintained that the process of land acquisition for the proposed Defense City would likely to be too long and too costly compared to a scattered-site approach.[109]

## Labor Backs Housing Reorganization

While labor awaited action on Reuther's Defense City proposal, a dispute arose with the Mutual Division over a contract offer made by the Currier Lumber Company for 300 prefabricated dwellings for a site in Wayne, Michigan. Westbrook refused to award the contract to Patrick Currier, owner of the company, even though he was the low bidder. He had been advised to take this action by Sidney Hillman, who feared labor unrest between the AFL and the CIO over the latter's effort to establish itself in the building trades through the "back door" of prefabrication. Shortly after, Hillman reached a "stabilization agreement" with the AFL and the CIO, in which AFL-affiliated trade and craft unions would enjoy something of a monopoly on defense building in exchange for their forfeiting of overtime and other concessions. The case came at time when the number of labor critics from both the Left and the Right was growing, and it attracted the attention of Senator Harry Truman and his committee of senatorial investigators, who seemed convinced that the Currier case was an example of how the president was being misled by Hillman into granting labor too much influence. Hundreds of letters, telegrams, and press articles called on the administration to award the contract to Currier, who had a history of labor troubles and had hired CIO-affiliated construction workers in order to be permitted to bid on the job. Currier never got his contract and Wayne, Michigan, never got its mutual housing.[110]

As 1941 drew to a close, it became more and more difficult for labor and housing reform advocates to separate criticism of Palmer's handling of the Defense City proposal from larger issues of defense housing policy. On December 2, 1941, the *New York Times* reported that the "feud" between Palmer and Carmody, one of "the most deep-seated in the field," had contributed to the reluctance of the House to approve the defense housing appropriation that the president had requested months earlier.[111] To prod congressional action on the funding request, presidential adviser Samuel Rosenman announced on December 4, 1941, that Roosevelt had asked him to devise a way of "smoothing out the confusion and conflict among bureaus that have slowed up the [entire] defense housing program."[112] The press speculated that if an administrative housecleaning took place, Palmer would likely keep his job because Rosenman's wife Dorothy, head of the National Committee on the Housing Emergency, regarded him as critical to maintaining the "balance between public and private housing."[113]

Rosenman's announcement not only put the Defense City proposal in jeopardy but threatened the very existence of the mutual housing program. Westbrook telegraphed architect Richard Neutra in California to inform him that the fate of the Mutual Division was now "up in the air" and its elimination was possible. Neutra expressed frustration that he was "in the dark" in trying to interpret the rumors and bits of information that made their way to the West Coast from Washington. Westbrook's telegram left him and his wife Dione feeling "flat and sad," Neutra later told David Williams.[114] The list of individuals considered likely to take over the housing program made him "gloomy," and the couple worried that the program's possible elimination would create an "anxious time" for Williams, who had been "working so hard" on it.[115]

R. J. Thomas responded to the December 7, 1941, Japanese attack on Pearl Harbor with a demand that Palmer seek immediate executive authorization for 10,000 units of Lanham housing so work on Defense City could begin. Fed up with Palmer's assurances that he was "making a 'study' of the situation," the union boss made a special pre-Christmas plea to President Roosevelt for his intervention, but Roosevelt took no action because, UAW members were told, "Churchill was here and nothing could be done" while the two world leaders formulated military strategy.[116]

Thomas charged that Palmer was opposed to publicly funded housing development, including mutual housing, because it "may tend to seriously diminish private construction." Speaking of the Mutual Plan, Palmer stated in February 1942 that a "development of this character in Detroit" offered the possibility of widespread implications and "may aggravate already difficult housing situations elsewhere," by which he meant declining real estate values in neighborhoods in the old urban core.[117]

Pushed to the breaking point, the UAW called for Palmer's removal, branding him one of the "agents of Hitler in America" and claiming that he did not wish to "interfere with private builders and real estate operators who were busy, then and now, building low cost homes for high prices and high profits." *The Distributor* informed workers that "Nazi or no Nazi, Charles F. Palmer played the role of a Fascist when he set about spiking the Defense City project."[118] The UAW favored the consolidation of all federal housing agencies into one to "straighten out the whole confused picture in respect to public housing agencies." It envisioned all of the "good people in the FWA, USHA, FSA, etc. [gathered together in] one set-up responsible for the whole job."[119]

Thomas encouraged the reorganization of the federal housing bureaucracy despite Stonorov's perceptive prediction that such an action would likely diminish labor's influence in housing and doom the Defense City proposal. The architect told Deverall, "we had better all make up our minds that we will stick together or our housing dreams will result in the same housing[—]scattered shacks (demountables)."[120] The CIO Housing Committee met to quickly assemble "a definite CIO program to smash the housing bottleneck by smashing Palmer."[121]

According to *The Distributor*, shortly after Pearl Harbor Thomas had met with President Roosevelt regarding the Willow Run housing situation and the need to reorganize the federal housing apparatus "so as to gear it for war."[122] Notably absent from this report was any mention of the stalled Defense City project. At the time of this meeting, members of the UAW's Housing Committee were attending a gathering sponsored by the National Public Housing Conference with other union leaders, trading accounts of how their efforts to secure defense housing had been stymied by Palmer. The labor leaders agreed that Palmer had to be removed from office because he was "deadly opposed" to mutual housing and wished to curry favor with real estate interests by building "demountable houses and PBA houses—large scale barracks which are rented." Palmer, according to all attending the conference, had called the Camden Plan illegal. "He said it was impractical. Finally he said he didn't like it . . . and that was that."[123]

*The Distributor* asserted that the Mutual Plan was "democracy applied to housing," offering workers "a voice in how they will live." Critics had gone to great lengths to make sure it was "hamstrung at every turn. Palmer blocked it at every turn. His real estate friends were horried [*sic*] by the CIO boys who just kept screaming for Mutual Home Ownership projects." The weekly also underscored the difference between Carmody and Palmer. Carmody was a friend to labor who "believed in democracy and fair play [and the] Mutual Home Ownership Plan." Palmer was against labor and had "undermined and destroyed [Carmody]. . . . [He] had Carmody liquidated" because, it was alleged, the DDHC head had influential friends in real estate development.[124] The UAW was forced to call for both the removal of Palmer in a "chuck Chuck" campaign and the reorganization of the federal housing bureaucracy.[125]

During the first half of 1941 the scarcity of experienced production workers in defense industries gave labor a brief and unprecedented period of influence in the policy-making process. The AFL and the CIO, in a loose alliance, worked to make Congress and the public aware of the need for housing for middle- income (later referred to as moderate-income) householders who did not seek or qualify for low-income public housing but could not afford to purchase a home. Because labor found Palmer to be anything but a friend to the needy defense worker, the urgency of his immediate removal was one area of agreement between the members of over two hundred AFL and CIO union locals that attended the February 1942 War Workers' Housing Conference.

Sponsored by the California Planning Association and the Citizens Housing Council of Los Angeles, the conference featured a welcome from Governor Culbert Olson and addresses from Carey McWilliams, chief of California's Division of Immigration and Housing, and Richard Deverall of the UAW. Monsignor

Thomas J. O'Dwyer, chairman of the Citizens Housing Council, presided. Labor attendees were united in their demand that public agencies step in because the private sector had failed to provide adequate numbers of affordable rental housing units. The conference delegates agreed that at least 85 percent of defense housing aid should be allotted to rental housing that would be available to residents to buy under the Mutual Plan.[126]

The War Workers' Housing Conference and other expressions of support for mutual housing worried real estate developers and their political allies, who interpreted them as an indication that the coalition of labor and reform advocates that had brought the expansion of desegregated public housing to Los Angeles would put enough political pressure on the administration to bring about broader application of the Mutual Plan. The CIO's shipbuilding, steel, automobile, electrical, and construction workers' unions and the AFL's allied trade unions had to be stopped from using the conference as a steppingstone to a more organized demand for the construction of defense housing under the Mutual Plan.

# 5

# The Mutual Plan's "Arrested" Development

The labor leaders and liberal architects, planners, and housing reformers who lobbied for the removal of DDHC head Charles F. Palmer and for the reorganization of the federal housing bureaucracy claimed victory on February 24, 1942, when President Roosevelt issued an executive order creating the National Housing Agency (NHA). Harry C. Bates of the AFL and Richard L. G. Deverall of the UAW agreed that this "heralded the beginning of a large-scale, rapid-action program of public housing for industrial war workers," and they optimistically anticipated the "end of the hesitations, vacillations, and appeasement of real estate interests which had caused the provision of housing for workers to lag so far behind the building of industrial plants."[1]

Gathered at the May 1942 meeting of the National Public Housing Conference, labor leaders and housing reformers discussed their expectations for an expanded role for the Mutual Plan in the defense housing program. As Edith Elmer Wood, a prominent housing expert, explained, "Many workers [are] interested in something between ownership and renting and want the [mutual housing] experiments continued."[2] Labor soon discovered, however, that the reorganization plan was actually a victory for the real estate and financial interests who did not want wage earners to have anything "between ownership and renting." Westbrook and others who shared the New Deal–inspired goal of expanding the noncommercial housing market were replaced by or made subordinate to a new breed of housing administrators led by the head of the NHA, John B. Blandford. A World War I Navy veteran, mechanical engineer, and former Tennessee Valley Authority staff member, Blandford saw himself as a public administrator, not a housing reformer. He was far more at ease talking to groups of home builders, realtors, bankers, and those who represented Main Street interests than with labor leaders and liberal housing reformers. Blandford saw it as his responsibility to keep the commercial market profitable and bring traditional home ownership within the economic grasp of ordinary workers. He withdrew staff and financial support for mutual home ownership, communitarian housing design, resident involvement in community management, and other policy experiments and innovations such as open housing that he considered politically problematic. Westbrook later lamented that Blandford "opposed the [mutual housing] experiments from their beginning . . . [and] immediately attempted to convert them into standard public housing projects."[3]

Facing political pressure to show Congress that preparations for the postwar disposition of defense housing were under way, Blandford was forced to reconsider his early hardline stance against the Mutual Plan. Seeking an expeditious way to sell whole communities of multiunit defense housing with minimal resident displacement, he allowed federal housing officials to prepare a set of disposition policies and procedures that incorporated the Mutual Plan, as Westbrook had recommended. But he rejected Westbrook's suggestion to integrate the Mutual Plan into his larger plans for aiding the low- and middle-income households that would be affected by anticipated postwar urban renewal and infrastructure development. As far as Blandford was concerned, the sun would set on the Mutual Plan when the last unit of defense housing was sold and the whole experiment would soon be forgotten.

## Lanham Amendments Shift Housing Focus

For months prior to the announcement of the reorganization plan, there were signs that the Roosevelt administration could no longer look on housing as a target of economic and social class reform.[4] In January 1942, shortly after Congress returned from its holiday recess, Representative Lanham secured passage of a series of amendments to his October 1940 defense housing bill, one of which was a slight increase in the money that could be spent to construct a unit of housing in the continental United States, to $3,750. Despite the objections of labor, Lanham inserted a provision requiring the construction of temporary dwellings unless a "need extending beyond the emergency" could be demonstrated. Federal housing officials were required to consult with local housing and planning officials before any Lanham-funded housing was built, presumably to allow them more time to gather the forces needed to keep the number to a minimum.[5]

In its original form, the Lanham Act contained an ambiguous passage requiring the disposition of dwellings in the "public interest." A 1942 amendment required that housing funded under the law be sold for "full market value" as soon as postwar conditions allowed. It specifically prohibited the conveyance of Lanham-funded units to local public housing authorities without congressional authorization in an attempt to assuage critics who claimed that the defense public housing program would ultimately strengthen the low-income public housing program. Lanham maintained that the 1942 amendments were in keeping with the original intent of his bill. Defense housing, he said, was never supposed to be subsidized but was always intended to be sold immediately after the war to "recoup for the Treasury as much of this expenditure as possible."[6]

Lanham's proposed amendments offended public housing supporters in both houses of Congress, who spoke out against them but with little effect. Representative Adolph J. Sabath (D-IL) regarded Lanham's amendments as "discriminatory against municipalities and people of the lowest income." By discouraging conveyance to public housing authorities, he argued, Lanham wished to ensure that "private real estate operators may purchase [the Lanham projects] without any restrictions."[7]

Among those who urged members of Congress to reject the 1942 Lanham Act amendments was the New York attorney and activist Charles Abrams. He saw the bill as part of a larger effort to further discredit public housing.[8] The National Public Housing Conference (NPHC) agreed, warning that the "temporary homes of today may be the slums of tomorrow. We must rebuild, not reslum, America."[9] The National Association of Housing Officials questioned the motives of those who wanted to make the conversion of defense housing to low-income housing as difficult as possible and called the congressional authorization requirement "too cumbersome to be practical."[10]

*Pencil Points* observed that when temporary housing was "forced" on the Portland, Oregon, area, the results were "unhappy and unsuccessful, save as an extravagant educational experience." The city now faced the "terrific postwar problem of preventing its unexpected temporary communities from becoming vicious slums to be added to its prewar slums, which came through all the new housing efforts untouched."[11] The Pittsburgh Housing Authority and the Allegheny County Housing Authority, agencies that assumed expanded roles as a result of the national defense housing program, regarded temporary defense housing as a waste of labor and financial resources. The privately funded Pittsburgh Housing Association branded the Lanham amendments' supporters as "reactionary forces" and regarded their action as "willful political bigotry."[12]

The amendments to the Lanham Act and rumors of a pending action to reorganize the entire federal housing bureaucracy made the Mutual Division's future uncertain. Baird Snyder, assistant administrator of the Federal Works Agency (FWA), took full advantage of the situation to pull the underpinning from beneath mutual housing. His efforts to maneuver a quiet retreat from the commitments and promises made by Westbrook and "liquidate" the Mutual Division prompted residents of the pilot projects to turn to their unions and elected representatives for help. When M. M. Miniard, chairman of the Montgomery County, Ohio, CIO Housing Committee, requested written assurance from Snyder that Greenmont Village would be sold to the residents under the Mutual Plan, his request was accompanied by forty-three handwritten letters from defense workers residing in the community. The union's letter-writing campaign failed to extract a promise from Snyder that he would honor earlier Camden Plan commitments.[13]

Carl Bersing of the CIO's Philadelphia Industrial Union Council was similarly frustrated in his efforts to clarify the future of the Mutual Plan with Snyder. In February 1942 he complained that Snyder refused to confirm his intention to uphold the Mutual Division's promises to build a community center at Pennypack Woods and give the residents an opportunity to vote whether to begin negotiations for its purchase under the Camden Plan. Bersing stated that the "CIO locally and nationally will and does insist that undertakings and agreements of this type be honored and carried out." He took pains to impress on Snyder that the CIO expected to continue working in concert with federal housing officials to implement the Camden Plan at Pennypack Woods as they had under Carmody: "Many thousands of workers have followed the development of this project and are watching and waiting for the community building to be finished in time for occupancy."[14]

The CIO opposed Snyder's decision, similarly made without consultation with labor, to cancel plans to develop two Coatesville, Pennsylvania, Lanham projects under the Camden Plan. Bersing reminded Snyder that Arthur F. Anderson, Philadelphia representative of the Steel Workers' Organizing Committee, and Charles Lukens Huston Jr., personnel manager of Lukens Steel Corporation, had journeyed together to Washington, for the specific purpose of obtaining assurance that the community would be developed by the Mutual Division and sold to the steelworkers under the Camden Plan.[15] "I am shocked to discover a gross breach of faith by your Agency," Bersing wrote. Surely the assistant administrator was "aware of the fact that most cordial and cooperative relations have existed for some time between the FWA and the labor movement." Bersing gave Snyder an opportunity to rectify matters by acknowledging that a "mistake" had been made. The CIO would overlook these "grave errors" if he would pledge to honor the promises made to the workers.[16]

Snyder felt no compulsion to mend any "breach of faith" in CIO strongholds such as Coatesville or Lackawanna, New York, where local steel workers had also been promised mutual housing. Coatesville was the proposed location of the Camden Plan project for African Americans approved by the president in November 1941. The community's 100 dwelling units were expected to bring the nationwide total of Lanham-built dwellings—"attractive, modern, and efficiently planned," open to African American occupancy—to 4,844.[17]

Despite the city's pressing need for decent affordable housing open to African Americans, in April 1942 city leaders remained "at a loss to understand what is holding up the Federal housing project." All they knew was that months earlier Westbrook had come to town, purchased a tract of land on behalf of the FWA, and met with the leaders to discuss the agency's defense housing plans. Neither he nor anyone else from the Mutual Division ever returned.[18] In December 1942 representatives from the FPHA arrived, seeking approval from Coatesville's War Housing and Home Utilization Committee to build a Lanham-funded community of 100 dwelling units for African American defense workers on a site "near the Welded Steel Shapes property in the East End."

A community for white steel workers was to be located on the land purchased by Westbrook and reduced in size from the 300 units the CIO had earlier recommended to 150 units. The announcement prompted James A. Haines of the United Steel Workers Union to observe that the CIO had "first started the drive for federal homes here more than two years ago" and the proposal had been "booted around ever since." The local press did not investigate the reasons that the FWA backed out of its agreement with Lukens Steel and the Steel Workers Organizing Committee to sell the two communities under the Mutual Plan.[19]

The plans that George Howe, Louis I. Kahn, and Oscar Stonorov developed for the Mutual Division's George Washington Carver Courts called for "ground-freed" dwelling units clustered around an interior green space. The community, which was built by the Mutual Division's successor agency, won architectural praise from the Museum of Modern Art and was featured in both a traveling exhibit and a museum publication.[20] Several miles away, the Public Buildings Administration built the architecturally undistinguished Brandywine Homes for white steel workers. Neither community had been developed under the Mutual Plan.[21]

The CIO was unable to force Snyder to build the Lanham projects promised to workers in Coatesville and elsewhere under the Mutual Plan. It enjoyed more success in pressuring him to uphold the promises made to residents of the eight pilot projects. The UAW stated that Snyder "discovered to his loss that he was fighting something bigger than either himself or Palmer." Labor was optimistic that mutual housing would remain a federal housing program priority when the anticipated reshuffling took place. UAW officials interpreted Westbrook's arrival in Detroit on February 19, 1942, as a member of a delegation led by Frederic Delano, chairman of the National Resources Planning Board, as an indication that mutual housing might be built at Willow Run. The "Mutual Home Ownership plan developed by the Colonel [Westbrook]" was to have been one of the topics of discussion that day, but the meeting was overshadowed by debate over the racial designation of the Sojourner Truth Homes.[22] By that time, "only Walter P. Reuther of the UWA-CIO held out for construction of a 'model city' near the bomber plant," and a series of smaller, scattered-site mutual housing communities seemed more likely.[23]

## February 24, 1942: The Axe Falls on Community Modernism

On February 24, President Roosevelt ordered the transfer of the FWA's public housing responsibilities and more than a dozen other programs and agencies, including Westbrook's Mutual Division, to the newly created National Housing Agency's Federal Public Housing Authority (FPHA), according to a plan developed by presidential adviser Samuel I. Rosenman.[24] The UAW claimed credit for helping to bring about this "drastic shake-up of housing," stating that Roosevelt "went down the line with the UAW-CIO 100%. Every recommendation which Pres. R.J. Thomas gave to Roosevelt two weeks ago at the White House was followed out." The union was thankful that the "real estate boys have lost their monopoly on war housing. Now we will house for victory—not for profit."[25]

The reorganization and centralization plan put both Snyder and Palmer out of their jobs, and the UAW celebrated: "You, the rank and file of the UAW-CIO, by your splendid support of Pres. Thomas' fight, have cleaned out two of the top fascists in Washington!"[26] The union reported that if the ever delaying Palmer went abroad as requested by the president to study "[the] housing situation in England as he studied the Willow Run situation, the war workers in America may breathe easily. He will not return until after the war is won by our country."[27]

The labor leaders who took credit for precipitating the February 1942 reorganization of the federal housing bureaucracy assumed that President Roosevelt would appoint a housing administrator who agreed with their view that, although home ownership for workers was a long-term goal, short-term noncommercial housing options were needed for those who could afford to take on the economic risk. The UAW advised war workers that with "Palmer and Snyder out, it is quite plain that the chances for Mutual Home Ownership are good. But the fight must go on."[28]

*The Distributor* assured workers that they were "entitled to secure a Mutual Home Ownership project. It is necessary if you are to produce the guns, tanks, and planes necessary to defeat Fascism." The UAW warned that to "get a mutual home ownership project you will have to organize. You will have to learn more about housing. You will have to know more about your housing situation so that you can advise with Washington." UAW workers were encouraged to write to President Roosevelt and his new appointees to "tell them that you insist on Mutual Home Ownership" because it provided good housing and protection for war workers, and saved the government money. It meant "the extension of democracy, and that in turn means the production of worker morale needed to defeat Fascism."[29]

Union leaders greeted Blandford and his initial choice as FPHA commissioner, Leon Keyserling, formerly a member of Senator Robert Wagner's staff, as allies in their bid to increase mutual home ownership opportunities.[30] However, they soon discovered that the reorganization plan was a victory not for labor but for those who sought to keep the housing options of middle-income households confined to the commercial market and to curtail the expansion of mutual housing opportunities. There was a new "subtheme" for the federal housing program—one that sought to "establish a peaceful and profitable understanding with the private housing industry as to goals and methods."[31]

NHA administrator John Blandford won support from banking, real estate, and home-building interests by emphasizing his plans to seek ways to maximize the growth of the commercial market and encourage middle- or moderate-income wage earners to undertake the economic responsibility of home ownership. Shortly after taking office, he transferred responsibility for the eight pilot projects from the NHA's central administrative offices in Washington to their respective field offices. The pilot projects were administratively isolated from headquarters and from each other as a tactic to force their residents into giving up on the idea that they would ever own their communities on a cooperative basis.[32]

Two months after the administrative shake-up, further evidence of the declining importance of the Mutual Plan emerged from Willow Run. When the Detroit Housing Commission announced that the FPHA would provide $35 million to construct "seven projects, each one a virtual village in itself" in the Willow Run vicinity, no mention was made of the Mutual Plan. Mayer & Whittlesey; Skidmore, Owings, Merrill & Andrew; Stonorov & Kahn; Winn, Roensch & Brezner; and the Housing Associates of the University of Michigan would each be responsible for a "sub-town," with the architectural firm of Saarinen & Swanson designing a commercial and civic center. Former TVA site planner Tracey B. Augur of the FPHA was brought to Detroit to serve as a consultant on the proposed project, and began meeting with local officials and industrialists.[33] The proposal was opposed by Henry Ford, who, according to Ford Motor Company's Harry H. Bennett, regarded the construction of anything but temporary dwellings for Willow Run workers as an "unnecessary, wasteful and extravagant use of government funds."[34]

The emphasis that Ford and other allied business interests placed on temporary housing offered an opportunity for architect David Williams, now working for the FPHA, to promote the prototype demountable housing he had designed for the Mutual Division. Together with Roy A. Worden, Karl R. Schwarz, and associate William P. Jones, he designed a dwelling to "free the housewife for war work" using a minimum of strategic material. The resulting design was tested by shipbuilding workers at the Mutual Division's 600-unit Multimax Village in Beaumont, Texas.[35] The *Architectural Forum* admired the Multimax design and claimed that it came "closest to illustrating the kind of shelter that is required" to help bring the war to a successful conclusion.[36] In May 1942, just three months after the agency reorganization plan took effect, G. Gresham Griggs, chief of the Mutual Division's Management Section, now under the direction of the FPHA, wrote to Williams: "I only hope you can start something in Detroit which will attract the notice and accomplish the purposes as in Beaumont." Blandford, however, did not favor the construction of a series of metro-area developments modeled on Multimax Village.[37]

Architect Alan Mather explained that Ford and allied business and real estate interests favored temporary Lanham housing and opposed the construction of permanent planned communities because they did not want an influx of UAW workers into the area who would be urged by their union to vote for Democratic Party candidates, thus weakening local Republican political and economic influence. In July 1942 George Meader, Washtenaw County's prosecuting attorney, told the Truman Committee that a permanent settlement of workers near the Willow Run plant would eventually become "a repository for the flotsam and jetsam of humanity and . . . be a perpetual eyesore and source of public attention both as to law enforcement, social work, and public assistance."[38]

Meader was opposed to Defense City because of the potential impact that it and mutual home ownership might have on city real estate values and suburban growth patterns. Plans for the speculative development of outlying areas would be jeopardized if Defense City and the Mutual Division's pilot projects set a pattern for postwar development. With $3.25 billion worth of FHA-insured mortgages on residential property mostly in city neighborhoods, vested financial interests needed metro Detroit's workers to remain willing to take on a home mortgage as a way to limit the availability of noncommercial market alternatives such as mutual home ownership.[39]

Mather's proposed garden cities and Reuther's call for a mutually owned Defense City threatened plans for the postwar speculative development of metro Detroit made by "hundreds of hard men, the mighty men of the Board of Commerce." He said they had "voices like the grinding of gears [and] shrewd eyes [that] look through glasses calculating." The Detroit-based architect was dismayed but not surprised when, in October 1942, after reviewing plans for housing submitted by some of the original proposed Defense City architects, including Stonorov and Kahn, the UAW agreed with the FPHA on a revised plan for Willow Run where dormitories and temporary housing outnumbered permanent family dwellings.[40]

"It was the UAW-CIO that weakened," Mather sadly noted. "The UAW backed away from its demand first, for Reuther's Defense City proposal, and secondly for 6,000 units of permanent housing." Both were cast aside as "part of a strategy to smooth the political waters for a favorable outcome to contract negotiations that took place between June and November of 1942." Mather regarded the UAW's decision to relinquish its demand for the construction of the mutually owned Defense City and agree to temporary dwellings as evidence of a "growing opportunism" within its ranks. The UAW, like other CIO unions, responded to growing political hostility by focusing its attention on gaining recognition, negotiating contracts and wage increases, and other so-called bread-and-butter issues, limiting the resources devoted to social and economic justice issues such as housing and segregation.[41]

## Mutual Housing Is "Held in Suspense"

Once John Blandford took the helm of the federal housing bureaucracy, Congress no longer feared that Lanham funds would be used to promote the postwar growth of noncommercial middle-income housing. "All has been sweetness and light, so much so that Congressmen now refer to the dark days of housing as B.B. [before Blandford]," the *Architectural Forum* observed in July 1942. Blandford's requests for additional housing appropriations raised "nary a peep of objection," whereas previously "a dog-and-cat fight" accompanied each request. Housing's shift to the right was also evident in the leadership selected for the

FPHA. USHA legal counsel Leon H. Keyserling was widely expected to become "public houser no. 1" and serve as FPHA commissioner. However, because his "contacts with housing . . . [were] more sociological rather than engineering," the post was given to Herbert Emmerich.[42]

The hostility that FWA acting administrator Baird Snyder harbored toward the Mutual Plan was transferred to the FPHA. Westbrook later observed that, as a result of the reorganization plan, the eight pilot projects were "placed in the unsympathetic, misunderstanding hands" of FPHA officials, and the "expressed wish of Mr. Roosevelt for the huge mutual project in Detroit was conveniently forgotten . . . [and] scores of requests from different parts of the country for similar projects were brushed aside with practiced bureaucratic efficiency. The purposes for which the eight pattern projects were undertaken were ignored by the PHA high command."[43]

The National Public Housing Conference agreed that the war was used as a "pretext for scuttling . . . [the] work of agencies engaged in social undertakings."[44] FPHA staff member Ruth M. Little observed that in "the months preceding and immediately after the establishment of [the] NHA the development of Mutual Ownership was arrested." The Mutual Plan was "held in suspense pending [a] decision as to whether the changed circumstances would permit its continuance."[45]

Architect and planner Garrett Eckbo, who had won acclaim for his work for the Farm Security Administration, recalled that FPHA decision makers used the January 1942 amendments to the Lanham Act to justify shelving the Mutual Plan because Congress now wanted the emphasis shifted to temporary housing that would be razed at the war's end. "No theories or 'schools of thought' of any member of the staff of the Federal Public Housing Authority, or of any Local Housing Authority," Eckbo was informed, "should be allowed to interfere with this clear expression of will of the law-making body."[46]

Given what he saw as the increasing inhospitable political climate for the Mutual Plan, Westbrook "declined an offer of appointment as Assistant Commissioner under the new set-up" and announced his intention to seek overseas duty with the U.S. Army.[47] On March 7, 1942, while still acting director of the Mutual Division, he tried to convince Blandford that the Mutual Plan could be useful to him by placing it in a larger political context. He explained that the Mutual Division was created to "furnish patterns . . . [for] all phases of the housing industry," including site and neighborhood planning, architecture, the use of prefabricated building components or mass-production building methods, financing, and resident participation in community management. The ideas and methods worked out in the Mutual Division's "housing laboratory" were intended as starting points for public and privately funded urban redevelopment when the war ended.[48]

Westbrook described how organized labor and community-based housing organizations from all over the county rallied behind mutual home ownership and favored broader application of the Camden Plan. They convinced Baird

Snyder to verbally authorize lease agreements (with the option for mutual sale) for four of the pilot projects, but were unable to persuade him to reverse his refusal to allow the construction of a combined total of 1,950 units under the Mutual Plan for workers in Cheektowaga, New York, Compton, California, and Coatesville, Pennsylvania.[49]

Westbrook suggested that Blandford prepare for the postwar disposition of Lanham-funded housing by restarting the stalled mutual sales process at the eight pilot projects. The Mutual Division had already developed "merchandising and fiscal policies and procedures for Mutual Ownership" to facilitate their postwar sale to mutual housing associations. Staff members from the FWA's legal and accounting divisions had worked with union representatives of defense housing committees to start preparing the contracts and other documents "necessary for putting the Mutual Ownership Program into effect." Although this process was, Westbrook acknowledged, incomplete when the reorganization plan went into effect, the Mutual Division had made substantial progress. All Blandford had to do, Westbrook implied, was direct the FPHA staff to pick up where the Mutual Division staff had left off, complete the lease-to-own agreements, and proceed with the implementation of the Camden Plan as originally conceived.[50] Westbrook also suggested that Blandford give the residents of *all* of the permanent defense housing developments a chance to buy their homes under the Mutual Plan when the war ended. Mutual housing associations, he said, "provide the best method of disposition."[51]

Westbrook urged Blandford to use the highly acclaimed Multimax Village design as a blueprint wherever the need for war workers' housing persisted. More important, he encouraged Blandford to begin looking ahead and consider the Mutual Plan's "implications as they relate to post-war slum clearance." Now was the time for the administrator to identify potential investors willing to "extend the production of private low cost housing at a profit to all, possibly, with the aid of coordinated and contributed public works."[52] Convinced he had done all he could for the eight pilot projects and the Mutual Plan, Westbrook went to New Zealand, where he served as president of the U.S. Joint Purchasing Board, a procurement agency created in June 1942.[53]

## Vinton Comes to the Rescue of Mutual Housing

Blandford welcomed the January 1942 decision by Congress to require war housing officials to build temporary war workers' housing unless special circumstances warranted permanent construction. When it came time to fulfill the legislative requirement to liquidate the stockpile of Lanham-funded housing, disposal of the temporary structures would present far fewer problems than would permanent dwellings. Home builders and real estate investors pressed for the same liquidation process that had been used in the previous war—commercial market sales. War workers and returning veterans who were now eligible to live in Lanham housing were fearful of rent increases or eviction and appealed to federal housing officials and their elected representatives for assurance that their homes would not be sold out from under them, and they had good reason to be concerned. John Lutes of the Walnut Grove Mutual Housing Association observed in 1946 that the experience and background of many of the staff employed in the FPHA's disposition branch were in the "speculative real estate business." If they had had their way, the housing would have been "sold on the auction block to the highest bidder" because the residents—the men and women who served on the front lines of industry—were of "little concern" in the debate over disposition policy in Congress.[54]

Encouraged by FPHA commissioner Herbert Emmerich, Blandford authorized the pilot projects to resume their path toward mutual ownership. Early in his career as a staff member at the City Homes Corporation, Emmerich had concluded that the lack of ethnic, religious, and occupational homogeneity at Sunnyside Gardens in Queens, New York, was among the reasons that its efforts to establish cooperative ownership had floundered.[55] He saw merit in Westbrook's March 1942 suggestion that the FPHA create a disposition task force or division and move quickly to develop a "clear-cut policy with respect to [the] ultimate disposition" of Lanham housing. Westbrook had advised him that if policies and procedures were immediately established, "most of the controversies that have plagued the program from the beginning will disappear."[56]

Emmerich asked staff economist Warren J. Vinton, one of the FPHA's most trusted and experienced staff members, to give the Mutual Plan his assessment as a means of disposing of the Mutual Division's eight communities. Vinton, whose career began with the USHA, provided the FPHA with a link to its New Deal predecessor agencies and offered institutional memory. In April 1942, after a thorough review of the Mutual Division's "Suggested General Principles Governing Execution and Operation of a Mutual Home Ownership Project," Vinton informed Emmerich that he found the Mutual Plan to be hurriedly assembled and lacking in certain financial and legal safeguards but its major shortcomings could be remedied. He offered eleven pages of revisions and refinements that if implemented would make the Mutual Plan a "sound financial scheme" and ensure that when the FPHA used it as the basis for the disposal of Lanham housing, it would not "be a party to a scheme which appears to invite financial disaster within a limited number of years."[57]

Vinton wanted to help mutual home ownership associations succeed financially, pay off their mortgages, and maintain the communities as they aged and required expensive improvements and upgrades. He questioned the ability of Camden, South Bend, Grand Prairie, and other host cities to offer the associations stability as they adjusted to a peacetime economy and weathered larger economic downturns. Vinton recommended tightening and refining the provisions calling for the establishment and use of reserve accounts by resident-shareholders who, because of injury, illness, or unemployment, might temporarily fall behind on their monthly payment and then look to the mutual housing association for repairs and upkeep.[58]

The refinements made to the Mutual Plan by Vinton were welcomed by National Public Housing Conference president Mary K. Simkhovitch, who regarded mutual housing as the "most promising method of accommodating that large group of American workers earning about $37 a week—which the Bureau of Labor Statistics says is the current average of workers in the war industries." She "*earnestly recommended*" to Emmerich the use of the Camden Plan projects as "garden colonies" or prototypes for postwar communities for "the income group just above those served by [federally] subsidized housing." The "enthusiasm of American workers . . . [and the] splendid vigor and tenacity [of labor leaders] . . . augurs well for [the] steady expansion and the gradual achievement of a workable and sound formula for the development of sample projects in many parts of the country during the war emergency."[59]

Simkhovitch encouraged Emmerich to "preserve [Westbrook's] promising beginnings" and build on them for middle-income families whose housing needs were not fulfilled by "the normal operations of commercial enterprise, nor through the through the low-cost housing projects of the large insurance companies." Recognizing the need for oversight, the National Public Housing Conference suggested that local public housing authorities mentor the fledgling mutual housing associations and provide them with managerial advice and technical assistance until they paid off their mortgages.[60]

Simkhovitch agreed with Westbrook that the Mutual Plan should play a central role in planning for postwar housing development. If sizable public works projects were needed to facilitate the readjustment of the economy to peacetime production and restore economic and social vitality to the cities, mutual housing offered an opportunity for low- and moderate-income families to gain an economic stake in their new dwellings and neighborhoods and participate in their management. At that time, neither Simkhovitch nor Westbrook realized that the architects of postwar housing policy, including NHA head John Blandford, would assign the Mutual Plan a specific, well-defined role in Lanham disposition policy and nothing more.

Far away in New Zealand and relying on bits and pieces of information as it came to him, Westbrook struggled with the new political realities influencing housing policy and implementation back in Washington. His reaction to the changes the FPHA had made to the Mutual Plan suggest that he was more concerned about the plan's postwar potential than how it could be adapted to serve the short-term goal of expediting the disposition of Lanham housing. In August 1942, shortly before he left for New Zealand, Westbrook wrote to John Carmody, now the head of the U.S. Maritime Commission, to inform him that the Mutual Plan was "being subject to certain drastic changes which are contrary to the original basic ideas." Even though the exact terms of the mutual sale agreement had not been "worked out in detail," he said, agreement had been reached on "a set of general principles." Westbrook wanted Carmody to advise Blandford that "understandings were in fact reached with representatives of the various tenant groups."[61]

Carmody disappointed Westbrook by declining to take the matter up with Blandford because, he said, Blandford might "look upon any such advice as unwarranted interference with his own administrative responsibility." Carmody tried to appease Westbrook with a compliment: "I commend you for your continued interest in a program that is so wholesome and so fundamentally sound and so close to your heart," and he expressed the hope that Westbrook's military duties would not keep him from "participating in discussions that will lead to a constructive solution."[62]

Westbrook's note prompted Carmody to write John Green of the Shipbuilding Workers to tell him that he shared Westbrook's "deep disappointment" with the FPHA for the "attempts made to defeat the fine objectives that you and the workers of Camden and Kearney had made sacrifices to achieve." He expressed confidence that as union president Green would "appreciate how delicate a matter it is for any official to interfere in the administration of his successor" and expressed hope that "you and the workers who struggled to get a new plan of defense housing into operation do not get cheated at this stage of the war."[63]

The Vinton-revised Mutual Plan circulated throughout the federal housing bureaucracy and among housing experts such as Abraham Kazan for comment.[64] In October 1942 the FPHA released a document, "Proposed Method of Application of Mutual Ownership Plan to Lanham Act Projects," to explain the procedure that would be followed by residents of the pilot projects who, at the conclusion of their two-year leasing period, wished to exercise their option to purchase their community from the FPHA. As part of Vinton's effort to financially and legally safeguard the public interest should the mutual housing corporation fail, residents were required to establish and maintain a number of reserve funds, including a "Reserve Fund for Vacancy and Collection Losses" and a "Reserve for Repairs, Maintenance, and Replacement." Vinton maintained that the changes he made to the Mutual Plan provided greater likelihood of financial stability for the mutual housing associations as corporations and managers of residential real estate.[65]

## The Winfield Park Scandal Discredits Mutual Housing

On February 15, 1942, just days before President Roosevelt ordered the reorganization of the federal housing bureaucracy, the FWA agreed to lease Winfield Park to the Winfield Park Mutual Housing Association. At that time, the Shipbuilding Workers Local 16 Housing Committee was unaware that Winfield Park's general contractor, Clifford MacEvoy, taking advantage of the relaxed oversight that apparently arose with rumors of the pending reorganization of the federal housing bureaucracy, was cutting corners on materials and allowing shoddy workmanship. The shipyard workers and their wives who had successfully demanded basement laundry sinks either did not notice or did not get the chance to observe that MacEvoy and his crews were cheating them and the public. A short time after members of Local 16 began moving into Winfield Park, sagging floors, leaking pipes, flooded basements, and other problems forced the relocation of twenty-eight families.

The Senate investigative committee created by Harry S. Truman to look into the matter made clear its displeasure with the FWA for allowing CIO unionists to have a voice in every phase of defense housing development, from design to construction and eventual ownership. Its hearings, which took place while Westbrook was overseas, revealed that Westbrook had allowed Winfield Park architect John T. Rowland to leave certain architectural and engineering plans and specifications unfinished and had authorized MacEvoy to be paid upon 97 percent completion of work on the development. Westbrook signed off on Winfield Park in February 1942, days before the president ordered the reorganization plan to take effect, amid rising tensions between the AFL and the CIO over the use of mass production and prefabrication in defense housing. FPHA Region II director John Taylor Eagan, who assumed responsibility for the Winfield project, testified that, because Westbrook had accepted it on behalf of the FWA, he never checked MacEvoy's work.[66] In May 1942, when a staff member from the FPHA Construction Division examined the property, he found it was in "very poor shape" and predicted it would remain so unless "radical changes" were made.[67] In November 1942 the *New York Times* reported that only about 315 families resided at the 700-unit community because many of the dwelling units were unfit for habitation.[68]

The board of directors of Winfield Park's mutual housing association tried without success to get firm commitments from the FPHA regarding when the dwellings would be fixed and who would accept financial responsibility for the repairs. Some believed that the mutual housing association should be allowed to renegotiate the terms of the lease in light of the condition of the units. In April 1943 the FPHA threatened to cancel its lease with the Winfield Park Mutual Housing Association because the board was not meeting as required or maintaining records as agreed. The FPHA hired a new contractor to repair the flaws and defects in construction, and gradually Winfield Park's many vacancies were filled. However, relations between the FPHA and the mutual association remained tense.[69] The Winfield Park scandal concerned the CIO Housing Committee because the Mutual Plan "and its future are of great concern to several CIO internationals."[70]

In 1945 the FPHA would require replacement of the entire Winfield board, a move that in the view of Sidney J. Wood, a public trustee on the board, was intended to undermine the mutual association and "turn the Winfield electorate over to a sectarian Union County political leadership lock, stock, and barrel." There was, he stated, no "bonafide [*sic*] interest in Mutual Housing" among those who now saw the economic value of Winfield Park. The political leaders Wood referred to had persuaded the legislature to make Winfield Park an independent borough and were out to destroy mutual housing. He predicted that mutual home ownership would survive only as the "frustrated dream . . . [of] ideological workers who dared to hope for home security and decent living quarters, to say nothing of the chance to rear their children in healthful surroundings," and he prayed for the forgiveness of those who did not know what they were doing. The residents' loyalty to the Mutual Plan, he believed, was unshaken.[71]

Blandford sent a signal to the FPHA staff that he attached little importance to the fate of the eight pilot projects by transferring responsibility for them to the agency's regional field offices with little or no support or direction from NHA headquarters in Washington. John Taylor Egan, director of the FPHA's Region II office, who had jurisdiction over the four Mid-Atlantic projects, testified to the Truman Committee that he was "not at all familiar with the method of operations or the whole concept of this Mutual Ownership." Egan's understanding of the terms of the Camden Plan was, he admitted, "based on gathering information here and there." He could not tell the committee "just what the details of those arrangements were or what the plan was."[72]

Egan was not the only FPHA staff member who knew little about the communities he was supposedly preparing for eventual mutual home ownership. When asked about the mutual housing program, Lorimer C. Graef, the FPHA's manager of housing, replied that he "was not too familiar with the plan itself."[73]

Despite indifference or hostility toward the Mutual Plan in the FPHA, Emmerich reported in March 1943 that he was "proceeding with the necessary steps," to skip over the leasing period and sell Audubon Park to the Audubon Park Mutual Housing Corporation for $1,488,850. A down payment would not be required and, on terms similar to those previously negotiated by Westbrook and Green, the corporation merely had to sign a note promising repayment within forty-five years at 3 percent interest. The purchase price of the other seven projects would be at "fair market value" as determined by a "board of appraisers" in a procedure similar to that adopted by the Defense Plant Corporation. For unspecified reasons, however, the deal did not take place.[74]

Westbrook was still in New Zealand when, on July 1, 1943, the Walnut Grove Mutual Housing Corporation signed a lease agreement with a purchase option from the FPHA. On October 1, 1943, the Greenmont Mutual Housing Corporation and the FPHA completed a similar agreement.[75] Westbrook welcomed the news and emphasized the importance of recruiting dedicated, sympathetic community members to join the three FPHA representatives and three resident-elected representatives on the mutual housing associations' boards of directors. He was particularly eager to secure the support of individuals with a business background or connections to lend further legitimacy to mutual housing associations as private, tax-paying corporations that would pay their own way and not seek public subsidies for operations. The Walnut Grove Mutual Housing Association board thought that their government representative, H. Milton Colvin of the Defense Homes Corporation, was so vital to their success that they later made him an honorary member of the housing corporation. According to Colvin, it had been his "great desire to have an outstanding Mutual Ownership housing project established in my native state of Indiana," and he took "great satisfaction" in knowing that Walnut Grove was an "example for other groups to follow."[76]

Herbert Emmerich informed John Blandford that as the FPHA staff worked out the details of the sale of the pilot projects, he was beginning to consider whether the Mutual Plan "ought to be extended to other appropriate cases" and promised more on the idea after more study.[77] Catherine Bauer, who had stayed on as a consultant after the USHA had been superseded by the FPHA, encouraged Emmerich to apply the Mutual Plan to other permanent housing developments, observing that support for mutual or cooperative home ownership had grown during the war years among "the fairly well-to-do families with some capital who would have been potential individual home purchasers" and those with "little or no capital but with fair pay and job stability."[78]

## Mutual Housing Seeks a Place in Postwar Housing Plans

As early as 1943 the role of housing and urban development in the postwar economy had become a topic of concern for both President Roosevelt and key members of Congress, such as Republican Senator Robert Taft of Ohio. The issue of how much housing would be needed to accommodate postwar needs was debated everywhere, from the halls of Congress to the pages of popular magazines.[79] In November 1943 Frank Burns of the National Association of Home Builders; Loula D. Lasker, associate editor of *The Survey*; and the FPHA's Warren J. Vinton debated postwar housing at a National Housing Conference meeting in New York City. Burns argued that postwar federal aid ought to be directed to programs that made it possible for private builders to supply adequate numbers of dwellings to suit the budget and taste of every family that dreamed of home ownership. Lasker urged those who aspired to home ownership to exercise caution as the nation approached what would likely be a long and rocky phase of postwar economic and social readjustment. Home ownership came with no guarantee of property appreciation; rather, it involved an economic risk that many industrial workers could not afford when facing the prospect of job loss or underemployment when the war ended.[80]

The FPHA's Warren Vinton, who offered the last word in the debate, presented mutual home ownership as a third option—a means of "combining the desirable features of home ownership with the advantages of large-scale neighborhood operations." He explained that as a result of recent refinements, the Mutual Plan now embodied "the principal features of other sound cooperative enterprises as well as some novel elements." When describing how the plan's features worked to the economic and social benefit of wage earners, Vinton, a housing economist, used some of Westbrook's phrases in his promotional efforts, noting that it "secures all the traditional privileges of ownership such as privacy, assured tenancy and the right, within proper limits, of doing as [the home owner] pleases with his house." At the same time, the cooperative home owner "has the benefits of living in a protected neighborhood, democratically controlled and operated by himself and his neighbors for their own use and benefit."[81]

Vinton's message—that mutual or cooperative ownership offered another option for war workers, returning veterans, and other middle-income housing consumers to consider—was not embraced by the FPHA. John Blandford emphasized the need for Congress to create financial incentives for home builders and bankers that would make it possible for wage earners to afford a home mortgage, and he said as little as possible about postwar plans to resume the construction of low-income public housing. His polices and approach won favor from those who looked to the commercial market to help the economy make a transition to consumer production when the war ended. For example, Herbert U. Nelson of the National Association of Real Estate Boards, called home ownership the "bedrock of democracy" and emphasized that "there can be no alternative or substitute for our time-honored institution."[82]

Evidence that the Mutual Plan would not be accorded a place in postwar housing policy emerged on a number of different fronts. In late1943 the newly organized National Association of Home Builders suggested a commercial market alternative to the postwar construction of public housing by local housing authorities under the Wagner-Steagall Act. It favored the "extension of federal credit to private interests and the reassembly of land by cities with broad powers of eminent domain." Families who could not pay the market rate for housing in redeveloped areas should be granted rent certificates issued by "local relief boards." No consideration was to be given to how the payment of such certificates to private, nonprofit, resident-controlled housing cooperatives or mutual housing corporations would allow them to function as economic and social anchors in neighborhoods undergoing economic or social transition or in those targeted for redevelopment.[83]

In March 1944 the shipbuilding and construction magnate Henry Kaiser told attendees of the National Conference on Postwar Housing in Chicago that he expected home building to be a leading sector in the postwar economy. The celebrated industrialist looked forward to a new level of collaboration between government, business, and labor to help everyday Americans realize their dreams of home ownership. Kaiser accurately predicted that the most enduring legacy of the Lanham program would be its role in promoting new or innovative building methods and materials. Wartime advances would be used make cities "modern, safe, efficient and beautiful," he said, but he and other prominent postwar residential developers, such as William Levitt and Sons, would use what they had learned in the war housing program to promote traditional home ownership in the suburbs, not to revitalize city neighborhoods with mutual housing.[84]

When asked to speculate about the changes in store for urban housing once the war ended, labor leader John Green saw little prospect for the growth of mutual ownership. In May 1944 he told the Citizens' Housing Council of the Cosmopolitan Club of New York City that he had never seen mutual housing as a "cure-all" but rather as a step toward the growth of a noncommercial housing sector that would help revitalize and renew U.S. cities. Despite strong labor interest in the mutual housing program, said Green, the FPHA limited it "in the main to the few projects which were developed with our cooperation. . . . [It] died an abortive death before it really got underway on an extensive scale."[85]

Further evidence that mutual housing had failed to permeate the mainstream national conscience came in 1944 in the G.I. Roundtable Series on public policy issues created by the American Historical Association in collaboration with the U.S. Armed Forces Institute. The G.I. series emphasized that war workers and veterans would be rewarded for their service to the nation with a chance to become traditional, not mutual, home owners. In the series pamphlet "Shall I Build a House After the War?" a husband and wife are depicted seated at a dining table. She has a picture in her mind of the quaint Cape Cod–style suburban home they will presumably buy, and he is contemplating a swanky urban high-rise where they will presumably rent an apartment. Mutual home ownership at a planned urban community such as Audubon Village or Avion Village was not presented or suggested as an option as it was in the earlier housing "debate" published by the National Housing Conference.[86]

Mutual housing had no role in planning for postwar war housing except as a method of disposing of war housing. In April 1944 the FPHA's Harold W. Lautner told his colleague, Warren Vinton, that the agency was preparing to sell the permanent defense housing communities to mutual housing associations at a "fair market price" with a forty-five year mortgage at 3 percent interest. Lautner acknowledged "much pressure on us for this statement on Mutual Ownership," presumably from residents of Lanham housing.[87]

In May 1944 Westbrook was contacted by a member of the Federal Home Loan Bank Board who had visited a number of Mutual Division pilot projects and found "unanimous enthusiasm and understanding on the part of the occupants." His report and the fact that "both the C.I.O. and the A.F.L. had placed Mutual Ownership at the top of their lists of post-war activities," prompted the bank board to ask Westbrook to prepare a pamphlet on mutual home ownership for distribution to its "2700 member bank institutions with the suggestion that the principles of Mutual Ownership housing be considered by them in their post-war home building plans."[88] Westbrook gathered up-to-date information from the management at Westacres, Walnut Grove, and Greenmont, but the pamphlet he produced did not convince Blandford or other administration officials that the Mutual Plan should be implemented after the war.[89]

Westbrook's efforts to win expanded application of the Mutual Plan benefited from the work of Richard J. Wagner, chief of the Mutual Ownership Section of the FPHA's Management Standards Division, who served as the agency's representative on the board of directors of both Walnut Grove and Greenmont Village. Wagner regarded the two communities as evidence of the Mutual Plan's "possible success" and sought to eliminate one of the plan's "weak spots"—the lack of funds for educating residents and potential residents, many of whom lacked "a complete understanding of how the plan function[ed]" and how a non-profit corporation operated. FPHA officials needed to take measures to prepare future community leaders and prevent "the dissention which may arise among the tenant members of the corporation from hindering the successful functioning of the plan."[90]

Recognizing the need to establish the Mutual Plan's independence from the war housing program, Wagner favored confining its application to "cases where the tenants or other groups of consumers indicate an interest." The FPHA staff should not "promote the plan" among Lanham housing residents, he stated, "but advise interested groups upon request. If further experience warrants, then consideration can be given to the place Mutual Ownership should occupy in the overall housing program."[91]

Wagner wanted to establish some distance between the Mutual Plan and the Lanham program to improve the plan's prospects for further implementation. He shared the view expressed by Westbrook back in 1942 that the Mutual Plan might be best used to help low- and middle-income families who would lose their homes to the postwar slum clearance and urban revitalization that would likely be needed for economic recovery. Wagner's interest in applying the Mutual Plan to urban renewal prompted him to develop a six-point plan for mutual home ownership for middle- or moderate-income urban dwellers as "a means of restoring existing blighted areas or ones threatened with becoming blighted areas."

Wagner recommended that substandard properties seized by municipalities under eminent domain be conveyed to "municipally sponsored and supervised mutual housing corporations" at a price that took into consideration how the city would "be benefited by the provision of decent housing at reasonable rents." Public funds would be used to improve the public infrastructure and private funds would be directed to "either remodel or rebuild" privately owned structures. Depending on the level of municipal contribution, maximum income limits would have to be set to ensure "initial occupancy" of the communities by families who could otherwise afford only substandard housing. Screening procedures would make sure that successful applicants were those "capable of making the required monthly payments and participating in a cooperative endeavor."[92]

It was Wagner's belief that the Mutual Plan could be used for both privately and publicly funded postwar urban development and revitalization. Public funds could be lent directly to mutual housing associations for the construction of housing and "organizational expenses" subject to federal oversight and approval, with the goal of "making the program as private as possible eliminating the need for direct government financing or construction."[93] Like Westbrook before him, Wagner was unable to arrange a marriage between the Mutual Plan and urban renewal. The plan failed to secure an early place for itself in postwar planning, but was viewed as a way to bring about the disposition of Lanham housing with minimum resident displacement and political discord.

Westbrook charged that the FPHA delayed the sale of the communities built under the Mutual Plan after the "agreed-upon probationary period" and the communities were "sadly mauled and referred to by their unnatural sponsors only in deprecatory whispers." Despite the agency's shortsightedness, he said, the pilot projects stood as "empirical evidence of the vitality and validity of the principles they were intended to demonstrate."[94]

In May 1945, shortly after Westbrook's discharge from the Army, he and his wife hosted a dinner at the United Nations Club attended by House Speaker Sam Rayburn; Representative and Mrs. Estes Kefauver; Howard Hunter, Westbrook's old WPA boss; and others.[95] The presence of old friends and acquaintances might have made it seem as though little had changed in the years he was in the military, when in fact much was different. In the new political climate, federal housing policy makers no longer looked to the New Deal and the mobilization period for inspiration for postwar housing. Seeking to distance themselves from the earlier reform impulse, they scrutinized the terms and arrangements that the FWA made with mutual housing associations interested in purchasing Lanham housing. Seeking to locate, expose, and eradicate any vestiges of the New Deal emphasis on noncommercial housing, members of Congress found the Mutual Plan a handy whipping boy in their criticism of President Harry S. Truman's Fair Deal housing aims.

# 6

# No Fair Deal for Mutual Housing

Lawrence Westbrook returned from the South Pacific in 1945 to find the new president, Congress, and the country preoccupied with the scarcity of affordable housing. Five months after taking office, in his September 6, 1945, "Message on Reconversion," marking the "transition from the New Deal to the Fair Deal," President Harry S. Truman pledged his support for a "decent" house for every American family. To realize what would later become a national goal, Truman gave his support to the bipartisan Wagner-Ellender-Taft (W-E-T) Bill, which allowed the FHA to insure long-term mortgages with reduced down payment requirements and provide loan guarantees for builders of rental housing, grants for farm housing and urban redevelopment, and funds for research to reduce housing production costs. The bill also called for the resumption of construction of federally subsidized public housing.[1]

Passage of the W-E-T Bill seemed likely in light of its bipartisan sponsorship, White House support, and the persistent shortage of housing in cities and towns across the United States that forced homecoming veterans, former war workers, and others to "double up" with family or friends or reside in legally or illegally converted garages, sheds, attics, basements, and makeshift apartments.[2] The Senate ratified the bill in April 1946, but Representative Jesse P. Wolcott, the Michigan Republican who chaired the Banking and Currency Committee, refused to allow it to go to the House floor for a vote unless the public housing provisions were removed. It was not until 1949 that a slightly altered version, known as the Taft-Ellender-Wagner (T-E-W) Bill, was enacted and Congress authorized the resumption of public housing construction.[3]

During the next four years of legislative stalemate, Westbrook tried to convince President Truman and members of Congress that cooperative and mutual housing could help them solve the veterans' housing crisis, remedy the major shortcomings of the federally subsidized public housing program, and assist households that would be displaced by urban renewal projects. Part of the reason for his lack of success was that public perceptions of housing and the federal government's role in the housing market had changed since January 1937, when President Roosevelt spoke of "one-third of a nation ill-housed." Bipartisan consensus was now found in industrialization of residential home building and in helping veterans, former war workers, and others realize the American Dream of home ownership. The federal government's role was to remove as much economic risk as possible so home builders and consumers could enter the market with confidence. The calamities and injustices that befell Mr. Blandings in his attempt to build his Connecticut dream house amused and delighted audiences (in both print and film), but only because novelist Eric Hodgins made his protagonist a securely employed professional who had the economic means to meet or overcome his problems, not a struggling-to-get-adjusted veteran or former bomber plant worker.[4]

In 1947 the newly appointed chief of the Housing and Home Finance Agency (HHFA), Raymond M. Foley, a former FHA official, emphasized the need for programs that helped wage earners become home owners by acquiring commercial-market mortgages. The limited-dividend housing corporations, cooperatives, and other initiatives used by New Deal policy makers to close the gap between home owners and renters were of little interest to Fair Deal housing officials. Indeed, Foley took pains to politically distance himself and the HHFA from Audubon Village, Avion Village, and the New Deal's other troublesome progeny, but that assignment proved to be more difficult than either he or his successors anticipated.[5]

## Westbrook Seeks a Place for Mutual Housing

Discharged from the Army in October 1945, Lawrence Westbrook went about reestablishing himself in Washington without the benefit of an administrative appointment. He discovered that home front rationing, price controls, and shortages of consumer goods and services had helped to keep many Depression-era and wartime cooperatives going. Students, veterans, and other groups established cooperative bookstores and groceries. Democratic Congressmen Jerry Voorhis of California and Wright Patman of Texas expressed and fanned the continuing interest in cooperative housing with a conference in late 1945 that sparked formation of the National Mutual Housing Association (NMHA), and followed up with bills proposing aid for cooperative housing development for both veterans and middle-income workers generally who did not qualify for public housing and could not afford to buy a home of their own.[6]

Westbrook brought his case for the inclusion of mutual housing in postwar plans to the American people with the assistance of his old friend George Creel, who had advised him years earlier when setting up the WPA's public relations office. In February 1946 *Collier's* published "No Down Payment" by Westbrook "as told to George Creel," complete with color cartoons illustrating how mutual home ownership worked.

In the *Collier's* article, Westbrook and Creel presented the cooperative communities of Westacres, Greenmont Village, Walnut Grove, and Oak Park (in Dayton, Ohio) as evidence that mutual housing offered a workable alternative for middle-income householders unable to take on the economic obligations of commercial home financing and ownership. However, they emphasized that "bureaucrats don't like mutual home ownership because it will put many of them out of their jobs. Real estate speculators, as can be imagined . . . have no fondness for it, and banks and insurance companies have not yet shaken the timidities of the depression years."[7]

Nonetheless, Westbrook and Creel made a case for the Mutual Plan as the best means of disposing of Lanham housing and solving the postwar housing shortage. It would help keep inflation in check because it offered a means of expanding the supply of housing in a more systematic fashion. Mutual housing, they wrote, held "larger promise" for market stability and growth than "old methods that brought so many defaults and foreclosures." "Take mutual homeownership or leave it," the pair advised, but if "we refuse to profit by experience . . . [and] [go] ahead with postwar housing on the theory that the old methods will do the trick, the long-heralded housing boom is bound to boomerang."[8]

The appearance of "No Down Payment" helped Westbrook transform the Trans-American Development Corporation, his international land and natural resources development firm, into what he described as a "service organization for the development and financing of mutual home ownership projects anywhere in the United States."[9] Westbrook thought it reasonable that a portion of the 275 Lanham projects nationwide that the National Cooperative Mutual Housing Association estimated were "suitable for permanent use and could be organized as mutuals" might become his clients and help spearhead a movement to fold the Mutual Plan into both public and private redevelopment projects.[10] Still, the FPHA's Lanham housing disposition process remained fraught with difficulties, even after the agency issued the *Manual of Policy and Procedure* in1946, offering advice on writing bylaws, membership applications, and mutual home ownership contracts to guide those who formed mutual housing associations for the purchase of Lanham housing.[11]

Before release of the disposition manual, residents, veterans, and others interested in obtaining Lanham properties found widespread indifference to the idea in the FPHA regional offices and neglect of the problem in Washington. In Cleveland, for example, Werner Laging led a delegation to the FPHA regional office to discuss the purchase of Greenmont Village under the Mutual Plan. Staff members not only told him that they did not know how to do that but also, reported Laging, expressed no interest in asking the Washington office for advice. There was nothing they could do to help the Greenmont residents. This experience convinced Laging of the need for an "autonomous mutual home ownership administration" to clarify the "very confusing" Lanham disposition procedures for the regional offices so as to "make mutual ownership available to responsible citizens of any community regardless of social, racial, or economic status."[12]

Stories like this led not only to the publication of the disposition manual but also to a reshuffling of personnel in Washington. The Truman administration, in August 1946, removed FPHA commissioner Philip Klutznick and replaced him with Dillon S. Myer, who had previously served as director of the War Relocation Authority and now took over the task of developing and implementing a plan to liquidate the stockpile of Lanham housing.[13] A month later Myer told the Cooperative League of the USA that he took mutual ownership seriously and that he believed in it. He also announced that he would make available for mutual housing a significant number of Lanham projects, that he would expedite the disposition process, and that he looked forward to the tenants' "enlightened ownership" of Lanham homes.[14]

Myer's message encouraged the Cooperative League's John Carson, who expressed the hope that now, with Myer at the helm, "past misunderstandings should be buried in accepting the challenge of more and better homes needed today." To meet the challenge, he urged labor, cooperative organizations, "religious, social service," and other groups to "rally behind [the] Federal Public [Housing Authority] and Mutual Housing and get this job done."[15]

Myer's interest in mutual housing prompted him to visit Dayton and Laging's Greenmont Village project. While there, he asked H. M. Miniard, the community's manager, to provide detailed information on the terms of the Greenmont Village Mutual Housing Corporation's original lease-to-purchase agreement. Miniard reassured Myer that while mutual housing was in its fledgling stage and there were few options for commercial financing, publicly funded loans and administrative and technical support were crucial. He believed that once the second generation of mutual housing associations was established, there would be greater private sector willingness to invest in cooperative housing development.[16]

Miniard tried to convince Myer that the sale of Lanham housing under the Mutual Plan would bring "a saving to the government . . . [and] satisfaction and expectation" to residents. It would "encourage deserved democratic growth in the field. The shining example of the Mutual Housing Plan in operation will gain the support of all of those on the side of progress, and will foster further investment by the government FOR THE PEOPLE."[17]

Myer's support for mutual housing resulted in improved communications and more consistency in the implementation of policy directives, but it still remained necessary for residents to spend their time and limited economic resources in prolonged political tugs of war with each other and members of Congress, federal housing officials, realtors, bankers, and others who wished to prevent the sale of defense housing to mutual associations. In July 1947 the *Chicago Daily Tribune* offered a rare behind-the-scenes look as the residents of the 250-unit Kingsford Heights, a defense housing development in La Porte, Indiana, decided whether they wanted to become mutual home owners. William Oestreich, a fireman at the Kingsford ordnance plant, Urias C. Johnson, a grocer, and Donald Swanson, an insurance salesman, led the mutual purchase effort and enjoyed the support of roughly half the town. Another 128 families opposed the sale of Kingsford Heights to the association because they somehow thought it possible to acquire fee simple ownership. Some residents, such as E. J. Laun, postmaster and storekeeper, opposed the sale not because they objected to the mutual home ownership concept but because they believed the community was not worth the $359,000 sales price.[18]

Infant mutual housing associations that did not know about or could not afford to hire Westbrook's Trans-American Development Corporation relied on labor, veteran, religious, and civic organizations to obtain free or affordable legal, financial, and property management advice and guidance. Labor union leaders and Bryn J. Hovde, a University of Pittsburgh faculty member and former county housing administrator, helped the residents of Pittsburgh-area Lanham housing developments organize and buy their communities under the Mutual Plan. Thomas J. Fitzpatrick of the United Electrical, Radio, and Machine Workers of America believed that it was necessary to put pressure on government leaders to back mutual housing associations seeking to purchase local defense housing developments. In a July 14, 1947, letter, he emphasized that acquisition of Lanham projects by mutual housing associations was preferable to sales to private investors who were likely to "double or triple rents, evict tenants and eventually convert the projects into slums" as well as depress local real estate values.[19]

Many Lanham project residents who wanted to buy their communities on a mutual basis faced opposition from within and outside the community. The Bureau of Labor Statistics found that bitter divisions emerged between residents who wanted to purchase a community under the Mutual Plan and those who wanted to "continue as renters, had that been possible." Some residents did not like the "idea of holding only a lease as evidence of ownership." At Shalercrest, in Shaler Township, Pennsylvania, the proposed sale of the community under the Mutual Plan deeply divided the community. The local police were summoned to the home of Mrs. Robert Gasner when a brick was thrown through her window. She accused members of the Shalercrest Housing Association, which was trying to buy the community under the Mutual Plan over the opposition of a group known as "the Majority Rules Association."[20]

Mutual housing associations also faced opposition from outside of the community from local industrialists, realtors, bankers, private home-building contractors, and others interested in obtaining Lanham housing developments as investments. Members of a few public housing and urban redevelopment agencies opposed the sale of these developments under the Mutual Plan because they hoped to secure congressional authorization to convert them to low-income housing. Mounting political pressure prompted the Richmond,

California, City Council to reverse its initial plans to request congressional permission to turn Atchison Village into low-income housing.[21] The board of directors of the Norfolk Housing Authority tried to prevent the sale of the 2,200-unit Broad Creek Village to a mutual housing association formed by residents and veterans not because its members were opposed to the Mutual Plan but because they questioned whether the association could afford needed renovations and upkeep on 2,600 demountable dwellings. Opponents told the House Subcommittee on Government Operations that there was a "very grave question" as to whether the Mutual Plan could be applied successfully to unusually large projects such as Broad Creek Village. In Norfolk and elsewhere, when mutual housing opponents claimed they were acting to preserve the "local 'public interest,'" their real aim was to prevent any decline in local real estate values.[22]

## Wolcott Takes Aim against Mutual Housing

The more the FPHA worked to clarify its procedure for the liquidation of wartime public housing, the more politicized the process became. Mutual housing's most influential postwar opponent was Representative Jesse Wolcott of Michigan, the ranking Republican on the House Banking and Currency Committee. Wolcott's campaign against the Mutual Plan began in earnest shortly after the February 2, 1947, announcement that members of the Winfield Park Mutual Housing Corporation would soon be voting on whether to exercise their option to purchase the community under the Mutual Plan. Once the subject of a 1942 Truman Committee investigation, Winfield Park now had "a waiting list of 1,000 would-be tenants" and was, as the *New York Times* observed, "no longer a white elephant." Situated in a rapidly developing suburban region within the economic and cultural orbit of New York City, it was regarded as a highly desirable and affordable family-oriented residential community. If the residents voted to purchase, the mutual housing association would be granted a twenty-five-year mortgage from the FPHA.[23]

Wolcott and Iowa Representative Ben F. Jensen, the Republican chairman of the House Subcommittee on Government Operations, sent a letter to FPHA commissioner Dillon Myer shortly after the Banking and Currency Committee and the Operations Subcommittee unanimously passed a joint resolution on February 25, 1947, calling for cash sales of "permanent war housing units" to mutual housing associations. Determined to terminate mutual housing associations' access to public credit, Representatives Wolcott and Jensen warned that they intended to prepare a bill that would proscribe how war housing was to be disposed and put an end to the financing of ventures such as mutual housing.[24] Myer's response to the congressmen reflected his awareness of the latitude that the FPHA and its parent agency, the NHA, had been granted by Congress in determining the disposition of Lanham projects. He judiciously volunteered to refrain from "consummating certain types of sales for a reasonable period of time" while Congress considered legislative changes to the program. At the same time, he refused to capitulate entirely to its demands and stated his intention to go through with sales agreements that had already been negotiated.[25]

The Wolcott-Jensen letter functioned as intended, throwing a monkey wrench into the sales process. A joint delegation of members of the board of directors of both the Audubon Park and the Bellmawr Park mutual housing corporations hurried to Washington to meet with HHFA administrator Raymond Foley and protest the denial of the mortgage they had been promised. In a letter, Daniel Baskin, secretary of the board of trustees of the Bellmawr Park Mutual Housing Association, accused the FPHA of a "breach of faith" in its contract negotiations. The proposed cash requirement was contrary to the understanding that project residents had reached with the Mutual Division and was intended, he said, for the sole purpose of derailing or delaying sales to mutual housing associations.[26] On February 13 and 14, 1948, a member of the Bellmawr Park board met with Congressman Wolcott and other members of the Banking and Currency Committee to inform them that they had broken the residents' "good faith." Requiring cash sales was inimical to the Mutual Plan and created "extreme hardship" for the residents. Assisted by Congressman Charles A. Wolverton, a sixteen-term New Jersey Republican from Camden, the Bellmawr Park group took their case to the White House and met with Truman administration aide David Stowe in an effort to force the FPHA to grant them the mortgage promised under the Mutual Plan.[27]

Negotiations for the sale of Bellmawr Park were continuing when, on April 12, 1947, the Walnut Grove Mutual Housing Corporation became the first of the eight original Camden Plan projects to be acquired by the residents on a mutual basis. Walnut Grove was sold to its residents for $750,000, with the deal secured by a forty-five year mortgage from the FPHA at 3 percent interest. Unlike the case of Bellmawr Park, the sale of Walnut Grove and two projects in Compton, California, and Ogden, Utah, not originally built under the Camden Plan, had progressed to the point where Dillon Myer felt justified in his refusal to stop it to appease Wolcott and Jensen.[28]

"Innocent on its face," columnist Drew Pearson cautioned his readers, Wolcott and Jensen's cash-only policy delivered a "big advantage for the real estate operators, who can afford to put up the spot cash for the multiple-unit surplus housing projects." Wolcott and Jensen delivered yet another "swift kick in the pants for war veterans," Pearson wrote, "knowing full well that [mutual ownership] organizations cannot compete on a cash basis with big real estate syndicates."[29]

In June 1947 Wolcott tried to justify his actions by alleging that FPHA expenses were "very loosely controlled" and that labor unions exercised "undue influence" on staff decisions.[30] On June 18, 1947, he prevailed on the House to pass a bill that stripped the FHPA of responsibility for the liquidation of war housing and required cash sales of Lanham projects, but the bill died in the Senate. Of Wolcott's effort residents of Nor-Wayne, a Michigan defense housing development, observed that its goal had been the creation of a "gravy-train for speculators at the expense of the public."[31]

Wolcott found another opportunity to check the growth of mutual housing when the Truman administration announced a plan to replace the wartime NHA with a new, permanent federal housing agency. Truman had proposed Reorganization Plan No. 3 on May 27, 1947, as "one part of a wholesale modernization of the government's bureaucracy." In a message that accompanied the plan, the president reiterated the need for the United States to "alleviate the housing shortage and achieve our national objective of a decent home and suitable living environment for every American family."[32]

Reorganization Plan No. 3 called for replacement of the wartime NHA with a new permanent entity, the Housing and Home Finance Agency (HHFA) to consolidate all federal housing activities. The HHFA's constituent agencies would be the Federal Loan Bank Board, the Federal Housing Administration, and the Public Housing Administration (PHA), which was to assume responsibility for the disposition of Roosevelt-era housing. The reorganization plan was to go into effect unless both the House and the Senate voted within sixty days to kill it. Because of Wolcott's efforts, it died in the House on June 18, 1947.[33]

On June 26, 1947, the day the Senate Banking and Currency Committee was scheduled to vote on Reorganization Plan No. 3, House Appropriations Committee chairman John Taber (R-NY) charged that the FPHA had made "little or no progress in the disposal of permanent war housing" because agency officials sought to "perpetuate them as mutual low cost projects to the present tenants in a manner that will keep them under Government supervision for 65 years." Taber implied that FPHA staff members promoted mutual housing because they had fallen under the sway of left-wing labor activists and communist sympathizers.[34] An earlier report prepared by his committee had alleged that the FPHA had created a "socialized scheme of disposition to mutual organizations which completely ignore any veterans' preference, unless the veteran was already an occupant."[35]

Taber's charges did not convince the Senate to derail Reorganization Plan No. 3. The creation of the HHFA was one of the administration's rare bipartisan victories—the last granted Truman during the First Session of the Eightieth Congress.[36]

Reorganization Plan No. 3 went into effect in July 1947, and one month later Truman appointed Raymond Foley, a former public relations expert and director of the FHA's Michigan office, as HHFA administrator. Housing analyst Catherine Bauer was dismayed with the choice. Foley was an "FHA safe man" who, she claimed, presided over "a timid, stodgy and unimaginative agency" and did little to free it from an "atmosphere of shell-shock, fear and demoralization." Foley's selection served as an unwelcome reminder to Bauer and other liberals of just how far and how rapidly the goals of federal housing policy had shifted away from communitarian reform.[37]

Convinced that Representative Wolcott's ultimate goal was to halt sales to mutual housing associations, PHA commissioner Dillon Myer attempted to appease him with Public Regulation No. 1, announced on August 27, 1947, which required mutual housing organizations to pay cash for publicly funded housing and consult with local government housing and planning bodies. Public Regulation No. 1 was an immediate and crushing blow to mutual housing associations nationwide. Not even the pilot projects were spared.

Fearful that Public Regulation No. 1's cash-only requirement might affect the ability of the Winfield Park Mutual Housing Corporation to obtain the mortgage it was promised, in October 1947 the residents sought advice from United Textile Workers Union leader John W. Edelman and New Jersey's Independent Labor Union Conference. Union workers were encouraged to write to their congressional representatives for help in making sure credit would be available to the residents of Winfield Park as originally promised.[38]

Before Public Regulation No. 1, PHA officials had offered to sell the 300-unit Fulmor Heights in Hatboro, Pennsylvania, to a mutual housing association organized by the residents. Because the deal to purchase the community with a forty-year, $800,000 mortgage at 3.5 percent interest was not finalized before the regulation went into effect, PHA officials now required the mutual association to find private funds in order to proceed with a cash sale.[39]

The Gropius and Breuer–designed Aluminum City Terrace, known far and wide for its "radical architecture," was one of the mutual housing associations whose future was threatened by Public Regulation No. 1.[40] *Task*, a journal that promoted modern architecture and planning, took up the Aluminum City cause, noting that the "triumphant survivor of every obstacle to its construction and final occupancy" had become the subject of a new political controversy with an "overwhelming number" of residents' votes "to form a mutual housing association to buy it."[41] The FPHA offered to sell Aluminum City Terrace to the mutual housing association if it paid 10 percent of the purchase price up front and accepted a thirty-year mortgage at 3 percent interest. Before the agreement was officially in place, however, new terms of sale allowed under Public Regulation No. 1 required the association to buy the community for cash and give preference in the sale of shares to veterans over residents. After appealing to HHFA administrator Raymond Foley for exemption, the association was given permission to offer shares to residents before offering them to veterans but was still required to pay in cash.[42]

The Aluminum City Terrace Mutual Housing Association offered membership to any resident who paid a $50 membership fee regardless of whether the head of the household was a veteran. During a thirty-day period, 125 residents joined, and the $3,150 they raised was sufficient to secure an option to purchase the property from the PHA. The association now had ninety days to convince

168 veterans to pay a total of $350 by August 31, 1948.[43] Resident Grace Girardi, whose father had helped organize the mutual association, later recalled that mutual home ownership, as a "new concept . . . was very scary for these people to accept. . . . Many of them did not have $350 at that time."[44]

The Aluminum City Terrace Mutual Housing Association received help in finding a bank willing to provide a mortgage from Attorney J. Alfred Wilner, Professor Bryn J. Hovde, Monsignor Charles Owen Rice, and resident Benjamin Fisher, director of research for the Aluminum (later Steel) Workers of America.[45] CIO leaders also put pressure on the FHA to insure a mortgage covering up to 90 percent of the $560,513 purchase price.[46] An FHA regional director provided "valuable advice and guidance." Shortly before the closing, representatives from both the FHA and the bank created some last-minute drama, but eight months of tense negotiations ultimately came to a successful conclusion. On September 30, 1948, the Aluminum City Terrace Mutual Housing Association became the first of its kind to use a private sector, FHA-insured mortgage to purchase defense housing.[47]

The Aluminum City Terrace Mutual Housing Association issued a statement that it was "not really possible to fully describe the 8-month period" of intense negotiations with the PHA. Many members had joined to make "possible the defeat of many hostile groups" and solve "extremely intricate problems." After raking the residents and their attorney over the coals, federal housing officials were finally satisfied. Bernard L. Grove of the HHFA's Legislative Counsel Branch informed PHA regional directors in September 1948 that the contracts and bylaws of the Aluminum City Terrace Mutual Housing Association and its FHA mortgage insurance agreement should "serve as a guide for handling all problems of a general nature relating to sales of projects" under the Mutual Plan.[48]

The mutual housing campaign at Nor-Wayne, a 1,189-unit Lanham-funded community in Westland, Michigan, housing many UAW workers and veterans, was also crippled by Public Regulation No. 1. After repeated attempts to communicate with Foley to discuss efforts to buy their community on a mutual basis, in August 1947 the residents turned to Democratic representative John J. Lesinski, informing him that they suspected that the delays arose at least in part because Foley wanted the development sold to private investors. Lesinski wrote to President Truman asking him to back the sale of Nor-Wayne to its residents. His constituents not only wanted to purchase their community under the Mutual Plan but, as industrial unionists, also wished to see it "set a pattern for [the] nation."[49] The National Cooperative Mutual Association argued that the residents were "justified in their view that what happened to one mutual ownership association in Wayne, Michigan, might just affect other groups seeking to buy their Lanham Act homes nationwide."[50]

When asked about the Nor-Wayne case, Foley told the members of the Senate Banking and Currency Committee that his policy regarding mutual housing associations was "neither to promote nor discourage the formation of such corporations" even though he admitted that they were "the only practical device by which occupants and prospective occupants can achieve home ownership on projects that are not suitable for sale in individual units." The mutual sales effort at Nor-Wayne ultimately failed.[51]

In July 1947 the PHA began reporting on its Lanham housing disposition progress to Congress in a quarterly *Disposition Directory of Public Housing* (known as an S-104 report). Greenmont Village, Walnut Grove, an unnamed 200-unit project in Alameda, California (likely Woodstock Homes), and Fulmor Heights were identified as having been sold to "non-profit corporations." Three additional mutual housing associations awaited final closing, and ten communities were in preliminary negotiations. Included among the latter was the 600-unit, Richard J. Neutra–designed Channel Heights in San Pedro, California, considered the architectural jewel of the Lanham program.[52]

In June 1948 the two pilot projects in Texas, Avion Village and Dallas Park, were sold to mutual housing associations organized by residents. During negotiations over the purchase of Avion Village, Westbrook wrote to assure the residents that they were doing the right thing, reminding them that the mutual home ownership concept was not untried: Pontiac's Westacres "has been operated over nine years, and the basic principles of mutual home ownership have been tested there and proven beyond question." Mutual home ownership, Westbrook wrote, would make it possible for Avion Village householders to enjoy the flexibility offered by renting and at the same time secure the economic and social advantages of home ownership. Westbrook sent a copy of his Avion Village message to Richard Wagner of the PHA; Charles McGuerin of the NMHA, now known as the National Cooperative-Mutual Housing Association; Senator Allan J. Ellender (D-LA); and Jerry Voorhis of the Cooperative League of the USA.[53]

The sale of Avion Village and Dallas Park came as a relief to Westbrook, who observed that his successors in the FPHA had done "their utmost to discredit both the idea of mutual home ownership and the men responsible for its conception. For years they resisted, upon one pretext or another, the sale of the projects to private corporations, this being an essential feature of the mutual ownership plan." Mutual housing corporations formed by residents had been allowed to purchase their communities as a result of the "continued insistence of the local sponsors originally selected by the Federal Works Agency," which were mainly labor unions.[54]

When John Carmody heard of the sale of the two pilot communities, he sent a congratulatory letter to Westbrook, recalling a visit he made to Dallas Park shortly after the FPHA inherited the mutual housing program. He found the residents upset that "the housing authority was trying to kill off the mutual ownership idea. 'They will have to kill the tenants first' one man told me and his neighbors chimed in to the same general effect. They were completely sold on the project and on the mutual idea."[55] Dallas Park residents may not have been truly willing to die for a chance to buy their homes on a mutual basis, but they were aware of the many layers of opposition to their plans. They needed to negotiate the legislative and public policy obstacles that emerged from Washington and the FPHA's regional offices while facing resistance from outside and within the community. By December 1949 twenty-two publicly funded communities had been sold to their residents under the Mutual Plan.[56] Florence Parker of the Department of Labor found in July 1950 that twenty-six mutual housing associations had signed contracts with the PHA for the sale of a total of 9,627 units and that eleven mutual housing associations were negotiating mutual sales contracts for an additional 5,141 units.[57]

Westbrook promoted the Mutual Plan in the disposition of Lanham housing because he was convinced that it would be beneficial to both the residents and the public interest. The pairing proved to be more of a liability than a benefit for the plan. The meddling of powerful politicians such as Wolcott and Jensen and the seemingly endless stream of laws, rules, regulations, and procedures surrounding the sale of Lanham housing decreased the likelihood that the Mutual Plan would be applied at new publicly or privately funded postwar housing developments. The emergence of a second generation of Lanham projects from "the Federal cradle" did not, as Westbrook had hoped, pave the way for the Mutual Plan in the construction of postwar housing for veterans and low- and middle-income wage earners.[58]

## Mutual Housing for Veterans

According to the Department of Labor's Florence Parker, veterans responded to the "very difficult" housing situation they faced on returning home by embracing cooperation. Some were interested in the cooperative development of all types of housing ranging from "apartments, through single-family homes on city lots, to subsistence homesteads with land ranging up to several acres." A few veterans' cooperatives even planned to develop "outlying tracts, including the installation of utilities, streets, etc." All hoped to take advantage of preference in the allocation of scarce building supplies provided under the 1946 Veterans' Emergency Housing Act and by programs created by veterans housing expediter Wilson W. Wyatt.[59]

Westbrook played an active role in promoting the sale of "surplus" New Deal and war housing to veterans under the Mutual Plan. Shortly after the November 1945 Defense Homes Corporation's announcement that it intended to sell McLean Gardens and Naylor Gardens, two garden-style apartment developments in the District of Columbia, Post No. 1 of the American Veterans of World War II (Amvets) expressed interest in purchasing them on a mutual basis. Amvet legal counsel William A. Roberts organized the Veterans' Cooperative Housing Association (VCHA) in early January 1946 and immediately bid on both developments.[60] Westbrook was either hired or volunteered to help the VHCA to lease and then purchase McLean Gardens under the Mutual Plan—a "cooperative housing scheme," according to the *Washington Post*, that was "similar to one afforded Dayton, Ohio, war workers." Under the tutelage of Westbrook, Ray Sawyer of Amvets Post No. 1, a major who had served on the staff of General "Hap" Arnold, was speaking of Walnut Grove when he told Defense Homes Corporation officials that South Bend workers had recently bought a "comparable project" from the federal government at a price determined by an outside appraiser with no down payment required.[61]

Westbrook and journalist Dorothy Thompson, a personal friend and a supporter of the Amvets, toured McLean Gardens in a show of support for the VCHA's bid to purchase the 720-unit apartment complex on a mutual basis. Shortly before this, Senator Edwin C. Johnson (D-CO), who headed the Senate Finance Subcommittee on Veterans Legislation, had visited and expressed the hope that the veterans' mutual housing initiative would be so successful that "it could serve as a model for similar veteran housing schemes all over the country."[62]

Despite the impressive show of support for the VCHA, representatives from the Defense Homes Corporation and the Reconstruction Finance Corporation (RFC) (which had originally financed the two developments) questioned the VCHA's ability to purchase and cooperatively own and manage both properties, suggesting instead a merger with a rival cooperative group.[63] In February 1946, after the issue came to the attention of the House Committee on Expenditures, Congress passed a joint resolution mandating that veterans receive first preference in the sale of defense housing to mutual housing associations. This meant that mutual housing associations formed by veterans, like those set up by residents, had the right of first refusal.[64]

In April the RFC, the War Assets Administration, and the Defense Homes Corporation agreed to sell Naylor Gardens to the VCHA for $5,125,000. Residents who wished to stay could join the cooperative and veterans would be given first priority for vacancies. Within a short time of the agreement's announcement, the VCHA office was "swamped" with requests from veterans seeking membership.[65]

Newly formed organizations such as the Amvets and the American Veterans Committee (AVC) were more likely to pursue mutual housing opportunities than were the older, more politically conservative veteran groups such as the American Legion. The Amvets' Ray Sawyer said that he joined the organization because "old veterans' organizations are not militant enough."[66] In 1947 the James A. Manley Post of the Veterans of Foreign Wars helped veterans and former shipbuilding workers in Wilmington, North Carolina, organize a mutual housing association, Veterans' Homes, Inc., to purchase Lake Forest and Greenfield Terrace, with a combined 584 units, from the FPHA for $1.7 million.[67]

Veterans seeking to purchase Lanham housing received guidance and assistance from the National Housing Agency (NHA) with its 1946 publication of *Mutual Housing: a Veterans' Guide to Organizing, Financing, Constructing, and Operating Several Types of Cooperative Housing Associations with Special Reference to Available Federal Aids.* The booklet came in response to a "nation-wide demand by veterans groups for information and advice on cooperative and mutual housing enterprises." At the same time, Bureau of Labor Statistics Bulletin 858, originally issued in 1934, was revised and reissued in 1946 as *Organization and Management of Cooperative and Mutual Housing Associations.* It advised veterans who joined together to "purchase an existing property and operate it on a mutual basis" to adopt the "most conservative financing and reserve policies." It also counseled the recruitment of persons from their own "income group" and diversification of membership with persons employed in different field of business or industry in order to lessen the negative impact of strikes, slowdowns, or shutdowns.[68]

Publications such as *Mutual Housing: a Veterans' Guide* were intended to demystify the disposition process, but they left some convinced that the best way to obtain Lanham housing was to hire someone who knew how to negotiate the process. Convinced that it needed help in navigating the economic and political obstacles it faced in purchasing Greenbelt Homes in Greenbelt, Maryland, under the Mutual Plan, the Greenbelt Mutual Housing Association, consisting of residents and veterans, hired Lawrence Westbrook's Trans-American Development Corporation in October 1947.[69] Westbrook agreed to provide assistance in the "preparation of legal documents, review of site and dwelling unit plans and in the representation before F.H.A., N.H.A., C.P.A. [Civil Production Administration] and other federal agencies in Washington" in exchange for a "cash retainer for general services and a percentage charge for obtaining materials and supplies."[70]

Westbrook became involved in the proposed Mutual Plan sale of the famous suburb knowing of long-standing plans to develop more housing at Greenbelt. In 1940, architects Richard Neutra and David Williams, members of the board of directors of Housing Producers Cooperative Inc., a private organization that probably involved Westbrook behind the scenes, had been unsuccessful in reaching an agreement with an organization known as the Greenbelt Homeowners Cooperative for the construction of prefabricated, one-and-a-half story Cape Cod–style dwellings. The houses were to be produced by American Housing, Inc., and erected on lots originally set aside for future development by the Resettlement Administration.[71] Neutra appears to have judged the proposed expansion of Greenbelt development as consistent with his conviction that such housing ought to "be differentiated and properly fitted into different localities whether demountable, prefabricated or conventional in construction."[72]

Westbrook promised that if his clients decided they wanted to build new dwellings, his firm could cut through the bureaucratic red tape that encumbered so many of those seeking to procure building materials and clearances. Noting that the "lack of supplies is the real bottleneck in housing," Westbrook said, "We have a better set-up qualified to obtain building supplies than any other organization in the United States." Housing contractors would "submit to us a list of material and supplies that they cannot obtain from their customary sources," and Trans-American would "advise them which items we may be able to obtain for them. For performing this service we will charge a flat fee of 5% of the purchase cost."[73]

Westbrook was confident that his firm could help the Greenbelt Mutual Housing Association obtain the permissions, clearances, and building materials they needed because he had already secured the involvement of "some of the most outstanding people in government to perform the various services." Mutual housing corporations would find Alan Johnstone, the attorney who had served as FWA general counsel, ready to review their applications, permits, and other paperwork. The former Chief Architect of the United States, Gilbert Underwood, was ready to advise clients on community planning and architecture. Westbrook noted that, in addition to the "the valuable services and contacts that can be afforded by these gentlemen personally, they have large staffs of highly qualified and specialized personnel whose services, after hours, can be utilized to great advantage at relatively small cost."[74]

Careful not to leave anything to chance, Westbrook sought to build a popular base of support for the sale of Greenbelt under the Mutual Plan both within and outside the community and in its Washington environs. In November 1947 he and Dorothy Thompson met with the residents to assure them that mutual home ownership was the next best thing to traditional home ownership. Mutual housing's "principles," Thompson wrote, are "anti-private enterprise in the same sense that Sears Roebuck is anti-the enterprise of the door-to-door salesman, or that International Harvester is anti-the enterprise of the local blacksmith." Despite Westbrook's assistance, the Greenbelt Mutual Housing Association faced repeated delays and roadblocks.[75]

In March 1949 Greenbelt mayor Thomas J. Canning asked the Senate Banking Subcommittee to amend the bill introduced by Senator Joseph McCarthy (R-WI) and require the PHA to negotiate the sales of the Greenbelt towns under the Mutual Plan.[76] He also wanted residents and veterans to be given equal preference in the sale of shares in Greenbelt mutual associations and recommended that the bill require the sale of commercial buildings to the mutual associations to keep them from falling into the hands of real estate "speculators." When McCarthy's bill passed in May, it permitted, but did not require, sales to mutual associations formed by residents or veterans.[77]

Seven months after the bill's passage, Greenhills, Ohio, located about fifteen miles from Cincinnati, became the first Greenbelt town to be sold. The residents, who included both former war workers and veterans, had overcome the "psychological handicap of having Uncle Sam as a landlord" and formed the Greenhills Owners' Corporation. The group, represented by attorney Charles P. Taft, a Cincinnati municipal reformer, liberal Republican, and the brother of Senator Robert Taft, agreed to purchase the community under the Mutual Plan for $3.5 million. It paid $351,580 down and was granted a twenty-five year mortgage at 4 percent interest from the PHA. Greenhill residents had been closely divided in their support for the mutual sale; 317 families joined the mutual association and 310 declined. Nonetheless, the deal helped clear the "air of impermanence . . . [that had] hung over the community" since Congress had ordered its sale in 1948.[78]

Greenbelt's sale was delayed by a temporary freeze on the disposition of publicly funded housing precipitated by the outbreak of war in Korea in 1950. In 1952 the Greenbelt Mutual Housing Association was succeeded by a new organization, the Greenbelt Veterans Housing Corporation, which purchased most of Greenbelt in September 1952, including 1,579 dwelling units (excluding the commercial buildings and some apartment buildings) for $6,285,450. The PHA required the corporation to make a 10 percent down payment and granted it a twenty-five year mortgage at 4 percent interest. The corporation and the New York City–based Foundation for Cooperative Housing soon began work on a design for up to 2,000 dwellings that would be built over a ten-year period on 806 acres of the original undeveloped greenbelt it hoped to acquire from the PHA.[79]

Veterans seeking to purchase Lanham housing under the Mutual Plan found that HHFA administrator Raymond M. Foley could not be counted on for support. In April 1948 residents and veterans who had formed a mutual housing association to purchase the 139-unit Parkview Heights in Knox, Indiana, informed President Truman that Foley was insisting that they pay cash was willing to extend credit to a private investor. When the Parkview Heights group grew impatient waiting for a White House response, they turned to the American Legion, whose representative brought the issue to the attention of members of the House Subcommittee on Expenditures in the Executive Department on Behalf of Veterans. Legion national commander James F. O'Neil asked President Truman to make certain that Parkview Heights was sold to the mutual association. He also recommended that, because of their stonewalling of veterans' efforts to acquire housing under the Mutual Plan, both Foley and an unnamed assistant director of the Region III field office who directed the Parkview Heights negotiations be asked for their resignations.[80]

In September 1948 George McGill, a Kansas Democrat who was running for Senate, urged the president to look into a dispute over the sale of Hilltop Manor in Wichita.[81] Facing opposition from both the city government and real estate interests, residents of the community formed the Hilltop Manor Mutual Housing Association and hired former Kansas governor Payne Ratner as their legal counsel in a bid to purchase the community under the Mutual Plan. After protracted negotiations, the mutual association was given the opportunity to purchase 400 dwelling units of permanent construction for $1.1 million.[82]

Truman might have been more willing to take action to expedite sales to mutual housing associations in these and other cases had he been convinced of a broad base of support. Joseph Orendorff, who served as acting HHFA administrator when Foley was absent from Washington, told the president that veterans were "buying or participating in mutual purchases because of the fear of losing a place to live and not because of any real desire to achieve home ownership."[83]

Orendorff's claim that veterans were lukewarm in their support for mutual housing would have surprised New York governor Thomas E. Dewey. During his administration, New York became the first state to establish a mutual housing program for veterans under the direction of state housing commissioner Herman T. Stichman. Funded in part from the voluntary pooling of bonuses the State of New York paid to its veterans, the program was created roughly a year after Dewey had invited to his office the "more than 70 veterans"—those who had occupied the Senate chamber of the state legislature in October 1946 to protest the lack of housing aid—to discuss the housing situation.[84] As the *New York Times* reported, "veterans would organize mutual housing associations under the state's limited dividend laws which enable communities to grant tax exemption. In addition to State bonus checks, veterans will be encouraged to invest their terminal leave checks in such projects." In October of 1948, with veterans and other consumers worried about the escalating cost of housing, Stichman expressed the hope that mutual housing associations would "provide a gauge for measuring the savings possible in these days of inflated housing prices . . . [and become] true housing laboratories."[85]

The first development for middle-income veterans developed under New York State's limited-dividend plan was Bell Park Gardens, to be followed by Bell Park Manor, both located in Bayside, a leafy section of Queens. In Stichman's words, these "pilot projects" were meant to "prod private industry" and offer a yardstick for the costs of developing the garden apartment–type housing so popular with the public. They were also a test—albeit a quiet one—of integrated living in the urban fringe of eastern Queens.[86]

Given the nationwide attention devoted to the shortage of affordable housing and the promises made to homecoming veterans in 1945–1946, it was reasonable for Westbrook to believe that Congress and the Truman administration might make available to them a small amount of funding for the expansion of noncommercial housing. Westbrook believed that the construction of publicly or privately funded planned communities of prefabricated housing earmarked for mutual ownership by the residents would help solve the housing shortage, provide employment, and give veterans like his son Joel, an attorney and former army captain, a chance to create an organization that would bear their stamp.

The aid offered to service members under the Serviceman's Readjustment Act of 1944 (the G.I. Bill of Rights) and the programs created by veterans housing expediter Wilson Wyatt reinforced veterans' participation in the commercial residential market. Those who elected to build their own home needed to operate within the for-profit sector and use the products and services offered by architects, engineers, home-building contractors, home-building supply houses, bankers, and realtors if they were going to seek an FHA- or VA-secured commercial mortgage. Canada, too, steered its veterans toward home ownership but at the same time offered participation in a "state-assisted self-help housing" program designed to keep building costs as low as possible.[87] A successful cooperative housing program for veterans was created by the Nova Scotia Housing Commission, but it was not used as a model elsewhere because its promoters placed too much emphasis on its "cooperative character" and too little on the "element of 'sweat equity.'"[88]

## Mutual Housing, Not Fair Housing

The *Journal of Housing* welcomed the 1945 creation of the NMHA because it promised to address the needs of housing's "forgotten" people—those with incomes too high for admission to subsidized public housing but not high enough to afford adequate private housing.[89] Acknowledging that African Americans were among the forgotten people, the NMHA tried to cultivate support for cooperative housing among them by recommending that E.F.E. Williams, the New York and northern New Jersey "architect and planner of Negro communities," join architects Richard J. Neutra and Louis I. Kahn, labor leaders R. J. Thomas, John Edelman, and Harry Bates, and FPHA staff members on an NMHA advisory committee.[90]

The most important step the NMHA could have taken to build support for mutual and cooperative housing among African Americans would have been to encourage the building of desegregated mutual housing. But when it came time to build its own, privately funded mutual housing development, Oak Park in Dayton, Ohio, the NMHA followed the federal precedent set at nearby Greenmont Village and restricted application to whites. It might have furthered segregation in this way in order to secure an FHA loan guarantee. Oak Park's marketing was "directed and promoted by one of the top real estate men in Dayton," and it is possible that he believed that the financial future of the endeavor rested on maintaining the city's color line. The Oak Park project convinced one observer that the public would soon be hearing "as much about mutual housing plans in this county in the next few years" as it "heard about the REA over the past years." The NMHA showed that it was possible to attract private investment for the development of segregated housing under the Mutual Plan, but left unanswered the question of whether private funding could be obtained for desegregated mutual housing.[91]

Westbrook used his network of political connections to remove the political roadblocks and financial obstacles faced by mutual housing associations seeking to buy Lanham-built communities or by cooperatives planning to build new housing. Amid growing debate over the issue of fair housing in Washington and elsewhere, he worked to establish support for mutual associations and cooperatives within the larger confines of segregation and accepted clients for his Trans-American Development Corporation that regarded mutual housing as a way to uphold or extend the residential color line. In May 1946 he confided to his son Joel that the "race situation" had created an obstacle for a veterans' group that had formed a mutual housing association and hired his company to help them develop cooperative housing in the District of Columbia area. The veterans who founded the First Washington Mutual Homes Corporation had created their own obstacle by announcing plans to "build a project exclusively for white residents."[92]

Westbrook admitted that the AVC chapter would "not officially endorse this project because it violates the anti-discrimination provision of the AVC Charter. As individuals, however, the members of the Chapter, including the leaders, will strongly support our project."[93] In November 1946 First Washington Mutual Homes still had not acquired a site for its segregated, mutually owned community, and Westbrook sent FPHA commissioner Dillon Myer a request to discuss the possibility of the group acquiring land in the already racially segregated federal town of Greenbelt, Maryland.[94]

In Chicago, efforts to build a desegregated cooperative housing development faced repeated financial setbacks and delays. Plans for the development of Parkway Garden Homes, a series of mutually owned apartment buildings, were first announced in late 1945. The $5.8 million project was to be located on the site of the former "White City" amusement park on Chicago's South Side. Expected to be the city's "second largest privately funded Negro residential development," the project's initial financial backer was the Dining Car Workers Union. In March 1947 Parkway Garden Homes gained a new sponsor, the Community Development Trust created by architect Henry K. Holsman. Financial and other problems delayed the groundbreaking until October 1950.[95]

In his March 1946 article "Housing in a Democracy," Robert C. Weaver, a former New Deal housing official and private consultant who would later become the first secretary of the Department of Housing and Urban Development, wrote that cities needed cooperative housing because it made it possible for wage earners who could not afford or were otherwise excluded from home ownership to acquire an economic stake in their neighborhoods. He expressed the hope that mutual housing might "offer a convenient instrument for bringing African American and white occupants and building together." Weaver was one of only a small handful of housing policy makers who spoke and wrote of the need to take lessons learned from the New Deal and wartime experimentation and apply them to postwar plans for urban revitalization.[96]

Westbrook persisted in his effort to dodge the issue of mutual housing and racial segregation even when residents from projects that were designated as racially "mixed" expressed interest in obtaining their homes under the Mutual Plan. During the late 1940s and early 1950s, the residents of Glen Hazel Heights, a biracial defense housing community in Pittsburgh, were among the inhabitants of roughly a dozen area defense housing projects seeking Mutual Plan purchase of their homes. They organized a petition drive and obtained 689 signatures on a letter requesting that the PHA grant them more time to collect the down payment and comply with the agency's requirements. The PHA fulfilled their request, but in the end, instead of selling Glen Hazel Heights to its residents under the Mutual Plan, Congress authorized its conveyance to the Pittsburgh Housing Authority.[97] North Braddock Heights in North Braddock,

Pennsylvania, was one of only three mixed-race defense housing developments in the U.S. that were sold under the Mutual Plan. The mutual housing association was founded on an open-membership basis at the insistence of attorney J. Alfred Wilner.[98] Other mutually purchased defense housing developments in the area had been designated for white occupancy by federal housing officials when they were constructed.[99]

In Southern California, where the Los Angeles County Housing Authority had open housing policies in place, there were a number of defense worker communities where interest in the Mutual Plan was high. Attorney George E. Atkinson Jr. represented at least four mutual housing associations in the Greater Los Angeles area seeking to buy Wilmington's 384-unit Dana Strand for $1.1 million; the 600-unit Cabrillo Homes in Long Beach for $1.9 million; and two San Pedro–area developments—the 400-unit Normont Terrace and the 600-unit Channel Heights—for $1 million and $1.7 million. However, the authority ended up acquiring three of the four: Channel Heights, Normont Terrace, and Dana Strand Village. It is not known what happened to the mutual effort at Cabrillo Homes.[100]

The failure of residents' effort to obtain Channel Heights under the Mutual Plan was chronicled by shipbuilding worker and author Henry Kraus, who referred to Channel Heights as "Garden City" and employed pseudonyms for its residents in his 1951 book, *In the City Was a Garden*. A former member of the merchant marine known for his involvement in the UAW's famous sitdown strike in Flint, Michigan, Kraus was once identified in the *New York Times* as a "Communist party follower."[101]

The mutual housing campaign at Kraus's Garden City got off to an encouraging start at war's end with the establishment of an organizing committee made up of culturally diverse residents and newcomer veterans (not including Kraus, who planned to relocate). Some of the members had previously served on the tenants' council, which had been created by the Los Angeles County Housing Authority to foster both participation in community governance and resident acceptance of its policy of racial desegregation. The tenants' council proved to be an excellent training ground for the leadership and organization needed to achieve mutual home ownership. For example, Selena Daclan, a member of the council and a delegate to the Los Angeles Inter-Project Council, obtained information from the FPHA about the possible sale of the community on a mutual basis and distributed it to residents at the "Garden City" carnival in the summer of 1945.[102]

Kraus regarded the mutual home ownership effort as the "logical consequence of four years" of resident participation in project management. The sale of the community on a mutual basis, he claimed, would serve as a "monument" to the years of multicultural democratic participation in community governance.[103] Fellow resident Lennie Kaufman, editor of the community newspaper, regarded the purchase of Channel Heights on a cooperative basis as an unprecedented opportunity to make the community the "garden spot of California"—a model for postwar development.[104]

Operating on the advice that Selena Daclan had obtained from the FPHA, the mutual housing organizing committee gathered signatures documenting the residents' interest in purchasing their homes under the Mutual Plan and collected money to create the not-for-profit corporation. It also provided an opportunity for residents to learn about mutual home ownership by inviting an FPHA field office representative to a meeting to discuss buying the Neutra-designed community. In fact, the representative tried to talk the committee out of its plans, and Kraus noted with alarm that some residents left the meeting "disenchanted" with the idea of mutual housing.[105]

The lack of support from the FPHA proved to be only one of the problems faced by the Garden City proponents of mutual ownership. Herbert Spowart, an evangelical Baptist minister and nonresident who freely shared his anti-Catholic and anti-Semitic views, opposed mutual ownership, which he saw as a means of making permanent the open housing policy he abhorred.[106] Another opponent, Dean Sherman, a veteran with a military demeanor, had moved to Garden City just as the mutual housing initiative was getting under way. Suspected of keeping a list of political enemies in a "little black book," he formed an alliance with the Spowart and others who regarded the mutual housing association as a threat to racial segregation, traditional gender and family roles, Christianity, and democracy.[107]

Still, Kraus was convinced that the Mutual Plan offered strong appeal to Garden City residents who were economically or socially marginalized in the commercial market. He observed that roughly half of the residents who attended meetings on the purchase of Garden City under the Mutual Plan were racial or ethnic minorities. Selena Daclan, for example, was married to a Native Hawaiian, and she recognized that mutual housing could be a way to protect or unify families such as hers who faced housing market discrimination. Essie Rodney, an African American and mutual housing supporter, said, "Some of you people don't have to worry if the private landlords get this project but where will the rest of us go?" Kraus reported that many white families were content to remain as renters and regarded as excessive the "apprehension" expressed by families of color over being displaced from their homes.[108]

The growth of anti-Communism as a political issue across the United States and especially in Southern California aided opponents of the sale of Garden City to the mutual housing association. Sidney Burke, a real-life Channel Heights resident and left-wing activist, had attracted national publicity when efforts were made to deny him public housing because of his political views. The Burke case contributed to Congress passing the Gwinn Amendment in 1952, requiring a loyalty oath from public housing residents. Matters got even worse for Garden City mutual housing supporters when Selena Daclan admitted that she was a communist. Kraus saw this as a brave but ill-advised admission that prompted Sherman and his allies to successfully demand a complete change in leadership at a key time in negotiations and fund-raising.[109] Garden City, the pinnacle of community modernism, was portrayed by them as a safe harbor for communists, leftists, labor union militants, and advocates of racial mixing. In fact, from the outset all public housing had been branded by the "invisible congress" of the real estate lobby as "inefficient, alien, and un-American."[110]

Sherman and some members of the new steering committee introduced the lawyer they had chosen without consulting the rest and presented him as the one who would "take care of everything."[111] Attorney Lincoln Gregory had helped the mutual housing association at Liberty Mall (a pseudonym) in Lomita, California, purchase its community before all-cash sales were required. A Garden City resident who knew that the Lomita project was all white, asked him about his views of segregation. He replied that the "members of the corporation" would determine its racial policy.[112]

Without assistance from federal housing officials and private sector cooperative housing advocates such as Westbrook, residents of Lanham developments were left largely on their own to organize mutual housing associations, negotiate the purchase of their communities from the federal government, and obtain a commercial market mortgage. In late 1948 the PHA announced its intention to sell to mutual housing associations two Arlington, Virginia, developments built for African American war workers: the eighty-six-unit Paul Laurence Dunbar Homes and the forty-four-unit George Washington Carver Homes (not to be confused with Pennsylvania's George Washington Carver Courts). The Dunbar Mutual Homes Association sought private funds to purchase the Arlington County community, which had been built at a cost of $551,900 and was located about three miles from the new Pentagon building. The Carver Homes Mutual Association, a cooperative formed by forty residents and four nonresidents, agreed to the purchase price of $123,000 for eight, two-story cinderblock buildings. Members of the Arlington County Board of Commissioners tried to stop both sales by proposing that the developments be converted into low-income public housing. The two communities still had not been sold in June of 1949, when Elder Lightfoot Solomon Michaux, pastor of Arlington's Church of God and president of a housing development named Mayfair, announced the merger of the two groups, now to be known as the Veterans' Home Cooperative of Arlington, with goal of pursuing the purchase of both projects.[113]

The residents of the multi-racial Channel Heights in San Pedro, California and possibly other area defense housing developments might have been successful in buying the communities under the Mutual Plan if the PHA had been willing to extend mortgages to mutual housing associations instead of requiring cash sales. In response to an inquiry from James Cassells of the NMHA (now the National Cooperative Mutual Housing Association), Warren J. Lockwood, assistant to the FHA commissioner, stated that his agency had "never insured a project of mixed occupancy" and made the "unofficial and informal statement" that the FHA was unlikely to offer to insure a mixed-occupancy development because it would soon become "all Negro or all white."[114]

Lockwood's views aside, some FHA staff members, such as James A. Hewitt of the agency's Insuring Office, encouraged the construction of FHA-eligible cooperative housing developments for "Negroes and other minorities."[115] In November 1948 the PHA announced that it would sell certain Lanham projects to mutual housing associations that paid 10 percent down and accepted a twenty-year mortgage. This ruling was of potential value to African American Lanham residents whose mutual housing associations were unable to find private financing, but it is unclear if any actually benefited from it.[116] In 1952 the Bureau of Labor Statistics found that only a small handful of the housing cooperatives formed in 1949 and 1950 were officially committed to open membership. Many tried to avoid the issue, and some even purchased land with unenforceable racial covenants.[117]

## The Mutual Plan and Postwar Politics

In April 1946 Douglas Whitlock of the Producers Council and Edward R. Carr of the Home Builders Association of Metropolitan Washington accused the Truman administration of wanting to "socialize the country," with the housing program "serving as the opening wedge." Carr claimed that Truman's housing goals were at odds with the "ingrained desire of the American people" to own their own home as "a bulwark against the wave of collectivism" threatening the commercial market.[118]

Whitlock and Carr greatly exaggerated the threat to the commercial market posed by the "wave of collectivism." Between 1945 and 1949, Congress and the president devoted their energy and resources to legislation that would stimulate the production of an adequate supply of affordable housing by commercial home builders. Truman emphasized the creation of programs that would make it possible for veterans and other wage earners making \$2,000–\$4,000 per year to become home owners. Acknowledging that not all veterans and middle-income householders were ready to buy a house, Fair Deal legislation offered incentives for residential developers to construct middle-income rental housing as well.[119]

Speculative developers promoted detached, single-family dwellings on individual lots according to site plans that closely conformed to the standards set by the FHA and the VA for loan guarantees. Home builders such as William Levitt did not look to Avion Village and the defense communities as models for postwar development; instead, they achieved celebrity status by repudiating community modernism as un-American. Levitt and Sons, a company that perfected its mass-assembly construction methods building Lanham housing, negotiated sales on a one-on-one basis and did not welcome proposals from veteran, union, or cooperative groups.[120]

As Truman and Congress were authoring bills encouraging veterans and other wage earners to become home owners, a few calls for an alternative path were being heard. A handful of legislation containing provisions similar to those in the original W-E-T Bill was offered in Congress, but Truman took no special interest in increasing low- and middle-income access to cooperative home ownership. Not one postwar cooperative housing bill specifically called for residential development under the Mutual Plan.

In *A Housing Program for Now and Later*, released in February 1948, a joint committee of the National Public Housing Conference and the National Association of Housing Officials wrote that during the Great Depression and World War II the federal government had removed much of the financial risk faced by home lenders and builders through the FHA, the VA, and other programs, but now it refused to accept "parallel responsibility in the consumers' interest." Congress was unwilling to provide aid to housing cooperatives even though they were a "vast potential source of sound democratic initiative for moderate-cost housing."[121]

The CIO's National Housing Committee remained optimistic about cooperative housing's "vast potential" to help those who fell into the housing gap between subsidized housing and home ownership. In the UAW's April 1949 "Homes for People, Jobs for Prosperity, and Planes for Peace" initiative, committee chairman Walter Reuther called for a new "National Housing Authority . . . [that would] provide momentum, a framework for action, and goals . . . [that included] genuine cooperative housing developments." The proposed agency would "guide and encourage mutual home ownership" because it was the "best tested method for reducing management costs" while maintaining standards high enough to "minimize deterioration."[122]

Reuther's initiative did little to change the Truman administration's ambivalence towards cooperative housing. The sale of war housing proceeded, with federal housing officials neither actively promoting nor actively discouraging Mutual Plan purchases of the pilot projects or other Lanham developments. Residents and veterans who did organize to mutually purchase their communities stumbled along either on their own or with the help of individuals, who stood to gain little from the time and expertise invested, in negotiating the congressional and agency roadblocks erected to keep them from realizing their goal. "Years of discouraging rumors" that the federal government was or was not going to sell Success Park, a defense housing development near Bridgeport, Connecticut under the Mutual Plan took a heavy toll on group morale, and it was "not easy to keep the spirit of the hoped-for-cooperative alive. . . . [It was a] constant struggle . . . [to] keep the dream alive" for resident Irving Yurdin and a "small diligent group of supporters."[123]

Meanwhile, PHA officials were accused by Congress of delaying the disposition process to ensure that defense communities were sold to mutual housing associations. In May 1949 the House grew so dismayed with the lack of progress on Lanham housing disposition that it ordered the Government Operations Subcommittee of the Committee on Expenditures in the Executive Departments to investigate why only 24,535 out of a total of 191,116 units of permanent defense housing and 23,556 out of a total of 432,575 units of temporary housing had been sold since the war's end.[124]

Despite all the difficulties encountered, between September 1945 and June 1949 sixteen permanent projects totaling 4,566 dwelling units were sold to mutual housing associations. The smallest of these, Jackson Homes in Charlotte, North Carolina, had only 85 units and the largest, Dayton, Ohio's Greenmont Village, had 500. Nine projects, including four of the original pilots—Greenmont Village, Walnut Grove, Avion Village, and Dallas Park—were sold to mutual housing associations on credit, along with Grandview Acres in Ogden, Utah, Compton Village in Compton, California, Fulmor Heights in Hatboro, Pennsylvania, and two Wilmington, North Carolina, projects known together as Lake Forest. As a result of Public Regulation No. 1, cash sales were required of the mutual housing associations that purchased Jackson Homes and six other projects—Woodstock Homes in Alameda, California, Aluminum City Terrace in New Kensington, Pennsylvania, Quindaro Homes in Kansas City, Kansas, Oakland Heights Village in Meridian, Mississippi, Kingsford Heights in La Porte, Indiana, and Kenna Homes in South Charleston, West Virginia.[125]

The mutual and cooperative housing movement grew between 1945 and 1949, but its appeal suffered as opportunities for traditional home ownership increased and attitudes softened toward home mortgages and consumer indebtedness. Encouraged to regard the purchase of a house as a sensible investment because of the anticipated increase in its value over time, most saw no need to settle for the right to perpetual occupancy and the small rate of return on their original investment that mutual home ownership offered. For every mutual housing association that was successful in completing a purchase, there were probably two or three others that shared the fate of Channel Heights and St. Andrews Homes in Charleston, South Carolina, and dissolved under the weight of opposition from outside forces or internal division.[126]

In August 1949 the House Government Operations Subcommittee of the Committee on Expenditures in Executive Departments reported that "numerous complaints" had been made to Congress about the disposition of defense housing. It found that the PHA's policy of giving sales preference to mutual housing associations in the disposition of multiunit Lanham housing presented "many complicated problems and involve[d] costly disposition procedures." The PHA had very little experience in sales of small communities under the Mutual Plan, and the subcommittee had "grave doubts" about its ability to successfully apply what experience it had to large projects. Knowing sales under the Mutual Plan would be less popular with Congress than sales to investors, the subcommittee recommended that a "legislative determination" be made on whether the PHA would continue to grant preference to mutual housing associations.[127]

Westbrook's Mutual Plan might have been more readily incorporated into postwar housing programs for veterans and low- and middle-income households if it had *not* been incorporated into the Lanham disposition program. Once the Mutual Plan was tapped for Lanham and New Deal project disposition, it became difficult to distinguish it from the political controversy surrounding the sale of individual projects. The cost of the Truman administration's unwillingness to integrate mutual and cooperative housing into its plans for veterans, moderate-income householders, and those displaced by urban renewal or other infrastructure projects was high. The Housing Act of 1949 offered "simple solutions—new dwelling units and slum clearance—to solve the complex problems of American cities."[128]

Mutual housing was an example of the "New Deal's accepted fruit" that the Eightieth Congress left to "dry on the vine," or so it at least appeared until 1949, when the Republican lock on the omnibus W-E-T Bill was finally broken. Suddenly there was new reason for optimism among the backers of mutual and cooperative housing as the national housing focus shifted from the needs of low-income families to those of middle- or moderate-income households. The emergence of the second generation of mutual housing associations, led by Aluminum City Terrace, encouraged President Truman and members of Congress to undertake a major legislative bid to provide middle-income families with expanded cooperative housing opportunities.[129]

# 7

# Mutual Housing

## *"America's New Housing Economy"?*

In 1949, Elsie Danenberg published *Get Your Own Home the Co-operative Way*, offering 182 pages of "complete, authentic and up-to-date" information on the nationwide growth of the cooperative housing movement. Hers was "the actual story . . . [of the] more than 30,000 families" whose frustration with their commercial market choices prompted them to turn to "their community, their union, their church, their office, or even among their friends" for expertise and capital to form a housing cooperative. They achieved the American Dream of home ownership "by banding together into groups, or cooperatives, in order to purchase their land jointly, obtain materials in large quantities, and contract as a unit for architectural and building services, and for equipment and furnishings." Whether the residents "formed true and complete co-ops . . . some co-op features, . . . [or] only the loosest sort of association," Danenberg concluded, "all of them got houses of quality and beauty superior to anything they could have obtained under separate contracts."[1]

The cooperative housing activities of workers, veterans, and consumers chronicled by Danenberg, the U.S. Department of Labor's Florence Parker, and others helped to build and maintain Congressional support for cooperative housing aid. In January 1949 Congressman Wright Patman, an early sponsor of cooperative housing legislation, was invited to speak at the groundbreaking ceremony at Bannockburn, "the first housing development in the Washington area to be constructed by a cooperative group." The Bannockburn Cooperators, Inc., had acquired property just outside the District of Columbia in Glen Echo, Maryland, with an FHA-insured loan from the Mutual Life Insurance Company. The architects of the first group of twenty-four houses included Vernon DeMars, formerly of the Farm Security Administration (FSA). The closely watched experiment was seen as a "new venture that might set a future pattern for families in the middle-income group."[2]

The interest in cooperative housing expressed by veterans, consumers, and others convinced two U.S. senators that it was time to get it on a sound economic footing. In January 1950 Senator Burnet R. Maybank (D-SC), chairman of the powerful Committee on Banking and Currency, offered a friendly amendment to an earlier bill sponsored by his Senate colleague, John Sparkman (D-AL), calling for the creation of a public-private corporation called the National Mortgage Corporation for Housing Cooperatives (hereafter Cooperative Corporation). The proposed Cooperative Corporation would, Maybank believed, help to transform the U.S. housing market by making cooperatives the cornerstone of a noncommercial market that filled in the gaps left by the commercial market. The two southern Democrats had witnessed how the New Deal's Rural Electrification Administration, the Tennessee Valley Economic Development Corporation, the Santee Cooper (South Carolina) Public Service Authority (known as the "little TVA"), and other public-private initiatives had brought sweeping change to environmentally compromised and economically disadvantaged areas. Maybank and Sparkman believed that their Cooperative Corporation would help ailing U.S. cities by facilitating the development or redevelopment of centrally located sites with cooperatively owned communities of affordable, well-designed, and solidly constructed dwellings that would end the exodus of middle-income households to the suburbs.

Joel W. Schenker, the contractor whose Roth-Schenker Corporation had built Pennypack Woods and the mutually owned veterans' project Bell Park Gardens in Queens, New York, saw the creation of the proposed Cooperative Corporation as an acknowledgment that there was no better way of "solving, or even coming close to solving, the problem which besets America's lower middle-income families" than cooperative housing. The availability of low-interest loans to housing cooperatives would increase the options open to families of limited means, help achieve a "continual flow of fair-profit housing construction instead of a spasmodic risk pattern," and foster employment opportunities in architecture, planning, the building trades, and building supply houses. Cooperative housing was not "socialized housing" but "democracy in action," Schenker said. It should be "America's new housing economy."[3]

## Postwar Legislative Efforts to Promote Cooperative Housing

The postwar campaign to extend federal aid to private housing cooperatives began in 1945 with the Wagner-Ellender-Taft (W-E-T) Bill, which called for Federal Housing Administration (FHA) guarantees for private financing of housing cooperatives established for those in the "middle market or 'no-man's land' of housing."[4] James McEwan, president of the Indiana State CIO, urged passage of the bill so that mutual housing associations could more readily secure private funds to purchase Lanham housing. He also wanted the bill to make it possible for those displaced from their homes by anticipated slum clearance, highway building, and urban redevelopment to be eligible for aid to "form a mutual housing corporation and very well own their own homes and become the citizens we expect them to be." In April 1946 the Senate passed the W-E-T Bill with its cooperative housing provisions intact.[5]

The cooperative housing provisions contained in W-E-T engendered little controversy compared to those calling for a return to the construction of low-income public housing. Republicans and some Democrats opposed to resumption of the public housing program in its prewar form created four years of housing legislation gridlock. From 1945 until 1949, while action on W-E-T was blocked by the House, various cooperative housing proposals and bills circulated around Washington. In August 1947 Congress made it possible for the FHA to insure mortgages granted to mutual housing associations under Section 610 of the National Housing Act. The special summer session convened by President Truman in 1948 resulted in the passage of a bill co-sponsored by Representative Jesse Wolcott (R-MI) and Republican Senator Joseph McCarthy (R-WI) that contained some of the same cooperative provisions contained in the 1945 W-E-T Bill without the controversial public housing provisions. The resulting Housing Act of 1948 amended the National Housing Act and added Section 207(c) authorizing the FHA to guarantee up to 90 percent of the value of loans made to developers of moderate-income rental units, including housing cooperatives.

When the president signed the Housing Act of 1948 into law on July 1, he called it a "teeny-weeny" measure that paled in comparison to the comprehensive bill needed to help wage earners improve their housing and living standards.[6] Neither Donald Monson and Astrid Monson of the Detroit Plan Commission nor other housing analysts regarded the FHA as a cooperative-friendly agency and accurately predicted that it would give the Section 207(c) program "little emphasis." As the Bureau of Labor Statistics noted, "in the absence of special machinery and regulations" pertaining to cooperatives, few of those who applied received mortgage insurance.[7]

Westbrook and other cooperative housing supporters saw the liberalization of FHA regulations for housing cooperatives as a step in the right direction, but they remained convinced that a program of federal loans was essential for cooperative housing to become a mainstream housing choice for middle-income families. Support for loans to cooperatives gained ground in December 1948, when Senator Hubert H. Humphrey (D-MN) and Herbert U. Nelson of the National Association of Real Estate Boards (NAREB) engaged in a radio debate entitled "How Can We Get More Housing?" The two predictably disagreed about the need to resume public housing construction, but did agree on the need for Congress to make cooperative home ownership an option for Americans who were candidates neither for public housing nor for home ownership. Nelson called cooperative housing "the only road to home ownership for millions of American families" and pledged to support low-interest, long-term federal loans to stimulate private development of housing cooperatives for moderate-income households.[8]

NAREB tried to capitalize on public interest in cooperative housing to achieve its own economic and political ends. Drew Pearson of the *Washington Post* warned that interest in cooperative housing among the nation's realtors had come about only as a means of stopping Congress from resuming public housing construction. They wanted to replace the federal public housing program with what he called a "State-run 'cooperative housing' program."[9] Once it appeared that there was sufficient political support for Congress to fund the resumption of public housing construction, NAREB rethought the cooperative idea and, according to the *Washington Post*, quickly "shelved . . . [the] socialistic" plan.[10] T. H. Maenner, president of the association, acknowledged that his organization was interested only in cooperative housing as a "counter measure to public housing."[11]

## The Housing Act of 1949 Disappoints Cooperative Housing Advocates

In July President Truman reached the "high point of Fair Deal legislation" with the passage of the Housing Act of 1949, establishing the nation's first housing goal of "a decent home and suitable living environment for every American family." Intended to contribute to "the development and redevelopment of communities and to the advancement of the growth, wealth and security of the Nation," this act offered no evidence of congressional or administrative commitment to cooperative housing. Signed into law on July 15, 1949, it reactivated the public housing program along lines laid forth under the Wagner Act of 1937. No provision was made for the eventual resident ownership of the 810,000 dwelling units it authorized to be built over a six-year period.[12]

In the weeks that followed passage of the act, attention shifted to the housing needs of those whose income was "moderate" or slightly above what would qualify for public housing. The Senate Banking and Currency Committee noted a "spontaneous burst of interest in cooperative housing" among middle-income families whose annual "cash income was between $2,800 and $4,400," those who, unable to take on the risk of home ownership, were caught in the "large no man's land in the housing market."[13]

Housing activist Catherine Bauer welcomed the growth of interest in cooperative housing for middle-income households. Commenting on a report by the National Cooperative Mutual Housing Association claiming that roughly a hundred housing cooperative groups or developments were under way in the United States, she declared, "Nothing could be more important for the future of housing and community life in America than to implement this movement." The truth behind these "hopeful ventures" was that only "a handful—hardly half a dozen—have actually started construction on a more or less cooperative basis." Many lacked "solid financial resources of their own, a piece of land without zoning impediments or restrictive covenants, first-rate leadership and technical skills, and enough prestige and 'influence' of one kind or another to induce the Federal Housing Administration to work with them."[14]

Bauer identified four steps to be taken before cooperative housing could be reasonably expected to help middle-income families obtain better housing. First, housing cooperatives needed to secure long-term, low-interest loans from a federal agency "independent of the FHA" that was "seriously interested in promoting successful cooperative housing" and whose staff regarded cooperative housing without indifference or hostility. Second, competent advisers were needed to help housing cooperatives prepare for the financial obligations involved in planning and construction and in post-construction management of their property. Third, housing cooperatives required the services of knowledgeable architects and planners who offered "first-rate technical skill all along the way, from site selection to design and operation." Fourth, support and cooperation from local governments and their planning and zoning boards were needed if cooperative housing was ever to become a housing option for middle-income families.[15]

Bauer maintained that her four-point mutual housing program was not politically "unthinkable" and cited a number of bipartisan bills then pending that could help solidify the "healthy new demand in a hitherto untouched market." If the enactment of cooperative housing aid became a Truman administration priority, it would help solve the housing shortage, offer cities a tool for the retention of middle-income families, and create jobs. Middle-income cooperative housing, Bauer noted, showed veterans and labor that the administration was responsive to their needs. She argued it was "imperatively necessary" for cooperative housing to have its own "separate administrative organization" within the HHFA. Vested in traditional home ownership, the FHA could not be counted on to promote cooperative housing.[16]

## Senator Sparkman Champions Middle-Income Cooperative Home Ownership

Hopes for the enactment of cooperative housing aid grew during 1949 as a flurry of bills emerged in Congress from members of both parties. The most important of these was the February 1949 bill cosponsored by Republican Senators Ralph E. Flanders of Vermont, Charles W. Tobey of New Hampshire, and Irving M. Ives of New York, calling for the creation of a $3 million fund to provide direct loans for up to sixty years at 3 percent interest to build "60,000 housing units a year for families in the $2000 to $3000 income group." Shortly after, the Republican representative from New York, Jacob K. Javits, introduced a similar bill calling for federal loans for "large-scale development of cooperative and rental housing" for middle-income families.[17] FHA Commissioner Franklin D.

Richards was so convinced that Congress would create a cooperative housing loan program that in February 1949 he went on record favoring the creation of a program in his agency that would offer loans to qualified cooperative organizations "to build small homes" affordable for wage earners.[18] Richard's colleague, James A. Hewitt, director of the agency's Washington Insuring Office, "stressed the need for lower-cost rental and cooperative housing, particularly for Negroes and other minorities" at the first of a series of meetings held by the Housing and Home Finance Agency (HHFA) to encourage the construction of low-cost dwellings.[19]

By June 1949 a total of nineteen middle-income cooperative housing bills had been introduced by members of the House of Representatives, including at least one measure calling for the creation of a long-term, low-interest loan program to be administered by a "Cooperative Housing Administration housed within the HHFA" that would move cooperative home ownership into the mainstream of the housing market and benefit the nonprofit sector in much the same way that the FHA had helped the commercial residential market by promoting working-class home ownership.[20]

Senator John Sparkman (D-AL) emerged as the foremost champion of middle-income cooperative housing in the summer of 1949, when he proposed a bill calling for direct, long-term, low-interest loans to housing cooperatives as part of a larger middle-income housing bill. The son of tenant farmers and World War I veteran, Sparkman had been elected to the House in 1936 and joined the Senate in 1946. As chairman of the Senate Banking and Currency Committee's Subcommittee on Housing and Rents, he sought to increase the supply of affordable rental housing for veterans and wage earners and make it easier for them to become home owners. The Committee on Banking and Currency, chaired by Burnet R. Maybank (D-SC), observed that the expansion of FHA home mortgage insurance underwriting and the secondary mortgage market operations of the Federal National Mortgage Association had "without question" resulted in a "sizable volume of housing available for families in the highest income third." Now, the senator believed, it was time for Congress to fill the "big gap in our present housing program" and develop a "new avenue" for those in the middle, who qualified neither for public housing nor a commercial home mortgage.[21]

The Banking and Currency Committee anticipated a ready market for cooperative housing in and around big cities and "areas marked for urban redevelopment," where the demand for quality affordable housing usually exceeded the supply. Too often, the committee found, middle-income families, especially those with children, bought houses out of frustration with the lack of affordable rental market choices and risked ending up with an economic obligation they could hardly meet and a dwelling or neighborhood ill suited to their day-to-day needs.[22]

Sparkman was convinced that cooperative housing could become the housing of choice for moderate-income householders only if loans—not just FHA loan guarantees—were available for construction and start-up costs. It is hardly surprising that, as a result, Sparkman's middle-income housing bill and its program of direct long-term loans to housing cooperatives elicited a "frantic cry of grief" from real estate investors. NAREB called the bill a "bombshell" because of the damage it could potentially inflict on private mortgage-lending institutions and housing construction. Yet Maybank's Banking and Commerce Committee held firm against intense pressures from real estate, home-building, and banking interests and recommended the Sparkman bill for passage on August 11, 1949.[23]

American Labor Party member Vito Marcantonio of New York tried to kill the House version of the Middle-Income Bill in August 1949 by introducing an "antidiscrimination amendment" that would prevent racial discrimination in both public and private housing. "Good sense prevailed in the House," The *Washington Post* reported on August 26, when it voted to eliminate the Marcantonio amendment and the "dubious clause providing loans to housing cooperatives." According to Drew Pearson, the House version of the bill was "badly mangled by the real estate lobby, with the aid of their friend GOP representative Jesse Wolcott plus a deft assist" from Marcantonio.[24]

The *Post* tried to pick away at support for the cooperative loan provisions among members of the Senate Banking and Currency Committee, arguing that the Sparkman bill would likely result in "substantial losses" and require a "subsidy from taxpayers" and pointing out that the provisions were "vehemently assailed by the National Association of Home Builders."[25] Harry C. Bates of the AFL took issue with this argument, stating that federal loans had previously been made to cooperative electrification, irrigation, and other rural development projects both at home and abroad. The Sparkman bill "involved no element of subsidy" as alleged, but offered a "practical solution" that had already proven to be successful. Cooperative home ownership opportunities, Bates maintained, ought to be as commonplace for American workers as they were for workers in northern Europe.[26]

AFL and CIO housing advocates found common ground in their support of the Sparkman bill and were joined by representatives of veterans' organizations, including the American Legion, the Veterans of Foreign Wars, the Disabled American Veterans, the Jewish War Veterans, and the American Veterans Committee.[27] Catholic and Jewish organizations and secular social welfare groups also endorsed it. Monsignor John O'Grady of the National Conference of Catholic Charities claimed that labor, veterans, and social welfare organizations were "solidly behind" the cooperative aid program. He thought that the significance of the bill came not so much in the low-interest direct federal loans it proposed but "in the espousal by these organizations of the cooperative approach as being the solution to the housing problem for large numbers of middle-income families."[28]

Sparkman's bill enjoyed the support of Democrats such as Glen H. Taylor of Idaho, the singing cowboy turned politician who had joined the Senate in

1945. Taylor argued that broadening the definition of home owners to include cooperative home owners would prove beneficial to the "solid core of our nation—the factory workers, tradespeople, school teachers, office workers and the like."[29] Russell B. Long (D-LA) who had joined the Senate in 1948, spoke of middle-income families interested in cooperative home ownership as members of the "forgotten third" who had made "our nation what it is today." These families did not live in "storied mansions or slums. These are our average American families." No statistics were needed, he said, "to show that the welfare and prosperity of our Nation depends on this great middle-income group."[30]

Long promoted cooperative home ownership as an alternative to individually owned home for families who "work and serve in our offices, plants, and stores, in high-cost metropolitan areas." He wanted such families to have a chance to enjoy the advantages of living in "well-planned housing . . . [near] centers of urban employment, and served by school and other community facilities, and with space for their children to breathe and play and grow." The image of the "free-standing, vine-covered cottage of a half century ago is still inviting," he observed, but it was high time to admit it was "no longer practical."[31]

By mid-September of 1949, Sparkman's bill had enough backing from labor, veterans, and social advocacy groups to compel the *Washington Post* to further explain its opposition. Title III, the centerpiece of the Sparkman middle-income bill calling for loans to cooperatives, had to be eliminated in the name of fiscal restraint, according to a *Post* editorial because a federal subsidy "in all probability, would be involved." The paper claimed no objection to "the principle of cooperative housing" and supported congressional efforts to strengthen the FHA's ability to insure the mortgages that private financial institutions extended to housing cooperatives. But it noted that when the widely admired Amalgamated Clothing Workers housing cooperative began a major expansion project in 1947, it borrowed private funds and did not go "directly to the Federal Treasury."[32]

## European Study Tour Prompts Key Legislative Adjustments

Convinced that there was too much opposition to direct federal loans to middle-income housing cooperatives for his bill to pass, Sparkman withdrew Title III and announced plans to introduce a new bill in the following session that would allow his cooperative housing program to be "considered on its merits." To prepare, he and members of the Senate Banking and Currency Committee's Subcommittee on Housing and Rents—Ralph Flanders, the Republican from Vermont, Allen Frear Jr. (D-DE), Harry P. Cain (R-WA), and John W. Bricker (R-OH)—embarked on a Northern Europe study tour in October 1949, visiting housing cooperatives in Sweden, Denmark, Norway, England, the Netherlands, and France.[33] Senator Maybank, former mayor of Charleston and governor of South Carolina, was unable to travel with his colleagues and conducted his own European tour.[34] Herbert U. Nelson of NAREB; Herman T. Stichman of the New York State Commission; Donald Monson, senior architectural planner with the Detroit City Plan Commission; and Astrid Monson, senior economist with the Detroit City Plan Commission, were among the policy makers from the public and private sectors who went abroad in 1948–1949 to observe how European housing cooperatives worked and judge for themselves whether their approach could be adapted to American economic needs, social tastes, and political realities.[35]

Charles Abrams, a New York City attorney and prominent housing reformer, was delighted by all the high-level study devoted to the inner workings of European housing cooperatives and government finance programs. A U.S. program of government aid modeled on those in Scandinavia could, he argued, "be an important instrument . . . [to help] sustain employment in the building trades . . . [and promote] planned neighborhoods."[36] Abrams questioned the direct loan approach and favored the Scandinavian practice of offering secondary loans of public funds to qualified housing cooperatives that had secured a first mortgage in the private sector. Operating subsidies, Abrams suggested, could be made available to cooperative or nonprofit groups that successfully cleared blighted areas, rehoused those displaced by urban renewal, or "embark[ed] upon a social experiment such as mixed occupancy in an area where it is still a frontier." With proper attention and oversight, he added, cooperatives could "emerge as one of our great and most democratic institutions," paving the way for vibrant, multicultural communities.[37]

Sparkman, Maybank, and their supporters saw little likelihood that cooperatives awarded funds under the program would embark on "social experiments" with residential desegregation, in part because there was no precedent for doing so from earlier rural, suburban, and urban New Deal programs. Public funds had been lent to local not-for-profit or limited-dividend corporations and state and local agencies for the construction of segregated housing in and around Philadelphia, New York, Washington, D.C., and other cities despite a growing market demand for open housing. Nonetheless, the bill's backers assured southerners that there would never be much of a demand for cooperative housing in their districts and at the same time assured northern Congress members that the demand was likely to emerge from large cities such as New York, Chicago, and Los Angeles, where there were sizable numbers of liberals and low- and middle-income African Americans with limited housing choices.[38]

The subcommittee's European tour was "extremely helpful" said Sparkman, who returned home invigorated and convinced that the United States was "lagging behind the Scandinavian countries and Holland in providing adequate housing for its citizens." His Subcommittee on Housing and Rents produced a series of four reports on cooperative housing abroad and in the United States that contained detailed social and economic information on housing cooperatives in each of the countries visited. The first report, issued in February 1950, discussed Swedish postwar cooperative housing developments and their use of prefabricated housing to increase the pace of production and reduce costs, in much the same manner that Westbrook's Mutual Division had done in 1940–1942.[39]

Senator Maybank also benefited from his European trip. It taught him that "cooperatives do work in housing," making it possible for wage earners to "obtain substantial savings." He found no basis for the charges made by opponents that commercial home building and real estate would be seriously threatened if financial incentives were offered to housing cooperatives and other noncommercial entities for the construction of affordable housing. European cooperatives had not "usurped the entire housing field" and European commercial residential development continued.

The insights gleaned from overseas had encouraged Maybank and Sparkman to meet with HHFA head Raymond Foley and Truman aide David Lloyd in November 1949 to discuss the legislative implications of their fact finding. On December 14 Sparkman told members of the National Association of Housing Officials what he had learned and said he was "hopeful" for the passage of "workable" middle-income housing legislation.[40]

In early January 1950, just before the opening of the second session of the Eighty-first Congress, Senators Sparkman and Maybank and Representative Brent Spence (D-KY), a New Deal and Fair Deal supporter and chairman of the House Banking and Currency Committee, visited the White House. They came looking for the president's support for a series of proposed substitute amendments intended to "perfect and improve" Title III of Sparkman's middle-income housing bill. They also sought to "bring [the bill] more in line with the administration's housing views."[41] Maybank captured Truman's attention when he proposed the Cooperative Corporation to offer financial and technical assistance to housing cooperatives in place of the program of direct loans originally proposed. The president liked the "fully self-sustaining" concept because the Cooperative Corporation would protect the investment of public funds by requiring borrowers to pay into a restricted fund set aside to cover potential losses.[42]

With its modifications, the Cooperative Corporation was included in Sparkman's middle-income housing bill, which became the administration's Middle-Income Housing Bill. According to Drew Pearson, there was "considerable feeling" in Truman's voice whenever he spoke of this bill, which also strengthened the FHA's ability to insure private mortgage funds obtained by housing cooperatives. In Truman's estimation, it made for "a well-rounded housing program." Traditional home ownership was protected for the upper economic third, and more public housing would soon be available for the lowest economic third. The options open to the middle third would gradually increase as the Cooperative Corporation became operational.[43]

During his January 4, 1950, Annual Message to Congress on the State of the Union, Truman explained that now that the "groundwork for relieving the plight of lower-income families" had been laid by the Housing Act of 1949, it was time to address the needs of struggling middle-income families. He called on Congress to pass a bill authorizing a "vigorous program" of aid to housing cooperatives and other sponsors of nonprofit, affordable housing.[44] A few days later, in his Annual Budget Message to the Congress, Truman acknowledged that it would take time for cooperative home ownership to become firmly rooted or established among middle-income families. As he put it, cooperative housing had to be viewed initially "as experimental . . . [and could not] be expected to "attain a large volume in 1951." The president maintained that with "proper federal leadership and assistance," cooperative housing could be successful in providing middle-income families with "good housing at costs within their means."[45]

## Maybank's Public-Private Approach Fails to Appease the Opposition

Confident of backing from the Truman White House, Senator Maybank and Representative Spence returned from the holiday recess in January 1950 ready to "supplement" the low-income public housing bill passed during the first session of the Eighty-First Congress with a broad program of middle-income housing aid for the "butcher, the baker, [and] the candlestick maker—the clerks in the stores, the men who put gasoline in your car, the neighborhood grocer, the rank and file of labor, [and] the average young veteran." On January 7, 1950, companion Senate and House bills were introduced proposing the creation of the Cooperative Corporation to broaden the limited choices offered by the commercial real estate market to middle-income householders. The families of the bank clerk and the veteran might welcome the chance to stay in familiar city neighborhoods once Cooperative Corporation–backed cooperatives helped revitalize them with well-constructed and well-designed garden dwellings with as many as two, three, or four bedrooms sufficient for a consumer-oriented lifestyle.[46]

The new public-private approach embodied in Title III failed to appease the bill's critics. The *Washington Post* claimed that the bill was evidence that federal "welfare" spending would increase during 1951 despite the administration's claims to the contrary.[47] Senate Banking and Currency Committee hearings began on January 12, 1950, with the testimony of HHFA head Raymond Foley. He stated that the bill would remove the single biggest stumbling block faced by labor and other organizations—finding private sector funding for the construction of cooperative housing. The "much needed" measure would "round out our programs." Not surprisingly, Foley, who had been never been an advocate of cooperative housing, showed no passion for the cooperative loan program and failed to offer convincing testimony that there was a compelling need for cooperative housing for middle-income families whose neighborhoods were deteriorating or targeted for renewal or infrastructure improvements.[48]

Fearful of any measure that encouraged middle-income families to seek noncommercial market alternatives, Horace Russell, general counsel for the U.S. Savings and Loan League, called the bill "uneconomic and unrealistic" and "pure socialism to the extent of two billion dollars." Sparkman angrily retorted that the bill's supporters wanted merely to expand home ownership, not "mislead the people down the road to socialism."[49]

The Maybank-Sparkman Bill suffered a major setback on January 16, 1950, when Thomas McCabe, chairman of the Federal Reserve Bank Board, testified to the likelihood that it would contribute to inflation. Determined to keep housing cooperatives from gaining access to noncommercial financing, he recommended a "full and fair trail on an experimental basis with financing on the FHA plan, rather than the establishment of the new Government lending institution on a permanent basis."[50] The *Washington Post* played up McCabe's inflationary claim and reiterated its support for private funding. The federal government could not afford to provide cooperative housing aid through the Cooperative Corporation, it said, because "federal expenses for worthy causes" had already "piled up at a shocking rate."[51]

Concerned about the effect that growing cooperative home ownership might have on the middle-income real estate market and the demand for home mortgages, the U.S. Chamber of Commerce announced that it anticipated an adverse economic impact on housing if the Cooperative Corporation was established.[52] Cincinnati's William A. Reckman of the American Bankers Association charged that the middle-income housing bill would result in the "socialization of credit and the ultimate destruction of the private enterprise system." He predicted a "huge bureaucracy . . . [and] inflationary pressures" resulting from the creation of the proposed Cooperative Corporation.[53] Harry Held of the National Association of Mutual Savings Banks agreed, stating that direct loans to housing cooperatives were "unsound and unwarranted."[54]

Clarke Daniel, an African American housing developer and president of the Home Builders Association of Metropolitan Washington, argued that low-interest government loans for cooperatives would result in a "vast surplus of rental units on the market" followed by "foreclosure after foreclosure." Then, he said, the "taxpayer will get it in the neck because Uncle Sam has insured" the projects. Daniel also depicted the Democrat-sponsored measure as a "vote-getting scheme aimed directly at the elimination of the FHA" and wondered why cooperative housing beneficiaries should receive "special privileges." Daniel spoke for both white and African American builders, who feared that the demand for both single-family dwellings and rental units would be adversely affected by middle-income housing cooperatives. He recognized that the pending bill would subsidize cooperatives sponsored by unions and other groups that had one foot in the private market and the other in the public market. As a private developer of housing for affluent people of color, he did not welcome competition with his for-profit ventures.[55]

Such criticisms took their toll. On February 10, 1950, the Senate Banking and Currency Committee voted seven to six to delay action on the Middle-Income Housing Bill until February 23 so the Committee could weigh its potential economic drawbacks and secure additional opinions from the Federal Reserve Board. Monsignor O'Grady, quoted in the *Washington Post*, was convinced that the two-week delay "gave the building industry additional time to fight the measure . . . [and meant] serious trouble" for the bill's passage.[56]

Other signs pointed in the same gloomy direction for the Cooperative Corporation and Title III of the Middle-Income Housing Bill. Senator John Bricker, former Ohio governor, 1944 Republican vice-presidential nominee who had been elected to the Senate in 1946, and opponent of the Fair Deal, was willing to support cooperative housing only if it would result in the elimination of the low-income public housing program. On February 11, 1950, he announced his intention to offer an amendment to strike Title III from the bill because it would open vast "possibilities for political favoritism" for the Truman administration.[57]

The *Washington Post* reinforced Bricker's attack on the Cooperative Corporation by putting developer Clarke Daniel back in the spotlight. Daniel scoffed at Raymond Foley's claim that cooperatives could build housing at lower costs than commercial home builders, and he offered $5,000 to the charity of Foley's choice if a cooperative could build a unit at less cost than Daniel could.[58] Daniel also claimed to have found ten "bad points" in the bill, including the absence of "grassroots demand for such a proposal for huge public spending." The president and his fellow Democrats backed cooperative housing, Daniel charged, as "a payoff to rich labor unions, topped by the CIO, and [to] professional lobbyists on the payrolls of some veterans' organizations," not because the issue enjoyed popular support.[59]

Daniel argued that another "bad point" of the bill involved the future maintenance and upkeep of cooperative housing. Communities of cooperative home owners he claimed, could not "hope for American standards of service, maintenance, recreational facilities and other basic factors enjoyed by private home owners and tenants in private apartments." Instead, they would have to "cut their own grass, repair the boiler breaks, sweep their own corridors, haul trash—all things that are automatically provided by the private enterprise system." And, he added, many cooperative residents would refuse do to "their share" of this maintenance work, leading to the creation of a shoddy neighborhood.[60]

The *Washington Post* not only publicized Daniel's complaints but also stated that the nation's leading real estate, home-building, and banking firms and organizations were united in their opposition to the proposed Cooperative Corporation. NAREB, the Mortgage Bankers' Association, the U.S. Savings and Loan League, and the National Association of Home Builders were all against the bill, raising questions about how many middle-income householders stood to benefit from it and about the effectiveness of cooperative housing associations in creating cost savings. *Home Builders Monthly* called the expenditure of so much time on "such a poor piece of legislation" an "American tragedy." Congress's job, it asserted, was to liberalize the terms for FHA mortgage insurance available to housing cooperatives that secured private sector financing—nothing more or less.[61]

Given the lineup of well-financed real estate, home-building, and banking interests opposed to Title III, it is hardly surprising that the Federal Reserve Board, as one observer put it, "passed a cold-water sponge over the Administration's 'middle-income' housing bill." the board's chairman, Thomas McCabe, told the Senate Banking and Currency Committee that the Cooperative Corporation's 3 percent interest would give an unfair advantage to housing cooperatives because it was a lower rate than that for VA- and FHA-insured loans. He reiterated the need to confine federal aid to FHA mortgage insurance.[62]

Supporters of the bill reacted furiously to McCabe's statements, particularly because the bill did not set the rate of interest but offered a way for its determination.[63] McCabe faced "two solid hours of questioning" by Senator Paul Douglas (D-IL), who demanded to know why McCabe and the Federal Reserve Board considered the $2 billion that would ultimately be made available to the Cooperative Corporation inflationary but not the $3.25 billion provided in the same bill for the FHA. He speculated that the FHA had outlived its usefulness, an observation that was shared by Westbrook and others.[64]

Senator Sparkman, who understood the damage that McCabe's testimony had done to the prospects for Title III, emphasized that the proposed Cooperative Corporation would begin operations on a modest scale. The $300 million lent during the first year of its operation would build an estimated 35,000 units at a cost of about $8,000 each. He estimated that the funds available would allow it to make forty- to sixty-year low-interest mortgages to about seventy middle-income housing cooperatives (not individuals)—less than two per state.[65]

On February 23 the Senate Banking and Currency Committee voted nine to four to report the more modest bill out with Title III still intact. Its report went out of its way and at some length (forty-two pages) to mollify critics of middle-income urban cooperative housing, especially rabid antisocialists and fervent opponents of racial integration, particularly among southern Democrats who could kill the proposal if they wished. The Cooperative Corporation would obtain its initial working capital when $100 million of capital stock was purchased with public funds. When $50 million was raised through private sale of stock, the government stock would begin to be retired until the entire sum was returned to the federal treasury, after which the corporation would become entirely private. The report emphasized that the Cooperative Corporation would operate in much the same way that the FHA mortgage insurance system and the federal home loan banks facilitated private investment in housing cooperatives.

The committee also compared the advance of funds to the Cooperative Corporation to those that Congress had made available to the Home Owners' Loan Corporation when economic depression threatened the loss of millions of homes to mortgage foreclosure. The Cooperative Corporation idea, its report said, rested on "more than 15 years' experience with the Federal Housing Administration and the Federal home loans," two programs widely recognized as "successful means of governmental assistance to private enterprise."[66] It estimated that roughly 60 percent of the prospective prime Title III families lived in New York City, Washington, Baltimore, Newark, Philadelphia, Chicago, and Los Angeles, and that 40 percent of that total lived in just three metropolitan areas, New York, Baltimore, and Washington. To appease coalitions of white downtown interest groups and suburbanites who wanted to clear slums but were leery of public housing, the committee's report stressed that cooperative housing would address the high cost of family rentals, a situation that presented "almost insuperable obstacles in the way of such redevelopment programs."[67]

Committee chairman Burnet Maybank emphasized that cooperative housing's most fertile ground was in specialized big-city housing markets in New York and Washington and, to a lesser extent, in northeastern or southern border cities. In making this statement, he pointedly omitted deep South cities, including two with notoriously poor housing conditions of which he was quite aware—Charleston and New Orleans. He did so doubtless as a means of reassuring certain of his colleagues that cooperative housing, especially in racially integrated communities, posed no threat to their turf because of unfavorable market scenarios.

Another main point of the committee's report was that Title III would provide "technical advice and assistance" to housing cooperatives to ensure the establishment of viable and stable not-for-profit corporations. Maybank and Sparkman included this provision and stressed it to reassure skeptics that the Cooperative Corporation would insist on high standards of planning and architecture and provide advance funds to secure the advice of financial advisers, architects, and planning consultants in their effort to comply with planning regulations, zoning requirements, and building codes.[68]

Four Committee members opposed the bill, including William J. Fulbright (D-AR), who issued a terse statement echoing McCabe's concerns about inflation and fiscal responsibility; John Bricker (R-OH); Homer E. Capehart (R-IN); and A. Willis Robertson (D-VA), who was socially and fiscally conservative and closely allied to the political organization assembled by Senator Harry Byrd. Bricker had already gained attention by urging the racial integration of federal housing programs, a ploy to keep southerners from voting for the Housing Act of 1949. Now, he, Capeheart, and Robertson, in an eight-page statement, waved the red flag. There would always be middle-income families "priced out of the market" for housing unless the United States became like "socialist Great Britain" and subsidized "the housing of two-thirds of the population." After all, he and his fellow dissenters asserted, middle-income families who practiced "thrift and initiative" managed to become home owners and buy "television sets and other expensive products" without federal subsidies. If Congress created the Cooperative Corporation, it "would be just as logical for the Federal Government," to help strapped middle-income families by establishing "nonprofit purchasing corporations to sell cars on the basis of no money down and a 3-percent loan for the maximum life of the car."[69]

## Pulling Out all the Stops to Defeat Cooperative Housing Aid

During the heated debate over the middle-income bill on the Senate floor, Republican Senators Irving Ives of New York and Charles Tobey of New Hampshire offered a substitute amendment for Title III that would have assigned the FHA a central role in the cooperative housing program. However, because Sparkman and Maybank did not seize on it as an opportunity to work out a bipartisan agreement, it failed.[70] On March 11, 1950, Democratic National Committee chairman William M. Boyle Jr. showed just how far apart the two parties stood on the issue of federal loans to housing cooperatives when he urged his party members to stand firm against the "real estate lobby and Republican opponents of this measure."[71] In response Douglas Whitlock, chairman of the Building Products Institute, warned a group of legislators assembled at the Congressional Country Club that Title III had the potential to "destroy our mortgage system." If Congress, he added, did not strike it from the bill, it would be guilty of "encouraging people to walk away from their present obligations and the American way of living to join these collectivist groups," such as the CIO, which Whitlock regarded as the instigators of the Cooperative Corporation scheme.[72]

The House Appropriations Committee helped to erode what was left of support for Title III with the March 13 release of an FHA report predicting that 1951 would be a banner year for housing construction. Home builders across the country, the report said, were planning to increase the number of dwellings produced in the "lower-priced rental and lower-priced sales field." The implication was that few middle-income families would need or want mutual home ownership when many could take the path to fee-simple ownership with a long-term mortgage.[73] In any case, a "stiff floor fight" was anticipated by Representative Albert Rains (D-AL), who expressed doubt that the bill would pass even if what the *Washington Post* called the "disparity of interest rates between loans for cooperative purposes and those for veterans and others under the FHA" was rectified.[74]

On March 15, 1950, the day of the Senate vote on the bill, the *Washington Post* ran two pieces intended to derail Title III. According to Ysabel and Robert Rennie, authors of a regularly featured economics column, "However well intended . . . [the bill was a] clumsy attempt to get middle-income housing . . . [having] unsettling effects on our control of credit, the costs of building, our debt structure, and on the whole [international] debt structure."[75] On the editorial page, the *Post* reinforced the idea that the Cooperative Corporation was not needed because traditional home ownership opportunities had trickled down to the average wage earner. In the final analysis, the bill presented the "danger of upsetting the mortgage market with overly liberal credit pushed out through Government guarantees."[76]

The campaign waged against Title III had its desired effect. On a motion by Republican John Bricker, the Senate voted forty-three to thirty-eight in favor of eliminating it. Truman aide David D. Lloyd later said that the "real estate lobby did a terrific pressure job . . . [and] distinguished itself" with the number of editorials against Title III it was able to get into the press such as the *Washington Post*, *Life*, and *Newsweek*.[77] The Senate passed the bill after the Title III provisions calling for the creation of the Cooperative Corporation were stricken.[78]

## The House Vote on the Middle-Income Bill

Cooperative housing advocates knew they faced an uphill battle to keep the House from following suit on its version of the Middle-Income Housing Bill. AFL president William Green urged representatives to stand firm against the real estate lobby, and CIO affiliate unions barraged House members with letters and telegrams urging them to back the bill's cooperative housing provisions.[79] Green was interviewed by Sparkman and Representatives Albert M. Cole (R-TN) and Frank Buchanan (R-PA) on Washington's WQQW radio station on March 18, just days before the House vote, and House Speaker Sam Rayburn conferred by telephone with President Truman in Key West. Truman aide David Lloyd had advised the president that if he and the Democrats took pains to prevent the bill from becoming a "partisan issue," there was still hope that House Republicans in northern states such as Wisconsin might support it. Events soon revealed that Lloyd was overly optimistic.[80]

On March 20, 1950, Truman sent a telegram to Congress the day before the House debate on the bill commenced, urging its adoption. The bill, he wrote, offered "great benefits to the country which transcend any partisan considerations" by expanding home ownership opportunities for families whose income fell between $2,800 and $4,400,[81] adding that it would "stimulate home ownership through the use of cooperative methods to achieve savings in the cost of financing and construction methods which have long been successfully used in other fields of endeavor."[82]

Ignoring the president's request, Jesse P. Wolcott (R-MI) engineered the House "assault" on the bill, defending his opposition to Title III by arguing that it was "inflationary . . . discriminatory . . . socialistic and a threat to free enterprise."[83] On March 22, 1950, the House voted 218 to 155 in a roll call vote to strike Title III, and with that the prospect for the Cooperative Corporation ended. Wolcott was able to convince 137 Republicans and 81 Democrats to vote with him against Title III; 141 Democrats, 13 Republicans, and 1 American Labor Party member voted for it.[84]

The press presented the failure of Title III's passage as a black eye for the Truman administration. The *New York Times* described the defeat of the "pioneering cooperative program" as a "crushing blow to the Truman Fair Deal program."[85] The *Los Angeles Times* called it a "thumping setback" for the president, one of the "worst defeats the administration has suffered," and reported that Truman had "tried hard to save the cooperative program" but proved no match for the opposition. "Almost to a man, Republicans opposed the coop plan, and they were joined by a sizable block of Democrats, mostly from the South."[86]

## What Went Wrong for the Cooperative Corporation

Florence Parker, the Labor Department's housing expert, tried to put the best face on the outcome for Title III, but understood the full impact of its elimination. As long as federal aid emphasized loan guarantees over low-interest long-term loans, cooperative housing would never form the basis of the newly reconstituted noncommercial market as Maybank and Sparkman had envisioned it. Cooperative housing would remain on the real estate market's economic margins.

The failure of the Cooperative Corporation had implications for the urban renewal program. Passage of the original version of Title III might have resulted in a more balanced public-private approach to the burgeoning growth of the suburbs and the deterioration of central city neighborhoods and commercial and manufacturing districts. If housing cooperatives backed by the Cooperative Corporation had been invited to collaborate with government agencies, other nonprofits, and for-profit commercial developers such as James Rouse, who dominated the urban renewal process in U.S. cities in the 1950s and 1960s, there might have been more grassroots buy-in for the beleaguered federal program.

Cities that received federal urban renewal aid would have been able to rely on the Cooperative Corporation to help them stabilize targeted neighborhoods by working with local residents to plan redevelopment projects that included opportunities for middle-income families to cooperatively own an affordable new or newly refurbished dwelling or garden apartment. Middle-income housing cooperatives that enjoyed Cooperative Corporation funds and expertise would have built housing of quality, size, and design sufficient to persuade families to stay in centrally located urban neighborhoods. The Cooperative Corporation would have given cooperative home ownership a chance to become a "normal" and healthy part of American urban life and not a socialistic threat to the interests of private real estate financiers. If the amount of financial aid Congress would have allowed the Cooperative Corporation to offer were to increase over time, cooperative ownership might have become the housing choice of moderate-income households who found traditional ownership too risky.

## Cooperative Housing after the Failure of the Cooperative Corporation

Following the defeat of Title III, some advocates kept up the fight, although briefly and ineffectively. The AFL, the CIO, the Cooperative League of the USA, and the National Public Housing Conference in 1950 helped to create what they hoped would become a stronger organizational apparatus for the cause, the National Association of Housing Cooperatives.[87] Senator Sparkman continued to push the idea of the Cooperative Corporation in speeches to liberal organizations such as the Women's National Democratic Club, but he did not launch another legislative campaign to secure federal loans for housing cooperatives.[88]

Lawrence Westbrook also gave up hope for the Cooperative Corporation and the idea of direct federal aid to cooperatives. As a close friend of Sam Rayburn, he worked hard behind the scenes in the failed fight in 1949–1950, but now devoted most of his time to Democratic Party politics. He served briefly as assistant chairman of the Democratic National Party, where he sought to increase the level of "harmony" among Democrats in Congress in part by seeking "their advice and counsel on a day-to-day basis."[89] He lost that job, however, in a scandal involving charges of influence peddling to secure profit for a company he ran by abetting the sale of Portuguese tungsten to the government.[90] The *Washington Post* called him a "five percenter" and a prime and "depressing bit of evidence of the moral vacuum in which so many men of influence in Washington move," and Dwight D. Eisenhower, in his 1952 presidential campaign, cited the Westbrook case as an example of "the sort of crookedness [that] goes on and on in Washington." Westbrook felt compelled to cut back his crusade for direct federal aid for housing cooperatives, and for the next eight years he devoted considerable time and money to his legal vindication. This goal was achieved in 1960 when the U.S. Court of Claims unanimously ruled that Westbrook had not engaged in wrongdoing and ruled in his favor concerning the breach of the original contract.[91]

The Housing Act of 1950 strengthened the ability of the FHA to insure cooperative housing mortgages through the creation of the Section 213 program. The FHA established a Cooperative Housing Division in its Washington office and organized the staff into legal, land planning, architectural, technical, and management advisory sections. The division was advised by a "public interest group" to include representatives from labor unions, veterans' groups, community groups, and housing associations, but did little to promote cooperative home ownership to middle-income families.[92]

Had Title III of the Housing Act of 1950 been passed, cooperative housing might have played a far more important role in urban renewal not only in New York City but in smaller cities as well. Plans for cooperative housing developments containing a mix of apartment types—singles, doubles, triples, and even quadruples—were included in a number of early Title I urban redevelopment grants in New York, such as the ambitious Morningside Heights project in Manhattan, which involved the New York City Housing Authority, Columbia University, and a number of prominent organizations. But elsewhere in the nation there was little interest in middle-income cooperative housing. During the 1950s and 1960s, the United Housing Foundation and a small group of housing advocacy organizations developed middle-income housing cooperatives with private funds guaranteed by the FHA under Section 213, but the vast majority of these projects were in New York City. If nonprofit or limited-dividend housing corporations had been able to seek loans, loan guarantees, and technical assistance from the proposed Cooperative Corporation, middle-income housing cooperatives might had been established in other cities where the market demand was high, such as Boston, Washington, Chicago, Los Angeles, and San Francisco.[93]

## Lanham Disposition Ends with an Emphasis on Mutual Housing

In April 1950 Congress amended the Lanham Act to allow the sale of defense housing developments to mutual housing associations. One month later, Section 607 was added to the act, making possible the sale of defense housing to mutual groups with "no down payments, 45 years' amortization, and 3 percent interest."[94] That same year, the Department of Labor reported that thirty-four wartime housing projects with a combined total of about 15,000 dwelling units had been or were about to be sold to mutual associations. By January 1951 five of the eight pilot projects—Greenmont Village, Walnut Grove, Avion Village, Dallas Park, and Winfield Park—had "successfully negotiated a purchase contract." The Audubon Park Mutual Housing Association was still leasing the community from the Public Housing Administration (PHA) because of a dispute over sewage disposal, and Bellmawr Park and Pennypack Woods were as yet under PHA management because of a lack of waivers of compliance with local building codes.[95]

Attorney M. H. Goldstein, described as an "able and emphatic speaker," waged a prolonged campaign on behalf of Bellmawr Park residents who were committed to the Mutual Plan. He forced HFFA head Raymond Foley and his staff to concede that the PHA was "not bound to make a cash sale" and could still legally extend the promised mortgage to Bellmawr Park's mutual housing association despite Public Regulation No. 1. This important concession notwithstanding, sales negotiations dragged on and were temporarily suspended by the 1950 freeze on housing disposition prompted by the outbreak of the Korean War. The sales process went on for months, and some residents grew discouraged and abandoned the cause of mutual ownership. The defectors, who fruitlessly hoped to convince the PHA to sell the dwellings on an individual basis, were nearly successful in derailing years of negotiations and keeping the mutual association from meeting the required percentage of resident participation. Ultimately, however, the mutual associations at both Bellmawr Park and Pennypack Woods got their promised mortgages, in 1952.[96]

The PHA expected the Section 213 program and the 1950 Lanham Act amendment to result in an increase in FHA mortgage underwriting for mutual housing developments. By June 1952 ten projects had been sold to mutual associations with private financing. The rate of interest paid varied from 3 to 4.5 percent. According to a Bureau of Labor Statistics report, the source of the funds included "a regular lending agency, a savings bank, a life insurance company, a trust company, and a public employees' retirement fund."[97]

To speed up the pace of the disposition program, federal housing officials became more willing to give mortgages to mutual housing associations, and by

1956 the PHA or its predecessor agencies had extended mortgages to fifty-nine of them.[98] The associations negotiated different terms with the PHA depending on the appraised value of the real estate, the length of the amortization period, the size of the down payment, the rate of interest, and other factors. PHA officials became so eager to conclude the disposition of Lanham housing that they began financing the sale of communities of temporary construction. This decision likely worried Westbrook, who had consistently emphasized the need for housing cooperatives to adopt high standards of quality in design and construction and, up until the Winfield Park scandal that resulted in the need for thousands of dollars to repair shoddy workmanship, had managed to steer clear of "flimsy construction in purely war-born places, which were likely to be abandoned after the war."[99]

In 1956 residents of a temporary defense housing community in Glenolden, Pennsylvania known as Glendale Heights formed the mutual Glendale Heights Ownership Association. After making a down payment equivalent to $350 per dwelling unit, the association purchased the community from the PHA for $3 million with a twenty-five year mortgage at 4 percent interest.[100] As was the case with numerous similar Lanham communities, the effort to organize the Glendale Heights mutual association was filled with tension and melodrama.

Resident George Damon recalled that when the community voted to purchase the property from the federal government on a mutual basis, federal housing officials were granting first preference to veterans and second preference to residents. Representatives of the Veterans of Foreign Wars and other local veterans' organizations were interested in obtaining Glendale Heights on a mutual basis for their members to the exclusion of the original residents. Even though he was a WWII veteran, Damon opposed the initiative. He said, "I'm all for veterans, but I had just got done fighting a war against throwing people out of their homes." It did not make sense to him that those who had served on the war's battlefields should displace the veterans of the industrial home front.[101] When the veterans' group failed to assemble the $87,000 needed for a down payment, Glendale Heights' residents swung into action and convinced roughly two-thirds of their neighbors to join the effort. A key element in securing community support for the sale was the PHA's willingness to offer a mortgage to the ownership association.[102]

A lack of affordable housing options convinced many skeptical residents to join the mutual effort. Those who elected not to purchase a share were given notice that they had to move. William Hall recalled that over 300 families refused to join the mutual housing association at Success Village in Bridgeport, Connecticut, and board members spent "close to a year in court" evicting them. Ultimately, said Hall, some realized that they had made a mistake and tried to come back. When they were told that the project was sold out, Hall "tried not to gloat."[103]

Mutual housing advocates encountered resistance from outside and within their community. In 1952 when Stan Sheenan stood on the bed of a flatbed truck urging residents to "stand together" so Pennypack Woods could be purchased under the Mutual Plan, some residents "cheered, some booed, [and] two pitched eggs," according to one report.[104] In 1955 the mutual organization that formed to buy two adjoining Connecticut defense housing projects, Success Park and Canaan Village, and administer them as a single entity to be known as Success Village became "demoralized" as negotiations dragged on year and after year. A highly publicized challenge from Charles DuCharme of the Success Village Veterans-Tenants Committee delayed the sale. The sale was completed after the residents who backed the Mutual Plan hired a consulting firm, Federal Cooperative Housing, Inc., and retained law firms in Bridgeport and Washington.[105]

Residents who backed the sale of their homes under the Mutual Plan clashed with each other over the terms and implications of the letters, contracts, manuals, and other directives received by their legal and financial advisers and the PHA. Many found it difficult to put aside their many differences and bond around the shared goal of mutual ownership of their homes. What made things more difficult was that the dwellings in some communities did not conform to the personal expectations and beliefs of many concerning what a house and its surrounding neighborhood should look like and who should live there. Residents were better able to put their differences aside and come together in communities where all worked together and belonged to the same union. At Kramer Homes in Center Line, Michigan, a mutual housing supporter told the local news daily that the residents were so unified by the goal of mutual housing that an opponent "could not drive a wedge between them."[106]

It is possible that when residents of Woodstock Homes in Alameda, California, observed how freely accusations of communist and other un-American sympathies were made against those who supported the mutual sale of Channel Heights and other communities, they decided to be proactive, naming their successful, two-year mutual housing campaign "Operation Democracy."[107] On the East Coast, opponents rallied against mutual housing as a "form of socialized living." For example, the Pennypack Woods Civic Association claimed that the community was "sick to the core of fake deadlines, high pressure methods, half-truths, and downright lies" propagated by the Pennypack Woods Home Ownership Association and its left-leaning membership in their bid to buy the community under the Mutual Plan. On June 20, 1952, just days before the controversial sale was to close, the *Philadelphia Daily News* alleged that the mutual group's leader had been involved with a group tied to a Chinese organization deemed subversive by the U.S. House Committee on Un-American Activities. This was Oliver Haskell, the former manager of Banning Homes, a defense housing project administered by the Los Angeles County Housing Authority, who had been hired as the director of the Pennypack Woods Home Ownership Association on the recommendation of his former colleague, Drayton Bryant of the Philadelphia Housing Authority. The Philadelphia commander of the Veterans of Foreign Wars and Senator Patrick A. McCarran (D-NV) were among those who demanded a full investigation of the matter, but in the end no probe took place.[108]

The Pennypack Woods Home Ownership Association was permitted to conclude the sale as planned as long as it agreed to sack Haskell even though he professed his innocence. A resident complained nonetheless that the association had exaggerated the level of resident support and had failed to "get rid of Oliver Haskel [*sic*] . . . [and] stop dealing with Drayton Bryant" as the PHA had required. Mrs. Joseph H. Moore Jr. doubted that the "Communist Tinge" at Pennypack Woods could be "dissolved" even with the removal of the two men. Ultimately, the residents' "voices . . . prevailed against political opposition" and the Home Ownership Association closed the sale of Pennypack Woods on August 1, 1952.[109]

According to Glendale Heights resident George Damon, the problems faced by mutual housing proponents did not end when the purchase was completed. The "first five years were a struggle" because of the residents' lack of experience in administering a cooperative and maintaining a residential community and because of changes in the region's industrial manufacturing base. When the mutual housing association was negotiating the purchase, fifty-eight resident-shareholders were Westinghouse employees who happened to be on strike. Shortly after the strike ended, workers, from two other local firms went on strike, creating more financial uncertainty for the fledgling mutual housing association. "The upshot was we survived," said Damon.[110]

Survival was a theme emphasized by the *Saturday Evening Post* in its 1960 profile of Dayton, Ohio's Overlook Homes, another temporary Lanham community acquired by the residents on a mutual basis at roughly the same time as the Glendale Heights purchase. Overlook Homes could have been the model for Merry Hill, the Detroit defense workers' housing project inhabited by the Kentucky "hillbilly" migrant family in Harriet Arnow's highly acclaimed novel *The Dollmaker*. The *Post* reported that many of Overlook residents shared the experience of migrating from rural Appalachia to work in defense industries. Unified by bonds of color, class, and culture, they organized the mutual housing association, raised the down payment, and, with legal assistance from Attorney Norman E. Routzohn, purchased the community from the PHA on a mutual basis. On completion of the sale, the Overlook Mutual Housing Association immediately began a multiphase project to improve its dwellings by upgrading electrical work, laying better foundations, and improving the community's appearance (see Figure 7.1). In spite of improvements, however, resentment toward the mutual association persisted, as evidenced by nearby property owners who claimed that their real estate values would be higher if the community had been removed as originally planned.[111]

During the first half of the 1950s, when newly formed mutual housing associations were negotiating mortgage agreements with the PHA, Dallas Park became the first and to date the only community built by Westbrook's Mutual Division that rejected the Mutual Plan. Trouble began brewing shortly after the

**Figure 7.1** Overlook Homes in Riverside, Ohio, is one of only a handful of temporary defense housing communities that were sold to residents under the Mutual Plan. In 1960 the *Saturday Evening Post* found that community residents had made a successful transition from tenants to joint owners. Photograph by the author.

departure of the managers, Raymond Holder and Romie Stewart. According to a published report, a lawsuit filed by six shareholder-residents in 1954 alleged that board of directors president Leslie B. Lester and manager W. F. Elkins Jr. had "illegally offered properties of the corporation for sale in a move to dissolve the corporation." Ultimately, however, the plaintiffs reached a settlement when it was shown that they stood alone in their support for mutual ownership; 294 shareholders voted to "convert" to a "private ownership plan." An unidentified insurance company offered to lend money to shareholders who wished to buy their units, making it possible for the mutual housing association to pay off its $550,054 PHA mortgage.[112] The dissolution of the Dallas Park Mutual Housing Association brought no public commentary from Westbrook or any other mutual housing supporter, but it offered a sobering lesson about how quickly residents would abandon nonprofit housing when faced with possibility they could make money off their homes.

As the 1950s came to a close, the mutual housing associations that had been forced to find a commercial-market mortgage a decade earlier, began to mark their first decade of operation. Western Pennsylvania's Aluminum City Terrace, whose Bauhaus design had created such controversy in 1942, had become one of New Kensington's most socially vibrant neighborhoods. According to a 1957 report in the local *Valley Daily News*, adults, teenagers, and an estimated "1000 children" actively participated in kindergarten, scouting, and other recreational and social events. The *ACT Bulletin* kept residents informed of happenings in the community. Then resident manager Louise Boggs said that there was "nothing more interesting to me than cooperative housing, and I try to devote all my spare time to it."[113]

On July 6, 1958, the *New York Times* announced that disposition of Lanham housing was complete as of June 30, 1958. The last remaining Lanham-funded communities had been sold to "tenant cooperatives that would operate the projects for the benefit of their members."[114] The end of the Lanham disposition process was also noted in housing circles. According to the July 1958 *Journal of Housing*, "It's Official! WWII Housing Program Ended June 30." The liquidation program resulted in $600 million in sales, including sales made to cooperatives, educational institutions, and other nonprofit entities.[115]

## Kennedy Makes Loans to Cooperatives Possible

Although the Maybank-Sparkman-Spence campaign to establish the Cooperative Corporation had failed, it was to have unanticipated consequences. For one, it helped cooperative housing gain legitimacy so that it no longer seemed unusual or experimental. Beginning in the 1960s, various nonprofit and limited-dividend housing initiatives, including cooperatives, were more routinely deemed eligible for federal housing and community development funding. Westbrook responded to the1960 election of Democrat John F. Kennedy as president with enthusiasm in part because the former Massachusetts senator had shown an appreciation for the complexity of the issues facing urban America during his presidential campaign against Vice-President Richard M. Nixon.[116] Kennedy charged that Nixon's "sudden campaign time interest" in housing and urban renewal was "hardly convincing." America's "cities and suburbs require active programs around the clock," he argued, "not promises six weeks before the election." Kennedy laid out a ten-year program to achieve the 1949 national housing goal of a "decent home for every American family." He emphasized to voters that his program would "provide rental as well as sales housing, expand cooperative housing," and encourage "effective rehabilitation of existing homes."[117]

In November 1960, just weeks after Kennedy defeated Nixon, Westbrook sent him a memorandum offering a nine-page analysis of federal housing programs and suggestions for their improvement. He argued that the FHA and certain other programs and agencies created during the Great Depression and the war had outlived their usefulness and were now used to protect home builders and financial institutions from economic loss, doing little to keep failed home owners from creating economically and socially blighted neighborhoods that further destabilized cities. Westbrook reminded Kennedy that cooperative home ownership was a sound, proven alternative path to home ownership for the millions of middle-income Americans who had just helped elect him to office.

Westbrook explained that the FHA insured few cooperative or mutual housing projects because home-building organizations such as the American Association of Home Builders, home lending institutions, and realtors discouraged the practice by creating the "general impression that cooperative housing is a communistic conception, closely akin to the communes of China and the state socialism of Russia." The residents of these cooperatives had to band together to "overcome the obstacles interposed by vested housing interests, including the majority of FHA administrative personnel."[118] In Westbrook's opinion, as he told Kennedy, it was better to use federal funds to increase cooperative housing opportunities than to expand the rental housing market through incentives to speculative developers for the reason that cooperatives could function as social anchors in changing neighborhoods and help middle-income households lower housing construction and financing costs.[119] With the goal of "halting and preventing [the] further growth of slums," Westbrook urged the president-elect to establish an "ad hoc Housing Commission" to frame "new housing legislation" and create a "sound redevelopment plan" that encouraged home ownership.[120]

Westbrook did not suggest that the Kennedy try to convince Congress to authorize establishment of the Cooperative Corporation, despite the claim of attorney David L. Krooth of the Foundation for Cooperative Housing that the high cost of funds on the commercial financial market hampered cooperative housing's ability to contribute to the renewal of America's cities. Instead, in April 1960 Westbrook told members of the National Association of Housing Officials that cooperative housing needed long-term, low-interest federal loans to help "low in come [*sic*] families displaced from urban renewal or even many families with moderate incomes."[121]

In March of 1961, shortly after taking office, Kennedy proposed a "vast" stimulus program for housing to help those struggling through the economic "slump" and to assist cities in their revitalization efforts. He sought to make home ownership more affordable by calling for FHA insurance for forty-year mortgages for low-cost homes that required no down payment. The president wanted the FHA to be authorized to offer 100 percent loan guarantees to cooperatives and nonprofit corporations for the construction or rehabilitation of low and moderate-income housing. He also proposed the creation of a cabinet-level post to oversee programs for housing and urban affairs.[122]

On June 30, 1961, when President Kennedy signed the Housing Act into law, he called it the "most important and far-reaching Federal legislation in the field of housing since the enactment of the Housing Act of 1949." He gave credit for this "opportunity for [a] giant step forward toward better cities and improved housing" to Representative Brent Spence and Senator John Sparkman, who had "shepherded" the bill through the upper chamber. Both had been in Congress in 1950 and, Kennedy noted, remained committed to helping "forgotten families" who did not qualify for public housing and could not afford decent market-rate housing. He expressed hope that the new law would enhance other federal programs that "offer our communities and private builders and lenders the opportunity and the challenge to build the cities of tomorrow where families can live in dignity, free from both the squalor of the slums and the unbroken monotony of suburban sprawl."[123]

The Housing Act of 1961 did not infuse life into the cooperative housing movement to the extent that Westbrook and his backers hoped. This was because it delivered too little too late. The act lacked a provision calling for the establishment of a Cooperative Corporation, and by this time most middle-income household heads, the ideal candidates for cooperative housing, could obtain mortgages. Direct and indirect federal subsidies had made the American Dream of traditional, fee-simple home ownership more affordable and less risky economically than it was in the days when Westbrook, John Green, Walter Reuther, and others first began to seriously advocate the subsidizing of cooperative housing.

By the early 1960s, moreover, members of Congress who in 1950 had regarded the proposed Cooperative Corporation as a threat to the profitability of the commercial market no longer worried that any FHA cooperative housing program, no matter how generous, was going to lure many middle-income households away from the commercial market. Home builders, bankers, and realtors were confident that demand for cooperative aid would remain largely confined to specialized housing markets in New York City and a small handful of other cities. There was no longer any credible threat that many middle-income families would abandon the commercial market to pursue cooperative or other noncommercial market options. Realtors and home builders encouraged wage earners to put aside the fear of debt that had plagued their Depression-scared parents and accept the commercial market mortgage as the standard route to home ownership.[124]

## Secretary George Romney Returns to Cooperative Housing

President Richard M. Nixon appointed George Romney as Secretary of Housing and Urban Development (HUD) in 1969, five years after Westbrook's January 1964 death.[125] The former automobile executive and Michigan governor secured the adoption of a program similar to Westbrook's mutual housing plan, called Operation Breakthrough. Romney's scheme consisted of five parts: AFL-CIO support, prefabricated "modular" housing, comprehensive community planning, modern design, and cooperative ownership. HUD tested the concept in several cities, including Seattle, Washington, and Kalamazoo, Michigan, but the pilot projects failed to live up to expectations and saddled their host communities with dwellings that were poorly designed and costly to maintain. Since this failure, no federal administration has taken up the legacy of Westbrook's mutual housing ideas.[126]

There was a brief time between the early 1930s and the early 1950s when cooperative housing could have become the United States' "new housing economy." But the 1950 proposal for the establishment of the Cooperative Corporation remains the high-water mark of public effort to seed the growth of low- and moderate-income housing cooperatives in urban neighborhoods. Federal, state, and local housing and redevelopment officials during this time needed every tool at their disposal to stem the tide of central city decline and runaway suburban sprawl. Cooperative housing could have been one of the most effective ways of handling these aspects of the so-called urban crisis, but the staunch and unremitting opposition to the idea from the commercial real estate industry, abetted by Cold War and anti-communist rhetoric, ended any threat of federal activism in the great game of urban real estate manipulation.

# Epilogue

The communities of manufactured dwellings built between 1971 and 1973 as part of HUD secretary George Romney's Operation Breakthrough did not spark a revival of interest in cooperative housing. The ill-fated experimental program discouraged further federal involvement in the creation of housing cooperatives. Across the United States, however, in the early twenty-first century, thirty-seven mutual housing associations are flourishing. They remain, for the most part, places where self-reliance and individualism strike a sensible balance, places where, according to a *New York Times* reporter, people "pitch in" for the welfare of their personal community.[1]

Until very recently, most of the mutual housing associations did their best to remain in the shadows and out of public view. In 1957 William Hall, president of the board of directors at Success Village in Bridgeport, Connecticut, predicted that as a "pilot co-op project for the country," his community would be studied by federal housing officials to determine if it would "continue to prove a success."[2] He was mistaken. By the early 1970s most of the mutual housing associations had ceased to publicize or promote themselves and, like many other communities across the country, responded to economic, political, and social change by turning inward.[3] Over time, they adapted the formal policies and procedures mandated or recommended by federal housing officials to secure their financial survival and protect their ability to control their membership. Shareholders passed their shares in the mutual association from one family generation to the next. In the early years, shares that were returned to the corporation were usually quickly purchased by someone who was related to or known by an existing shareholder. Applicants for residence at one of the mutual associations rarely "came in off the street" and almost always had prior knowledge of the community. At age ninety-two, Jean Oliveri recalled that when her husband came home from the service, at the suggestion of his brother, they considered Kramer Homes in Center Line, Michigan, in the hopes of finding a good place to raise their two young sons: "That was 1949. We're still here."[4]

Mutual housing associations also turned inward because most were located in cities that suffered from economic and social decline and environmental degradation as a result of postwar public policy and corporate decision making. When I visited Western Pennsylvania's Electric Heights in 1985, its residents were for the first time confronting the end of more than a century of mining, smelting, forging, and processing of soft coal and heavy metals that had wreaked havoc on their air, soil, and water quality and taken a costly toll on their physical and emotional health and that of others who lived and worked in the Monongahela and Ohio river valleys.[5] Electric Heights and the other mutual housing associations located on Pittsburgh's industrial and commercial periphery were struggling to hold their own economically and socially as industry, commerce, and the residential population migrated out of the old mill towns into suburban areas and beyond. Unemployment and the decline in labor union membership threatened to adversely affect individual participation in mutual housing governance.[6]

In 2014 I tried to connect with or, in many cases, reconnect with all of the communities built during the Roosevelt administration that were sold under the Mutual Plan. Through letters, telephone calls, email messages, and personal visits, I was able to confirm that thirty-five are still in operation (see the Appendix). During this process, I discovered that a few, including Walnut Grove in South Bend, Indiana, had altered their bylaws to permit members to sell their shares on the commercial real estate market.[7] Stonybrook Gardens, a war workers' project in Stratford, Connecticut, that was sold to real estate investors after the war, became a mutual housing association in 1965 with the assistance of federal housing officials. At that time, the nearby Success Village and other Bridgeport-area mutual housing associations had been successfully operating for a decade.[8] In January 2014 western Pennsylvania's Van Buren Mutual Housing Corporation filed for bankruptcy protection. Quindaro Homes in Kansas City, Kansas, and Grandview Acres in Ogden, Utah, were no longer nonprofit corporations. Grandview Acres was converted to condominiums in 2001 after heated community debate.[9] Visitors to the Rosie the Riveter/World War II Home Front National Historic Park in Richmond, California, observe the mutually owned Atchison Village and learn how the city—and its housing market—were transformed by the wartime shipbuilding boom. Quite a few of the mutual communities have become naturally occurring retirement communities, and one has declared itself a "55+ community."[10]

For nearly three-quarters of a century, mutual housing associations have operated with minimal outside assistance, oversight, or notice from local, state, or federal housing officials, or real estate managers and developers. The following sections suggest some of the ways mutual housing associations have both benefited and suffered from the turn inward.

## Community Formation

The creation of social bonds among residents was facilitated by a community's design and layout, a community center, and, in the case of larger projects, a school or commercial center. Sports and recreational programs helped residents who did not work with each other to become acquainted.

In 1945 Columbia University sociologist Robert K. Merton and his Craft Town Study colleagues found "intensive community and political life to an exceptional degree" at Winfield Park. They also found that ideological interest in the mutual ownership concept had subsided fairly quickly. Newcomers sought cheap rent and their lack of zeal for the mutual housing association put them at odds with members of the "pioneer" generation who had lived in Winfield Park since its troubled infancy and admired the CIO for tackling complex economic and political issues such as affordable housing. In 1965 Rutgers University researchers concluded that the scandal surrounding the construction of Winfield Park and the legislative decision to force it to become an independent borough "apparently left an indelible impression on the minds of early inhabitants and upon their neighbors." A "residue of distrust and suspicion" remained two decades later despite a "community spirit . . . [of] an unusually intense nature."[11]

The bonds that existed between neighbors and coworkers were both strengthened and tested by the process of organizing the mutual housing association, completing the necessary paperwork, raising the needed funds, and making a sales offer. In 1957 William Hall of Success Village, two-term president of the board of directors, observed that it was necessary for the "tenants to have faith in the co-op and for the co-op to have faith in the residents." He described Success Village as a "community within a community."[12]

Riverside, Ohio's Overlook Homes, a mutual ownership community, was presented to the readers of the *Saturday Evening Post* in 1960 as a throwback to a time when the values most prized in American society—self reliance and cooperation—were in perfect balance. At Overlook Homes, where, according to one resident, "everyone is working class like me," a shared occupational culture helped residents bridge their local and regional differences.[13] During the early 1980s, when Pennypack Woods in Philadelphia was about to celebrate thirty years of mutual ownership, a reporter described it as an "animation of Norman Rockwell's freckled America, where pesky young boys tug little girls' pigtails, pimply teenagers lift weights in the morning and then accompany grandma to the Saturday matinee and children grow up to become the heads of their own recycled households." Pennypack's residents had created an island community and were "intent on deflecting the glint and glare of the ugly world outside."[14]

In 1982 a *Pittsburgh Press* reporter found a "sense of unity and protectiveness" among the 600 families at the "tightly-knit" Electric Heights. Pearl E. Mock, a seventy-one-year-old widow, regarded the neighbors who were "just a screen door away" as her family because they helped her with the yard and household chores that she was unable to do on her own. At Electric Heights, she said, "we do for each other." Pauline Thompson, who had moved to Electric Heights as a child, said, "I was the happiest person here." Jack W. Moucheron, who was raised in Electric Heights before becoming manager, agreed that it was a "great place to grow up in." Residents were neither in the country nor in the city but had "the best of both worlds." He conceded that growing up with others in such close quarters could be frustrating, but said that such circumstances brought people together to make "a unit."[15]

The mutual housing communities that had elementary schools attracted scores of applications from families with small children. The schools played a vital role in creating a sense of community identity among residents. When an accidental fire destroyed the Winfield Park Elementary School in 1995, the entire community mourned its loss. Long-time manager Paul Grieg told a *New York Times* reporter that the fire was a terrible blow to the community's morale because Winfield Park "does not have a church. It was the hub. It was the very core of the community." The school was eventually rebuilt even though there are far fewer children in Winfield Park now than there were in the 1950s and 1960s.[16]

The architecture, design, and layout of Mutual Plan communities contributed to a sense of community identity that was sometimes, but not always, beneficial. As youths growing up in Walnut Grove during the 1950s and 1960s, Alan Hartwick and Steven Tyler recalled a feeling of us and them; residents of Walnut Grove were both part of and apart from the larger city of South Bend. Similarly, youths raised in Audubon Park were known as "Park Boys" to those from the Borough of Audubon and other outsiders.[17]

## Social Cohesion

Workers and their families were and still are drawn to mutual home ownership by its affordability. In July 1941 shortly after completing a thirty-day sheet metal training course, Ralph McSpadden was hired by the North American Aviation Company. McSpadden and his wife Tommie felt fortunate to secure a two-bedroom apartment at Avion Village for their family. They moved in as soon as it was ready in October 1941 and remained there through their retirement. Tommie McSpadden recalled that she "did not really know all about mutual ownership" in the beginning. "All I knew was that it was inexpensive."[18]

Couples like the McSpaddens soon learned that the low cost of living offered by mutual housing came with strings attached—expectations of community responsibility and participation. Many residents became or chose to remain mutual home owners because of this informal network of assistance and support. Aluminum City Terrace resident Josephine Purpura told the *Pittsburgh Press* in 1983 that the community was a "really nice place to live. It's really nice to know that if something is wrong, you can just knock on a door and someone will help." Neighbor and fellow original shareholder Ray Kennedy agreed. He planned on remaining for the rest of his life, saying, "I have been here for 40 years, and I'll be here for another 40 unless they throw me out."[19] Pat McCreery, an Audubon Park Borough Township clerk who became a shareholder in the Audubon Park Mutual Housing Association in 1957, said, "It's really nice here. It's an excellent place to raise kids because people look out for each other. I've had the same neighbors for thirty years."[20]

Crime rates are low at most of the mutual housing associations, and codes of behavior, particularly for youth, are monitored by the entire community. Rule violations are addressed informally and involve the board of directors only as necessary. In 1989 George Damon, who had lived in Glendale Heights in Delaware County, Pennsylvania for forty-four years, stated that management becomes involved in cases if a family fails to discipline a child engaging in delinquent or antisocial behavior: "The board of directors will tell you, look, either you straighten 'little Johnny' out or we're going to cancel your membership and throw you out of here."[21] In 2007 a twenty-year-old who grew up at Aluminum City Terrace and was presumably "raised by the village" remarked that there was "never any trouble, everyone greets each other, and the most crime we had was when someone [was] siphoning gas."[22]

According to the *Bridgeport Sunday Herald*, Success Park and Canaan Village were "not too different from most public housing projects. . . . [There was] very little evidence that there was any real pride of occupancy" until they became jointly owned by the residents. Within a short time, crime, vandalism, and litter decreased and pride of ownership became evident in its appearance.[23]

Fran Headman, who moved to Pennypack Woods in 1950 and began her tenure as manager in 1976, acknowledged that the "all for one, one for all" philosophy of mutual housing had limited appeal and that cooperative home ownership is not for everybody. Pennypack Woods offered "a good, comfortable way to live," but the cost was more than just the monthly fees. The shareholders owed an obligation to each other and the mutual housing association. The return, according to Headman, is that "people feel secure. Most of the people who live here love it."[24]

Pennypack Woods resident Missy Barth also valued the informal surveillance or monitoring system that functioned in the community mainly to protect children, the elderly, and others who might need assistance. Acknowledging that neighborliness and security come at the cost of a certain amount of anonymity, she said, "People know your business here," which not all residents care for. "We have one common denominator here," said the late Paul Greig, long-serving manager of the Winfield Park Mutual Housing Corporation. "Everybody must work for the community."[25]

In a 2013 blog, Bradley Shane Bowling recalled that his grandparents had lived at Greenmont Village from 1942 until their deaths in the 1990s. During the first six years that his parents were married, his mother and father had lived there as well. As a "child of the village" he and his wife, whose children are grown and gone, got priority in obtaining a share. He fondly recalled playing in the common area. "Don't be surprised if I die there,"[26] he said.

## Architecture and Planning

During the 1940s art and architecture critics and students regarded Aluminum City Terrace as a litmus test of workers' response to modern design. *Task* reported that the redwood siding selected by Gropius and Breuer was disliked by residents who traced their ethnic roots to Southern and Eastern Europe, where "unpainted wood—was like the old county."[27] Ben Fisher, director of research for the CIO's Aluminum Workers Organizing Committee (later the United Steel Workers Union), whose family was one of a handful of white-collar residents, recalled during the 1980s that the dwelling units were too small to accommodate the furniture and home appliances most of his neighbors hoped to acquire.[28]

The *Architectural Forum* found that residents of Aluminum City, the "storm center of one of the most violent controversies over Federal housing," were slowly coming to appreciate the work of the famous Bauhaus architects. There was "growing tenant approval of the project—in the face of outside criticism and in the face of the tenants' own prejudices before living there." One resident said that she was initially put off by modern design but now liked it: "I am just crazy about it. I think it's ideal for the average family."[29] In 1952 the Bureau of Labor Statistics stated that the community, once the "object of derision in a region not so accustomed to the modern style . . . [had] not only become accepted but was a matter of local pride."[30]

Architecture and planning reinforced the goals of mutual housing. "In this community, some of the most perplexing social and civic problems common to modern industrial life have been solved or made less severe," wrote an admirer of Avion Village in Grand Prairie, Texas.[31] The design and orientation of the dwelling units encouraged residents to extend their living space to the outdoors. Debbie Stasulli, a resident of Audubon Park, said in 1998, "It is almost like being down the [Jersey] Shore, where everyone takes their walks at night. We all live very close together in these houses, so we really get to know each other really well."[32]

A resident of Greenmont Village in Kettering, Ohio, said that the community's attributes—"school, church, market, activity center, friends with great character, sports minded, school honors, and a team atmosphere"—positively shaped her childhood. She and her fellow Greenmont Villagers "had it all."[33] The shared green space was particularly important in forging community bonds, especially among young people. A former Kramer Homes resident fondly recalled living in a "true neighborhood" from 1965 to 1977. There were "lots of kids to play with" and the field in the middle of the community was full of daily activity. "Red Rover . . . [and] many baseball, football, and games of war were played in that field . . . until the street lights came on" and he was expected to return home.[34]

## Administrative Responsibilities

Under Westbrook's Mutual Plan, the first generation of mutual housing associations moved incrementally toward mutual home ownership by leasing and later purchasing their communities from the federal government. During the leasing phase, each mutual housing association had a board of directors made up of resident, community, and federally appointed members.[35] Most of the Lanham projects sold to mutual housing associations did not have the benefit of the leasing phase to ease the transition from public housing to mutual home ownership with its mortgage and real estate taxes. Residents were expected to immediately pitch in and serve on the board if elected and on other committees or to volunteer in community organizations such as fire companies.

Some mutual housing associations benefited from the aid of labor union officials who assisted with federal legal and financial compliance. The residents of Channel Heights and several other Los Angeles defense housing developments were advised by attorney George Atkinson, and those in Greater Pittsburgh were helped by J. Alfred Wilner. Some mutual associations spent years negotiating with the federal government. Those that did not form until the early 1950s, such as Electric Heights, were often able to wrap up negotiations fairly quickly largely because there was precedent to follow and federal housing officials were under pressure from Congress to complete the disposition process. In September 1956, shortly after receiving word from the Public Housing Administration (PHA) that it was going to sell Electric Heights, a group of residents met to establish a mutual housing association and elect a provisional board of directors. The following year, the association was granted a twenty-two-year mortgage at 4.75 percent interest.[36]

Federal housing officials did not require or encourage the newly-formed mutual housing associations to collaborate, nor did they arrange mentoring or guidance from established housing cooperatives as the fledglings struggled to establish themselves. In the early years, board members and managers from nearby mutual housing associations met or called each other to trade ideas, advice, policies, and knowledge. For example, in 1965 residents from Audubon Park, Bellmawr Park, Pennypack Woods, and Winfield Park organized a Delaware River Valley mutual housing group. In 1966, they joined with several other mutual housing associations to form the Eastern Cooperative Housing Organization (ECHO).[37] In 1977 twenty-four Lanham mutual housing associations in thirteen states and the District of Columbia were members of the National Association of Housing Cooperatives. By the 1990s most of the mutual associations had drifted apart, and only a few continued to meet or consult with each other; few were active members of state, regional, or national cooperative housing organizations.

The mutual associations that came together in state and regional organizations often exchanged community newspapers and newsletters and ideas on how to improve communications. Before computers, there were numerous ways besides print used to reach members, including closed-circuit and community-access television, bulletin boards, and telephone trees. Even the communities that have an Internet presence and use social media must maintain the more traditional forms of community news exchange because many of the older residents are not computer literate.[38]

According to one mutual community manager, governance is difficult, and the mutual housing association is "messy as a democracy."[39] The mutual associations see the willingness of residents to participate in community governance as up and down. Many experience difficulty getting residents to run for board of directors, serve on standing committees, or even attend quarterly membership meetings. Mutual associations with a high percentage of residents over the age of sixty-five report that the same people tend to run for the board and serve on committees year after year. Even those with a sizable population of younger residents often struggle with participation. Younger residents say they are too busy with their jobs or careers, families, or other activities to be more active participants in the affairs of the mutual association.[40]

The shareholders "come out of the woodwork," mutual association managers agree, whenever they feel their interests are threatened. Rumors circulate, telephone calls are made, letters and emails are written, and membership meetings can become "pretty charged" whenever bylaw changes are proposed or capital projects that will result in increased monthly fees are on the agenda.[41] The residents often divide into factions and heated arguments take place. A Dallas newspaper reported that Romie Stewart, the manager of Dallas Park, successfully broke up a fight between residents when tempers flared at a 1948 meeting.[42]

The frequency and intensity of clashes between shareholders, boards, and managers make it difficult for mutual housing associations to hire and retain staff. Bellmawr Park, managed by Pat Levins for fifty-one years, and Winfield Park, managed by the late Paul Grieg for thirty-plus years, are not typical of most mutual housing associations. It is far more common to see a series of managers. In some cases, the need for an honest, competent, affordable manager has prompted mutual associations to recruit from within the community, usually from the board of directors. A number of "children of the village" are now running their communities. Denise Balderama, for example, grew up at Audubon Park, left, and returned; soon after her homecoming she was recruited to serve as manager. After working in that capacity for several years, she became manager of Winfield Park. Balderama has now come back to Audubon Park for the second time and serves on the board of directors.[43] Dennis Champine, manager of Kramer Homes, grew up nearby in South Warren, Michigan, and played sports against boys who grew up in the community.[44]

Balderama observed that one of the features of Westbrook's original mutual housing plan that has proved beneficial to residents is the exchange of dwelling units. At Audubon Park and other mutual housing associations where there are two-story units, residents occasionally exchange them for one-story units. In such circumstances, the family moving into the larger unit is required to reimburse the family moving into the smaller one "the amount represented by the difference in equity." The exchange policy and the presence of relatives and friends who look after each other make it possible for many residents to remain in their homes into advanced age. Annie Green, the widow of Shipbuilding Workers president John Green and a member of one of Audubon Park's original families, remained in the community in her old age because she was able to exchange a two-story dwelling unit for a one-story unit.[45]

## Resident Selection and Education

In 1945, when defense contracts were canceled and war plants closed, some mutual associations saw a "substantial turn-over." Families unwilling to join the mutual housing association were asked to leave. Some found it difficult to gather the necessary number of signatures required by the PHA to show commitment to the Mutual Plan and raise the down payment. For many residents who backed mutual housing, an initial expression of interest did not mean that they were going to support the mutual initiative over the long haul and pay assessments according to a timetable set by federal housing authorities.[46]

Accusations of communism were used to undermine residents' efforts to successfully negotiate the sale of their communities under the Mutual Plan. By October 1950 the board of directors of Pennypack Woods had retained a former Los Angeles County Housing Authority official named Drayton Bryant to assist in its purchase negotiations. Board members were favorably impressed with Bryant, who helped them negotiate with the PHA on several "stiff points," such as requiring an escrow account containing a full year's taxes and property insurance premiums in advance. Bryant would be forced to resign from the staff of the Philadelphia Housing Authority in 1952 after he was accused of being a communist.[47]

Lanham housing residents refused to be talked out of pursuing the mutual sale of their communities by allegations of communist influence; they understood that "anti-Communism, antisocialism, and a general un-Americanism . . . [had been] hallmarks of the critics of public housing" since the program began, long before "Senator Joseph McCarthy's political vituperation of the 1950s."[48] The residents of Greenmont Village formed a mutual housing corporation with the assistance of the United Electrical, Radio, and Machine Workers of America, a union that was expelled from the CIO for its communist-dominated leadership shortly after.[49] Under the watchful eye of the CIO, Allegheny County, Pennsylvania, housing officials endorsed the sale of over a dozen of the region's best-designed Lanham developments to mutual housing associations. They sought congressional authorization to convert Clairton's Blair Houses, the only defense housing development in the county reserved for people of color, into federally subsidized public housing in response to the lack of low-income market options.

Sold at a time of selective enforcement of fair housing laws, regulations, and court rulings throughout the country, it is hardly surprising that the PHA allowed mutual associations to isolate themselves from the larger national demand for open housing. The results of this lack of enforcement can be dramatically seen in many of the mutual housing developments. A resident of Baltimore's Armistead Gardens, whose mother had lived in the community for over fifty years, regarded the community as "its own little bubble [with] a long history of racism." Race relations were poor in part because "no one really moves out." Residential persistence created a nice "sense of community," but it was also isolating. Few residents pursued economic and social mobility. They sought economic and social stability, but in the process lost something important to Armistead Gardens' future—"integration . . . with other communities."[50]

On the outskirts of Camden, New Jersey, the city where Westbrook and Green built the first pilot project in 1941, mutual home ownership has strongly influenced patterns of settlement. On the north side of New Jersey Route 168 is Fairview, the World War I shipbuilding workers' enclave widely admired for its Colonial Revival architecture and town square community planning. Subdivided and sold to residents and investors in the 1920s, Fairview was a tightly knit white working-class community whose residents adopted various strategies such as two-wage-earner households to economically adjust to the regional demise of shipbuilding and maritime trades and commerce. During the 1970 and 1980s, the community's more affluent residents began to move out and it was unable to maintain a balance of low- and middle-income renters and owners. Fairview followed the same a pattern of decline as other similar neighborhoods in shipbuilding and maritime commercial centers from Bath, Maine, to Norfolk, Virginia, and beyond.

On the south side of the highway, across from Fairview and just outside Camden's city limits, is the tiny Borough of Audubon Park. There are no vacant dwellings or signs of blight, and many of the dwelling units have been enlarged or embellished as much as regulations will allow. As the author of a 1964 historical sketch of Audubon Park noted, the residents "own it and govern it; that is why it has been successful."[51] In 1991, a reporter from the *Philadelphia Inquirer* described Audubon Park as Camden County's "most racially exclusive municipality," calling "white inside and out": the houses are "almost exclusively white. So are the residents who inhabit them."[52] Lee Daniels, Audubon Borough clerk, called Audubon Park "closed" and said that its residents were "very reticent about discussing [racial] matters in public." Audubon Park manager John Rogers conceded that the board of directors operated in a "very, very low-key manner. They don't want any publicity or anything else."[53]

Mutual associations sought to avoid the accusations of discrimination and legal suits faced by Pennypack Woods and other mutually owned communities. During the early 1970s and 1980s, Pennypack Woods was the subject of a Department of Justice investigation for racial discrimination under both the Civil Rights Act and the Fair Housing Act. It was also sued in U.S. District Court in Philadelphia by Michael Meyers, an employee of the National Association for the Advancement of Colored People. The community was allowed to continue giving preference to relatives of current residents, but the issue of discrimination would emerge again and again.[54]

The "mixed"-occupancy defense housing developments in the Pittsburgh area that were sold to mutual housing associations were slow to alter the pattern of internal segregation established under federal rule. African American steel workers who resided at North Braddock Heights were originally assigned units that were below road level. In 1969, when Christine Slappy of Midland, Pennsylvania, was considering moving to the mutually-owned Midland Heights, she found that the "complex was divided into a section for Blacks and a section for whites."[55] In 1973 she filed a complaint with the Pennsylvania Human Relations Commission. That same year, the commission ordered Van Buren Homes, Inc., also located in Beaver County, to stop its segregation practices. Until that time, families of color had been assigned to L Street and M Street, which were separated from the rest of the community by a stream. In 2001, the African American residents of Van Buren Homes alleged that the mutual housing association had not approved an application from a person of color in twenty-three years.[56]

Located nearby Van Buren Homes is Mount Vernon Homes, a 75-unit defense housing development designated for African American occupancy by federal housing officials. In 1955 the community was sold to the Mount Vernon Homes Tenant Association, Inc. Among it leaders have been southern-born men who worked at Jones and Laughlin Steel Company and played an active role in the United Steel Workers Union local and nearby churches. Home to the 1970s and 1980s college and professional football star Tony Dorsett, it is probably the only African American mutual housing association still in operation in the United States.[57]

Audubon Park and other mutual communities used their control of the purchase of shares to bar applicants perceived as threats to community and financial stability. A "stone's throw" away from each other, the economic and social differences between Fairview and Audubon Park reveal both the potential of mutual housing to help residents adjust to economic and social change and the need for oversight of the application process and resident education programs.

North Braddock Heights, a biracial Lanham development in metropolitan Pittsburgh acquired by residents on a mutual basis, has become less diverse over time.[58] The late Rufus Simpson, who served in several leadership positions during his long residence, said that the children of African American shareholders seldom formed their own households in the mutual association because they relocated for employment, anticipated greater economic and social gain from purchasing a house, or both.[59] Legal challenges to discriminatory practices in resident selection begun in the 1970s at Pennypack Woods and elsewhere resulted in temporary oversight of application practices and procedures.[60]

Most, but not all, mutual associations have been white enclaves. By 1960, the 925 apartments at Success Village were jointly owned, according to the *Bridgeport Sunday Herald*, by a "mixed population of industrial workers, teachers, businessmen, and older and retired . . . people [who] made investments of money, time, labor, and faith so that they might have a good home that is theirs." The residents included "some 3,000 human beings of just about every racial, religious, national and economic background . . . [who had] found and developed a democratic way of life that is a credit to them and a boon to the community." Despite all of the factions and divisions among the board members and within the community, "things get worked out and the solutions found are usually the best available." The mutual housing association was an "amazing success."[61]

Located in northern California's Bay area, Atchison Village, like the larger city of Richmond, became more diverse in order to survive.[62] For the past several years, meeting notices and newsletters have been produced in English and Spanish and there are bilingual staff members. Resident Esthela Diaz said in 2008 that at Atchison Village she was more than "just the Mexican lady." She liked raising her daughters in the community because they could see gay or lesbian couples "together being happy."[63]

## Financial Oversight

During World War II and the Cold War, in industrial cities like Dayton, Ohio, housing suitable for a family was difficult to obtain. A former Greenmont Village resident recalled that the community had a "good reptuatuon [*sic*] from the start. My father lived back there as a kid and loved it. . . . [He said that] at one time there was a waiting list to get in."[64] Bruce Duncan "Utah" Phillips, the late labor organizer and folk singer who lived briefly in Greenmont Village and attended the Greenmont Village Elementary School, remembered that when the planes first took off, "they flew low over Greenmont, and all the kids playing in the schoolyard would jump up and down and wave."[65]

During the 1970s, when plant closures and unemployment began to accelerate, some mutual associations struggled financially or faced an uphill battle in convincing shareholders to think ahead and make the improvements and upgrades needed to keep mutual communities appreciating. According to one observer, at Atchison Village shareholders faced "intense challenges" in maintaining the community's aging building stock.[66] Kenna Homes, a mutually owned community in South Charleston, West Virginia, responded to economic hard times by deferring maintenance and allowing its appearance to become dated; residents are now working to rectify the situation.[67]

Built in haste over half a century ago without regard for local building codes and often with wartime, so-called "victory" building materials, both buildings and utility systems in many Lanham communities have been criticized by local home builders and realtors. The sale of Pennypack Woods was delayed until 1952 because it did not conform to local building and safety codes. A member of the local home builders' association called the community "bandbox fire hazards." Resident George Smith stated that he did not believe "that there will be a Pennypack Woods at the end of forty-five years," implying that it would have collapsed or burned down by that time.[68]

Shareholders at Greenmont Village, Avion Village, and Kramer Homes have agreed to assess money to cover the cost of altering the original flat roofs and changing the siding on homes in their communities (see Figure E.1). New furnaces at Walnut Grove required residents to temporarily pay higher monthly fees. Greenbelt residents became so divided over a proposed $20 million rehabilitation project (stretched over three decades) that Benjamin Abramowitz, an original shareholder, took legal action to stop it. Challenging the very nature and authority of the mutual housing association, he argued unsuccessfully that the mutual housing association was not a cooperative but "merely 'mutual housing,' something similar to a condominium arrangement."[69]

Rutgers University researchers found that opposition to improvement projects at Winfield Park was mainly from the elderly and others who lived on a tight budget. Disputes over long-term maintenance attest to the need for

**Figure E.1** The Kramer Homes community in Center Line, Michigan, was purchased under the Mutual Plan in 1949. The dwelling units, designed by the father and son architects Eliel and Eero Saarinen, once had flat roofs and vertical wood siding. Photograph by the author.

**Figure E.2** Residents who enlarge or renovate their dwelling units must gain approval or work within guidelines established by the mutual housing association. Here work takes place on a dwelling at Winfield Park, New Jersey. Photograph by Michael J. Chiarappa.

a program suggested by the National Association of Housing Cooperatives in 1967 that would provide low-interest loans for such improvements. Still, the lack of such a program does not stop residents from undertaking approved additions and renovations at their own expense (see Figure E.2).[70]

Managers often struggle to convince residents of the need to create reserve accounts for major maintenance or capital improvement programs. Residents claim that they cannot afford higher monthly fees, but at the same time a few are able to make other major purchases such as a recreational vehicles, boats, or second homes. The affordability of the communities has resulted in many mutual housing associations becoming naturally occurring retirement communities. The lack of younger shareholders will affect communities' ability to govern themselves, educate the next generation of mutual home owners, and pay for infrastructure and improvement projects. A man whose parents had resided at Kramer Homes for forty-six years regretted that the community had turned into "retiree acres" and thought that it needed more young shareholders.[71]

One result of affordability is residential persistence. During the 1950s an early 1960s, when housing options were still fairly limited, "the majority of mutual housing associations had waiting lists," according to the Bureau of Labor Statistics. In 1975 Zola McConnaughey, manager of Greenmont Village, called the list of people waiting to purchase a share in the community "staggering," but she did not want to talk about the community because whenever she did her office was "swamped with inquiries." McConnaughey thought it was "kind of cruel to talk it up" because the chances of "finding a place here are so slim." The demand for shares in Greenmont Village among the children of the first generation was great enough that the board of directors agreed to give first preference to a "child of the village" or a "parent of the village." The arrangement made possible the return of Candy Oxley and her husband, who had lived in Greenmont Village for seven years before they left in 1971 to purchase a house. Eighteen months later, the couple returned with a new appreciation of "just how good we have it here," where their support network included parents, a brother-in-law, and an aunt, uncle, and cousin.[72]

Winfield Park also had many shareholders who were related by blood or marriage. In 1995 eighty-year-old Walter Pierre said that three generations of his family had attended the Winfield Park Elementary School. The "whole town . . . [was] based on family—uncles, aunts, cousins, grandfathers, [and] grandmothers." At that time there were twenty-nine "descendants" waiting for apartments, and an average of thirty units a year changed hands.[73] In 1991, when called upon to explain the community's lack of racial diversity, manager William Cullen responded that all applicants had to "go on a long waiting list. . . . It takes years and years to get in here."[74]

Today, formal and informal waiting lists still exist for mutual associations in markets were there is a strong demand for affordable housing. However, for associations in old industrial districts or in remote corners of the urban periphery, waiting lists are no longer an issue. For the first time since their establishment, some are beginning to advertise and offer financial incentives, such as gift cards, to residents who successfully recruit a new shareholder. Although they were advised to prepare for the day when "selling" the idea of mutual housing to prospective members might be necessary to keep the corporation financially healthy, few did so.[75]

Cheryl Sobr, bookkeeper for the Aluminum City Terrace Housing Association, said that residents carefully guard their ability to control access to the community and regard it as "one heck of a place to live because they never leave." With its activity center, two playgrounds, and wooded area, the community offers a "nice living environment," despite the poor economic conditions in New Kensington and the larger area.[76] Within easy commuting distance to downtown Philadelphia and its growing suburbs, Audubon Park's affordability makes it the "best kept secret in New Jersey."[77] In Wilmington, North Carolina, where recent growth has increased the need for affordable housing, there is considerable interest in living at Lake Forest, a mutual housing association originally formed by veterans in 1947. Navy veteran John Walker recalled his residence there from 1949 to 1953. He mentioned a friend who remained in the community for "forty-five or fifty years and upon her death willed her unit to her son who owns it to this day."[78]

## Documentation, Preservation, and Commemoration

The communities sold under the Mutual Plan vary in awareness of their historical significance. Community milestones, marked with celebrations and community histories, and web sites are intended largely for insiders who already know about the mutual association. The Winfield Cultural Heritage Commission published *History of Winfield* in 1976, the same year that thousands of other communities celebrated the Bicentennial. In August 2001, Winfield Park celebrated its sixtieth anniversary with a parade whose grand marshal was Leona H. Burke, a member of one of the "pioneer" families. Burke had served as the first president of the Winfield Park Volunteer Fire Department Ladies Auxiliary, a key women's group. Her late husband had been involved in the creation of the Fire Department and helped to make it the community's foremost adult social organization.[79]

Until recently, little attention had been given to the documentation, preservation, and commemoration of twentieth-century publicly financed housing. The HOPE VI program, sponsored by the Department of Housing and Urban Development (HUD) has resulted in a reduction of over 200,000 dwelling units, including those built during the Roosevelt administration. In 1999 the Park Service released guidelines for those seeking to nominate public housing developments for listing on the National Register of Historic Places. A study of federally funded low-income communities by Dawn Jourdan revealed that "less than a dozen projects have been listed." Jourdan found that in the case of Philadelphia's Carl Mackley Houses and St. Louis's Neighborhood Gardens, a National Register listing rested not on "the significance of the structures or the architects who designed them" but on how they "illustrated the intellectual and aesthetic judgment of the 1930s." She cautioned that a listing was no guarantee that a publicly funded development would be spared from destruction. Despite the scarcity of affordable housing in Atlanta and New Orleans, public housing developments listed on the National Register have been razed in both cities. Atlanta's Techwood Homes was torn down under pressure from business and real estate interests who saw it as inconsistent with the image they wished to project to Olympic visitors.[80]

Support for documenting, preserving, and interpreting Roosevelt-era communities sold under the Mutual Plan is gaining ground, and efforts toward local, state, and federal recognition and protection have commenced. Greenbelt, Maryland, the only one of the Greenbelt towns still mutually owned, was designated a national historic landmark in 1997 in recognition of its sixtieth anniversary. The Greenbelt Museum offers visitors an opportunity to visit a dwelling unit in the original town furnished with period pieces. Community life, not mutual ownership, is the key interpretive theme. The Tugwell Room at the Greenbelt Branch of the Prince George's County Library System makes research material on the famous garden suburb available to real and virtual visitors.[81]

In 1994 Aluminum City Terrace and another mutually owned western Pennsylvania defense housing development, Munhall Homesteads, were documented by the National Park Service's Historic American Engineering Record with measured drawings, photographs, and historical research.[82] A state historical maker was erected at Avion Village in the mid-1990s, and in 2010 Greenmont Village was included in the Ohio Historic Inventory sponsored by the State Historic Preservation Office.[83] New Jersey's State Historic Preservation Office helped Bellmawr Park to be listed on the National Register before federal and state transportation officials agreed to widen U.S 295. As a result, plans for the project include reconstruction of six buildings belonging to the Bellmawr Park Mutual Housing Corporation.[84]

One of the most important opportunities for the public to learn about the success of mutual housing came in 2000, when Atchison Village became a "living part" of the Rosie the Riveter/World War II Home Front National Historic Park.[85] The Richmond, California, City Council designated the community as one of its historical resources in 2001, and two years later Atchison Village was listed on the National Register. Despite mixed emotions in the community about the village's inclusion in the National Park, most residents have embraced the idea. By 2006 volunteers with the Atchison Village Historical Project were conducting interviews with residents who had helped form the mutual corporation.[86] Historical material regularly appears in the appropriately named community newsletter, the *Atchison Riveter*, which in 2014 was used in an effort to retrieve the "ledger-sized bound books" dating from the corporation's earliest days that had been missing from the documents/map room for over a year. According to Marie Kochaver, History Committee chairwoman, the corporation's goal was to keep the archives "safeguarded . . . protected . . . and catalogued."[87]

If the case for preservation of publicly financed residential communities is to be won, it will be necessary for advocates to place them in a larger historical context encompassing their changing economic, political, social, and cultural roles.[88] A leading scholar of preservation has said that the rising generation of preservationists must have "courage to stand up to sacred cows such as economic growth and the real estate market" and envision "an order of things different from the current one; boldness to make seemingly impractical proposals; and patience to see them through."[89]

Today most mutual housing residents think of their communities as safe, close-knit, and stable.[90] For example, Samuel Urick III, a physician who spent the first five years of his life at Linmar Homes in Aliquippa, Pennsylvania, believes that the community helped instill in him the desire to help others, particularly the elderly. He wrote in 2013 that his "journey towards pursuing a doctorate in people began in an end unit apartment at 221 Linmar Homes, Aliquippa, long before I began to pursue a doctorate in medicine."[91]

Residents are proud that their mutual housing corporations have withstood the test of time. In 1948 a writer observed that although the "growing pains" of Greenmont's infancy had "not been forgotten," the residents had made "a fine start [toward] the development of a cooperative community where people live in harmony and provide for their own spiritual, recreational and social needs." By "living and working together," residents can "make a better community, and through making better communities we can make a better world."[92]

Grace Girardi, an Aluminum City Terrace resident, spoke in similar terms forty years later when she said that the important thing about her community was that its residents were "still working together after 40 years to build a better place."[93] George Damon, who was among the original resident-shareholders of Glendale Heights, told the *Philadelphia Inquirer* in 1989, "We're so damned proud of what we've done here . . . We can't begin to describe our feelings about this place."[94] One of Damon's fellow residents, Betty Manuel, tried to describe how she felt about Glendale Heights after thirty-nine years of residence: "I would not move for all the tea in China."[95] And Walter Chambers, an early resident of Audubon Park who was an electrician at New York Ship, the once sprawling Camden shipyard, said, "Who'd have figured . . . that the New York Ship would be gone and we'd still be here."[96]

The sharp divisions that continue to divide the residents of mutual housing communities are largely overlooked on a day-to-day basis. Time alters memory, and few mutual housing residents are aware that over half a century ago, their parents and grandparents were regarded as an economic and social threat for backing mutual housing. Only a small handful of area residents recall the Borough of Audubon's opposition to the construction of Audubon Park. In South Bend, most have forgotten or are unaware that Walnut Grove was built over the heated protests of some of the city's most affluent residents, who saw the arrival of defense workers as detrimental to real estate values. No one knew any more that Greenmont Village was built as a model for postwar development and offered an alternative to the "explosion of substandard jerry-building in Dayton's suburban fringe, resulting in the city being surrounding by a ring of suburban slums." The clock and the cypress clock tower have vanished from Bellmawr Park's community center and will soon be forgotten (see Figure E.3).[97]

The shareholders at Greenmont Village signaled that it was time for them to open up to the outside world when a majority voted to hire a property management company instead of employing its own administrative and maintenance staff. The more tangible symbol of a break with the past was the 2004 decision to alter the "distinctive flat roofs built by the U.S. government" and gradually replace them with peaked roofs for better "protection against leaks, better ventilation and storage, and durability." Board member Winford South told the *Dayton Daily News* that by making such physical alterations the residents were "really changing history here," but he said that it was necessary in order to bring the community's dwelling units—the corporation's main source of income—"into the 21st century."[98] In Center Line, Michigan, Kramer Homes, the mutually owned community designed by Swanson and the Saarinens, has also completely altered its original look, replacing the flat roofs and the vertical redwood siding. In June 2014 the dwelling units were undergoing yet another

**Figure E.3** The cypress-sheathed clock tower that once served as the visual focal point of Bellmawr Park, New Jersey, was removed from the community building because of maintenance problems. The community building includes a meeting room large enough to accommodate all shareholders and houses the administrative offices of the Bellmawr Park Mutual Housing Corporation; a maintenance shop is attached. Photograph by Michael J. Chiarappa.

"aesthetic transformation . . . being updated for the community's existing and future 'shareholders.'"[99]

If, as one manager said, "stay[ing] incognito" was a successful strategy for so many years, why are some mutual housing associations beginning to take steps to connect or re-connect with the outside world?[100] At both Audubon Park and Winfield Park, where the mutual association is the borough's only source of property tax revenue, rising administrative costs precipitated discussion about consolidation of services in the metropolitan area. A 1990 study that estimated the cost of the Borough of Audubon and Audubon Park sharing law enforcement services put a temporary end to the discussion, but ultimately Audubon Park began sharing police costs with another nearby borough.[101]

Pennypack Woods was once described as a place where "nearly all the lawns are country club green and the living is, well, cheap."[102] Alan Hartwick, a Grand Rapids, Michigan, filmmaker, was raised in Walnut Grove with the notion that it was a "cheap place to live." Years later, he discovered that that it meant much more. Walnut Grove, Avion Village, Electric Heights, and other mutual housing associations should have occupied the center stage of federal housing policy at the end of the war. Instead, PHA housing officials relegated them to the sidelines to protect the profitability of middle-income commercial housing and to retain the top-down structure of low-income public housing. The first and second generations of mutual housing associations faded into obscurity while millions of moderate-income families took advantage of federal home ownership incentives because federal housing officials saw no role for cooperative and other noncommercial housing initiatives in realization of the national housing goal of a "decent home" for all.

A 2008 Kramer Homes resident, reflecting on his involvement "in housing cooperatives for more than 30 years," suggested that it was time for HUD to "go back to funding new housing of this type for the multitudes of people who need low cost and safe communities."[103] In *Baltimore City's Past Present and Future* blog, Spence Lean noted that, in contrast to nearby public housing developments, the city's mutually owned Armistead Gardens Homes was a success that yet to be duplicated. Instead of using HOPE VI funds to tear down the city's public housing developments, Lean asked, why not learn from Armistead Gardens and "turn public housing residents into home owners" with "minimal displacement" and thereby ultimately save the city money? He suggested McCullough Homes as the ideal place to begin applying Armistead's lessons to public housing because of its location in an area that has and continues to attract investment in its infrastructure and services.[104] The contribution that Westbrook's mutual housing program made toward the development of a "coherent" federal housing policy has finally been recognized, and the time has come for it to be reconsidered by policy makers.

# Appendix

The following is a list of residential communities built during the Roosevelt administration owned by mutual housing associations (arranged in chronological order of sale).

**1947**

**Fulmor Heights Home Ownership Association**
201 Fitch Road
Hatboro, PA 19040
Telephone: 215-675-1626 | Fax: 215-675-3548
Email: Fulmorheightsoffice@comcast.net
300 units

**Greenmont Village Mutual Housing Association**
20 Rembrandt Boulevard
Kettering, OH
Telephone: 937-252-9941 | Fax: 937-252-9970
Email: greenmontvillage@sbcglobal.net
500 units

**Lake Forest, Inc.**
250 Pinecrest Parkway
Wilmington, NC 28401
Telephone: 910-762-8522
584 units (combined Lake Forest and Greenfield Terrace)

**Walnut Grove Mutual Housing Association**
2717 Woodmere Lane
South Bend, IN 46615
Telephone: 574-233-9454 | Fax: 574-233-9410
250 units

1948

**Aluminum City Terrace Housing Association**
136 1/2 Aluminum City Terrace
New Kensington, PA 15068
Telephone: 724-335-1861
Email: aluminumcityterrace@comcast.net
250 units

**Avion Village**
800 Skyline Drive
Grand Prairie, TX 75051
Telephone: 972-262-1544
Email: avion@um.att.com
300 units

**Kenna Homes Cooperative Corporation**
410 Kenna Drive
South Charleston, WV 25309
Telephone: 304-768-0063
http://www.kennahomes.com

**Woodstock Homes**
1711 2nd Street
Alameda, CA 94501
Telephone: 510-769-8844
Email: woodstockcorp@comcast.net
200 units

1949

**Hilltop Manor Mutual Housing, Inc.**
1411 South Oliver Street
Wichita, KS 67218
Telephone: 316-684-5141
400 units

**Kramer Homes Co-operative**
8830 East 10 Mile Road
Center Line, MI 48015
Telephone: 586-757-1240
500 units

1950

**Winfield Park Mutual Housing Corporation**
Wavecrest Avenue
Winfield, NJ 07036
Telephone: 908-486-5012
700 units

1952

**Bellmawr Park Mutual Housing Corporation**
31 Peach Road
Bellmawr, NJ 08031
Telephone: 856-931-2001
500 units

**Pennypack Woods Home Ownership Association**
8724 Crispin Drive
Philadelphia, PA 19136
Telephone: 215-331-5828
1,000 units

1954

**Anthony Wayne Terrace Housing Association**
300 Harmony Road
Baden, PA 15005
Telephone: 724-869-2195
200 units

**Audubon Park Mutual Housing Corporation**
20 Road C #1
Audubon, NJ 08106
Telephone: 856-547-4550
499 units

**Linmar Homes**
1336 Tyler Street
Aliquippa, PA 15001
Telephone: 724-375-2602
250 units

**Shalercrest Housing Association, Inc.**
272 Mount Vernon Drive
Pittsburgh, PA 15223
Telephone: 412-822-7137
251 units

1955

**Bridgeport Mutual Gardens Apartments**
**Community Cooperative Development Foundation, Inc.**
49 Cannon Street, 3rd Floor
Bridgeport, CT 06604-4251
Telephone: 216-231-8067
772 units

**Chartiers Terrace**
1 Victory Drive
Carnegie, PA 15106
Telephone: 412-276-4555
200 units

**Dravosburg Housing Association**
42 Scott Drive
Dravosburg, PA 15034
Telephone: 412-466-4601
250 units

**Glendale Heights Ownership Association**
498 South Andrews Avenue
Glenolden, PA 19036
Telephone: 610-583-0611
250 units

**Lacock Housing Association, Inc.**
76 Lacock Dwellings
Rochester, PA 15074
Telephone: 724-775-3457
75 units

**Midland Heights Homes, Inc.**
Midland Heights Circle
Midland, PA 15059
Telephone: 724-643-1980
280 units

**Mount Vernon Tenant Association, Inc.**
46 Mount Vernon Drive
Aliquippa, PA 15001
Telephone: 724-375-0604
75 units

**Munhall Homesteads**
601 Longfellow Drive
Homestead, PA 15120
Telephone: 412-461-4547
397 units

**North Braddock Heights Mutual Housing Association**
Wolf Avenue
Braddock, PA 15104
Telephone: 412-824-1211
200 units

**Riverview Homes Association**
321 Utah Avenue
West Mifflin, PA 15122
Telephone: 412-469-2600 | Fax: 412-469-8268
Email: info@riverviewhomesassociation.com
450 units

**Success Village Apartments, Inc.**
100 Court Drive
Bridgeport, CT 06610
Telephone: 203-336-2545
924 apartments (combined Success Park and Canaan Village)

**Tamaqui Village, Inc.**
126 West Tamaqui Drive
Beaver, PA 15009
Telephone: 724-774-5527
125 units

**Van Buren Homes, Inc.**
D Street
Beaver, PA 15998
Telephone: 724-774-8673 | Fax: 724-774-8699
Email: info@vanburenhomes.net
400 units

1956

**Armistead Homes Corporation**
5222 Erdman Avenue
Baltimore, MD 21205
Telephone: 410-483-1300
1,500 units

**Atchison Village Mutual Homes Corporation**
Collins & Curry Streets
Richmond, CA 94801
Telephone: 510-234-9054 | Fax: 510-234-9072
Email: avmhc2@yahoo.com
450 units

**Electric Heights Housing Association**
76 Harper Drive
Turtle Creek, PA 15145
Telephone 412-823-4040
600 units

**Overlook Mutual Homes, Inc.**
61 Colin Kelly Drive
Riverside, OH 45431
Telephone: 937-252-5693
738 units

**Potomac Heights Mutual Homeowners Association**
200 Cedar Lane
Indian Head, MD 20640
Telephone: 301-743-3031 | Fax: 301-684-2445
Email: phmhoa.comcast.net
484 units

1957

**Greenbelt Homes, Inc.**
One Hamilton Place
Greenbelt, MD 20770
Telephone: 301-474-4161 | Fax: 301-474-4006

Email: www.ghi.coop
1,600 units

1965

**Stonybrook Gardens Cooperative, Inc.**
55 Singer Court
Stratford, CT 06614
Telephone: 203-375-5056
400 units

# Note on Sources

From October 1940 until President Franklin D. Roosevelt ordered the reorganization of the federal housing bureaucracy on February 24, 1942, at least sixteen federal agencies were involved in the construction of defense housing. Records pertaining to the defense housing activities of federal agencies, such as the U.S. Housing Authority, that existed before mobilization are easier to locate at the National Archives and Records Administration (NARA) II facility in College Park, Maryland, than are those pertaining to the activities of the administrative subunits created by federal works administrator John M. Carmody in the midst of the housing crisis. The records of Lawrence Westbrook's Mutual Ownership Defense Housing Division and Clark Foreman's Defense Housing Division were apparently merged into those of their succeeding agencies, including the National Housing Agency's Federal Public Housing Authority, the Housing and Home Finance Agency's Public Housing Administration, and later the Department of Housing and Urban Affairs.

Confusion over the exact names of Roosevelt-era agencies and the lines of agency organization and succession further complicates the research process. Researchers frustrated by the difficulty of locating the administrative records of agencies that built or sold defense housing will be relieved to find that at both NARA and the Library of Congress maps, still and motion pictures, architectural drawings, and other visual resources pertaining to the Lanham housing program can be readily located.

Three of the presidential Libraries administered by NARA—the Franklin D. Roosevelt Library, the Harry S. Truman Library, and the Dwight D. Eisenhower Library—offer useful material. With the exception of the effort in early 1950 to create the National Mortgage Corporation for Housing Cooperatives, President Truman was not deeply involved with mutual or cooperative housing initiatives. He and President Eisenhower were asked for assistance by Lanham housing residents, veterans, and others seeking to purchase wartime housing. All of the presidential libraries offer access to the papers of administration officials and assistants who were involved in the Lanham program. Some, such as John Carmody, whose papers are at the Roosevelt Library, were interviewed as part of various oral history programs and projects that focused on prominent New Dealers.

Lawrence Westbrook's papers are located at the Carroll Library at Baylor University in Waco, Texas, not far from the cotton fields his family once cultivated. There will be disappointment for researchers seeking a deeper understanding of when, where, why, and how he developed the Mutual Home Ownership Plan and the nature of his relationship with labor leader John Green and the architects he hired to design the eight pilot projects. Enmeshed in political controversy and scandal from the outset of his career, Westbrook was a man of action, not words, who cultivated a positive image of the agencies and programs he directed.

The records of the Industrial Union of Marine and Shipbuilding Workers of America (IUMSWA), housed at the University of Maryland, offer insight into the union's efforts to promote mutual housing and show that housing was just one of numerous issues that captured John Green's attention. Additional insight into labor's role in the promotion of mutual housing can be gained at Wayne State University's Walter P. Reuther Library, with its the archives of the United Automobile Workers Union. R. J. Thomas and Reuther were both actively involved in the promotion of mutual housing. Catherine Bauer Wurster's papers at the University of California at Berkeley's Bancroft Library document her support for mutual housing and the involvement of labor-friendly reformers and reform groups as well as leading architects and planners. The Walter Gropius Papers at Harvard University's Houghton Library, the Oscar Stonorov Papers at the University of Wyoming, the Richard Neutra Papers at the University of California at Los Angeles, and the David R. Williams Papers at the University of Louisiana at Lafayette are among the collections that researchers interested in the design and planning of the mutual housing communities should consult.

The Bemis Foundation records located at the Massachusetts Institute of Technology provide an opportunity to gain an understanding of the movement to industrialize housing production. The collection documents show how the prospect of prefabricated or "factory-built" housing stirred passions among government officials, bankers, realtors, home builders, labor leaders, and consumer advocates.

The local public housing authorities that built and oversaw Lanham projects on behalf of federal housing officials and agencies vary widely in their treatment of noncurrent records. Some, such as the Wilmington Housing Authority in Wilmington, North Carolina, have done a good job safeguarding their records and have fairly complete sets of board meeting minutes as well as publications and other material. Others, such as the Camden Housing Authority, lost custody of or discarded a great deal of material. The same can be said for the mutual housing associations themselves. Some have been careful to protect material pertaining to their creation and the sale of the community; others, suffering from a lack of storage space, have discarded it. As private, nonprofit corporations, the mutual associations are required only to have certain tax information available for public inspection and are not obligated to grant researchers access to their office files.

The Internet offers the possibility of access to records that have hitherto been unknown and the oral testimony of individuals involved in the creation and administration of mutual housing. It is my hope that this study will inspire support for efforts to better document and interpret the history of mutual housing in the United States.

# Notes

## INTRODUCTION

1. Jane Jacobs used the term in her famous book *The Death and Life of Great American Cities* (New York: Random House, 1961). Electric Heights shows how residents readily altered their system of community surveillance to suit the design of their homes and the layout of their community.

2. John Hoerr, *And the Wolf Finally Came: The Decline and Fall of the American Steel Industry* (Pittsburgh: University of Pittsburgh Press, 1988). See also "Deindustrialization—A Panel Discussion," *Pennsylvania History* 58 (1991): 181–211; Jefferson Cowie and Joseph Heathcott, *Beyond the Ruins: The Meanings of Deindustrialization* (Ithaca, NY: ILR Press, 2003); John T. Cumbler, *A Social History of Economic Decline: Business, Politics, and Work in Trenton* (New Brunswick, NJ: Rutgers University Press, 1989); Howard Gillette Jr., *Camden after the Fall: Decline and Renewal in a Post-industrial City* (Philadelphia: University of Pennsylvania Press, 2005); Steve High and David W. Lewis, *Corporate Wasteland: The Landscape and Memory of Deindustrialization* (Ithaca, NY: Cornell University Press, 2007); Sherry Linkon and John Russo, *Steeltown, U.S.A.: Work and Memory in Youngstown* (Lawrence: University Press of Kansas, 2002); and Thomas J. Sugrue, *The Origins of Urban Crisis: Race and Inequity in Postwar Detroit* (Princeton, NJ: Princeton University Press, 1996).

3. U.S. Department of Labor, Bureau of Labor Statistics, *Cooperative Housing in the United States, 1949 and 1950*, Bulletin 1093, Housing and Home Finance Agency, Housing Research Paper 24 (Washington, DC: Government Printing Office, 1952), 2–3. Florence Parker and her team noted a small number of privately funded postwar housing initiatives calling themselves mutual housing associations. She included them in her cooperative studies, but did not lump them with the mutual associations created to buy public property.

4. Sarah Jo Peterson, *Planning the Home Front: Building Bombers and Communities at Willow Run* (Chicago: University of Chicago Press, 2013).

5. Jeanne Gang and Greg Lindsay, "Designing a Fix for Housing," *New York Times*, February 10, 2012, A27. On the history of low-income housing programs, see Timothy L. McDonnell, *The Wagner Housing Act: A Case Study of the Legislative Process* (Chicago: Loyola University Press, 1957); Nicholas Dagen Bloom, *Public Housing That Works: New York in the Twentieth Century* (Philadelphia: University of Pennsylvania Press, 2008); Mary Susan Cole, "Catherine Bauer and the Public Housing Movement, 1926–1937" (Ph.D. diss., George Washington University, 1975), 465–468; Joseph Heathcott, "The Strange Career of Public Housing: Policy, Planning, and the American Metropolis in the Twentieth Century," *Journal of the American Planning Association* 78, no. 4 (2012): 360–375; D. Bradford Hunt, *Blueprint for Disaster: The Unraveling of Chicago Public Housing* (Chicago: University of Chicago Press, 2009); Jacqueline Leavitt, "The Interrelated History of Cooperatives and Public Housing from the Thirties to the Fifties," in *The Hidden History of Housing Cooperatives*, ed. Allan Heskin and Jacqueline Leavitt (Davis: University of California Press, 1995), 89–90; and Lawrence Vale, *From the Puritans to the Projects: Public Housing and Public Neighbors* (Cambridge, MA: Harvard University Press, 2000). On recent issues in public housing, see J. S. Fuerst, *When Public Housing Was Paradise: Building Community in Chicago* (Urbana: University of Illinois Press, 2005); Rhonda Y. Williams, *The Politics of Public Housing: Black Women's Struggles against Inequality* (Oxford: Oxford University Press, 2004); Lawrence J. Vale, *Reclaiming Public Housing: A Half Century of Struggle in Three Neighborhoods* (Cambridge, MA: Harvard University Press, 2002); and Sudhir Alladi Venkatesh, *American Project: The Rise and Fall of a Modern Ghetto* (Cambridge, MA: Harvard University Press, 2000).

6. David M. Kennedy, "What the New Deal Did," *Political Science Quarterly* 124, no. 2 (2009): 256.

7. Resettlement Administration, *Greenbelt Towns* (Washington, DC: Resettlement Administration, 1936), unpaged.

8. Gail Radford, *Modern Housing for America: Policy Struggles in the New Deal Era* (Chicago: University of Chicago Press, 1996), 1.

9. Joseph Heathcott, "The City Quietly Remade: National Programs and Local Agendas in the Movement to Clear the Slums, 1942–1952," *Journal of Urban History* 34, no. 2 (2008): 223.

10. Todd M. Michney, "Constrained Communities: Black Cleveland's Experience with World War II Public Housing," *Journal of Social History* 40, no. 4 (2007): 934. Michney was specifically referring to African Americans in Cleveland, but his thesis reflects the larger case nationwide.

11. Frank Rahill, "Johnny Green, Stabilizer," *Commonweal* 36 (June 1942): 156.

12. On the "triple dream" of home ownership—home, neighborhood, and community, see Dolores Hayden, *Building Suburbia: Greenfields and Urban Growth* (New York: Pantheon, 2003), 5. Vanport, Oregon, a temporary city built for shipyard workers between Vancouver and Portland, was used by Hayden as an example of a community-centered place of residence—the antithesis of places like Levittown. See Dolores Hayden, *Redesigning the American Dream: The Future of Housing, Work and Family Life* (New York: Norton, 1985; rev. ed., 2002), 19–27. For an alternative treatment of Vanport, see Heather Fryer, *Perimeters of Democracy: Inverse Utopias and the Wartime Social Landscape in the American West* (Lincoln: University of Nebraska Press, 2010). On postwar housing design, see Avi Friedman, "The Evolution of Design Characteristics during the Post–Second World War Housing Boom: The U.S. Experience," *Journal of Design History* 8, no. 2 (1995): 131–146.

13. National Housing Agency, *Fourth Annual Report, 1945* (Washington, DC: Government Printing Office, 1946), 210.

14. To Westbrook's disappointment, cooperative housing played a minor role in postwar urban renewal. See Eric Avila and Mark H. Rose, "Race, Culture, Politics, and Urban Renewal: An Introduction," *Journal of Urban History* 35, no. 3 (2009): 335–347; Robert Fogelson, *Downtown: Its Rise and Fall, 1880–1950* (New Haven, CT: Yale University Press, 2001); Marc Weis, "The Origins and Legacy of Urban Renewal," in *Federal Housing Policy and Programs: Past and Present*, ed. J. Paul Mitchell (New Brunswick, NJ: Rutgers University Press, 1985), 253–275; and Samuel Zipp, "The Roots and Routes of Urban Renewal," *Journal of Urban History* 39, no. 3 (2012): 366–391.

15. This idea was first suggested by Zane Miller in a June 2014 email exchange with the author.

16. "Government Giving Up New Towns," *The Ledger* (Lakeland, FL), October 1, 1978, 14.

17. Sukumar Ganapati, "Enabling Housing Cooperatives: Policy Lessons from Sweden, India, and the United States," *International Journal of Urban and Regional Research* 34, no. 2 (2010): 365–380.

18. Heskin and Leavitt, *Hidden History of Housing Cooperatives*. See also Jonathan E. Zimmer, *From Rental to Cooperative: Improving Low and Moderate Income Housing* (Beverly Hills, CA: Sage, 1977).

19. Pennypack Woods Home Ownership Association, "History and Background of MHO," Pennypack Woods Historical File, Philadelphia, 4.

20. Ibid.

21. Obama quoted in Dionne Searcey and Robert Gebeloff, "More Fall Out as Middle Class Shrinks Further," *New York Times*, January 26, 2015, B4. See also Jonathan Weisman, "Obama to Outline Proposals to Bolster a Lagging Housing Sector," *New York Times*, January 8, 2015, A14; and Jesse Eisinger, "A Push for a Greater Government Role in Housing Finance," *New York Times*, January 29, 2015, B9.

## CHAPTER 1

1. Edward Alden Jewell, "Housing Exhibition Has Opening Today," *New York Times*, October 16, 1934, 21. The exhibit was co-sponsored by the NYC Housing Authority, the Columbia University Housing Orientation Study, the Lavanburg Foundation, and the Welfare Council. See also Judith C. Rohrer, "'Housing on Trial': The Museum of Modern Art and the Campaign for Public Housing in the U.S., 1932–1952" (Ph.D. diss., Emory University, 2004), 105–112, 118–130.

2. Gaia Caramellino, "Negotiating Modern Architecture during the New Deal: MoMA Exhibitions on Public Housing," *Journal of the American Institute of Planning* 78, no. 4 (2012): 376. See also Alice Graeme, "Museum of Modern Art Exhibiting PWA Models," *Washington Post*, June 21, 1936, TM5; and Rohrer, "'Housing on Trial,'" 144. On opposition to the PWA, see Jo Ann E. Argersinger, "Contested Visions of American Democracy: Citizenship, Public Housing, and the International Arena," *Journal of Urban Planning* 36, no. 3 (2010): 797–799.

3. On the impact of the New Deal on housing, see Robert Moore Fisher, *Twenty Years of Public Housing* (New York: Harper, 1959), 73–125; Lawrence M. Friedman, *Government and Slum Housing: A Century of Frustration* (Chicago: Rand McNally, 1968), 116–117; Mark I. Gelfand, *A Nation of Cities: The Federal Government and Urban*

*America, 1934–1975* (New York: Oxford University Press, 1975); R. Allen Hays, *The Federal Government and Urban Housing: Ideology and Change in Public Policy* (Albany: State University of New York Press, 1995), 83–94; Kenneth Jackson, *Crabgrass Frontier: The Suburbanization of the United States* (New York: Oxford University Press, 1985), 172–229; and Nathaniel S. Keith, *Politics and the Housing Crisis since 1930* (New York: Universe Books, 1973). Overviews by industry insiders include Joseph B. Mason, *History of Housing in the U.S., 1930–1980* (Houston: Gulf Publishing, 1982); and the more recent and less biased Kent W. Colton, *Housing in the Twenty-First Century: Achieving Common Ground* (Cambridge, MA: Harvard University Press, 2003).

4. Paul K. Conkin, *Tomorrow a New World: The New Deal Community Program* (Ithaca, NY: Cornell University Press for the American Historical Association, 1959), 81–89.

5. Ibid., 267–271.

6. Cathy D. Knepper, *Greenbelt: A Living Legacy of the New Deal* (Baltimore: Johns Hopkins University Press, 2001).

7. Robert Fairbanks, *Making Better Citizens: Housing Reform and the Community Development Strategy in Cincinnati, 1890–1960* (Urbana: University of Illinois Press, 1988), 1–3.

8. On agrarian politics, see Worth Robert Miller and Stacy G. Ulberg, "Building a Populist Coalition in Texas, 1892–1896," *Journal of Southern History* 74, no. 2 (2008): 255–296; and Elizabeth Sanders, *Roots of Reform: Farmers, Workers, and the American State, 1877–1917* (Chicago: University of Chicago Press, 1999), 40–62, 128–137, 292–294.

9. Obituary for Lawrence Westbrook, *New York Times*, January 26, 1964, 81.

10. For a fictional account of the creation of the Texas Cotton Growers Cooperative, see Dorothy Scarborough, *Can't Get a Red Bird* (New York: Harper and Brothers, 1929).

11. "Report of the Texas Rehabilitation and Relief Commission to the Senate Investigating Committee of the 43rd Legislature First Called Session," typescript, n.d., 494–495, Office of the Governor, Archives and Information Services Division, Texas State Library and Archives Commission (hereafter Texas Archives), Austin.

12. "Forester to Represent 'Ma' Ferguson Here," *Washington Post*, April 2, 1933, 3; and "Opportunities Now Beckon Country Women as They Beckoned Pioneer Forebears [*sic*]," *Washington Post*, June 26, 1934, 12. See also James Terry Booker, "The Woodlake Cooperative Community: A New Deal Experiment in Rural Living for the Unemployed" (master's thesis, Texas A&M University, 1976), 11–13. Westbrook reported that FERA's Jacob Crane and "a group from WPA and Agriculture went to Europe for several months to make a survey of cooperatives." See Lawrence Westbrook, untitled typescript, July 31, 1939, 7, Lawrence Westbrook Papers, The Texas Collection, Carroll Library, Baylor University, Waco, TX (hereafter Westbrook Papers), 2E444, FF 30.

13. Conkin, *Tomorrow a New World*, 132.

14. Michael Glen Wade, "David Reichard Williams: Avant-Garde Architect and Community Planner, 1890–1962" (Ph.D. diss., University of Southeastern Louisiana, 1978), 72. See also "Rural Industrial Community Projects: Woodlake, Texas; Osceola, Arkansas; and Red House, West Virginia," *Architectural Record* 77 (1935): 12; and Lawrence Westbrook, "The Program of Rural Rehabilitation of the FERA," *Journal of Farm Economics* 17, no. 1 (1935): 89–91. The Woodlake film was made by the Texas Emergency Relief Commission.

15. Wade, "David Reichard Williams," 232. At roughly the same time, a few Texas cities were pursuing federal housing aid through the Public Works Administration. See Robert B. Fairbanks, "Public Housing for the City as a Whole: The Texas Experience,

1934–1955," *Southwest Historical Quarterly* 103, no. 4 (2000): 402–420. Woodlake homesteaders got an opportunity for wage labor in garment manufacturing. See "Pants in Texas and Flowers in New York," *Chicago Tribune*, August 11, 1934, 8.

16. George R. Donnell to Lawrence Westbrook, February 11, 1957, Westbrook Papers, 2E442, FF 18.

17. *Journal of the Senate of Texas, Forty-Third Legislature, First Called Session*, 1933, 550–551 (testimony of Lawrence Westbrook on S.R. 9). Westbrook reported on the difficulties encountered in getting county relief boards to follow uniform accounting and reporting procedures. See *Report of the Texas Rehabilitation and Relief Commission to the Senate Investigating Committee of the 43rd Legislature First Called Session*; and "Ferguson's Passing Forecast in Texas," *New York Times*, February 18, 1934, E7. On Westbrook's replacement, see "Adam Johnson to Direct Relief," *Dallas Morning News*, February 2, 1934, 1.

18. T. R. B., "Washington Notes," *New Republic*, October 20, 1937, 300.

19. Federal Emergency Relief Administration, *Purpose and Activities of the Federal Emergency Relief Administration* (Washington, DC: Federal Emergency Relief Administration 1934), 6.

20. "Vast Land Area Doomed by U.S. to Withdrawal," *Washington Post*, February 5, 1935, 2. See also Michelle Landis Dauber, *The Sympathetic State: Disaster Relief and the Origins of the American Welfare State* (Chicago: University of Chicago Press, 2013), 112–129.

21. *American Magazine* quoted in "Among the Magazines," *Washington Post*, February 23, 1936, B7.

22. "Harry Hopkins," *Fortune*, July 1935, 64. When Hopkins gathered his key advisers together—Westbrook, Corrington Gill, Aubrey Williams, and Jacob Baker—they allowed him to "think out loud." Their meetings were "really lecture periods" that concluded with spirited card games. *American Magazine* quoted in "Among the Magazines." Westbrook remained friends with Hopkins until the latter's death in 1946.

23. Photo caption, *Washington Post*, November 8, 1934, 9.

24. Pine Mountain Valley was a rural industrial community in Georgia. See Wilma E. Van Dusseldorp, "Who Builds Pine Mountain Valley" (n.p.: Federal Emergency Relief Corporation of Georgia, 1936). A dispute over the use of FERA funds with controller general J. R. McCarl did not prevent Hopkins from approving fifty new communities in late 1934 and expressing his wish to "see the number of rural-industrial communities multiplied as rapidly as our united forces are able to proceed on a sound basis." Hopkins quoted in "Farm-Work Units Approved by FERA," *New York Times*, November 26, 1934, 2. Westbrook and Williams planned six rural rehabilitation communities for Texas. See "Architects Lay Plans for Texas Farm Colonies," *Los Angeles Times*, January 21, 1934, D8; and Booker, "Woodlake Cooperative Community," 50.

25. Herman Clarence Nixon, *Forty Acres and Steel Mules* (Chapel Hill: University of North Carolina Press, 1938), 15, 39. Like Westbrook, Nixon was the son of a cotton planter.

26. Gail Radford, *The Rise of the Public Authority: Statebuilding and Economic Development in Twentieth-Century America* (Chicago: University of Chicago Press, 2013), 10–38.

27. Rural Rehabilitation Division, "Establishment of Community Organizations," typescript, n.d., Warren J. Vinton Papers, Olin Library, Cornell University, Ithaca, NY (hereafter Vinton Papers), RG 2946, Box 3.

28. Morgan Baker, "The Federal Diary," *Washington Post*, November 30, 1934, 28.

29. Westbrook, "Program of Rural Rehabilitation of the FERA," 89–100; and "Housing Plan to Be Pushed by President," *Washington Post*, October 18, 1934, 1. Notice of the radio broadcast appeared in "Outstanding Events Today," *Washington Post*, November 14, 1934, 23. On a proposal to allow veterans who received disability payments to participate in the rural rehabilitation program, see "Homes in Rural Sections Seen Aid to Veterans," *Washington Post*, December 25, 1934, 2.

30. Conkin, *Tomorrow a New World*, 199–201.

31. "U.S. Families Soon to Settle Alaskan Valley," *Washington Post*, March 9, 1935, 6.

32. [David R. Williams], "Organized Rural Communities: Federal Emergency Relief Administration, Division of Rural Rehabilitation; Plans and Instructions," typescript, n.d., 3, Westbrook Papers, 2E444, FF 43. See also Wade, "David R. Williams," 189, 192–198. Walter G. Metschke, an architect and draftsman, recalled that Williams, who "resembled a skid row bum in appearance" except for his "meticulously waxed" moustache, "was a genius at his profession." See Memoirs of Walter G. Metschke, comp. Chicago Architects Oral History project, 1977, 27, available at www.digital-libraries.saic.edu/cdm/ref/collection/caoh/id/8498, accessed January 8, 2015. For a flattering sketch of Williams, see Wellington Brink, "David Reichard Williams: Advance-Guard Architect," *Holland's, the Magazine of the South*, Papers of David R. Williams, Edith Garland Dupré Library, University of Louisiana, Lafayette (hereafter Williams Papers), FF 2-16. On the National Youth Administration recreation center, see Letter to Louis Haley from William E. Flanagan, May 21, 1941, Williams Papers, FF 2-16. See also Arnold Alanen, "Midwesterners in the Matanuska Valley: Colonizing Rural Alaska in the 1930s," *People, Power and Places: Perspectives in Vernacular Architecture* (Knoxville: University of Tennessee Press, 2000), 55.

33. Williams wrote to his wife, Lyle, that the experience gave him a keener understanding of the problems involved in "taking people off relief and suddenly making them think they're heroes and rich ones at that. It doesn't work." See Williams quoted in Wade, "David Reichard Williams," 288.

34. Arville Schaleben, "Our New Pioneers," *American Magazine* 121 (January 1936): 23. The Matanuska Colony was administered under Westbrook's direction until January 1939, when it was transferred to the Department of the Interior. See Marvin Albert Halldorson, "The Matanuska Colonization Project" (master's thesis, University of Colorado, 1936), 85. A copy of Hopkins's report to Congress was reproduced in app. B.

35. M. L. Wilson, "A New Land-Use Program: The Place of Subsistence Homesteads," *Journal of Land and Public Utility Economics* 10, no. 1 (1934): 12. See also M. L. Wilson, "The Place of Subsistence Agriculture in Our National Economy," *Journal of Farm Economics* 16, no. 1 (1934): 73–84.

36. Conkin, *Tomorrow a New World*, 121.

37. Wilson, "Place of Subsistence Homesteads," 74. See also Russell Lord and Paul H. Johnstone, eds., *A Place on Earth: A Critical Assessment of Subsistence Homesteads* (Washington, DC: U.S. Department of Agriculture, Bureau of Economics. 1942), pt. 2; Timothy Miller, *The Quest for Utopia in Twentieth-Century America*, vol. 1, *1900–1960* (Syracuse, NY: Syracuse University Press, 1998), 129–134; John Franklin Carter, "Back to the Land: The Work of the Resettlement Administration," *Housing* 23, no. 3 (1935): 227–235; and Oliver C. Winston, "Subsistence Homesteads Projects: Their Past, Present and Future," *Journal of Housing* 3, no. 10 (1946): 223–225. On Cumberland Homesteads, see Delos D. Hughes, "The Housing Ideal at Cumberland Homesteads," *Tennessee Historical Quarterly* 60, no. 1 (2001): 38–53. On Arthurdale, see "The Arthurdale Experiment," *New Republic*, June 22, 1942, 849; "Eden Liquidated—New Deal's First Venture in

Resettlement Is Written Off at Big Loss," *Business Week*, July 27, 1946, 22–26; and Blair Bolles, "Resettling America," *American Mercury* 39 (1936): 338–345. On Penderlea, see Marcia G. Synnott, "Hugh MacRae, Penderlea, and the Model Farm Communities Movement," *Proceedings of the South Carolina Historical Association* (1987): 53–65.

38. Harold L. Ickes, *Back to Work: The Story of the PWA* (New York: Macmillan, 1935), 178–194. See also Leon Dure Jr., "Housing Plan to Be Pushed by President," *Washington Post*, October 18, 1934, 1.

39. Urs Buttiker, *Louis I. Kahn: Light and Space* (New York: Whitney Library of Design, 1994), 35. See also Lee E. Cooper, "Garment Workers Soon to Occupy Jersey Homesteads," *New York Times*, June 6, 1936, RE1. In 1945 the community changed its name to Roosevelt.

40. Bruce L. Melvin, "Housing Standards for Subsistence Homesteads," *Architectural Record* 77 (January 1935): 9. See also Alison K. Hoagland and Margaret M. Mulrooney, *Norvelt and Penn-Craft: Subsistence Homestead Communities of the 1930s* (Washington, DC: Historic America Building Survey / Historic American Engineering Record, National Park Service, 1991), 17–18.

41. Fred Carroll, "The Racial Politics of Place: Jim Crow, the New Deal, and Suburban Housing on the Virginia Peninsula," *Journal of Urban History* 40, no. 3 (2014): 514–535; and Conkin, *Tomorrow a New World*, 199–201. On the involvement of African American architect Hilyard R. Robinson, see "War-Torn Europe Gave Hilyard Robinson Idea for Career as Housing Pioneer," *Chicago Defender*, May 8, 1943, 5.

42. Wilson, "Land-Use Program," 3. On federalization, see Edith Elmer Wood, "The Development of Legislation," *Social Work Year Book 1937*, reprinted in *Public Housing in America*, comp. M. B. Schnapper, *The Reference Shelf No. 13* (New York: Wilson, 1939), 77–78; "Ickes Orders Federalization of Homesteads," *Journal-Herald* (Dayton, OH), June 15, 1934, Dayton Public Library Clipping File 77-94; and Lord and Johnstone, *Place on Earth*, 45.

43. In her comparison of the economic and social programs undertaken by the United States and Italy during the Great Depression, Ghirardo accused Westbrook and his colleagues of clinging to "an idealized image of rural life." See Diane Yvonne Ghirardo, *Building New Communities: New Deal America and Fascist Italy* (Princeton, NJ: Princeton University Press, 1989), 124.

44. The Division of Subsistence Homesteads purchased prefabricated homes for Arthurdale with the support of Eleanor Roosevelt. See Hughes, "Housing Ideal at Cumberland Homesteads," 49; and Jeanne S. Rymer, "Arthurdale: A Social Experiment in the 1930s: Foundations, Fantasies, Furniture, and Failures," *West Virginia History* 46, no. 1–4 (1985–1986): 89–102. Jersey Homesteads, also financed by the Division of Subsistence Homesteads, offered dwellings designed by Louis I. Kahn and Alfred Katsner that were made of precast concrete. See Buttiker, *Louis I. Kahn*, 34–35; and Helen Schwartz, *The New Jersey House* (New Brunswick, NJ: Rutgers University Press, 1983), 159.

45. On the FSA, see Burnham Kelly, *The Prefabrication of Houses* (Cambridge, MA: MIT Press, 1951), 35–36; "FSA Prefabricates $930 Homes for Missouri Sharecroppers," *Architectural Forum* 69 (November 1938): 393–398; Farm Security Administration, "Experiments in Rammed Earth Construction," mimeograph, National Archives and Records Administration, College Park, MD, RG 196, Box 15; Conkin, *Tomorrow a New World*, 171; and C. B. Baldwin, "Farm Security Administration's Sixth Year in Rural Housing," in *NAHO Housing Yearbook, 1941*, 251, 255. On the FSA's wartime prefabs, see "Plan Standards for Defense Housing," 77; and "More for Martin," *Architectural Forum* 75 (December 1941): 44.

46. Ernest K. Lindley, "Low-Cost Housing," *Washington Post*, April 7, 1939, 11.

47. Federal Housing Administration, *Fort Wayne Housing Plan: A Low-Cost Fifty-House Program Begun in 1938 by the Housing Authority of Fort Wayne, Indiana to Reduce Social Welfare Costs* (Washington, DC: Federal Housing Administration, 1938). See also John Edelman, "Low Cost Slums," typescript, n.d., The John Edelman Collection, Walter P. Reuther Library, Wayne State University, Detroit, Box 101, FF 5; Kelly, *Prefabrication of Houses*, 36–37; "Fort Wayne, IND. Tries New Type of Slum Clearance," *Chicago Daily Tribune*, August 7, 1938, B9; "Fifty Plywood Panel Houses Built at the Rate of One a Day," *Architectural Record* 85 (March 1939): 38–40; "Minimum Houses for Four, Cost $900," *Christian Science Monitor*, November 14, 1939, 8; and Loula D. Lasker, "Fort Wayne's Fifty Houses," in *Public Housing in America*, 141–148. The AFL opposed the use of WPA labor on the project. See American Federation of Labor, *History, Encyclopedia, and Reference Book*, vol. 3, pt. 1 (Washington, DC: American Federation of Labor–Congress of Industrial Organizations, 1960), 1141. Alan Mather called the dwellings "shacks." See Alan Mather, "The Threshing Floor," *Pencil Points* 21 (April 1940): 20. The Fort Wayne houses are an exception to Marc Weiss's finding that the FHA improved working-class housing standards. See Marc A. Weiss, "Developing and Financing the 'Garden Metropolis': Urban Planning and Housing Policy in Twentieth-Century America," *Planning Perspectives* 5, no. 3 (1990): 307–319. For an endorsement of the project, see William F. Hall, "Challenge of the Fort Wayne Plan," in *Public Housing in America*, 319–325.

48. Kelly, *Prefabrication of Houses*, 33. Harvard University professor James B. Ford maintained that the Bureau of Standards ought to be the federal agency to test building materials and construction techniques. See James B. Ford, "Advantages and Disadvantages of Government Action," in *Public Housing in America*, 105.

49. Lescaze quoted in "Lescaze Calls Pre-fabrication Still Far Away," *Washington Post*, July 17, 1938, R2.

50. Dione Neutra quoted in Thomas Hines, *Richard Neutra and the Search for Modern Architecture* (Berkeley: University of California Press, 1994), 189. The issues of design, finance, and tenure typically dominate debate about the influence of European housing policy on the United States. See Argersinger, "Contested Visions," 797.

51. On RA communities, see Conkin, *Tomorrow a New World*, 267–271; Gwendolyn Wright, *Building the Dream: A Social History of Housing in America* (Cambridge, MA: MIT Press, 1983), 222; Carter, "Back to the Land," 227–235; Bruce Melvin, "Stake in the Land," *Review of Reviews* 95 (July 1936): 48–50; Bernard Sternsher, *Rexford Tugwell and the New Deal* (New Brunswick, NJ: Rutgers University Press, 1964), 265; and Wade, "David Reichard Williams," 236–237.

52. Sidney Baldwin, *Poverty and Politics: The Rise and Decline of the Farm Security Administration* (Chapel Hill: University of North Carolina Press, 1968), 97. Tugwell wrote in his diary that Westbrook's "attitude was very good," even though he had been told by Hopkins that "Rural Rehabilitation was to be handed over" to him. Westbrook was told by Hopkins that it was necessary to "separate him completely" from the Rural Rehabilitation program even though it "really almost belonged to him personally." *The Diary of Rexford G. Tugwell: The New Deal, 1932–1935*, ed. Michael Vincent Namorato (New York: Greenwood, 1992), 239.

53. Resettlement Administration, *Greenbelt Towns* (Washington, DC: Resettlement Administration, 1936), preface.

54. Ibid.

55. Conkin, *Tomorrow a New World*, 155. See also Joseph L. Arnold, *The New Deal in the Suburbs: A History of the Greenbelt Town Program, 1935–1954* (Columbus: Ohio State University Press, 1971); Robert Fairbanks, "Greenhills: Model for Metropolitan Development," *Queen City Heritage* 48, no. 4 (1990–1991): 10–11; Arnold R. Alanen and Joseph A. Eden, *Main Street Ready-Made: The New Deal Community of Greendale, Wisconsin* (Madison: State Historical Society of Wisconsin, 1987); Carol A. Christensen, *The American Garden City and the New Towns Movement* (Ann Arbor: UMI Research Press, 1986); and Daniel Schaffer, "The American Garden City: Lost Ideals," in *The Garden City: Past, Present, and Future*, ed. Stephen V. Ward (London: Spon, 1992), chap. 7.

56. Daniel Pearlstein, "Sweeping Six Percent Philanthropy Away: The New Deal in Sunnyside Gardens," *Journal of Planning History* 9, no. 3 (2010): 170–182.

57. Joel Schwartz, "Tenement Renewal in the 1930s: The District-Improvement Ideas of Arthur C. Holden," *Journal of Planning History* 1, no. 4 (2002): 290–310.

58. Westbrook, untitled typescript, 5.

59. Harry Barnard, *Independent Man: The Life of Senator James Couzens* (New York: Charles Scribner's Sons, 1958), 293. Barnard argued that Couzens was immediately "sorry he made this housing gift" (p. 293). Ford built camps and communities for those involved in extractive industries—including forest products. See Greg Grandin, *Fordlandia: The Rise and Fall of Henry Ford's Jungle City* (New York: Metropolitan, 2009), 30–65.

60. FERA funds were channeled through the Michigan State Relief Administration. See "Westacres," *Architectural Record* 80 (October 1936): 253. Westbrook quoted by Elsie Danenberg, *Get Your Own Home the Co-operative Way* (New York: Greenberg, 1949), 142.

61. [Oakland Housing, Inc.], *Westacres, 1936–1986*, [West Bloomfield Township, MI: n.d.], 1, Walter P. Reuther Library and Archives, Wayne State University, Detroit. See also Oakland Housing, Inc., *Once in a Lifetime* (Oakland Housing, Inc., n.d.).

62. *Westacres, 1936–1986*, 2. Residents agreed to repay the $4,400 mortgage provided by Oakland Housing over twenty or thirty years at 3 percent interest. In 1938–1939 Jenks and Arthur T. Wilson completed the WPA's Real Property Survey for Pontiac. See also "Couzens to Finance Homes for Workers," *New York Times*, June 20, 1935, 17; Lawrence Westbrook as told to George Creel, "No Down Payment," *Collier's*, February 2, 1946, 28; U.S. Department of Labor, Bureau of Labor Statistics, *Non-profit Housing Projects in the United States*, Bulletin 896 (Washington, DC: Government Printing Office, 1947), 32–39; and Danenberg, *Get Your Own Home the Co-operative Way*, 155.

63. Some units were occupied in March 1936. See *Westacres, 1936–1986*, 2. See also Robert E. Grese, "Jens Jensen: The Landscape Architect as Conservationist," in *Midwest Landscape Architecture*, ed. William Tishler (Urbana: University of Illinois Press, 2000), 117–140; and Miriam E. Rutz, "Genevieve Gillette: From Thrift Gardens to National Parks," in *Midwest Landscape Architecture*, 215–229.

64. Lawrence Westbrook, "Housing for Medium-Income Families," address to the National Public Housing Conference, typescript, n.d., 4, Vinton Papers, Box 19.

65. "Cooperatives Ask Federal Aid Credit," *New York Times*, October 11, 1936, N1. See also "W.P.A. Rural Director Calls It Quits," *Los Angeles Times*, June 21, 1936, 9; and "Westbrook Quits WPA Post," *New York Times*, June 20, 1936, 7. Westbrook negotiated an arrangement with the WPA (likely through Harry Hopkins) whereby he continued to direct the Matanuska Colony, the Pine Mountain Valley Colony in Georgia, the Dyess Colony in Arkansas, and Cherry Lake Farms in Florida after he left the WPA in the summer of 1936. See Westbrook, untitled typescript, 7.

66. On neighborhood planning, see Donald Leslie Johnson, "Origin of the Neighborhood Unit," *Planning Perspectives* 17, no. 3 (2002): 227–245. On Sunnyside and Radburn, see Daniel Schaffer, *Garden Cities for America: The Radburn Experience* (Philadelphia: Temple University Press, 1982). On the Park Living concept, see Richard J. Neutra, "Peace Can Gain from War's Forced Changes," *Pencil Points* 23 (November 1942): 31, 34.

67. "Cooperative Guinea Pig," January 1941, clipping, in Lawrence Westbrook to Herbert Emmerich, March 7, 1942, appendix, Westbrook Papers, 2E444, FF 50.

68. Neutra quoted in "Architect Neutra Builds for Family," *Los Angeles Times*, September 29, 1957, D9.

69. Neutra quoted in "Camden Plan," *California Arts and Architecture*, clipping, in Westbrook to Emmerich. Emphasis in original.

70. Lisa Ann Greenhouse, "Oskar Stonorov: Building Community on Shifting Ground" (master's thesis, George Washington University, 1997), 35; and James Ford, "American Architecture on the March," *Christian Science Monitor*, February 24, 1940, WM8.

71. "Neither for Sale nor Rent," *Architectural Forum* 74 (June 1941): 443. See also Westbrook as told to Creel, "No Down Payment," 26–28.

72. Senate Temporary National Economic Committee, *Toward More Housing; Monograph No. 8*, 77th Cong., 3rd Sess. (Washington, DC: Government Printing Office, 1940). See also "Neither for Sale nor Rent," 443. The *Engineering News-Record* erroneously reported that after he left the WPA, Westbrook "engaged in private practice with cooperative housing developments in the Southwest." See "Houses Built in Jig-Time," *Engineering News-Record*, May 5, 1941, 55. In 1937 Westbrook was appointed by the Senate Agriculture Committee to investigate the American Cotton Cooperative Association, an organization he helped found. See "Appoints Col. Westbrook," *New York Times*, August 1, 1937, 40. Shortly before, Westbrook had been considered for the appointment of a special investigator to examine relief expenditures in Washington, D.C. See "Investigator on D.C. Relief to Be Named," *Washington Post*, April 7, 1937, X16; and "Action Is Sped on District Bill by Conferees," *Washington Post*, March 10, 1938, 23.

73. Byrd quoted in Robert C. Albright, "Byrd Attacks 'Sinful Waste' at Greenbelt," *New York Times*, July 5, 1937, 1; and Conkin, *Tomorrow a New World*, 130.

74. In 1940, Westbrook was a "failed revolutionary" according to journalist David J. Foster. See David J. Foster, "In the Northeast, F.D.R.'s New Deal Housing Project," *Northeast News Gleaner*, August 16, 1995, 1.

75. The term "one-third of a nation ill housed" was drawn from President Roosevelt's second inaugural address of March 1937. The Federal Theater Project's ". . . One-Third of a Nation" was a stage production described as "A Living Newspaper about Housing." See George Kondolf to drama editor, "From the Drama Mailbag," *New York Times*, March 13, 1938, 166. Former U.S. housing administrator Nathan Straus called his postwar housing program "Two-Thirds of a Nation." See Nathan Straus, *Two-Thirds of a Nation: A Housing Program* (New York: Knopf, 1951).

76. Howard O. Hunter to Lawrence Westbrook, October 16, 1940, Westbrook Papers, 2E441, FF 4. The original letter is damaged.

77. Lawrence Westbrook to Howard O. Hunter, October 7, 1940, 1–2, Papers of John M. Carmody, President Franklin D. Roosevelt Library, Hyde Park, NY, Box 117.

78. Alexander von Hoffman, "The End of the Dream: The Political Struggle of America's Public Housers," *Journal of Planning History* 4, no. 3 (2005): 243.

79. Westbrook to Hunter, 2.

## CHAPTER 2

1. John H. Faley, "The Federal Home Loan Bank Board—1940," *1941 Housing Yearbook* (Chicago: National Association of Housing Officials, 1941), 267.

2. "National Unofficial Housing Agencies," *1941 Housing Yearbook* (Chicago: National Association of Housing Officials, 1941), 299.

3. "Building for Defense . . . Headway and Headaches," *Architectural Forum* 74 (June 1941): 425–429.

4. American Federation of Labor, *Proceedings of the Thirty-Fourth Annual Convention of the American Federation of Labor* (Washington, DC: American Federation of Labor, 1914), 355.

5. *Housing the Shipbuilders: Constructed during the War under the Direction of the United States Shipping Board, Emergency Fleet Corporation, Passenger Transportation and Housing Division* (Philadelphia: U.S. Shipping Board, 1920), 1; and U.S. Department of Labor, Bureau of Industrial Housing and Transportation, *Report of the United States Housing Corporation* (Washington, DC: Government Printing Office, 1920), 1:42. See also Robert Macieski, "The Home of the Workingman Is the Balance Wheel of Democracy," *Journal of Urban History* 26, no. 6 (2000): 715–740; Bruce Bustard, "Homes for War Workers: Federal Housing Policy during World War I," *Prologue* 24, no. 1 (1992): 33–43; and Nicholas Adams, "The United States Housing Corporation's Munitions Worker Suburb in Bethlehem, Pennsylvania and Its Architectural Context," *Pennsylvania Magazine of History and Biography* 108, no. 1 (1984): 59–86.

6. Gail Radford, *Modern Housing for America: Policy Struggles in the New Deal Era* (Chicago: University of Chicago Press, 1996), 44.

7. P.L. 76-849, October 14, 1940.

8. John M. Carmody to Lawrence Westbrook, August 24, 1942, Papers of John M. Carmody, President Franklin D. Roosevelt Library, Hyde Park, NY (hereafter Carmody Papers), Box 72. See also The Reminiscences of John M. Carmody (1954), Oral History Collection, Columbia University, New York, 595.

9. Johnston Birchall, "The Hidden History of Cooperative Housing in Britain," in *The Hidden History of Housing Cooperatives*, ed. Allan Heskin and Jacqueline Leavitt (Davis: University of California Press, 1995), 55–60.

10. Green quoted in "'Neither Subsidies nor Guarantees': Text of Statement by President Green on Need for Defense Housing," *Shipyard Worker* 5, no. 10 (September 6, 1940): 2. On the Glasgow rent strike, see Sean Damer, "State, Class and Housing: Glasgow, 1885-1919," in *Housing, Social Policy and the State*, ed. Joseph Melling (London: Croom Helm, 1980), 73–112; Joseph Melling, *Rent Strikes: Peoples' Struggle for Housing in West Scotland, 1890–1916* (Edinburgh: Polygon, 1983), 1–49; Joseph Melling, "Clydeside Housing and the Evolution of State Rent Control, 1900–1930," in *Housing, Social Policy and the State*, ed. Joseph Melling (London: Croom Helm, 1980), 139–167; and John Butt, "Working-Class Housing in Glasgow, 1851–1914," in *The History of Working-Class Housing: A Symposium*, ed. Stanley D. Chapman (Totowa, NJ: Rowman and Littlefield, 1971): 55–92.

11. Frank Rahill, "Johnny Green, Stabilizer," *Commonweal* 36 (June 1942): 155.

12. Electus D. Litchfield, "Yorkship Village," *American Review of Reviews* (December 1919): 601. See also Michael Lang, "International Influences on Urban Design: The Impact of Aesthetics of British Guild Socialism on Yorkship Village in Camden, New Jersey," *Planning History* 15, no. 1 (1993): 21–31.

13. "Government Housing Chaos," *The Nation* 108 (1919): 84–85. On the sale of World War I housing, see Mel Scott, *American City Planning since 1890: A History*

*Commemorating the Fiftieth Anniversary of the American Institute of Planners* (Berkeley: University of California Press, 1969), 172. On Yorkship Village, see "An Open Letter to the Public from Joseph P. Day," typescript, n.d., Camden County Historical Society, Fairview Vertical File, Camden, NJ. See also "Auction of 1898 Houses," *Washington Post*, November 2, 1921, 6; and "Shipboard to Sell the Towns It Built," *New York Times*, November 2, 1921, 9.

14. "Auction Shipyard Houses," *New York Times*, December 11, 1921, 20. See also "World's Greatest Auction Sale Ends," *New York Times*, December 15, 1921, 21; and "A $3,822,200 Auction," *New York Times*, December 18, 1921, 1.

15. Jinbin Park, "The Legacy of Conservative Reform: Making the First Public Housing in Philadelphia, 1890–1940" (Ph.D. diss., University of Pennsylvania, 2002), 163.

16. John Green wrote the speech to the National Public Housing Conference, which was held on April 25–26, 1941, but it was delivered by Henry Andreas. See Records of the Industrial Union of Marine and Shipbuilding Workers of America, University of Maryland Special Collections Library, College Park (hereafter IUMSWA Records), Series 5, Box 1.

17. Rahill, "Johnny Green, Stabilizer," 155.

18. Ibid.

19. David Palmer, *Organizing the Shipyards: Union Strategy in Three Northeast Ports* (Ithaca, NY: Cornell University Press, 1998), 15.

20. Rahill, "Johnny Green, Stabilizer," 155. Some shipbuilding workers tried to use the company union to gain concessions, but Green rejected that strategy and created an independent organization with an anticapitalist preamble that was later amended. See Palmer, *Organizing the Shipyards*, 34.

21. Ibid., 15–24.

22. Ibid.

23. "Shipyard Strike Called in Camden," *New York Times*, March 27, 1934, 3; and "7 War Ships Tied Up by Camden Strike," *New York Times*, March 28, 1934, 32.

24. Radford, *Modern Housing for America*, 111–144. See also Eric J. Sandeen, "The Design of Public Housing in the New Deal: Oskar Stonorov and the Carl Mackley Houses," *American Quarterly* 37, no. 5 (1985): 645–667; and Park, "Legacy of Conservative Reform," 182–186. On Stonorov, see Ursula Cliff, "Oskar Stonorov, Public Housing Pioneer," *Design and Environment* 2, no. 3 (1971): 50–57. Based in part on the "brilliant jobs" Katsner had completed for the RA, Edelman hired him to design the Textile Workers Union of America's postwar housing development in Front Royal, Virginia. See John Edelman, "Memo to Archives," April 18, 1963, The John Edelman Collection, Walter P. Reuther Library, Wayne State University, Detroit, Box 38.

25. Palmer, *Organizing the Shipyards*, 10. See also Thomas R. Heinrich, *Ships for the Seven Seas: Philadelphia Shipbuilding in the Age of Industrial Capitalism* (Baltimore: Johns Hopkins University Press, 1997); and Philip S. Foner, *Organized Labor and the Black Worker, 1619–1973* (New York: Praeger, 1974), 264.

26. Charles F. Hollopeter, "How Labor Led in Camden," *Public Housing* 3, no. 3 (1941): 6. Mary Susan Cole attributed support for public housing aid in Camden during the 1930s to the Camden Plan, which she erroneously associated with World War I. See Mary Susan Cole, "Catherine Bauer and the Public Housing Movement, 1926–1937" (Ph.D. diss., George Washington University, 1975), 368n1.

27. Bauer quoted in Cole, "Catherine Bauer," 258, 494.

28. "Shipyard Rejects Arbitration Plan," *New York Times*, July 22, 1935, 31.

29. "Shipyard Reopens but Few Go Back," *New York Times*, July 24, 1935, 37.

30. Ibid.

31. "Violence Marks Shipyard Strike," *New York Times*, July 25, 1935, 3; and Green quoted in "Shipyard Closed Again in Camden," *New York Times*, July 26, 1935, 2.

32. Holthusen quoted in "Look to U.S. to End Shipyard Strike," *New York Times*, July 28, 1935, NR.

33. Metten and Van Gelder quoted in "Shipyard Strike Is Laid to Reds," *New York Times*, July 30, 1935, 39; and Green quoted in "Metten Charges Denied," *New York Times*, July 30, 1935, 39.

34. The program was federalized because developers sought to use it to "unload on the government land for which they could find no other purchaser and at values far in excess of its appraised value." See Mabel L. Walker, *Urban Blight and Slums: Economic and Legal Factors in Their Origin, Reclamation, and Prevention* (Cambridge, MA: Harvard University Press, 1938), 320. Architect and planner Henry Churchill endorsed the decision. See Henry Churchill, "Housing Is Up to the Tenants," *New Republic*, August 15, 1934, 20. In December 1934 Ickes reported that one limited-dividend project was completed, five were under construction, and two were scheduled for construction. See Harold L. Ickes, "The Federal Housing Program," *New Republic*, December 19, 1934, 155–157. See also Edith Elmer Wood, *Slums and Blighted Areas in the U.S.*, U.S. Federal Emergency Administration of Public Works, Housing Division Pamphlet 1 (Washington, DC: Government Printing Office, 1935); *Urban Housing: The Story of the PWA Housing Division, 1933–1936*, U.S. Federal Emergency Administration of Public Works, Housing Division Pamphlet 2 (Washington, DC: Government Printing Office, 1936); and Horatio B. Hackett, "The Housing Activities of the Public Works Administration," *Housing* 23, no. 1 (1935): 29–37. The USHA reported that its predecessor agency completed seven projects. See U.S. Housing Authority, *Labor and Housing* (Washington, DC: Federal Works Agency, n.d.), 3.

35. Jack Levin, *Your Congress and American Housing: The Actions of Congress on Housing from 1892 to 1951* (Washington, DC: Government Printing Office, 1952), 6. Figures vary from fifty to fifty-three depending on the source. On the transfer of PWA developments to local public housing authorities, see Horatio B. Hackett, "Municipal Cooperation Leads PWA's Program of Slum Clearance and Low-Rent Housing," *American City* 50 (February 1935): 52–54. When Indianapolis's Lockefield Garden Apartments development was converted into USHA-subsidized public housing, 180 families exceeded income restrictions. Four months later, less than one-third had relocated. Those who had left either doubled up with other families or moved to substandard dwellings. See Citizens' Housing Committee, *Housing in Indianapolis: A Report of the Citizens' Housing Committee*, mimeograph, February 1940, 7, Indiana State Library, Indianapolis. Westfield Acres was razed in 2000 with funds from the Hope VI program. Archival material that was removed from the development's Camden Housing Authority office has apparently vanished. See Marc Levy, "Camden Projects' Legacy Lives On," *Philadelphia Inquirer*, December 17, 2000.

36. Lisa Ann Greenhouse, "Oskar Stonorov: Building Community on Shifting Ground" (master's thesis, George Washington University, 1997), 23. Stonorov worked out of Camden's Labor Temple, where workers often directed questions to him regarding the design. See Greenhouse, "Oskar Stonorov," 20, 25.

37. Greenwood recalled in a 1962 interview that before starting work on the mural she "went through the canning factories and hosiery factories and shipyard workers' docks. I saw the actual workers building the housing project." See oral interview with Marion Greenwood, January 31, 1964, Archives of American Art, Smithsonian

Institution, available at hppt://www.aaa.si.edu/collections/interviews/oral-history-inter view, accessed June 17, 2013.

38. American Federation of Labor, *History, Encyclopedia and Reference Book*, vol. 3, pt. 1 (Washington, DC: American Federation of Labor, 1960), 1192–1193. See also *Hearings Before the Senate Committee on Education and Labor on S. 4424*, 74th Cong., 2nd Sess. (statement of Harry Bates) (Washington, DC: Government Printing Office, 1936), 43. Jo Ann Argersinger claimed labor was initially divided on public housing. See Jo Ann E. Argersinger, "Contested Visions of American Democracy: Citizenship, Public Housing, and the International Arena," *Journal of Urban Planning* 36, no. 3 (2010): 800–801. The inadequacy of funds for PWA housing prompted the head of the NYC Housing Authority, Langdon Post, to remark in September 1935 that the program stood on the "brink of being a total failure." See "U.S. Housing Plan Attacked by Post," *New York Times*, September 18, 1935, 17.

39. *Hearings Before the Committee on Education and Labor on S. 2392*, 74th Cong., 1st Sess. (statement of Catherine Bauer) (Washington, DC: Government Printing Office, 1935), 91. See also Cole, "Catherine Bauer," 272–276; Gail Radford, *Modern Housing for America: Policy Struggles in the New Deal Era* (Chicago: University of Chicago Press, 1996), 185–186; and H. Peter Overlander and Eva Newbrun, *Houser: The Life and Work of Catherine Bauer* (Vancouver: University of British Columbia Press, 1999), 131–135.

40. Public Housing Committee, U.S. Building and Loan League, "Report by the Public Housing Committee of the U.S. Building and Loan League," in *Public Housing in America*, comp. M. B. Schnapper, *The Reference Shelf No. 13* (New York: Wilson, 1939), 201–202. See also Radford, *Modern Housing for America*, 185; Samuel Zipp, "The Roots and Routes of Urban Renewal," *Journal of Urban History* 39, no. 3 (2012): 380; and D. Brad Hunt, "Was the 1937 U.S. Housing Act a Pyrrhic Victory?" *Journal of Planning History* 4, no. 3 (2005): 195–221.

41. Lee E. Cooper, "Housing Authorities Soon to Be at Work in New York and New Jersey Communities," *New York Times*, March 30, 1938, 39. Labor was part of a coalition that advocated for the creation of the Housing Authority of Baltimore City. See Deborah Weiner, "From Modern Victory to Postmodern Defeat: Two Baltimore Housing Projects," *Maryland Historian* 26, no. 2 (1995): 25.

42. Hollopeter, "How Labor Led in Camden," 7. Westfield Acres, designed by Hettel, Stonorov and Associates, and the community center at Branch Village, designed by Hettel, Stonorov, and Radey, were featured in an exhibit on housing by the Museum of Modern Art. See "Circulating Exhibition on Homes and Housing," n.d., Archives of the Museum of Modern Art, New York, New York Research File 11.1/64(5).

43. John Green, "Organized Labor and Housing," typescript, May 23, 1944, 6, IUMSWA Records, Series 1, Box 5.

44. Local housing authorities were exempted from the provisions of the U.S. Housing Act that required them to raze an equal number of substandard dwelling units and clear slums. The defense housing developments built under P.L. 671 were to be converted into low-income public housing developments at the end of the war. See "USHA Provides Homes Now and in the Future," *Public Housing* 2, no. 42 (1941): 1. On AFL support for P.L. 671, see Harry C. Bates, "Housing Defense Workers," *American Federationist* 48 (August 1941): 9, 31.

45. Carmody expressed regret that, when President Roosevelt was considering appointing Palmer as defense housing coordinator, he was consulted and spoke in favor

of the appointment. See Oscar Stonorov to John M. Carmody, Carmody's handwritten notation, October 1, 1941, Carmody Papers, Box 72.

46. Homes were advertised for sale in suburban-like settings in the *Shipyard Worker*. See "Inganamort 40-Features Homes," *Shipyard Worker* 6 (November 7, 1941): D; and "Defense Workers Live Rent Free," *Shipyard Worker* 6 (May 8, 1942): 6, IUMSWA Records, Series 8, Box 4.

47. John Green, "New Homes for Old," *CIO News*, May 13, 1940, 3; John Green to Anthony Wayne Smith, March 15, 1940, IUMSWA Records, Series 1, Subseries 2, Box 1; Industrial Union of Marine and Shipbuilding Workers of America, "Prewar and Wartime Living Standards of Shipyard Workers," typescript, November 1, 1944, U.S. Department of Labor Library, Washington, DC; John T. Jones to John Green, telegram, February 27, 1940, IUMSWA Records, Series 1, Subseries 2, Box 2; and "Home Owners Tell Their Woes," *Shipyard Worker* 4, no. 25 (1940): 5. The AFL also cautioned against home ownership among defense workers. See American Federation of Labor, *Report of the Proceedings of the Sixty-First Annual Convention of the AFL* (Washington, DC: American Federation of Labor, 1941), 657.

48. Green, "New Homes for Old," 7.

49. Ibid.

50. Ibid.

51. "'Neither Subsidies nor Guarantees,'" 2.

52. *Hearings Before the Committee on Public Buildings and Grounds on H.R. 10412*, No. 11, 76th Cong., 3rd Sess. (statement of John Green) (Washington, DC: Government Printing Office, 1940), 68. Green requested federal aid in July. See "Union Seeks 7500 Homes," *Shipyard Worker* 5, no. 2 (July 12, 1940): 1–2. On housing shortages in Camden and other shipbuilding centers, see "Workers Urge Defense Housing for 5 Cities," *Public Housing* 2 (July 1940): 4; Alan Mather, "Slow Progress in Housing for Shipyard Workers," *Pencil Points* 22 (January 1941): 47–52; and "Survey Finds on 3 p.c. of Camden's 31,447 Dwelling Units Vacant," *Courier-Post* (Camden, NJ), January 27, 1941, Camden County Historical Society Vertical File, Camden, NJ. Early in the war New Jersey was a leader in defense contracting. See "Building for Defense," *Architectural Forum* 74 (March 1941): 171.

53. *Hearings Before the Committee on Public Buildings and Grounds on H.R. 10412* (statement of John Green), 68. See also "Housing Demanded by CIO at Kearny," *Courier-Post* (Camden, NJ), January 27, 1941. Shipbuilding workers and dockworkers shared similar housing problems. Compare Elizabeth Ogg, *Longshoremen and Their Homes* (New York: Greenwich House, 1939). On New York Ship and Federal Ship, see David Palmer, "Organizing the Shipyards: Unionization at New York Ship, Federal Ship, and Fore River, 1898–1945" (Ph.D. diss., Brandeis University, 1990).

54. "'Neither Subsidies nor Guarantees,'" 2. See also "Pres. Green to Confer with Gov't Heads, Today, to Break Housing Jam," *Shipyard Worker* 5, no. 9 (August 30, 1940): 1; and "Deadlock on Housing Sought by IUMSWA Seen Broken by Pres. Green in 3-Day Drive," *Shipyard Worker* 5, no. 10 (September 6, 1940): 1. In 1935 Green and delegations of shipbuilding workers were going to Washington, D.C., to make direct appeals to Congress or the White House by "camping on President Roosevelt's doorstep." See "Strikers Off to Capital," *New York Times*, August 15, 1935, 39.

55. R. J. Thomas, *Housing for Defense* (Detroit: United Automobile Workers Union, 1942), 18, 28.

56. Ibid., 28.

57. Mather, "Slow Progress," 50.

58. Reminiscences of John M. Carmody, 594–595.

59. John M. Carmody to Lawrence Westbrook, August 24, 1942, Carmody Papers, Box 72.

60. "Green Pushed Union Demand," Supplement to *Courier-Post* (Camden, NJ), December 13, 1941, 9.

61. On the Lanham Act, P.L. 849, 76th Cong., 3rd Sess. (1940), its amendments, and other related measures, see *Defense Housing Digest: A Summary of Laws, Regulations, and Results* (Chicago: National Association of Housing Officials, 1940). On debate over defense housing legislation, see "Congress in Housing Snarl," *Business Week*, September 14, 1940, 20.

62. Philip J. Funigiello, *The Challenge to Urban Liberalism: Federal-City Relations during World War II* (Knoxville: University of Tennessee Press, 1978), 5. See also Charles Abrams, "Housing the War Workers," *New Republic*, December 29, 1941, 886.

63. "War Housing," *The Distributor*, March 15, 1942, 4.

64. Andreas quoted in *Proceedings of the Seventh National Conference of the Industrial Union of Marine and Shipbuilding Workers of America* (Camden, NJ: Industrial Union of Marine and Shipbuilding Workers of America, 1941), 65. See also "12 Projects Slated in Defense Housing," *New York Times*, November 30, 1940, 8.

65. Lawrence Westbrook to John B. Blandford Jr., March 7, 1942, 2, Lawrence Westbrook Papers, The Texas Collection, Carroll Library, Baylor University, Waco, TX (hereafter Westbrook Papers), 2E444, FF 50. See also "FWA Cuts Pattern for Co-op Housing," *Public Housing Progress* (January 1941), unpaged; and "Officers' Report to the Seventh National Convention," 11–12, IUMSWA Records, Series 4, Subseries 1, Box 1. Thomas was grateful that the mutual housing plan was "receiving wide national publicity" but dismayed that the "part played by the union is being generally overlooked." See Thomas, *Housing for Defense*, 28.

66. Sarah Jo Peterson, *Planning the Home Front: Building Bombers and Communities at Willow Run* (Chicago: University of Chicago Press, 2013), 90–95. On the dream house ideal, see John Archer, *Architecture and Suburbia: From English Villa to American Dream House, 1690–2000* (Minneapolis: University of Minnesota Press, 2005), 260–289. See also Tom Martinson, *American Dreamscapes: The Pursuit of Happiness in Postwar Suburbia* (New York: Carroll and Graf, 2000); Dolores Hayden, *Redesigning the Dream: The Future of Housing, Work, and Family Life* (New York: Norton, 1984; rev. ed., 2002); and Jan Cohn, *The Palace or the Poorhouse: The American House as Cultural Symbol* (East Lansing: Michigan State University Press, 1979).

67. "Housing's Forgotten People," *Walnut Grove Gazette* 1, no. 1 (December 1944): Walnut Grove Mutual Housing Association History File, South Bend, IN, 1. See also Marvin M. Miniard, "Mutual Ownership: The Workingmen's Plan," *Walnut Grove Gazette* 1, no. 1 (December 1944): 1.

68. Lawrence Westbrook, "Housing for Medium-Income Families," typescript of address to the National Public Housing Conference, n.d., 6, Warren J. Vinton Papers, Olin Library, Cornell University, Ithaca, NY (hereafter Vinton Papers), Box 19, FF 42. See also Lawrence Westbrook, "Explanation of the Proposed 'Camden Plan,'" Press Release No. 83, March 21, 1941, Vinton Papers, Box 19, FF 42; and Lawrence Westbrook, "Home Ownership by Workers Made Feasible," *Labor Information Bulletin* 8, no. 9 (1941): 10–11.

69. Lawrence Westbrook to Howard O. Hunter, October 7, 1940, Carmody Papers, Box 72. On the bottom of Howard's letter of transmittal, Carmody wrote in longhand, "This plan of Lawrence Westbrook became the basis for the Federal Works' Mutual Housing program. It was under this plan that Audubon in Camden, N.J. was built (and

later projects in five or six cities—Dallas, Tex. among them). I always have been surprised the plan has not spread more widely. JMC." See Howard O. Hunter to John M. Carmody, memorandum, October 10, 1940, Carmody Papers, Box 72.

70. Federal Works Agency, "Mutual Ownership Defense Housing," Release No. 9149, n.d., Vinton Papers, Box 19.

71. Lawrence Westbrook, "The Camden Plan of Rental Housing as Explained by Col. L. Westbrook, Assistant Administrator," typescript, n.d., 2, Carmody Papers, Box 103.

72. Westbrook and Green shared a commitment to all four of the "four distinct worlds," or realms, identified in Marc A. Weiss, "Developing and Financing the 'Garden Metropolis': Urban Planning and Housing Policy in Twentieth-Century America," *Planning Perspectives* 5, no. 3 (1990): 308.

73. John R. Lutes, "Cooperative Mutual Housing," speech before the National Cooperative League Congress, Columbus, Ohio, September 9, 1946, Leo Goodman Papers, Manuscript Division, Library of Congress, Box 36, FF 1.

74. Carmody to Westbrook, August 24, 1942. On the shortage of housing in the Philadelphia/Camden area before and during the war, see Charles F. Palmer's remarks in "U.S. Speeds Village," Supplement to *Courier-Post* (Camden, NJ), December 13, 1941, 2. Carmody assigned the Audubon project to Westbrook's Mutual Division on November 28, 1940, eight days after it was authorized by President Roosevelt. See U.S. Federal Works Agency, *Annual Report for 1941* (Washington, DC: Government Printing Office, 1942), 226, table 14. When Audubon Village opened, 900 families applied for the 499 available units. See "Tenants Buy Town in New House Plan," *New York Times*, November 9, 1941, 44.

75. Lawrence Westbrook, "The Housing Mess," typescript, Westbrook Papers, 2E444, FF 51. Westbrook testified that he and Lanham had met with Carmody and Hunter in 1940. See *Hearings Before the Committee on Banking and Currency on S. 1592*, Part 2, 79th Cong., 1st Sess. (testimony of Lawrence Westbrook) (Washington, DC: Government Printing Office, 1945), 1076. Lanham was an opponent of low-income public housing; see Lanham quoted in Nathan Straus, *The Seven Myths of Housing* (New York: Knopf, 1944), 210.

76. Lawrence Westbrook, typescript of statement of before the House Committee on Banking and Currency on H.R. 5631, Westbrook Papers, 2E444, FF 52.

77. *Hearings Before the Committee on Banking and Currency on S. 1592*, Part 2, 79th Cong., 1st Sess. (testimony of John Carson) (Washington, DC: Government Printing Office, 1946), 1067.

78. Carmody quoted in "Camden Plan."

79. Ibid.

80. Carmody quoted in "Landscape Architects Hear FWA Chief," *Washington Post*, January 28, 1941, 13.

81. Kathryn R. Murphy, "Housing for War Workers," *Monthly Labor Review* 54 (June 1942): 1266.

82. Frank E. Hill, "Housing Plan Suggested by Labor," *American Architect* 118 (September 22, 1920): 376.

## CHAPTER 3

1. On Kazan, see Peter Eisenstadt, *Rochdale Village: Robert Moses, 6,000 Families, and New York City's Great Experiment in Integrated Housing* (Ithaca, NY: Cornell University Press, 2010), chap. 1. In 1931 Stonorov tried to get work designing cooperative

housing for the Amalgamated Clothing Workers Union. See Richard Pommer, "The Architecture of Urban Housing in the United States during the Early 1930s," *Journal of the Society of Architectural Historians* 37, no. 4 (1978): 238n9. See also Andrew Dolkart, "Homes for People: Non-profit Cooperatives in New York, 1916–1929," *SITES* (May 1989): 20; and Richard Plunz, *The History of Housing in New York City* (New York: Columbia University Press, 1990), 165–167.

2. Donald C. Parson, *Making a Better World: Public Housing, the Red Scare, and the Direction of Modern Los Angeles* (Minneapolis: University of Minnesota Press, 2005), 34. See also Jean-Louis Cohen, *Architecture in Uniform: Designing and Building for the Second World War* (New Haven, CT: Yale University Press, 2011), 45.

3. Green conveyed his recommendations to Sidney Hillman verbally instead of by letter, asking Carmody to select "local architects" with "local experience," as Stonorov requested. The architect needlessly feared that this "typical Johnny Green gesture" might cost his firm the job. See Oscar Stonorov to John Edelman, October 25, 1940, Papers of Oscar Stonorov, Collection 04375, University of Wyoming American Heritage Center, Laramie (hereafter Stonorov Papers), Box 38, Folder 3. See also Lisa Ann Greenhouse, "Oskar Stonorov: Building Community on Shifting Ground" (master's thesis, George Washington University, 1997), 10.

4. "Building for Defense . . . Government Housing in a Hurry," *Architectural Forum* 75 (November 1941): 341. See also "FDR Approves Defense Housing Start; Camden Project Gets Underway," *Shipyard Worker* 5, no. 22 (November 29, 1940): 1, 5; and Lawrence Westbrook to Joseph Hettel and Oscar Stonorov, December 4, 1940, Stonorov Papers, Box 38, Folder 3. Westbrook was reported to have two "paintings" of Audubon Village but their whereabouts are unknown. See Gladys A. La Fetra to Eliot F. Noyes, January 13, 1942, Circulating Exhibition Album, Architecture, A4, Exhibition: Wartime Housing, Archives of the Museum of Modern Art, New York.

5. "Housing Work in Audubon to Start Today," *Morning Post* (Camden, NJ), January 6, 1941, 1, 4.

6. "Houses Built in Jig-Time," *Engineering News-Record*, May 5, 1941, 817; "25 Men Begin WPA Project to Prepare Site for Audubon Housing," *Morning Post* (Camden, NJ), January 7, 1941, 3; "Audubon Rulers O.K. Housing Plans," *Courier-Post* (Camden, NJ), January 8, 1941, 2; and "Ground Broken for Defense Housing Project in Audubon," *Courier-Post* (Camden, NJ), January 16, 1941, 3. In 1940 the FWA was called upon by the CIO to investigate claims that the AFL was forcing WPA workers to pay work permit fees at a California military base. See "WPA Work Fees Charged by CIO," *Christian Science Monitor*, December 24, 1942, 2.

7. The *Engineering News-Record* reported that the building was an "abandoned foundry." See "Houses in Jig-Time," 816. On the CIO dispute, see "Building for Defense . . . Headway and Headaches," *Architectural Forum* 75 (April 1941): 77, 80; and "Housing Cycle: Defense Urgencies Bring Advancement of New Techniques and at Same Time Result in a New Plan of Financing," *Business Week*, August 16, 1941, 42–46.

8. "Building for Defense . . . Government Housing in a Hurry," 344. On the Carmody agreement, see The Reminiscences of John M. Carmody (1954), Oral History Collection, Columbia University, New York, 630. Architect John Rowland indicated that Williams tried to adapt his designs for prefabrication, but ultimately abandoned the idea. See *Hearings Before the Senate Special Committee Investigating the National Defense Program Pursuant to S. 71*, 81st Cong., 2nd Sess. (testimony of John Rowland) (Washington, DC: Government Printing Office, 1950), 6078. The *Engineering News-Record* indicated "labor conditions" as the "probable" reason that prefabricated housing was not provided for

Winfield Park. See "FWA Speeds Construction of Prefabricated Housing," *Engineering News-Record*, July 10, 1941, 67. The Clifford L. MacEvoy Company completed the Winfield Park dwellings at a rate of two a day using "a precut lumber and site assembly technique for erection." See "Park Living Plan for Defense Housing," *Engineering News-Record*, November 20, 1941, 704.

9. Palmer quoted in "Palmer Proud of Record Set," in "U.S. Speeds Village of New Homes for Defense Workers," Supplement to the *Courier-Post* (Camden, NJ), December 13, 1941, 5. See also Daniel P. McDonnell, "Plant at Gloucester to Fabricate Houses," *Morning Post* (Camden, NJ), March 5, 1941, 1, 4.

10. "Work Is Hobby of Joseph Day," in "U.S. Speeds Village," Supplement to the *Courier-Post* (Camden, NJ), December 13, 1941, 6.

11. "20 Prefabricated Houses per Day—Built by Joseph Day," in "U.S. Speeds Village," Supplement to the *Courier-Post* (Camden, NJ), December 13, 1941, 7. Stonorov's interest in prefabrication is furthered evidenced by his work with Louis I. Kahn on the "Hotel for 194X" design. See Urs Buttiker, *Louis I. Kahn: Light and Space* (New York: Whitney Library of Design, 1994), 47.

12. "20 Prefabricated Houses per Day," 7.

13. "Building for Defense . . . Government Housing in a Hurry," 341.

14. Joseph P. Day to Franklin D. Roosevelt, December 5, 1941, Audubon Park Mutual Housing Corporation Historical File, Audubon Park, NJ.

15. Burns Roensch quoted in "Houses in Jig Time," 57. Roensch was with Westbrook, Hettel, and Stonorov when the bids from general contractors for Audubon Village were opened. See "9 Bids Are Open in Audubon Project," *Courier-Post* (Camden, NJ), February 4, 1941, 3; and "Audubon Housing Awarded on 'Negotiated Fixed Fee Basis,'" *Courier-Post* (Camden, NJ), February 6, 1941, 3. Wheeler's Arthur Hamburger established the schedule of field erection. See Lawrence Westbrook to Charles F. Palmer, May 5, 1941, National Archives and Records Administration, College Park, MD (hereafter NARA), RG 207, Box 21. The cost effectiveness of Audubon Village's prefab housing was questioned. See "500-House Experiment at Camden, New Jersey: FWA Defense Housing Project Tries Mutual Ownership Plan as Well as Prefabrication," *American Builder* 63 (August 1941): 53, 116; and Howard Robertson, "Defense Housing in the U.S.A.," *Architect and Building News*, February 27, 1942, 165.

16. "Building for Defense . . . Government Housing in a Hurry," 341.

17. "Never Before," advertisement, in "U.S. Speeds Village," Supplement to the *Courier-Post* (Camden, NJ), December 13, 1941, 4.

18. "Weigel Veteran at Rush Jobs," in "U.S. Speeds Village," Supplement to the *Courier-Post* (Camden, NJ), December 13, 1941, 8.

19. Ibid.

20. Ibid.

21. Weigel quoted in "Weigel Veteran at Rush Jobs," 8.

22. "Houses Built in Jig-Time," 817. See also the photograph of Audubon Village on the cover of the *Engineering News-Record*, July 10, 1941.

23. "More Housing Jobs Get 'Camden Plan' Financing," *Engineering News-Record*, October 30, 1941, 13.

24. "Houses Built in Jig-Time," 813.

25. "500-House Experiment at Camden, New Jersey," 52.

26. "Audubon Housing Plan," *Real Estate Record and Builders Guide*, November 15, 1941.

27. "Housing Essential to Defense Says President Roosevelt," in "U.S. Speeds Village," Supplement to the *Courier-Post* (Camden, NJ), December 13, 1941, 3.

28. Of the 499 units, 112, or 25 percent, had an attached one-car garage. "Village Called Only Signpost," in "U.S. Speeds Village," Supplement to the *Courier-Post* (Camden, NJ), December 13, 1941, 11.

29. "Plenty Fresh Air," *Shipyard Worker* 6 (May 9, 1941): D.

30. See the photograph of Audubon Village on the cover of "U.S. Speeds Village," Supplement to the *Courier-Post* (Camden, NJ), December 13, 1941.

31. Willis Winters, "Avion Village: Enduring Values of Community," *Texas Architect* 38, no. 3 (1988): 26. The support that war housing agencies gave to planning is largely overlooked. See Howard Gillette Jr., "The Evolution of Neighborhood Planning from the Progressive Era to the 1949 Housing Act," *Journal of Urban History* 9, no. 4 (1983): 421–444.

32. A shopping center, cooperative gas station, and tennis courts were included in the original site plan. Plans to improve the land fronting on Peters Creek and make it available to residents for recreation, linking the development to Camden County's ambitious Cooper River watershed improvement project, were also not realized. See "Building for Defense . . . Government Housing in a Hurry."

33. John F. Bauman, *Public Housing, Race, and Renewal: Urban Planning in Philadelphia, 1920–1974* (Philadelphia: Temple University Press, 1987), 72.

34. "500 Families Test New Housing Plan," *Trenton Evening News*, October 9, 1941, 5.

35. Elsie Danenberg, *Get Your Own Home the Co-operative Way* (New York: Greenberg, 1949), 154.

36. Frank Rahill, "Johnny Green, Stabilizer," *Commonweal* 36 (June 1942): 155.

37. "12,000 More Homes Needed for Defense Workers," in "U.S. Speeds Village," Supplement to the *Courier-Post* (Camden, NJ), December 13, 1941, 16.

38. "Housing Project, Bellmawr, New Jersey—Comments by the Architects," *Architectural Forum* 78 (January 1943): 74. Emphasis in original.

39. Ibid.

40. Ibid., 78.

41. The architects had previously attempted to "distill the culture of planning into a diagram that could be understood by anyone. Concentric rings were used to illustrate the connections between house planning, neighborhood planning, city planning, regional planning and national planning." See Andrew Shanken, *194X: Architecture, Planning, and Consumer Culture on the Home Front* (Minneapolis: University of Minnesota Press, 2009), 1–2. See also Cohen, *Architecture in Uniform*, 116; and Philip Nobel, "Who Built Mr. Blanding's Dream House?" in *Architecture and Film*, ed. Mark Lamster (Princeton, NJ: Princeton Architectural Press, 2013), 6–70. Thomas W. Hanchett argued that the Lanham Act encouraged local communities to plan. See Thomas W. Hanchett, "Roots of the 'Renaissance': Federal Incentives to Urban Planning, 1941–1947," paper presented at the Fourth Biennial Meeting of the Society for American and City Regional Planning History, 1991; copy in the author's possession. Perry R. Duis also found evidence that Chicago began planning for postwar development during the war. See Perry R. Duis, "Symbolic Unity and the Neighborhood: Chicago during World War II," *Journal of Urban History* 21, no. 2 (1995): 203–204. Historian Roger Lotchin found the war's influence on planning in California to be more "ambiguous." See Roger Lotchin, "World War II and Urban California," *Pacific Historical Review* 62, no. 2 (1993): 170. In Portland's case the influence of the war on planning was mixed. See Carl Abbott, "Portland and the Pacific

War: Planning from 1940 to 1945," *Urbanism Past and Present* 11 (Winter–Spring, 1980–1981): 12–24.

42. The *Philadelphia Record* quoted in "Brief on Behalf of the Pennypack Woods Home Ownership Association," mimeograph, Pennypack Mutual Housing Corporation Historical File, Philadelphia. The construction contract ran from September 6, 1941, to March 15, 1942, allowing the contractor 160 calendar days to complete the work.

43. M. Herbert Syme to Raymond Foley, February 18, 1949, 3, Pennypack Mutual Housing Corporation Historical File, Philadelphia. Emphasis in the original.

44. "History of Mutual Ownership at Pennypack Woods," *Pennypack Woods Chit Chat*, Special Edition, March 31, 1950, 1, General Pamphlet Collection, Part 30, Urban Archives Collection, Samuel L. Paley Library, Temple University, Philadelphia.

45. On Federal Ship, see "Strike Threatened at Jersey Shipyard," *Trenton Evening Times*, July 1, 1941, 20. Joseph Wright Sr. quoted in Christopher M. Loder, "A Town Just Like a Family," *Star-Ledger*, September 16, 1990, Winfield Park Mutual Housing Association Historical File, Winfield, NJ, 1.

46. "Development of a Park Site," *Architectural Record* 90 (November 1941): 86–87.

47. "Local 16 Group Okays Site for Defense Homes," *Shipyard Worker* 5, no. 44 (April 11, 1941): 1–2. See also "Union Political Lights to Fete Local 16 Homes," *Shipyard Worker* 5, no. 49 (May 23, 1941): 1; "Gets Jersey Housing Contract," *New York Times*, June 4, 1941, 37; and "Rapid Progress on Homes Lo 16 Sponsors," *Shipyard Worker* 5, no. 52 (June 27, 1941): 5. Details on the community's construction were featured in the *Architectural Record*, a leading professional journal, in November 1941. See "Housing for Defense: A Building Types Study," *Architectural Record* 90 (November 1941): 86–87. On site selection, see "Housing Plan Approved," *New York Times*, March 29, 1941, 17.

48. Rowland testified that the pitch of the roofs was reduced (presumably to make the dwelling units appear more modern) without his consultation. See *Hearings Before the Special Committee Investigating the National Defense Program Pursuant to S. 71*, 76th Cong., 2nd Sess. (testimony of John Rowland) (Washington, DC: Government Printing Office, 1942), 6081.

49. FWA, Mutual Ownership Defense Housing Division, groundbreaking program, June 7, 1941, Clark Township, New Jersey, Papers of John M. Carmody, President Franklin D. Roosevelt Library, Hyde Park, NY, Box 103.

50. *Hearings Before the Special Committee Investigating the National Defense Program Pursuant to S. 71* (testimony of Clifford MacEvoy), 6112–6113. MacEvoy built the housing; the Agostini Brothers Construction Company built the community building. See "To Build War Housing," *New York Times*, August 8, 1943, RE2.

51. "Defense Homes Get 135 Tenants," *New York Times*, December 2, 1941, 26. According to the FPHA, 81 units were occupied in November 1941, 141 units were occupied in December, and 181 were occupied in January 1942. See *Hearings Before the Special Committee Investigating the National Defense Program Pursuant to S. 71* (testimony of Lorimer C. Graef), 6049.

52. Leona Burke, interviewed by Kristin M. Szylvian and Matthew Weismantel, June 11, 2001, Winfield Park, NJ.

53. On Federal Ship, see "Strike Threatened at Jersey Shipyard," *Trenton Evening Times*, July 1, 1941, 20. Joseph Wright Sr. quoted in Christopher M. Loder, "Town Just Like a Family."

54. Dallas Chamber of Commerce, Defense Housing Committee, quoted in Holmes Green, "Dallas Builds a New City within a City," *Dallas Magazine*, March 1941, 10. On race and housing in wartime Dallas, see Andrew Wiese, *Places of Their Own: African*

*American Suburbanization in the Twentieth Century* (Chicago: University of Chicago Press, 2003), 196–199.

55. "Avion Village," typescript, n.d., Papers of Richard and Dione Neutra, Special Collections Library, University of California, Los Angeles (hereafter Neutra Papers), Box 21, FF 6. DeWitt was to pay Neutra $600 for serving as a consulting architect on the Avion project. Financial problems prompted him to delay paying Neutra his final $200 installment. See Richard J. Neutra to David R. Williams, June 30, 1941, Papers of David R. Williams, Edith Garland Dupré Library, University of Louisiana, Lafayette (hereafter Williams Papers), FF 2-16; and Neutra to Williams, August 4, 1941, Williams Papers, FF 2-17. Avion Village's construction contractor, Henry C. Beck, president of the Central Contracting Company, knew of DeWitt's financial troubles. See Henry C. Beck to David R. Williams, May 9, 1941, Williams Papers, FF 2-16. On DeWitt's bankruptcy, see Richard J. Neutra to David R. and Lyle Williams, April 8, 1942, Williams Papers, FF 2-18. For more on Neutra's role, see Cohen, *Architecture in Uniform*, 117.

56. "Federal Housing for Aviation Workers," *Architectural Forum* 75 (July 1941): 5; "Low-Cost Houses," *Architectural Forum* 75 (October 1941): 240–242; "Texas Workmen Build Finished Home in 58 Minutes," *Life*, June 9, 1941, 59–60, 63; "Ready for Unique Building Battle," *Dallas Times Herald*, May 15, 1941, clipping, Williams Papers, FF 16-15; "Race to Complete Fabricated Houses at Avion All Set," *Dallas News*, May 15, 1941, clipping, Williams Papers, FF 15-16; and "House-Building Battle in Grand Prairie Pasture to Make 1941 Banner Year," *Dallas Times Herald*, May 16, 1941, clipping, Williams Papers, FF 15-16. The contest was covered in wire service stories that appeared in newspapers in Washington, Indianapolis, Memphis, and other cities. See Avion Village Mutual Housing Corporation Historical File, Grand Prairie, TX. See also "Four-Room House Up in 58 Minutes," *Christian Science Monitor*, May 17, 1941, 1; "Aircraft Workers Get New Housing," *New York Times*, October 8, 1941, 41; "Defense Housing Being Erected on Mass-Output," *New York Times*, October 12, 1941, 6; "Houses for Defense," *Architectural Forum* 75 (November 1941): 327–329; Dave Williams, "Defense on the Home Front: Avion Village," *Dallas Magazine*, May 1941, 18–19; David Dillon, "Avion Village," in *Modernist Visions and the Contemporary American City* (Austin: Center for the Study of American Architecture, University of Texas, 1989), 5:118–120; and Kristin M. Szylvian, "Avion Village: Texas' World War II Housing Laboratory," *Legacies* 6 (Fall 1992): 28–34. Michael Glen Wade observed that, although Avion Village was for white workers, racially integrated crews were used for the contest as a show of "cooperation on behalf of national defense." See Michael Glen Wade, "David Reichard Williams: Avant-Garde Architect and Community Planner, 1890–1962" (Ph.D. diss., University of Southeastern Louisiana, 1978), 367. A Williams biographer said that Williams had the idea for the contest. See Muriel Quest McCarthy, *David R. Williams: Pioneer Architect* (Dallas: Southern Methodist University Press, 1984), 137.

57. Miles L. Colean, "Prefabrication Needs Architects," *Architectural Record* 90 (September 1941): 64–68. Architecture professor Barbara Brown Wilson called Avion Village an example of "sustainable" architecture. See Barbara Brown Wilson, "Before the 'Triple Bottom Line': New Deal Defense Housing as Proto-sustainability," *Journal of Planning History* 14, no. 1 (2015): 4–18.

58. Wade, "David Reichard Williams," 189, 192–198. For a flattering sketch of Williams, see Wellington Brink, "David Reichard Williams: Advance-Guard Architect," *Holland's, the Magazine of the South*, clipping, Williams Papers, FF 2-16. Williams had

previously designed a prefabricated National Youth Administration recreation center. See Louis Haley to William E. Flanagan, May 21, 1941, Williams Papers, FF 2-16.

59. Richard J. Neutra, *Buildings and Projects*, ed. W. Boesiger (Zurich: Girsberger, 1951). See also Esther McCoy, *Richard Neutra* (New York: Braziller, 1960). Neutra's Channel Heights featured prefabricated construction. See Harrison Stephens, "Los Angeles Completes 5 Lanham Act Projects," *Architect and Engineer* 13 (September 1943): 16.

60. "Mass-Production Homes Held Solution of Housing Poor," *Washington Post*, July 9, 1938, X2.

61. Neutra quoted in "Notes in Passing," *California Arts and Architecture* 59 (January 1942): 15. Temporary housing was future slum housing in the estimation of the USHA's Straus. See Nathan Straus, *The Seven Myths of Housing* (New York: Knopf, 1944), 211.

62. Wade, "David Reichard Williams," 359. McCarthy reported that Williams "went on to do twelve more permanent housing projects," including Pennypack Woods (identified as "Pennypack Park"), Kramer Homes, and an unnamed San Diego development. See McCarthy, *David R. Williams*, 137.

63. Beck to Williams, May 9, 1941. See also "Work Begins on Housing for Big Plant," *Dallas Morning News*, April 22, 1941, clipping, Williams Papers, FF 15-16; and "Building for Defense . . . Prefabricated Steel Walls," *Architectural Forum*, 2–5, 38. Sixteen units were constructed first to test the assembly procedure. See Winters, "Avion Village," 25, 28.

64. Beck to Williams, May 9, 1941.

65. Beck to Williams, May 9, 1941; and Irvin to Williams, July 9, 1941. On construction subcontracting, see Frank M. Roberts to Central Contracting Company, April 17, 1941, Williams Papers, FF 2-16. Beck's Central Contracting Company continued to receive detailed instructions on how to cut costs into April 1941. See Burns Roensch to Henry C. Beck, April 9, 1941, Williams Papers, FF 2-16.

66. Westbrook quoted in "Strikes Halt Defense Jobs," *Los Angeles Times*, July 24, 1941, 18. See also Beck to Williams, May 9, 1941; Carl Henry Monsees to Charles F. Palmer, memorandum, March 18, 1941, DDHC, NARA, RG 207, Box 11; and Monsees to Palmer, May 29, 1941, DDHC, NARA, RG 207, Box 20. The Houston Ready-Cut House Company also employed AFL workmen on "five demonstration houses" built at the Grand Prairie site in April 1941. See Frank M. Roberts, Houston Ready-Cut House Company, to Central Contracting Company, April 17, 1941, Williams Papers, FF 2-16. Sidney Hillman reported that AFL workers worked on prefabricated defense housing in Rahway, New Jersey, the site of Winfield Park. See *Hearings of the U.S. Senate Special Committee Investigating the National Defense Program Pursuant to S. Res. 71*, 76th Cong., 2nd Sess. (testimony of Sidney Hillman) (Washington, DC: Government Printing Office, 1942), 2511. Confident he would obtain defense- related building contracts, Beck had purchased vast amounts of building supplies before an A-1 priority certificate was necessary. See Memoirs of Walter G. Metschke, comp. Chicago Architects Oral History project, 1977, 27–28, available at www.digital-libraries.saic.edu/cdm/ref/collection/caoh/id/8498, accessed January 8, 2015.

67. Winters, "Avion Village," 24.

68. Roensch to Beck, April 9, 1941.

69. Ray Holder, "The Texas Mutuals," mimeographed typescript, Avion Village Mutual Housing Association Historical File, Grand Prairie, TX. Antonin Raymond endorsed the use of "movable partitions" in "Report to Dr. Clark Foreman on Experimental Housing Project No. PA-36044," typescript, n.d., Williams Papers, FF 34-15. The movable

wall panels and the carports that "doubled as modest architectural links between units" were "clear cut expressions for Neutra's crisp modernism." Dillon, "Avion Village," 118. A version of the Dillon article appeared in the *Dallas Morning News*, July 28, 1985, 7c. See also Colean, "Prefabrication Needs Architects," 64–68. Nineteenth-century American household organizer extraordinaire Catherine Beecher devised a movable wall partition to divide her parlor. See Dolores Hayden, *Building Suburbia: Greenfields and Urban Growth* (New York: Pantheon, 2003), 39.

70. Dillon, "Avion Village," 118. Eager to determine whether dwellings with open-beam ceilings offered better natural cooling than those with traditional ceilings, Williams compared the temperatures of two groups of dwelling units on Musick Way. The experiment confirmed his suspicion that the open ceilings found in many rural Texas farmhouses increased air flow and reduced the interior temperature. The experiment also convinced him of the importance of deep overhangs and insulation in home heating and cooling. See Nelson Irvin to David R. Williams, July 9, 1941, Williams Papers, FF 2-17. Williams had earlier lamented the fact that most architects felt compelled to call for the plastering of all walls and ceilings even when "simple, natural construction would look better, cost less and last longer." See D. R. Williams to Lawrence Westbrook, "Thoughts on Housing," typescript, n.d., 2, Lawrence Westbrook Papers, The Texas Collection, Carroll Library, Baylor University, Waco, TX (hereafter Westbrook Papers), 2E444, FF 43.

71. Williams wrote that Avion Village "was planned for park living by the Federal Works Agency, with the aid of local architect Roscoe P. DeWitt," with no mention of Neutra. See Williams, "Defense on the Home Front," 18. Elsewhere, including on the official set of project drawings, DeWitt was listed as the architect and Williams and Neutra as consulting architects. See "Low-Cost Houses," 240–242.

72. "Avion Village," Neutra Papers, Box 21, FF 6.

73. "Avion Village: A Defense Housing Plan," n.d., Avion Village Mutual Housing Association Historical File, Grand Prairie, TX.

74. Winters, "Avion Village," 24. Winters indicated that Neutra and Williams designed Avion Village. DeWitt was identified as the "resident architect" (p. 26).

75. Ronnie Stewart, a certified home economics teacher hired by Holder, turned the community building into a beehive of activity for children, teenagers, and adults. Stewart later succeeded Holder as manager of Avion Village. See "Built Fast but Last," *Dallas Morning News*, July 28, 1985, 1C, 7C; Winters, "Avion Village," 24–29; and Williams, "Defense on the Home Front," 18, 21. On the importance of community centers, see William H. Conrad, "Community Centres in United States War Housing Projects," *Journal of the Royal Architectural Institute of Canada* 22, no. 2 (1945): 33.

76. Holder, "Texas Mutuals," 6. Neutra proposed a garden with sculpture by Isamu Noguchi beneath the terrace. See Richard J. Neutra to David R. Williams, August 4, 1941, Williams Papers, FF 2-17.

77. Albert Mayer, "Why Dreary Housing Projects?" *Survey Graphic* 31 (February 1942): 84; and Albert Mayer, "Housing for Defense—And After," *New York Times Sunday Magazine*, September 21, 1941, 16. See also Bernard Taber, "War Housing: Exhibit at Museum of Modern Art," *New Republic*, May 18, 1942, 670; and Lewis Mumford, "War and Peace: Wartime Housing Show at the Museum of Modern Art," *New Yorker*, May 23, 1942, 56–58. On the private work done by defense housing architects Walter Gropius, Marcel Breuer, Richard J. Neutra, and William Lescaze in the late 1930s, see "Four American Houses," *Architectural Review* 86 (November 1939): 189–200. Elizabeth Mock concluded that the defense housing developments designed by Neutra and his

peers showed sensitivity to the "psychological and esthetic problems inherent in large-scale building." See Elizabeth Mock, ed., *Built in USA: 1932–1944* (New York: Museum of Modern Art, 1944), 23. Mock was Bauer's sister. The exhibit traveled to England. See "American Housing in War and Peace," *Journal of the Royal Institute of British Architects* 51 (July 1944): 227–230.

78. Tom Treanor, "The Home Front," *Los Angeles Times*, November 1, 1941, 1A.

79. "Avion Village Not Enough; Realtors Aid," *Dallas Morning News*, March 6, 1941, 6.

80. Arch Swank to Richard J. Neutra, August 21, 1941, Neutra Papers, Box 21, FF 6.

81. "Westbrook Is Silent on Housing," *Dallas Times Herald*, May 16, 1941, clipping, Williams Papers, FF 16-15. The pilot projects were often mistakenly reported to be of temporary construction. See "Avion Village Survives as a Corporation," *Grand Prairie Daily News*, March 2, 1986, 1; Matthew Weismantel, "The Mutual Ownership Defense Housing Program," 23, unpublished, copy in possession of author; Loder, "Town Just Like a Family," 1, 6; and Suzanne C. Russell, "There's No Place Like Home for Winfield Residents," *Home News Tribune*, July 24, 2002, Winfield Park Historical File.

82. "Plane Plant Workers to Have Colony of Own on Edge of Grand Prairie," photo caption, *Dallas Morning Herald*, March 2, 1941, clipping, Williams Papers, FF 16-15.

83. "With Benefit of Local Planning," *Architectural Record* 90 (November 1941): 85. See also Holder, "Texas Mutuals," 3.

84. The dwellings were complete by March 7, 1942. The city's work was to be done by March 15. See Lawrence Westbrook to John B. Blandford Jr., March 7, 1942, Appendix A, Westbrook Papers, 2E444, FF 50.

85. "With Benefit of Local Planning," 85; and Swank to Neutra. Swank described Roensch as someone "whom I trust as far as I can stretch concrete" (p. 3).

86. Holder, "Texas Mutuals," 5.

87. The Building and Housing Association was created in 1941 under the auspices of the Dallas Chamber of Commerce to prevent the construction of defense housing. See "Westbrook Is Silent on Housing," 16–15; and "Selecting 2nd Village Site Due Shortly," *Dallas Morning News*, May 17, 1941, clipping, Williams Papers, FF 16-15. The site plan included a series of satellite parking areas for automobiles as requested by the residents.

88. Holder, "Texas Mutuals," 8. On business support for public housing in Texas and the Southwest, see Robert Fairbanks, *The War on Slums in the Southwest: Public Housing and Slum Clearance in Texas, Arizona, and New Mexico, 1935–1965* (Philadelphia: Temple University Press, 2014), 1–7, 118–122, 156–157.

89. In 1934, the Dayton Metropolitan Housing Authority (Metro Housing) sought unsuccessfully to obtain funds from the PWA for low-income housing. By the time of mobilization, Metro Housing had obtained USHA financing for one development for African American families and one development for white families. See "Dayton's Federal Low-Rental Housing Project May Be Aid to 1200 Families," *Dayton Daily News*, n.d., Dayton Public Library Clipping File 2937-2941.

90. "Housing Project Start Predicted for Aug. 15," *Journal-Herald* (Dayton, OH), July 16, 1941, Dayton Public Library Clipping File 2932-2941.

91. *Hearings Before the Committee on Banking and Currency on S. 1592*, 79th Cong., 1st Sess. (statement of Albert J. Fitzgerald) (Washington, DC: Government Printing Office, 1945), 697.

92. *General Housing Act of 1945. Hearings Before the Committee on Banking and Currency on S. 1592* (statement of Werner Laging), 1108.

93. *The Story of Greenmont Village* (Dayton, OH: Greenmont Village Mutual Housing Association, 1948), 3. On CIO efforts to publicize the Camden Plan, see "All Angles of Housing Problem Clearly Analyzed in New Union Pamphlet," *CIO News*, October 13, 1941, 6; "Urge U.S. to Speed Pace of Workers' Housing Program," *CIO News*, November 17, 1941, 2; and M. M. Miniard quoted in "Housing," *Dayton Union News*, September 24, 1941, unpaged.

94. *Hearings Before the Committee on Banking and Currency on S. 1592* (statement of Charles McGuerin), 1090, 1092; and Lew Carr, "A New Village Is Rising," *Journal-Herald Spotlight* (Dayton, OH), February 8, 1942, 10, Dayton Public Library, Clipping File 2932-2941.

95. Editorial staff of the *Greenmont Forum*, "The Story of Greenmont Village," *Coop Housing*, June 1949, 5, Leo Goodman Papers, Manuscript Division, Library of Congress, Box 35, FF 1.

96. Carr, "A New Village Is Rising," 10.

97. *Hearings Before the Committee on Banking and Currency on S. 1592* (statement of Albert J. Fitzgerald), 697. Local business leaders were involved in the land acquisition. See "500 Dwellings to Be Built Near Dayton," *Journal-Herald* (Dayton, OH), July 1, 1941, Dayton Public Library Housing Clipping File 2937-2941.

98. Carr, "New Village Is Rising," 10. According to an undated report, "relief from monotony is obtained by interspersal [*sic*] of buildings of different heights, by the use of exterior paint in different pastel colors, and the varying use by the tenants of flowers and shrubs in the yards." See Bureau of Labor Statistics, "Mutual Home Ownership," 6, Warren J. Vinton Papers, Olin Library, Cornell University, Ithaca, NY (hereafter Vinton Papers), Box 19.

99. "U.S. Worries over Housing Problem Here," *South Bend Tribune*, January 29, 1941, South Bend Public Library Housing Clipping File, South Bend, IN. See also UAW Studebaker Local 5, *The Champion* 1, no. 8 (September 11, 1940), The John Edelman Collection, Walter P. Reuther Library, Wayne State University, Detroit, Box 101, FF 12; and David Thompson, "Housing Case Study 4: U.S. Unions Help Build Housing Cooperatives," *Co-operative News*, May 22, 2014, available at http://www.thenews.coop/85298/news/general/housing, accessed July 22, 2014.

100. "Realtors Get Challenge on Housing Needs," *South Bend Tribune*, January 30, 1941, South Bend Public Library Housing Clipping File, South Bend, IN.

101. Thomas quoted in "70-Acre Plot Sought; Work to Begin Soon," *South Bend Tribune*, February 6, 1941, South Bend Public Library Housing Clipping File, South Bend, IN.

102. "Housing Funds for Mishawaka," *South Bend Tribune*, May 27, 1941, South Bend Public Library Walnut Grove Clipping File, South Bend, IN. See also "'We Can Put Up 1,500 Homes,' Builders Say," *South Bend Tribune*, February 14, 1941, South Bend Public Library Housing Clipping File, South Bend, IN.

103. R. J. Thomas, *Housing for Defense* (Detroit: United Automobile Workers Union, 1942), 10. Boldface in the original.

104. "New Defense Homes Limited to Mishawaka," *South Bend Tribune*, May 29, 1941, and "System Lets Tenants Build Up Equities," *South Bend Tribune*, June 1, 1941, South Bend Public Library Housing Clipping File, South Bend, IN.

105. According to the UAW, "the government saved $32,000 because of cooperation with the UAW-CIO." See "War Housing," *The Distributor*, March 15, 1942, 5. See also "FWA Acquires Option on Land," *South Bend Tribune*, July 3, 1941, South Bend Public Library Walnut Grove Clipping File, South Bend, IN.

106. "Owners of Homes on East Jefferson Boulevard Object to Site for New Federal Housing Project," *South Bend Tribune*, June 22, 1941, South Bend Public Library Walnut Grove Clipping File, South Bend, IN.

107. On May 27, 1941, the day after President Roosevelt authorized construction, Carmody assigned responsibility for the 250-unit community to Westbrook's Mutual Ownership Defense Housing Division. See U.S. Federal Works Agency, *Annual Report for 1941*, 225, table 14. See also "Site for 250 Camden Plan Homes Named," *South Bend Tribune*, June 13, 1941, South Bend Public Library Walnut Grove Clipping File, South Bend, IN.

108. "FWA to Start New Housing Job in Month," *South Bend Tribune*, July 16, 1941, South Bend Public Library Walnut Grove Clipping File, South Bend, IN. Construction work on the community center at Walnut Grove commenced in September 1942. See "Walnut Grove Project Starts," *South Bend Tribune*, September 29, 1942. The center was dedicated in early May 1943. See "Community Building to Be Dedicated Thursday," *South Bend Tribune*, May 5, 1943, South Bend Public Library Walnut Grove Clipping File, South Bend, IN.

109. "Housing Plan Adds 231 Units," *South Bend Tribune*, July 21, 1941, South Bend Public Library Walnut Grove Clipping File, South Bend, IN.

110. "FWA to Start New Housing Job in Month."

111. "Back Tax Due from Housing Site Cut Half," *South Bend Tribune*, July 17, 1941, South Bend Public Library Walnut Grove Clipping File, South Bend, IN.

112. Ibid.

113. "Ground Broken for New Defense Homes," *South Bend Tribune*, October 14, 1941, South Bend Public Library Walnut Grove Clipping File, South Bend, IN.

114. Richard A. Meussel, "Appraisal Report for Walnut Grove Mutual Housing Project, NO. IND-12022, South Bend, Indiana, for the Federal Public Housing Authority, as of September 7, 1946," 1, Walnut Grove Mutual Housing Association Historical Files, South Bend, IN.

115. Ibid., 1. Another defense housing development that featured basements was Lucy Mallary Village in Springfield, Massachusetts, designed by architect Royal Barry Wills. See W. Clifford Harvey, "Lucy Mallary Village in Springfield—A Defense Project Stamped with Permanency," *Christian Science Monitor*, December 11, 1942, 5.

116. "250 Homes Ready in Month." One thousand families applied for the 250 vacancies. See *Hearings Before the Committee on Banking and Currency on S. 1592* (statement of James McEwan), 1100. Griggs served as the FPHA representative on the first board of directors of the Greenmont Mutual Housing Corporation and remained involved with mutual housing. See John W. Shively to Foley, Fitzpatrick, Dobbs, et al., interoffice memorandum, August 1, 1949, Papers of Raymond Foley, Harry S. Truman Presidential Library, Independence, MO, Box 3.

117. Harold B. Schultz, address to the National Cooperative-Mutual Housing Conference, May 9, 1946, Walnut Grove Mutual Housing Association Historical Files, South Bend, IN.

118. Frank and Violet Moore, interviewed by Michael Wright, February 8, 2001, South Bend, IN.

119. H. M. Goldstein to John M. Carmody and attached memorandum, May 21, 1941, 1–2, Vinton Papers, Box 9, FF 51. On the IUMSWA's wartime labor issues, see Nelson Lichtenstein, *Labor's War at Home: The CIO in World War II* (Cambridge: Cambridge University Press, 1982), 68, 97. On union reaction, see "Building for Defense . . . Headway and Headaches," 83; and Industrial Union of Marine and Shipbuilding Workers of

America, *Proceedings of the Seventh National Conference* (Camden, NJ: IUMSWA, 1941), 61–69, Records of the Industrial Union of Marine and Shipbuilding Workers of America, University of Maryland Special Collections Library, College Park (hereafter IUMSWA Records), Series 5, Box 1. See also "Camden Defense Homes Will Be Prefabricated," *Shipyard Worker* 5, no. 36 (March 7, 1941): 1; "IUMSWA 'Workers' Town? Government-Built Village of Audubon Park," *Business Week*, November 29, 1941, 30; "500-House Experiment at Camden, New Jersey," 53; and "Tenants Buy Town in New Home Plan," 44.

120. Goldstein to Carmody and attached memorandum, May 21, 1941, 2. See also "Local 1 Housing Group Fights Interest Charge on Gov't Homes Project," *Shipyard Worker* 5, no. 48 (May 30, 1941): 2.

121. John M. Carmody to Henry J. Andreas, June 14, 1941, Vinton Papers, Box 9, FF 51. Palmer used this same line of reasoning when arguing against the use of WPA labor on early Mutual Division projects.

122. Carmody to Andreas, June 14, 1941.

123. Resolution No. 27, indicating that the union wished to "avoid a repetition of the scandalous losses suffered by the Government in the resale of its defense housing projects after the last war, and of the unjustifiable losses that were in turn suffered by the defense workers who had originally bought these houses." See IUMSWA, untitled brief accompanying Resolution No. 27, *Proceedings of the Seventh National Conference*, 63–64.

124. H. M. Goldstein to John M. Carmody, June 21, 1941, Vinton Papers, Box 9, FF 51. On union disappointment with the housing, see "Building for Defense . . . Headway and Headaches," 83; and IUMSWA, *Proceedings of the Seventh National Conference*, 61–69. See also "Camden Defense Homes Will Be Prefabricated," *Shipyard Worker* 5, no. 36 (March 7, 1941): 1; "IUMSWA 'Workers' Town?" 30; "500-House Experiment at Camden, New Jersey," 53; and "Tenants Buy Town in New Home Plan," 44. On the popularity of neocolonial architecture, see Joseph B. Mason, "America's Builders Speak on Post-war Building," *American Builder and Building Age* 65, no. 5 (1943): 32. See also Bridget A. May, "Progressivism and the Colonial Revival: The Modern Colonial House," *Winterthur Portfolio* 26, no. 2–3 (1991): 107–122; and David Gephard, "The American Colonial Revival in the 1930s," *Winterthur Portfolio* 22, no. 2–3 (1987): 109–148.

125. Ironically, the Camden Plan made it possible for residents to "make a down payment on the red brick houses of the private real estate operators" because many of them were eligible to receive "reimbursement of a sufficient portion of the rental payments made by them while living in the Project." See Goldstein to Carmody, June 21, 1941.

126. IUMSWA, untitled brief accompanying Resolution No. 27, *Proceedings of the Seventh National Conference*, 65. Charles F. Palmer, "Defense Workers' Cooperative Housing," typescript, November 13, 1941, 4, Vinton Papers, Box 28.

127. IUMSWA, untitled brief accompanying Resolution No. 27, *Proceedings of the Seventh National Conference*, 63.

128. Ibid., 62.

129. "IUMSWA 'Workers' Town?" 30. Brick veneer was planned for some of the units. See "Bids to Be Offered Feb. 3 on Audubon Housing Project," *Courier-Post* (Camden, NJ), January 29, 1941, 11.

130. "Housing Hub-bub," *Business Week*, May 3, 1941, 32.

131. Simon quoted in "Town Bills U.S. for Added Cost of Housing Unit," *Chicago Daily Tribune*, May 18, 1941, 21.

132. "IUMSWA 'Workers' Town?" 30.

133. State of New Jersey, One Hundred and Sixty-Fifth Legislature, *Laws of 1941*, Chapter 360, August 6, 1941, 944–950. See also "Winfield Township, New Jersey," available at http://en.wilipedia.org.wiki/Winfield_Township,_New_Jersey, accessed July 21, 2014.

134. On July 3, 1947, the State Legislature voted to separate Audubon Village from Audubon if approved by voters in a special October 28, 1947, referendum election. See State of New Jersey, One Hundred and Seventy-First Legislature, *Laws of 1947*, Chapter 418, July 3, 1947, 1295–1298. See also "Housing Hub-bub," 32.

135. Shanken, *194X*, 1–2.

136. "Building for Defense . . . Government Housing in a Hurry," 341.

137. On Foreman's appointment, see "11 Defense Centers to Get U.S. Housing," *New York Times*, November 26, 1940, 12; and Ryan, "6,750 New Defense Houses Approved; Col. Westbrook and Clark Foreman Get Housing Posts," "The Federal Diary," *Washington Post*, November 26, 1940, X6. Allen W. Stephens, a contract negotiator who had worked on the PBA's prefabricated, demountable housing developments, was transferred to the DHD to help make the transition a smooth one. See "Building for Defense . . . Headway and Headaches," 338–340; and "Building for Defense . . . Government Housers Meet," *Architectural Forum* 74 (July 1941): 8.

138. Reviewer Dale Douglas said that the book could "serve as a miniature Bible for good Social Democrats." See Dale Douglas, "Defense, External and Internal," *New York Times*, November 3, 1940, B6.

139. Foreman gave Carmody credit for suggesting that he hire prominent architects, and overlooked or ignored how they had been hired by earlier New Deal and defense housing agencies, including the Mutual Division. It is not known why Foreman shunned Neutra. See Clark Foreman to Walter Creese, November 28, 1969, and Foreman to Creese, November 6, 1969, Creese Research Files, private collection of Alexander von Hoffman.

140. Murphy quoted in Robert R. Hagy Jr., "Even If It Does Cost a Million, You Have to Try It Yourself," *Pittsburgh Post-Gazette*, August 25, 1942, 11, available at http://news.google.newspapers?nid=1129&dat=19420825&id=ddkOAAAAIBAJ&sjid, accessed August 6, 2014.

141. *Hearings Before the Senate Special Committee Investigating the National Defense Program Pursuant to S. 71* (statement of John M. Carmody), 2327. For a list of demountable housing vendors, see "Half Demountable House Program Placed," *American Builder and Building Age* 64, no. 3 (1942): 82. The level of professional interest in demountable housing was underscored by "Defense Housing—1940," an exhibit prepared by the Washington, D.C., chapter of the American Institute of Architects. Here the "ghost town" argument favored by home-building interests was advanced. See "Defense Housing—1940," 121.

142. "Building for Defense . . . Headway and Headaches," 44; and "Improving Design of Defense Housing," *New York Times*, December 21, 1941, XI, 3.

143. William V. Reed to Charles F. Palmer, internal office memorandum, November 12, 1941, DDHC, NARA, RG 207, Box 23. See also "From Washington," *Architectural Record* 89 (March 1941): 16; and "Varied Use of Paint Livens Defense Housing Projects," *Christian Science Monitor*, December 10, 1941, 22. On the Homasote Company, see "Old Newspapers to New Houses," *Architectural Forum* 73 (December 1940): 531–535, 38; "Products and Practices—Vallejo Construction Data," *California Arts and Architecture* 58 (November 1941): 38; and Sally Carrigher, "Prefabrication and Good Architecture: A California Example," *Architect and Engineer* 153 (April 1943): 12–20, 22. See also William Wilson Wurster, "Carquinez Heights,"

*California Arts and Architecture* 58 (November 1941): 34–37; and "Real Estate Notes," *New York Times*, March 29, 1942, RE3.

144. Antonin Raymond, "Working with the USHA," *Pencil Points* 22 (November 1941): 693. On Wright's plans for prefabrication, see Talbot Wegg, "FLLW versus the USA," *AIA Journal* 53 (February 1970): 48–52; Zenia Kotval, "Opportunity Lost: A Clash between Politics and Design in Defense Housing in Pittsfield, Massachusetts," *Journal of Planning History* 2, no. 1 (2003): 25–46; and Peter S. Reed, "Enlisting Modernism," in *World War II and the American Dream: How Wartime Building Changed a Nation*, ed. Donald Albrecht (Washington, DC: National Building Museum; Cambridge, MA: MIT Press, 1995), 18. Wright called for the use of precast concrete slabs that would be used for dwelling units' floors and party walls in his quatrefoil plan. The Wright controversy was likely the subject of a comment made by Representative Lanham in the House of Representatives on January 15, 1942. Lanham quoted in Edmund R. Purves, "The Washington Situation," *The Octagon* 14 (January 1942): 7.

145. "Housing: Prefabrication's Chance," *Time*, March 16, 1942, 77.

146. Catherine Bauer to Herbert Emmerich, "Enclosure," April 1, 1942, Vinton Papers, Box 4.

147. Avi Friedman, "The Evolution of Design Characteristics during the Post–Second World War Housing Boom: The U.S. Experience," *Journal of Design History* 8, no. 2 (1995), 144.

148. John Green, speech before the National Public Housing Conference, April 25–26, 1941, IUMSWA Records, Series 5, Box 1. Henry J. Andreas delivered the speech for Green.

149. CIO Housing Committee statement quoted in "Camden Plan and Its Post-war Possibilities," *Architect and Engineer* 147 (October 1941): 55. Westbrook had a copy of the original report. See CIO Housing Committee, "Memoranda Submitted by the Housing Committee of the Congress of Industrial Organizations to the Office for Emergency Management on April 14, 1941," typescript, Westbrook Papers, 2E444, FF 50. See also Philip Murray to President Franklin D. Roosevelt, April 12, 1941, President Franklin D. Roosevelt Library, Hyde Park, NY, FDR Office File OF 63, Box 8.

150. "War Housing," *The Distributor*, 5–6.

151. National Housing Agency, *Fourth Annual Report for 1945* (Washington, DC: Government Printing Office, 1946), 210.

152. U.S. Federal Works Agency, *Annual Report for 1941*, 28.

## CHAPTER 4

1. Murray quoted in Henry C. Fleischer, "CIO Group Asks to Extend 'Mutual' Project Plan," *CIO News*, April 21, 1941, 8. See also "IUMSWA Housing Plan Backed by CIO Nationally," *Shipyard Worker* 5, no. 42 (April 18, 1941): 1.

2. Sarah Jo Peterson, *Planning the Home Front: Building Bombers and Communities at Willow Run* (Chicago: University of Chicago Press, 2013), 90. See also Sarah Jo Peterson, "The Politics of Land Use and Housing in World War II Michigan: Building Bombers and Community" (Ph.D. diss., Yale University, 2002).

3. "The Directors Column," *The Distributor*, March 15, 1942, 35.

4. National Public Housing Conference, "Resolution Adopted by the Board of Directors on 6 February 1942," National Archives and Records Administration, College Park, MD (hereafter NARA), RG 207, Series 22, Box 2.

5. National Committee on the Housing Emergency, *Recommendations of the National Committee on the Housing Emergency: A Program for Housing Workers in War Industries* (New York: National Committee on the Housing Emergency, 1942), 28.

6. Dorothy Rosenman, "Housing to Speed Production," *Architectural Record* 91 (April 1942): 45–46. See also Dorothy Rosenman, "Defense Housing—Are We Building Future Slums or Planned Communities?" *Architectural Record* 90 (November 1941): 56–57; and Dorothy Rosenman to Lawrence Westbrook, October 14, 1941, Lawrence Westbrook Papers, The Texas Collection, Carroll Library, Baylor University, Waco, TX (hereafter Westbrook Papers), 2E444, FF 50.

7. California Housing and Planning Association quoted in "Camden Plan and Its Post-war Possibilities," *California Arts and Architecture*, enclosure in Lawrence Westbrook to Herbert Emmerich, March 7, 1942, Westbrook Papers, 2E444, FF 50.

8. Catherine Bauer to Herbert Emmerich, "Enclosure," January 22, 1943, II-13, Warren J. Vinton Papers, Olin Library, Cornell University, Ithaca, NY (hereafter Vinton Papers), Box 4, FF 15.

9. Catherine Bauer to Herbert Emmerich, "Enclosure," April 1, 1942, A-3, Vinton Papers, Box 9, FF 14.

10. Ibid.

11. Catherine Bauer, "Outline of War Housing," *Task* 4 (1943): 8.

12. Ray Holder, "The Texas Westbrook Mutuals," typescript, n.d., 5, Avion Village Mutual Housing Association Historical File, Avion Village, Grand Prairie, TX.

13. Alpheus Winter to Francis Maloney, April 26, 1941, enclosure in Lawrence Westbrook to Charles F. Palmer, May 5, 1941, NARA, RG 207, Entry 22, Box 4. Westbrook addressed the occupant selection issue in an October 1941 policy statement. See "Suggested General Principles Governing Execution and Operation of Mutual Home Ownership Projects," typescript, October 17, 1941, FWA Release 7530, Vinton Papers, Box 19, FF 41; and Lawrence Westbrook to John B. Blandford, March 7, 1942, 4, Westbrook Papers. On opposition to public defense housing in Bridgeport, see "Bridgeport Workers Prefer These Privately Built Small Homes," *American Builder and Building Age* 63, no. 10 (1941): 74–76.

14. Lawrence Westbrook, "The Housing Mess," typescript, November 1954, 18, Westbrook Papers, 2E444, FF 51.

15. Robert Fairbanks, "The Fight against Slums in the Southwest, 1934–1954," paper presented at the Thirteenth International Planning History Conference, July 2008, 4–6, copy in author's possession; and Robert Fairbanks, *The War on the Slums in the Southwest: Public Housing and Slum Clearance in Texas, Arizona, and New Mexico* (Philadelphia: Temple University Press, 2014).

16. John M. Carmody to Lawrence Westbrook, February 13, 1942, Papers of John M. Carmody, President Franklin D. Roosevelt Library, Hyde Park, NY (hereafter Carmody Papers), Box 81; and Lawrence Westbrook to John M. Carmody, February 17, 1942, Carmody Papers, Box 103. See also John M. Carmody to Henry Kaiser, February 13, 1942, Carmody Papers, Box 72.

17. Albert Mayer, "Housing for Defense—And After," *New York Times Sunday Magazine*, September 21, 1941, 14, 16–17.

18. Edmund N. Bacon, "Wartime Housing," *Annals of the American Academy of Political and Social Science* 229 (September 1943): 137. Bacon did not include mutual housing in his postwar redevelopment plans for Philadelphia's Society Hill neighborhood.

19. "Neither for Sale nor Rent," *Architectural Forum* 74 (June 1941): 54.

20. Ibid., 443. In January 1941 Audubon Village was called "the most mystifying project" in the defense housing program. See "Building for Defense," *Architectural Forum* 74 (January 1941): 29.

21. "Neither for Sale nor Rent," 54.

22. Ibid., 445.

23. Ibid.

24. "New Jersey Area Has New Idea in Housing Being Tested by 500 Families," *Christian Science Monitor*, October 29, 1941, 21; and "Tenants Buy Town in New Home Plan," *New York Times*, November 9, 1941, 44.

25. Lew Carr, "A New Village Is Rising," *Journal-Herald Spotlight* (Dayton, OH), February 8, 1942, 10, Dayton Public Library Housing Clipping File 2932-2941, Dayton, OH.

26. "Project Stirs Wide Interest," in "U.S. Speeds Village for Defense Workers," Supplement to the *Courier-Post* (Camden, NJ), December 13, 1941, 8. See also "Other Projects under Plan," in "U.S. Speeds Village," 10.

27. "IUMSWA 'Workers' Town? Government-Built Village of Audubon Park," *Business Week*, November 29, 1941, 30.

28. "Not for Rent, Not for Sale," *Time*, June 21, 1941, 70, 72.

29. "This Month in Building," *Architectural Forum* 74 (August 1941): 3.

30. Alan Mather, "Backhousing for Bomber Plants," *Pencil Points* 23 (December 1942): 70.

31. Agnes Meyer, *Journey through Chaos* (New York: Harcourt, Brace, 1943), 34. See also Agnes Meyer, "Detroit's Willow Run Area Is a Nightmare . . . ," *Washington Post*, March 3, 1943, 6; and Lowell J. Carr and James E. Stermer, *Willow Run: A Study of Industrialization and Cultural Inadequacy* (New York: Harper, 1952), 97–119.

32. William G. Nicholas, "Labor's Responsibility in Housing," *Task* 4 (1943): 19.

33. Alan Mather, "Build Garden Cities Near Aircraft Plants!" *Common Sense* 2 (August 1941): 245.

34. International Union of United Automobile, Aircraft and Agricultural Implement Workers of America, *Homes for Workers in Planned Communities thru Collective Action* (Detroit: UAW-CIO, 1943), 29.

35. R. J. Thomas, *Housing for Defense* (Detroit: United Automobile Workers Union, 1942), 5–6.

36. Ibid., 28.

37. Carmody described being "unable to rise from the chair. It was a strange feeling—[a] complete inability to even get to my feet, much less stay on them." The Reminiscences of John M. Carmody (1954), Oral History Collection, Columbia University, New York, 629. John N. Edy was acting FWA administrator during Carmody's illness. "Building for Defense . . . Headway and Headaches," *Architectural Forum* 74 (December 1941): 422, 44.

38. Walter Reuther, *Memorandum on Defense City for Detroit Area*, September 26, 1941, 12–13, Carmody Papers, Box 103. The interest in housing betterment and modern architecture and planning shared by Reuther and Stonorov formed the basis of a relationship that would end with their deaths in a May 11, 1970, airplane crash. See Nelson Lichtenstein, *Walter Reuther: The Most Dangerous Man in Detroit* (New York: Basic Books, 1995), 172, 308–311.

39. Reuther, *Memorandum on Defense City*, 13.

40. Ibid., 11.

41. Ibid., 8–9. The need for housing open to African Americans was especially critical. See Dominic J. Capeci Jr., *Race Relations in Wartime Detroit: The Sojourner Truth Housing Controversy of 1942* (Philadelphia: Temple University Press, 1984).

42. Reuther, *Memorandum on Defense City*, 1.

43. Ibid., 5.

44. Ibid., 8. Emphasis in the original.

45. Ibid., 1, 9. Emphasis in the original.

46. Ibid., 1, 11. Emphasis in the original.

47. Ibid.

48. Ibid., 1, 9.

49. "Defense City," *The Distributor*, December 15, 1941, 7.

50. Reuther, *Memorandum on Defense City*, 12.

51. Mumford is twice mistakenly referred to as "Numford." See ibid., 13.

52. Ibid., 2.

53. Ibid., 11–12. The construction of housing to aid postwar economic reconversion was also advocated by others, such as the USHA's Nathan Straus. See Nathan Straus, *The Seven Myths of Housing* (New York: Knopf, 1944), 26, 217–219.

54. Catherine Bauer, "Housing for, of and by Workers," *Hosiery Worker* 12, no. 2 (May 11, 1934): 2.

55. "Defense City," 7.

56. Ibid.

57. Ibid.

58. Ibid., 9.

59. C. W. Farrier to C[harles]F[orest]P[almer], handwritten, n.d., Papers of Charles F. Palmer, Robert W. Woodruff Library, Emory University, Atlanta (hereafter Palmer Papers), Box 80, Item 4. See also Carl Henry Monsees to Charles F. Palmer, memorandum, March 18, 1941, NARA, RG 207, Box 11. WPA workers also worked on Avion Village and Pennypack Woods.

60. The FERA gave preference to local applicants who possessed "a collective homogeneity and integrity" because such families were believed to be most likely to "produce a high type of cooperative community life out of the economic, the social, the cultural, and the physical and mental health qualities which they possess." See [Williams], "Organized Rural Communities," typescript, n.d., 4, Westbrook Papers, 2E444, FF 43.

61. CIO Housing Committee, "Memorandum Submitted by the Housing Committee of the Congress of Industrial Organizations to the Office for Emergency Management on April 14, 1941," typescript, 3, Westbrook Papers, 2E444, FF 50. The NAHO indicated that those selected were "assured of employment in the local shipyard for a long time and are hence more inclined and able to participate in the ownership." See "Demonstration Projects," *NAHO News* 4, no. 1 (January 6, 1941): 4.

62. Palmer referred to the April 30 meeting in a July letter. See Charles F. Palmer to President Franklin D. Roosevelt, July 15, 1941, Palmer Papers, Box 83, Item 6.

63. "Gothic Gazebo," *Time*, January 5, 1942, 29.

64. Philip J. Funigiello, *The Challenge to Urban Liberalism: Federal-City Relations during World War II* (Knoxville: University of Tennessee Press, 1978), 83, 90, 108; and Doris Kearns Goodwin, *No Ordinary Time: Franklin and Eleanor Roosevelt: The Home Front in World War II* (New York: Simon and Schuster, 1994), 206.

65. Charles F. Palmer to Lawrence Westbrook, May 15, 1941, NARA, RG 207, Entry 22, Box 4.

66. Charles F. Palmer to John M. Carmody, May 26, 1941, Palmer Papers, Box 7, Item 2.

67. Palmer to Westbrook, May 15, 1941; Palmer to Carmody, May 26, 1941; John M. Carmody to Charles F. Palmer, June 17, 1941, NARA, RG 207, Entry 22, Box 4; Carl Major Wright to Jacob Crane, memorandum, July 1, 1941, Office of Emergency Management, DDHC, NARA, RG 207, Entry 22, Box 2; Charles F. Palmer to John Carmody, July 22, 1941, NARA, RG 207, Entry 22, Box 4; John M. Carmody to Charles F. Palmer, July 30, 1941, NARA, RG 207, Entry 22, Box 4; and Charles F. Palmer to John Carmody, August 7, 1941, NARA, RG 207, Entry 22, Box 4.

68. Carmody to Palmer, June 17, 1941.

69. Ibid.

70. Palmer to Roosevelt, July 15, 1941. See also Harry Knowlton to Charles F. Palmer, memorandum, September 17, 1941, NARA, RG 207, Entry 22, Box 2; and see Col. Cornelius Beard to Charles F. Palmer, memorandum, September 16, 1941, NARA, RG 207, Entry 22, Box 2.

71. Palmer to Carmody, July 22, 1941; Frank A. Vanderbilt Jr. to Charles F. Palmer, memorandum, July 24, 1941, NARA, RG 207, Entry 22, Box 4. On tenant selection and the IUMSWA, see John Green to Mrs. Charles Thomas, April 27, 1942, Records of the Industrial Union of Marine and Shipbuilding Workers of America, University of Maryland Special Collections Library, College Park, Series 5, Box 1.

72. Carmody to Palmer, July 30, 1941.

73. FWA, "Suggested General Principles Governing the Execution and Operation of Mutual Home Ownership Projects," mimeograph, October 17, 1941, 3, Vinton Papers, Box 19, FF 41.

74. Carmody quoted in "Camden Plan and Its Post-war Possibilities." The language used by Carmody is practically identical to Westbrook's. See Lawrence Westbrook, "Home Ownership by Workers Made Feasible," *Labor Information Bulletin* 8, no. 9 (1941): 10.

75. Westbrook, "What Is Wrong with Housing?" 12.

76. "Camden Plan and Its Post-war Possibilities," 55.

77. Palmer quoted in "Camden Plan and Its Post-war Possibilities." See also Division of Defense Housing Coordination, "Explanation of Proposed 'Camden Plan,'" Press Release No. 83, March 21, 1941, NARA, RG 207, Entry 22, Box 4.

78. Wright to Crane, July 1, 1941, 6.

79. Warren Jay Vinton to [Nathan Straus], memorandum, November 19, 1941, 2, Vinton Papers, Box 2.

80. "You Need a Housing Program," quoted in "War Housing," *The Distributor*, March 15, 1942, 7.

81. Ibid.

82. Ibid.

83. Dorothy Thompson, "On the Record," *Evening Star* (Washington, DC), July 4, 1941.

84. Ibid.

85. Federal Public Housing Authority, "The Mutual Home Ownership Program," mimeograph, January 3, 1946, NARA, RG 196, Box 14. A copy of the same document is in the Vinton Papers, Box 19.

86. "What Housing for Willow Run?" *Architectural Record* 92 (September 1942): 54.

87. "Defense City," 9.

88. Richard J. Deverall to Oscar Stonorov, October 19, 1941, Papers of Oscar Stonorov, Collection 04375, University of Wyoming American Heritage Center, Laramie (hereafter Stonorov Papers), Box 39.

89. Jerry Kluttz, "Carmody Resignation Reported in Housing Agency Shakeup," *Washington Post*, October 21, 1941, 1; and "Way Opened for Fleming to Become Head of FWA," *Washington Post*, October 24, 1941, 23.

90. Bauer, "Outline of War Housing," 5–6.

91. Charley Cherokee, "National Grapevine," *Chicago Defender*, August 16, 1941, 13. See also "Carmody Goes to Aid of Barred Workers: Carpenters Get Jobs," *Atlanta Daily World*, August 17, 1941, 1; and Charley Cherokee, "National Grapevine," *Chicago Defender*, September 20, 1940, 15. The USHA allowed local public housing authorities in San Francisco to build public housing for Chinese occupancy and those in Tucson and other cities to designate certain developments as Mexican.

92. Alvin White, "Federal Chiefs, Fair to Negro, Being Forced Out," *Chicago Defender*, January 24, 1942, 12.

93. Oscar Stonorov to Richard J. Deverall, October 22, 1941, Stonorov Papers, Box 39.

94. Sidney Hillman to President Franklin D. Roosevelt (draft), November 3, 1941, Stonorov Papers, Box 39. Stonorov told Reuther that he wrote the draft letter for Hillman. He also indicated that the letter was being used as the basis for an informational memorandum for Dr. Lubin and First Lady Eleanor Roosevelt. See Oscar Stonorov to Walter Reuther, November 7, 1941, Stonorov Papers, Box 39.

95. Hillman to President Roosevelt, November 3, 1941. For a drawing, see Nicholas, "Labor's Responsibility in Housing," 21. The day before the convention, Stonorov reported that they were "working like Beavers on the general presentation of the plan, a model of which I will bring with me to Detroit next Wednesday for the Convention." See Oscar Stonorov to Otis Winn, November 13, 1941, Stonorov Papers, Box 39.

96. Stonorov to Reuther, November 7, 1941.

97. Michael Harris to Roy Reuther, December 26, 1941, 8–13, Walter P. Reuther Library and Archives, Wayne State University, Detroit (hereafter Reuther Papers).

98. Peterson, *Planning the Home Front*, 91.

99. Stonorov worried that animosity, which he described as "some feeling," had developed between Hillman and Westbrook over the Currier Lumber Company contract dispute and would have a negative impact on Defense City. Oscar Stonorov to Walter Reuther, November 6, 1941, Stonorov Papers, Box 39.

100. Oscar Stonorov to Samuel Rosenman, draft memorandum, n.d., 3, Stonorov Papers, Box 39.

101. Ibid., 4.

102. Ibid., 3–4. The UAW's Richard Deverall pointed out that Stonorov used letterhead that was not printed in a union print shop. See Deverall to Stonorov, October 19, 1941.

103. Joel W. Schenker to Samuel Rosenman, September 10, 1941, Samuel I. Rosenman Papers, President Franklin D. Roosevelt Library, Hyde Park, NY, Series II, Box 9.

104. President Franklin D. Roosevelt to Sidney Hillman, November 6, 1941, Reuther Papers. See also Reuther, press release, November 11, 1941, 8–13, Reuther Papers; and associated newspaper clippings in The John Edelman Collection, Walter P. Reuther Library, Wayne State University, Detroit, Box 103, FF 21. The UAW claimed that the project was approved by FDR "in toto" on November 11, 1941. See "Willow Run," *The Distributor*, March 15, 1942, 15.

105. President Franklin D. Roosevelt to Sidney Hillman, November 14, 1941, Vinton Papers, Box 19, FF 43. FDR's endorsement letter was also quoted in "Defense City," 7.

106. Rolland J. Thomas to President Franklin D. Roosevelt, telegram, November 21, 1941, Stonorov Papers, Box 39. A photograph of the Stonorov model with Thomas,

Reuther, Deverall, Stonorov, Winn, John Green, and "GM Dept. Rep. Blackwood" was taken. See "Defense City," 9.

107. Roosevelt to Hillman, November 14, 1941.

108. Palmer to Smith quoted in "Willow Run," 15.

109. "Bomber City Row," *Newsweek*, July 6, 1942, 48; and "Housing Muddle: Willow Run, Michigan," *Business Week*, March 13, 1943, 75–76.

110. "Building for Defense . . . Headway and Headaches," *Architectural Forum* 75 (November 1941): 330.

111. Thomas J. Hamilton, "House Bars Vote on Housing Funds," *New York Times*, December 2, 1941, 13.

112. "Asks That Palmer Be Kept On in Housing," *New York Times*, December 4, 1941, 18.

113. Ibid.

114. Richard J. Neutra to Lyle and David R. Williams, December 13, 1941, Papers of David R. Williams, Edith Garland Dupré Library, University of Louisiana, Lafayette (hereafter Williams Papers), FF 2-17.

115. Richard Neutra to Lyle and David R. Williams, March 7, 1942, Williams Papers, FF 2-18.

116. "Willow Run," 16.

117. Ibid., 15.

118. Ibid.

119. Ibid., 16.

120. Oscar Stonorov to Richard J. Deverall, February 14, 1942, Stonorov Papers, Box 39. Thomas found backing for his call for a reorganization of federal housing from a strange political bedfellow, the National Association of Realtors executive secretary Herbert U. Nelson, an avowed public housing enemy. See "Urges One Agency to Direct Housing," *New York Times*, February 22, 1942, 22.

121. "Directors Column," 34.

122. "Willow Run," 16.

123. "War Housing," 5. Carmody expressed regret at approving Palmer for the post of defense housing coordinator. See Oscar Stonorov to John Carmody, October 1, 1941, Carmody Papers, Box 81.

124. "War Housing," 6–7.

125. "Detroit: A City Where Housing Emergencies Are Nothing New," 195.

126. "Directors Column," 35; "War Workers' Housing Conference Called," *Los Angeles Times*, February 15, 1942, A6; and "Billion Asked for Housing," *Los Angeles Times*, February 16, 1942, A1. On the impact of the war on California, see Greg Hise, *Magnetic Los Angeles: Planning the Twentieth-Century Metropolis* (Baltimore: Johns Hopkins University Press, 1997), 36–37, 114–132; Roger W. Lotchin, *Fortress California, 1910–1961: From Warfare to Welfare* (Champaign: University of Illinois Press, 1992); Roger W. Lotchin, ed., *The Way We Really Were: The Golden State in the Second Great War* (Champaign: University of Illinois Press, 2000); Roger W. Lotchin, *The Bad City in the Good War: San Francisco, Los Angeles, Oakland and San Diego* (Bloomington: Indiana University Press, 2003); Arthur C. Verge, *Paradise Transformed: Los Angeles during the Second World War* (Dubuque, IA: Kendall Hunt, 1993); and various articles in Roger Lotchin and Martin Schiesl, eds., *Fortress California at War: San Francisco, Los Angeles, Oakland and San Diego, 1941–1945*, special issue, *Pacific Historical Review* (August 1994): 277–420.

## CHAPTER 5

1. Edith Elmer Wood, "Close Harmony on Housing," *Journal of Home Economics* 34 (May 1942): 310.

2. Ibid.

3. Lawrence Westbrook, "The Housing Mess," typescript, n.d., 16, Lawrence Westbrook Papers, The Texas Collection, Carroll Library, Baylor University, Waco, TX (hereafter Westbrook Papers), 2E444, FF 51. See also "How Housing Needs Met Told," *Los Angeles Times*, February 12, 1943, A1.

4. Susan Dunn, *Roosevelt's Purge: How FDR Fought to Change the Democratic Party* (Cambridge, MA: Belknap, 2010).

5. P.L. 409, 77th Cong., 2nd Sess. See also Sarah Jo Peterson, *Planning the Home Front: Building Bombers and Communities at Willow Run* (Chicago: University of Chicago Press, 2013), 109.

6. U.S. Congress, House of Representatives, *Amendment of the Lanham Act, House Res. 6128*, 77th Cong., 1st Sess. (statement of Representative Frederick "Fritz" G. Lanham), *Congressional Record* 87 (1941): 9278.

7. U.S. Congress, House of Representatives, *Amendment of the Lanham Act, House Res. 6128*, 77th Cong., 1st Sess. (statement of Representative Adolph J. Sabath), *Congressional Record* 87 (1941): 9675.

8. Charles Abrams, *The Future of Housing* (New York: Harper and Brothers, 1946), 301.

9. National Public Housing Conference, "Program for National Public Housing Conference," National Archives and Records Administration, College Park, MD (hereafter NARA), RG 207, Series 22, Box 2.

10. National Association of Housing Officials, *Housing for the United States after the War* (Chicago: National Association of Housing Officials, 1946), 50.

11. Walter Gordon, "Cities While You Wait: 'Housing' in Washington and Oregon," *Pencil Points* 24 (April 1943): 48, 52.

12. Pittsburgh Housing Association, *Housing in Wartime Pittsburgh: A Summary of Activities, 1924–1943* (Pittsburgh: Pittsburgh Housing Association, 1943), 13.

13. "War Housing," *The Distributor*, March 15, 1942, 7. See also M. M. Miniard to Baird Snyder, February 13, 1942, NARA, RG 162, Box 33. Almost all of the forty-three letters follow a template likely provided by the union local. See FWA Records, NARA, RG 162, Box 33.

14. Carl Bersing to Baird Snyder III, February 18, 1942, Papers of Oscar Stonorov, Collection 04375, University of Wyoming American Heritage Center, Laramie (hereafter Stonorov Papers), Box 39.

15. Arthur F. Johnson to Oscar Stonorov, July 15, 1941, Stonorov Papers, Box 38; and C. L. Huston Jr. to Oscar Stonorov, July 22, 1941, Stonorov Papers, Box 38.

16. Carl Bersing to Baird Snyder III, February 18, 1942. Earlier, Stonorov had provided Lukens Steel Corporation officials with estimated monthly costs to workers if the proposed community was sold to them under the Camden Plan. See Oscar Stonorov to C. L. Huston, July 11, 1941, Stonorov Papers, Box 38.

17. "Coatesville's 100 Defense Homes O.K.'D," *Chicago Defender*, November 8, 1941, 3.

18. *Coatesville Record*, April 3, 1942, and June 18, 1942, Chester County Historical Society, Clan Township Lands File, Coatesville, PA (hereafter CTLF).

19. *Coatesville Record*, September 1, 1942, CTLF.

20. Elizabeth Mock, ed., *Built in USA: 1932–1944* (New York: Museum of Modern Art, 1944), 66. The community "receded from public attention" despite its distinguished architects. See Kostis Kourelis, "Louis Kahn's African-American Vernacular," *Society of Architectural Historians* (blog), March 26, 2014, available at http://sah.org/publications-and-reasearch/sah-blog/sah-blog2014/03/26/louis-kahn's, accessed August 6, 2014. Bloggers thought Kourelis's title was misleading.

21. *Coatesville Record*, April 28, 1942, and May 5, 1942, CTLF.

22. "The Directors Column," *The Distributor*, March 15, 1942, 35; and Peterson, *Planning the Home Front*, 116–117.

23. Alan Mather, "The Battle of Willow Run," *Common Sense* 12, no. 2 (1943): 41–42.

24. W. H. Lawrence, "President Merges Housing Agencies," *New York Times*, February 25, 1942, 24.

25. "Directors Column," 36.

26. Ibid.

27. "Willow Run," *The Distributor*, March 15, 1942, 16.

28. "War Housing," *The Distributor*, 7.

29. Ibid., 8.

30. Ibid., 7. Keyserling was originally named but for unknown reasons did not serve. Emmerich was given the post instead.

31. "Housing as Usual," *Business Week*, March 28, 1942, 24, 28–29.

32. "Housing Fund Bill Approved for FWA Solely," *Washington Post*, November 29, 1941, 4. See also "Local Authority Is Key to War Housing," *Public Housing* 3, no. 6 (1942): unpaged.

33. Frank B. Woodford, "Willow Run Poses Problems," *New York Times*, April 9, 1942, E10. See also Herman H. Field, "The Lesson of Willow Run," *Task* 4 (1944): 13.

34. Bennett quoted in "Ford Stirs War Housing Issue," *New York Times*, June 28, 1942, 25.

35. "War Housing," *Architectural Forum* 76 (May 1942): 285–291.

36. Ibid., 286.

37. G. Gresham Griggs to David R. Williams, May 26, 1942, Papers of David R. Williams, Edith Garland Dupré Library, University of Louisiana, Lafayette, FF 2-18.

38. *Hearings Before a Special Committee Investigating the National Defense Program*, Part 15, 77th Cong., 2nd Sess. (statement of George Meader, Exhibit 542) (Washington, DC: Government Printing Office, 1942), 5383.

39. Alan Mather, "Backhousing for Bomber Plants," *Pencil Points* 23 (December 1942): 70–71, 73–74. See also Margaret Crawford, "Daily Life on the Home Front: Women, Blacks, and the Struggle for Public Housing," in *World War II and the American Dream: How Wartime Building Changed a Nation*, ed. Donald Albrecht (Cambridge, MA: MIT Press and the American Building Museum, 1995), 112–117.

40. "What Housing for Willow Run?" *Architectural Record* 92 (September 1942): 3. See also Henry E. Riggs to William K. Divers, June 8, 1942, NARA, RG 196, Series 29, Box 3.

41. Mather, "Battle of Willow Run," 42.

42. "The Month in Building . . . News," *Architectural Forum* 77 (July 1942): 33–34.

43. Lawrence Westbrook to Dorothy Thompson, March 1, 1949, Westbrook Papers, 2E441, FF 13.

44. National Public Housing Conference, "Program for National Public Housing Conference," NARA, RG 207, Series 22, Box 2.

45. Warren J. Vinton, "Mutual Home Ownership Plan," typescript, Warren J. Vinton Papers, Olin Library, Cornell University, Ithaca, NY (hereafter Vinton Papers), Box 19.

46. FPHA quoted in Garrett Eckbo, "Site Planning," *Architectural Forum* 76 (May 1942): 265.

47. Lawrence Westbrook, "A New Method of Merchandising Homes," typescript, n.d., 13, Westbrook Papers, 2E444, FF 52.

48. Lawrence Westbrook to John B. Blandford, March 7, 1942, 1, Westbrook Papers, 2E444, FF 50.

49. Ibid., app. A.

50. The mutual sales procedure was described in "Suggested General Principles Governing Execution and Operation of Mutual Home Ownership Project." See Federal Works Agency, *Third Annual Report* (Washington, DC: Government Printing Office, 1942), 99, table A12.

51. Westbrook to Blandford, March 7, 1942, 7.

52. "Neither for Sale nor Rent," *Architectural Forum* 74 (June 1941): 445.

53. When the Order of the British Empire was conferred upon Westbrook, it was noted that the "amicable relations which existed between the officers of the Joint Purchasing Board and the New Zealand government were largely due to the efforts made by Colonel Westbrook to ensure the smooth working of the procurement organization." See "Reception at Legation Marks 'New Zealand Day,'" *Washington Post*, September 27, 1947, B5.

54. John R. Lutes, "Cooperative Mutual Housing," speech before the National Cooperative League Congress, Columbus, Ohio, September 9, 1946, Leo Goodman Papers, Manuscript Division, Library of Congress (hereafter Goodman Papers), Box 36, FF 1.

55. Herbert Emmerich, "The Problem of Low-Priced Cooperative Apartments: An Experiment at Sunnyside Gardens," *Journal of Land and Public Utility Economics* 1 (offprint, 1928), Papers of Herbert Emmerich, University of Virginia Library, Charlottesville, RG 21/38.711, Box 34.

56. Lawrence Westbrook to Herbert Emmerich, interoffice memorandum, March 30, 1942, Vinton Papers, Box 19.

57. Vinton, "Mutual Home Ownership Plan."

58. Ibid., 4.

59. Mary K. Simkhovitch to Herbert Emmerich, April 28, 1942, Vinton Papers, Box 19. Emphasis in the original.

60. Ibid.

61. Lawrence Westbrook to John M. Carmody, August 21, 1942, Papers of John M. Carmody, President Franklin D. Roosevelt Library, Hyde Park, NY (hereafter Carmody Papers), Box 81.

62. John M. Carmody to Lawrence Westbrook, August 24, 1942, Carmody Papers, Box 81.

63. John M. Carmody to John Green, August 27, 1942, Carmody Papers, Box 81.

64. Warren Jay Vinton to Herbert Emmerich, memorandum, August 14, 1942, Vinton Papers, Box 19. Emmerich wanted to know if Vinton had consulted with Abraham Kazan, Charles Ascher, and J. O. Walker. See Herbert Emmerich to Warren Jay Vinton, memorandum, August 19, 1942, Vinton Papers, Box 19.

65. Warren Jay Vinton, "Proposed Method of Application of Mutual Ownership Plan to Lanham Act Projects," typescript, October 12, 1942, Vinton Papers, Box 19. To Westbrook, the "most repugnant requirement" imposed by the FPHA was the charging of a so-called social rent instead of the slightly higher payments anticipated under the

original Camden Plan. Westbrook alleged that the policy was adopted to undermine mutual housing. The residents would "resist the increase necessary to purchase the project and operate it on a business basis." See Westbrook, "Housing Mess," 16.

66. "Large Housing Job in Jersey Scored," *New York Times*, November 20, 1942, 17. See also "U.S. Indicts 3 Firms for Housing Frauds," *New York Times*, March 31, 1943, 15; "Truman Committee Explores Housing Mess; Winfield Park Defense Housing Project at Linden, N.J.," *Life*, November 30, 1942, 45–46; and "Two Scandals: Winfield Park and Towanda Projects," *Time*, November 30, 1942, 85.

67. David Solomon to H. L. Campbell, memorandum, May 31, 1942, Goodman Papers, Box 34, FF 1.

68. "Only 315 of 700 Units Rented," *New York Times*, November 20, 1942, 17.

69. Abner D. Silverman to Thomas Cantillo, April 26, 1943, Goodman Papers, Box 39, FF 4.

70. Anthony Wayne Smith to John Merrill, April 12, 1943, Goodman Papers, Box 39, FF 4.

71. Sidney J. Wood to Board of Trustees of Winfield Park, June 12, 1945, Goodman Papers, Box 34, FF 4.

72. *Hearings Before a Special Committee Investigating the National Defense Program* (statement of John Taylor Egan), 6054.

73. *Hearings Before a Special Committee Investigating the National Defense Program* (statement of Lorimer C. Graef), 6045.

74. Herbert Emmerich to John B. Blandford, March 24, 1943, Vinton Papers, Box 19. In October 1944 the Audubon Park Mutual Housing Corporation asked the FPHA to cancel the agreement and negotiate a lease with option to purchase, similar to leases negotiated with the mutual housing corporations at Walnut Grove and Greenmont Village. The request was granted, but unfortunately it was not reported why it was made in the first place. See Vinton, "Mutual Ownership Housing Plan." The IUMSWA voted to strike against New York Ship in July 1945. See "Camden Shipbuilders to File Strike Notice," *Trenton Evening News*, July 24, 1945, 3. Labor problems continued for the union into 1947. See "Bids Truman End Shipyard Tieup," *Trenton Evening News*, August 11, 1947, 21.

75. "Residents Act to Purchase Greenmont Village," *Journal of Housing* 2, no. 11 (1945): 183; and "Eight Mutual Ownership Developments in Operation," *Journal of Housing* 2, no. 11 (1945): 183. The PHA's Central Office invited Fred Bell of the Cleveland Regional Office to present "Mutual Ownership Sales: How We Sold Greenmont" at a war housing sales conference held in January 1947. See Public Housing Administration, "Central Office Sales Conference Program," PHA Records, NARA, RG 196, Central Office Files, Series 374-208, Box 29.

76. H. Milton Colvin quoted in "Appointment of an Honorary Member," *Walnut Grove Gazette*, December 2, 1944, 6. A dispute arose in 1944 between the FPHA Region II office and the Winfield Park Mutual Housing Corporation that resulted in the former resuming management of the community. See "U.S. to Resume Rule of Winfield Housing," *New York Times*, April 7, 1944, 36.

77. Emmerich to Blandford, March 24, 1943.

78. Catherine Bauer, "Notes on a Postwar Housing and Planning Program," enclosure in Catherine Bauer to Herbert Emmerich, January 22, 1943, Vinton Papers, Box 4.

79. Richard O. Davies, *Housing Reform during the Truman Administration* (Columbia: University of Missouri Press, 1966).

80. Warren J. Vinton, "The Mutual Home Ownership Plan," in "On the Home Front—To Own or Not to Own?" *Tomorrow's Town* 1, no. 8 (1943): 3, Vinton Papers, Box 19.

81. Ibid., 3.

82. Nelson quoted in Home Builders Association of Metropolitan Washington, *The Answer to Public Housing* (Washington, DC: Home Builders Association of Metropolitan Washington, n.d.), 29.

83. Frank W. Cortright, "War Housing Items from the Capital," *American Builder* 65, no. 12 (1943): 64.

84. Russell B. Porter, "Kaiser Proposes Mass Housing Plan," *New York Times*, March 10, 1944, 16.

85. John Green, "Organized Labor and Housing," typescript, May 23, 1944, Records of the Industrial Union of Marine and Shipbuilding Workers of America, University of Maryland Special Collections Library, College Park, Series 1, Subseries 4, Box 5.

86. U.S. Army, Division of Information and Education, "Why Co-ops: What Are They? How Do They Work?" *GI Roundtable EM 23*, 1944; and "Shall I Buy a House after the War?" *GI Roundtable EM 23*, 1944, available at https://www.historians.org/about-aha-and-membership/aha-history-and-archives/gi-roundtable-series/pamphlets, accessed December 29, 2014.

87. Harold W. Lautner to Warren J. Vinton, memorandum, April 7, 1944, Vinton Papers, Box 19.

88. Lawrence Westbrook to Harry Hopkins, May 1, 1944, Westbrook Papers, 2E441, FF 13.

89. Lawrence Westbrook to William J. Norton, May 15, 1944, Westbrook Papers, 2E441, FF 13; Lawrence Westbrook to Philip Klutznick, June 10, 1944, Westbrook Papers, 2E441, FF 13; Lawrence Westbrook to Henry Andreas, June 5, 1944, Westbrook Papers, 2E441, FF 13; and Lawrence Westbrook to Henry Andreas, June 20, 1944, Westbrook Papers, 2E441, FF 13. Westbrook was later made an honorary member of the Walnut Grove board of directors. See "Appointment of an Honorary Member," *Walnut Grove Gazette*, 10.

90. Richard J. Wagner, "The Mutual Ownership Housing Plan," typescript, October 31, 1944, Part 6, PHA Records, Central Office of the Historian, NARA, RG 196, Series 374–208, Box 14.

91. Ibid., Part 1a.

92. Ibid., Part 4.

93. Ibid., Parts 5a and 5b.

94. Lawrence Westbrook, "Housing and Whatever Bomb," typescript, n.d., 14, Westbrook Papers, 2E444, FF 51.

95. "Mrs. Crawford Dinner Guest," *Washington Post*, May 27, 1945, S2.

## CHAPTER 6

1. "New Housing Bill Offered in Senate," *New York Times*, November 15, 1945, 38. Truman's speech was written by Rosenman. See Richard O. Davies, *Housing Reform during the Truman Administration* (Columbia: University of Missouri Press, 1966), 31–32.

2. "Housing Situation Here Goes from Critical to 'Desperate,'" *Washington Post*, January 18, 1946, 1.

3. Charles Hurd, "President Signs Housing Bill; Orders Work Begun at Once," *New York Times*, July 16, 1949, 1.

4. Eric Hodgins, *Mr. Blandings Builds His Dream House* (New York: Simon and Schuster, 2004, 1946).

5. "Housing Bill Approved by Senate Group," *Christian Science Monitor*, April 3, 1946, 1. The Senate bill included a provision allowing the Reconstruction Finance

Corporation (RFC) to make loans to mutual housing associations unable to obtain private-sector financing.

6. Attendees included FPHA commissioner Philip Klutznick, James Twohy of the Federal Home Loan Bank, John Carson of the Cooperative League of the USA, Boris Shishkin of the AFL, R. J. Thomas of the UAW, John Edelman of the United Textile Workers Union, Lee Johnson of the NPHC, and representatives from Walnut Grove and Greenmont Village. See "National Mutual Housing Association Organized," *Journal of Housing* 2, no. 11 (1945): 182–183; and "Prospectus for the Organization of a National Mutual Housing Association," n.d., Papers of R. J. Thomas, Walter P. Reuther Library and Archives, Wayne State University, Detroit (hereafter Thomas Papers), Box 24, FF 12. See also "Co-ops Active on All Fronts: FHA Financing Available," *Journal of Housing* 7, no. 5 (1950): 165. On Edelman, see John W. Edelman to Gilbert R. Wormwood, August 3, 1945, The John Edelman Collection, Walter P. Reuther Library, Wayne State University, Detroit (hereafter Edelman Papers), Box 34.

7. Lawrence Westbrook (as told to George Creel), "No Down Payment," *Collier's*, February 2, 1946, 28. Oak Park was developed under the Mutual Plan with private funds from the National Mutual Housing Association.

8. Ibid., 28. Westbrook sent a copy of the article to Carmody with a note in which he wrote, "I have attempted to give you that credit you so richly deserve." The colonel had not forgotten that Carmody had given him the chance to test the Camden Plan with Lanham funds in the first place. Lawrence Westbrook to John M. Carmody, January 10, 1946, Papers of John M. Carmody, President Franklin D. Roosevelt Library, Hyde Park, NY (hereafter Carmody Papers), Box 72.

9. Lawrence Westbrook to Dorothy Thompson, July 2, 1947, Lawrence Westbrook Papers, The Texas Collection, Carroll Library, Baylor University, Waco, TX (hereafter Westbrook Papers), 2E445, FF 52. Westbrook asked Thompson if she "would like to join us," presumably meaning invest in the company.

10. Dorothea Kahn, "Housing Shortage Booms Cooperative Building," *Christian Science Monitor*, February 11, 1947, 13.

11. "Wyatt, Wagner and Klutznick Will Speak at Housing Conference Here This Week," *New York Times*, March 10, 1946, R1. One month before the conference Thomas was in correspondence with Senator Tobey regarding loans to co-ops. See R. J. Thomas to Senator Charles W. Tobey, February 25, 1946, 24–29, Thomas Papers. "Mutual Housing Leaders Meet," *New York Times*, April 28, 1946, W1; and Philip M. Klutznick, *Manual of Policy and Procedure* (approved May 4, 1946), Section 3553.2, National Archives and Records Administration, College Park, MD (hereafter NARA), RG 207, Box 778.

12. *Hearings Before the Committee on Banking and Currency on S. 1109*, 78th Cong., 2nd Sess. (statement of Werner Laging) (Washington, DC: Government Printing Office, 1943), 1592; and *Hearings Before the Committee on Banking and Currency on S. 1592*, 79th Cong., 1st Sess. (statement of Lawrence Westbrook) (Washington, DC: Government Printing Office, 1945), 1079.

13. Myer's appointment was initially a "recess appointment." See "Taft Stops Appointment," *New York Times*, August 3, 1946, 13; and "Myer Gets Recess Housing Post," *New York Times*, August 11, 1946, 4.

14. Vinton quoted in W. V. Torma, "Report on Group Meeting on Cooperative and Mutual Housing Associations," typescript, September 12, 1946, 2, Warren J. Vinton Papers, Olin Library, Cornell University, Ithaca, NY (hereafter Vinton Papers), Box 19.

15. John Carson quoted in Torma, "Report on Group Meeting," 1.

16. M. M. Miniard to Dillon S. Myer, December 6, 1946, Vinton Papers, Box 19.

17. Ibid.

18. "New Deal 'Ghost Town' for Sale at Kingsbury," *Chicago Daily Tribune*, July 5, 1947, 3. See also "$13,000,000 Hamlet on Sale at $359,000," *New York Times*, July 6, 1947, 2. A few other mutual housing associations acquired other temporary projects. See "Workers Build Themselves a Dream," *Cooperative Housing* 3 (1966): 21.

19. Thomas J. Fitzpatrick to All District 6 Union Local, July 14, 1947, Fitzpatrick Correspondence, D4, UE Archives, University of Pittsburgh, Pittsburgh.

20. U.S. Department of Labor, Bureau of Labor Statistics, *Cooperative Housing in the United States, 1949 and 1950*, Bulletin 1093, Housing and Home Finance Agency, Housing Research Paper 24 (Washington, DC: Government Printing Office, 1952) (hereafter Bureau of Labor Statistics), 2–3; and "Groups at Odds over Shaler Housing Sale," *Pittsburgh Post-Gazette*, May 15, 1954, 11, available at http://news.google.com/newspapers?nid=1129&dat=19540515&id=vKFhAAAAIBAJ&sjid=5GoDAAAAIBAJ&pg=4862,3862014, accessed July 25, 2014.

21. Bureau of Labor Statistics, *Cooperative Housing*, 63; and "Atchison Village, A Critical Part of Richmond's History," available at http://atchisonvillage.org/history_201207201623_0001.pdf, accessed July 21, 2014.

22. House Subcommittee on Government Operations, "Study of the War Housing Disposal Program," *Program of the Housing and Home Finance Agency and the Public Housing Administration, Third Intermediate Report of the Committee on Expenditures in the Executive Departments* (Washington, DC: Government Printing Office, 1949), 53–54.

23. "700 Tenants Seek to Buy War Town," *New York Times*, February 3, 1947, 21. On Winfield Park's sale, see "To Buy Jersey Housing," *New York Times*, May 13, 1947, 43; "Tenants in Winfield Set to Buy Project," *New York Times*, September 5, 1948, R2; "Winfield Sale Awaited," *New York Times*, August 11, 1949, 35; "Would Cut U.S. Price on Winfield Housing," *New York Times*, August 21, 1949, R1; "Grants Winfield Delay," *New York Times*, September 13, 1949, 51; "U.S. Cuts Housing Price," *New York Times*, October 14, 1949, 47; "Price Set on Housing," *New York Times*, November 9, 1949, 48; "Defense Housing Sold," *New York Times*, November 18, 1949, 47; and "Winfield, N.J. Tenants Are Set to Acquire 700-Family Housing from Government," *New York Times*, December 17, 1950, R1.

24. Jesse P. Wolcott and Ben F. Jensen to Dillon S. Myer, February 25, 1947, quoted in House Subcommittee on Government Operations, "Study of the War Housing Disposal Program," 12–13.

25. Dillon S. Myer to Jesse P. Wolcott and Ben F. Jensen, February 28, 1947, quoted in House Subcommittee on Government Operations, "Study of the War Housing Disposal Program," 13–14.

26. Daniel A. Baskin to Charles Tobey, March 19, 1947, quoted in *Hearings Before the Committee on Banking and Currency on S. 287, S. 866, S. 701, S. 802, and S. 804*, 80th Cong., 1st Sess. (Washington, DC: Government Printing Office, 1947), 567. See also Arthur M. Blaine to Daniel A. Boskin (*sic*), March 17, 1947, Bellmawr Park Mutual Housing Corporation Clipping File, Bellmawr, NJ.

27. Bellmawr Park Mutual Housing Corporation, untitled typescript, [1952], 2, Bellmawr Park Mutual Housing Corporation Historical File, Bellmawr, NJ.

28. House Subcommittee on Government Operations, "Study of the War Housing Disposal Program." Walnut Grove was identified in February 1947 for possible ac-

quisition by the mutual housing association. See Kahn, "Housing Shortage Booms Cooperative Building," 13.

29. Drew Pearson, "The Washington Merry-Go-Round," *Washington Post*, March 25, 1947, 7.

30. Wolcott quoted in Josephine Ripley, "House Group Swings Ax on U.S. Housing Agencies," *Christian Science Monitor*, June 10, 1947, 8.

31. U.S. House of Representatives, *House Resolution 3492*, 80th Cong., 1st Sess. Ironically, Wolcott specified the FWA. See also Nor-Wayne Mutual Housing Committee to John J. Lesinski, August 7, 1947, Truman Official File, Truman Library, Independence, MO (hereafter Truman Library), OF 6, Box 246.

32. U.S. Congress, *House Concurrent Resolution 51*, 80th Cong., 1st Sess. See also "Text of President's Message on Housing Agency," *New York Times*, May 27, 1947, 14; "Truman Plan Puts Housing and Finance in New Setup," *Christian Science Monitor*, May 27, 1947, 15; Flex Belair Jr., "Top Housing Agency Asked of Congress by the President," *New York Times*, May 28, 1947, 1; and Mary Spargo, "Truman Asks One Agency for Housing," *Washington Post*, May 28, 1947, 1.

33. Cain quoted in Davies, *Housing Reform during the Truman Administration*, 63. The House Committee on Expenditures in the Executive Departments recommended that the house block the plan. See John D. Morris, "House Bars Reorganization Plan to Expand Labor Department," *New York Times*, June 11, 1947, 1.

34. Taber quoted in "Accepts Plan for Housing," *Washington Post*, June 27, 1947, 6.

35. "Interim Funds Proposed for U.S. Agencies," *Washington Post*, June 12, 1947, 1.

36. "Accepts Plan for Housing," 6. See also Davies, *Housing Reform during the Truman Administration*, 64–65.

37. Catherine Bauer, "The Middle Class Needs Houses Too," *New Republic*, August 29, 1949, 118–119.

38. John W. Edelman to Carl Hollerman, October 29, 1947, Edelman Papers, Box 34.

39. "Hatboro, PA Tenants Buy War Housing," *Journal of Housing* 4, no. 10 (1947): 303.

40. Robert R. Hagy Jr., "Even If It Does Cost a Million, You Have to Try It Yourself," *Pittsburgh Post-Gazette*, August 25, 1942, 11, available at http://news.google.newspapers?nid=1129&dat=19420825&id=ddkOAAAAIBAJ&sjid, accessed August 6, 2014.

41. Isabel Bayley, "New Kensington Saga," *Task* 5 (1945): 28. See also Jean-Louis Cohen, *Architecture in Uniform: Designing and Building for the Second World War* (New Haven, CT: Yale University Press, 2011), 114.

42. John T. Eagan to Raymond Foley, interoffice memorandum, October 5, 1948, NARA, RG 207, Box 778. See also "Aluminum City Terrace," *Journal of Housing* 10, no. 9 (1953): 331. Labor leader John Edelman informed Foley that twelve mutual housing associations, including Audubon Village, Bellmawr Park, and Pennypack Woods, were in existence prior to Public Regulation No. 1. See John W. Edelman to Raymond Foley, memorandum, October 5, 1948, NARA, RG 207, Box 778.

43. "Aluminum City Terrace," 331.

44. Mary Niederberger, "Aluminum City Lives On," *Pittsburgh Press* (Alle-Kiski edition), May 15, 1983, V1. See also Mary Niederberger, "Aluminum City: 35-Year-Old Co-op Proves Its Mettle," *Pittsburgh Post-Gazette*, May 19, 1983, E8; "Tenants Bid for Project," *Pittsburgh Post-Gazette*, March 8, 1948; and "Residents Buy Housing Unit from PHA," *Pittsburgh Post-Gazette*, March 17, 1948, Aluminum City Terrace Mutual Housing Association Clipping File, New Kensington, PA.

45. George E. Atkinson Jr. to Raymond Foley, June 3, 1948, NARA, RG 207, Box 778. See also "Walnut Grove Secretary Outlines Mutual Grove Ownership Plan," *Journal of Housing* 2, no. 11 (1945): 183.

46. By April 30, 1949, the FHA had insured nine "disposition mortgages," including Aluminum City Terrace. See House Subcommittee on Government Operations, "Study of the War Housing Disposal Program," 22. The FHA lowered its standards for multiunit dwellings so it could underwrite mortgages for the sale of defense housing units that were "one or two story row or semi-detached buildings of frame or masonry construction." The interiors of the Lanham-funded building were "more cheaply finished than in any of the other types of [cooperative] associations." See Florence E. Parker, "Cooperative Housing in the United States, Mid-1950," *Monthly Labor Review* 73 (September 1951): 263.

47. Bureau of Labor Statistics, *Cooperative Housing*, app. D, 188.

48. Bernard L. Grove to All PHA Regional Directors, interoffice memorandum, September 27, 1948, NARA, RG 207, Box 778. In a 1948 speech, Foley stated that the agency favored private financing of Lanham housing sales to mutual housing associations. See Raymond Foley, "Address to Mortgage Association Bankers of America," September 22, 1948, Papers of Raymond Foley, Harry S. Truman Presidential Library, Independence, MO (hereafter Foley Papers), Box 5.

49. John J. Lesinski to President Harry S. Truman, telegram, August 26, 1947, Office of the President, Truman Library, OF 63, Box 296; John J. Lesinski to President Harry S. Truman, August 27, 1947, Office of the President, Truman Library, OF 63, Box 296; and John Steelman to John J. Lesinski, September 17, 1947, Office of the President, Truman Library, OF 63, Box 296.

50. Kahn, "Housing Shortage Booms Cooperative Building," 13.

51. *Hearings on S. 1179, S. 1459 and H.R. 3492*, Part 6, 80th Cong., 1st Sess. (statement of Raymond Foley), 19, Foley Papers, Box 4. Now on the National Register of Historic Places, the Norwayne Historic District includes individually owned homes.

52. Housing and Home Finance Agency, Public Housing Administration, Budget and Statistical Division, *Disposition Directory as of July 31, 1947*, Report S-104, NARA, RG 196, Series 25, Boxes 112 and 113. S-104 reports continued to be issued at least until 1953. On Channel Heights, see Cohen, *Architecture in Uniform*, 117–120.

53. Lawrence Westbrook, "Benefits of Mutual Home Ownership—A Personal Message to the Residents of Avion Village," typescript, n.d., Westbrook Papers, 2E444, FF 51; and *Hearings Before the Committee on Banking and Currency on H.R. 6618 and H.R. 6742*, 81st Cong., 2nd Sess. (statement of Jerry Voorhis) (Washington, DC: Government Printing Office, 1950), 150–151, 158.

54. Lawrence Westbrook, "A New Method of Merchandising Homes," 14, Westbrook Papers, 2E444, FF 53.

55. John M. Carmody to Lawrence Westbrook, March 22, 1948, Carmody Papers, Box 72.

56. "Public Housing Projects Sold as Co-ops," typescript, February 7, 1950, Leo Goodman Papers, Manuscript Division, Library of Congress, Box 36, FF 1.

57. Parker, "Cooperative Housing in the United States, Mid-1950," 259, table 1. Eight mutual associations were started in 1947, two in 1948, eight in 1949, and one in 1950. See Bureau of Labor Statistics, *Cooperative Housing*, 10.

58. Elsie Danenberg, *Get Your Own Home the Co-operative Way* (New York: Greenberg, 1949), 143.

59. Florence Parker, "Developments in the Consumer Cooperative Movement in 1946," *Monthly Labor Review* 64, no. 3 (1947): 474; and Wilson W. Wyatt Sr., *Whistle Stops: Adventures in Public Life* (Lexington: University Press of Kentucky, 1985).

60. "Amvets Taking Housing Bid Protest to 'Hill,'" *Washington Post*, February 14, 1946, 5. See Holly K. Chamberlain, "Permanence in Time of War: Three Defense Homes Corporation Projects in the Washington Metropolitan Area," in *Housing Washington: Two Centuries of Residential Development and Planning in the National Capital Area*, ed. Richard Longstreth (Chicago: Center for American Places at Columbia College, 2010), 181–201.

61. "Veterans Plan New, 'Definite' McLean Offer," *Washington Post*, January 15, 1946, 4.

62. "Senator Johnson Backs Amvets' Housing Plan," *Washington Post*, January 2, 1946, 16; and Lawrence Westbrook, "Speech at McLean Gardens," n.d., Westbrook Papers, 2E445, FF 52. See also Westbrook, untitled speech to the chairwoman and members of the Veterans' Housing Committee, June 5, 1946, Westbrook Papers, 2E445, FF 52.

63. "All Fairlington Bids Rejected, Board Reveals," *Washington Post*, February 13, 1946, 1; "Homes for Veterans," *Washington Post*, February 19, 1946, 6; and "Sales of U.S. Housing Await Congress Stand," *Washington Post*, February 21, 1946, 8. See also Sam Stavisky, "McLean Gardens Fight Spotlights New Vet Unit," *Washington Post*, March 3, 1946, S6.

64. "Veterans Plan New, 'Definite' McLean Offer," 4. See also R. J. Thomas, *Problems and Answers* (Detroit: United Automobile Workers Union, 1945): 24–25. The joint resolution originated in the House in January 14, 1946, and was initiated by Congressman Carter Manasco (D-AL). Disposition priority remained an issue of contention despite the preparation of a 1946 manual outlining procedures. See Federal Public Housing Authority, *Manual of Policy and Procedure: Commissioner's Orders*, 1946, PHA Records, NARA, RG 196, Central Office of the Historian, Series 374-208, Box 10. Representative Edith Nourse Rogers (R-MA) correctly anticipated that the granting of veterans' preference would create problems for existing residents of Lanham projects who wished to purchase their homes under the Mutual Plan. See "Rep. Rogers Backs Mrs. McLean's View on Housing for GIs," *Washington Post*, February 19, 1946, 2.

65. "Veterans of District Clamor for Naylor Gardens Homes," *Washington Post*, April 24, 1946, 10. See also Lawrence Westbrook to Joel Westbrook, May 29, 1946, Westbrook Papers, 2E441, FF 13.

66. Sawyer quoted in "AMVETS Claim 50,000 Members," *Washington Post*, March 3, 1946, S6.

67. Danenberg, *Get Your Own Home the Co-operative Way*, 159; and "Veterans Acquire Housing Projects," *New York Times*, March 9, 1947, R2. The Wilmington Housing Authority (WHA) recommended the sale of the 584 dwelling units at Lake Forest as a single entity. See *Minutes of the Wilmington Housing Authority*, vol. 8, November 21, 1944, Wilmington, NC, 20, and November 20, 1945, vol. 8, 283; see also "Wilmington, North Carolina Vets Co-op Leases Lake Forest," *Journal of Housing* 4, no. 4 (1947): 99.

68. National Housing Agency, *A Veterans' Guide to Organizing, Financing, Constructing, and Operating Several Types of Cooperative Housing Associations with Special Reference to Available Federal Aids* (Washington, DC: National Housing Agency, 1946), preface. Controversy remained over Lanham sales priorities, especially where

veterans sought to exclude nonveterans as residents. See "Summary of Commissioner's Staff Meeting," typescript, October 1, 1946, NARA, RG 196, Box 6.

69. Danenberg, *Get Your Own Home the Co-operative Way*, 144.

70. Lawrence Westbrook to Joel Westbrook, July 29, 1946, Westbrook Papers, 2E441, FF 13. See also L. Westbrook to J. Westbrook, June 10, 1946, Westbrook Papers, 2E441, FF 10.

71. Housing Producers Cooperative, Inc., "Recommendations of the Housing Producers Cooperative," August 30, 1940, Papers of David R. Williams, Edith Garland Dupré Library, University of Louisiana, Lafayette, FF 34-15. The involvement of Neutra and Williams in the venture and the fact that Greenbelt was sold under a modified version of the Camden Plan suggest that Westbrook was involved behind the scenes.

72. Neutra quoted in "Notes in Passing," *California Arts and Architecture* 59 (January 1942): 15.

73. L. Westbrook to J. Westbrook, July 29, 1946.

74. According to Westbrook, the "opportunity for making a substantial amount of money is very great indeed." See L. Westbrook to J. Westbrook, July 29, 1946.

75. Dorothy Thompson, "Address to the Residents of Greenbelt, Maryland," typescript, November 10, 1947, 12, Westbrook Papers, 2E445, FF 52. See also Lawrence Westbrook to Dorothy Thompson, November 5, 1947, Westbrook Papers, 2E445, FF 52; and "Housing Move Grows," *Washington Post*, November 12, 1947, B2.

76. "Vets Housing Plan Urged by McCarthy," *Washington Post*, February 23, 1949, B11.

77. "Equal Preference for Veterans and Nonveterans in Buying Sought," *Washington Post*, March 25, 1949, B1; "Bill Passed to Permit Sale of Greenbelt," *Washington Post*, May 5, 1949, B1; and "Truman Signs Bill for Sale of Greenbelt," *Washington Post*, May 20, 1949, 19.

78. Merson quoted in Bellmawr Park Mutual Housing Corporation, "To the 500 Families of Bellmawr Park," [1952], Bellmawr Park Mutual Housing Corporation Historical File, Bellemawr, NJ. See also "Federal Homes Project Sold at 8 Million Loss," *Chicago Daily Tribune*, December 7, 1949, B13; and "U.S. Sells Ohio Town It Built in Depression," *New York Times*, December 7, 1949, 56.

79. A rival mutual association was created in early 1950 by six veterans who opposed the Greenbelt Veterans Housing Corporation's plans to continue to operate Greenbelt Consumers Services, which operated the commercial enterprises. See "New Turmoil Stirs Calm of Greenbelt," *Washington Post*, March 19, 1950, M16. Not included in the sale were 311 apartment units and roughly 1,700 acres of undeveloped land. The actual title transfer took place on December 30, 1952. See "Greenbelt's Top Worry 'Post-sale' Is Tax," *Washington Post*, October 31, 1951, 17; "P.H.A. Selling a 'Town,'" *New York Times*, January 4, 1952, 36; "U.S. to Open Greenbelt Sale Talks Again," *Washington Post*, January 4, 1952, B1; "Selling Prices for Greenbelt Homes Fixed," *Washington Post*, January 26, 1952, B1; "Contract Gets Nod of Group in Greenbelt," *Washington Post*, April 3, 1952, B2; "Petition Asks Greenbelt Sale Disapproval," *Washington Post*, April 21, 1952, B1; "Greenbelt, MD Sale Extended for Thirty Days," *Washington Post*, May 31, 1952, 15; "Greenbelt's Woes," letter to the editor, *Washington Post*, June 26, 1952, 14; "Sale Deadline at Greenbelt Declared Met," *Washington Post*, June 29, 1952, M16; "Greenbelt Group Moves with Care in Purchase Plan," *Washington Post*, July 3, 1952, 22; "U.S. Sells Town Ending Autopia of New Dealers," *Chicago Daily Tribune*, September 27, 1952, 16; "Veterans' Groups Buys Greenbelt," *Washington Post*, September 27, 1952, 15; "Greenbelt Houses Sold to Cooperative Group," *American City* 67 (October 1952): 125;

"Most Greenbelt Residents Seeking to Have Rent Raised," *Washington Post*, December 7, 1952, M21; and Harrison P. Hagemeyer, "Greenbelt, a New Deal Dream, Finally Sold by Government," *Washington Post*, December 31, 1952, 15. The apartment buildings were auctioned off in 1953. See "New Sale Set for Greenbelt," *Washington Post*, February 5, 1953, 8. On the proposed plan to build new housing, see "Group Plans 2000 Homes in Greenbelt," *Washington Post*, December 25, 1952, 18; and "Maryland Homes Planned in 'Co-op,'" *New York Times*, May 9, 1952, R10.

80. Louis Ludlow to Matthew J. Connelly, April 24, 1948, Office of the President, Truman Library, OF 63, Box 297; "Summary of Facts, Conclusions Thereon and Recommendations Submitted by the American Legion to the House Subcommittee on Expenditures in Executive Departments on Behalf of Veterans in Connection with the Knox, Indiana Housing Controversy," n.d., Office of the President, Truman Library, OF 63, Box 297; James F. O'Neil to President Harry S. Truman, May 11, 1948, Office of the President, Truman Library, OF 63, Box 297; *Investigation of Sale of Parkview Heights Housing Project at Knox, Indiana by the Public Housing Administration to Knox Homes, Inc, a Private Corporation: Hearings Before a Subcommittee of the Committee on Expenditures in the Executive Departments*, April 1948, Office of the President, Truman Library, OF 63, Box 297; and *Investigation of Sale of Parkview Heights . . . Eleventh Intermediate Report*, May 1948, Office of the President, Truman Library, OF 63, Box 297. American Legion Nicholson Post No. 38 formed the American Legion Housing Corporation, a cooperative, to help Baton Rouge veterans construct 250 prefabricated houses. See *Hearings Before the Committee on Banking and Currency on H.R. 6618 and H.R. 6742* (statement of Robert Dinger), 91–113.

81. George McGill to President Harry S. Truman, September 10, 1948, Office of the President, Truman Library, OF 63, Box 297. Because of the inability of the Hilltop group to get private financing, it was granted a mortgage from the PHA. See House Subcommittee on Government Operations, "Study of the War Housing Disposal Program," 49–51.

82. Julie Courtwright, "Want to Build a Miracle City? War Housing in Wichita," *Kansas History* 24, no. 4 (2000–2001): 233.

83. Joseph Orendorff to Raymond Foley, internal office memorandum, n.d., NARA, RG 207, Box 778. A petition protesting the sale of Broad Creek Village under the Mutual Plan was signed by 1,700 residents. The local housing authority was also opposed. See House Subcommittee on Government Operations, "Study of the War Housing Disposal Program," 53–54.

84. "Lawlessness at Albany," *New York Times*, October 21, 1946, 6.

85. Stichman quoted in Robert M. Hallett, "Veterans Housing Project Ready to Begin in Queens," *Christian Science Monitor*, October 21, 1948, 3.

86. "New York Backs Plan to Aid Veterans," *Christian Science Monitor*, October 9, 1947, 18. The League of Women Voters opposed use of the mutual housing program to build public support for the bond issue for bonuses. See "Bonus Warning Issued," *New York Times*, November 1, 1947, 17. Stichman quoted in Hallett, "Veterans Housing Project Ready to Begin in Queens," 3. See also "Mutual Housing Plan Seen Cutting Costs to Veterans Nearly 25%," *Wall Street Journal*, February 10, 1948, 2; "Depositary Named for Housing Funds," *New York Times*, February 16, 1948, 28; "460 Veterans Buying Suites," *New York Times*, June 13, 1948, R5; "Veterans' Apartments Available," *New York Times*, August 15, 1948, 20; Robert M. Hallett, "New York's Housing Programs," *Christian Science Monitor*, September 10, 1949, 18; "300 Seek Space in Smith Project," *New York*

*Times*, August 30, 1949, 29; and "Bell Park Cooperative Gets F.H.A. Commitment," *New York Times*, March 30, 1950, 52.

87. Tricia Shulist and Richard Harris, "Build Your Own Home: State-Assisted Self-Help Housing in Canada, 1942–1975," *Planning Perspectives* 7, no. 4 (2002): 345–373; and Richard Harris, *Building a Market: The Rise of the Home Improvement Industry, 1914–1960* (Chicago: University of Chicago Press, 2012), 235–265.

88. Richard Harris, "Flattered but Not Imitated: Cooperative Self-Help and the Nova Scotia Housing Commission, 1936–1973," *Acadiensis* 31, no. 1 (2001): 104.

89. National Mutual Housing Association, "Prospectus"; and Gilbert Wormwood, "Mutual Housing Association," typescript, July 27, 1945, Edelman Papers, Box 34. See also National Mutual Housing Association, *Rules and Regulations*, n.d., Thomas Papers, Box 24, FF 12.

90. National Mutual Housing Association, "Prospectus"; and Wormwood, "Mutual Housing Association."

91. *Hearings Before the Committee on Banking and Currency on S. 1592*, Part 2, 79th Cong., 1st Sess. (statement of John Carson), 1068.

92. L. Westbrook to J. Westbrook, July 29, 1946. See also L. Westbrook to J. Westbrook, June 10, 1946. Many of Westbrook's contemporaries, including prominent Democrats like Eleanor Roosevelt, supported housing desegregation and were active with the National Committee on Segregation in Washington. See Murrey Marder, "D.C. Business Accused of Maintaining Negro Ghetto," *Washington Post*, December 11, 1948, 1.

93. L. Westbrook to J. Westbrook, July 26, 1946, Westbrook Papers, 2E441, FF 13.

94. Lawrence Westbrook to Dillon S. Myer, November 27, 1946, Westbrook Papers, 2E441, FF 13; and Housing Producers Cooperative, "Recommendations of the Housing Producers Cooperative," August 30, 1940.

95. "'White City' Homes to Be Cooperative," *Chicago Tribune*, December 23, 1945, C4; and "Home Project Is Mortgaged for 6.8 Million," *Chicago Daily Tribune*, March 30, 1947, NWB. James Cassells of the National Mutual Housing Association was informed by the FHA's Warren J. Lockwood that the agency had "never insured a housing project of mixed occupancy." Lockwood added, "We cannot state in advance what our underwriting would would [*sic*] be except to make the unofficial and informal statement that we believe such projects would probably in a short period of time become all Negro or all white." See Lockwood quoted in James L. Hicks, "Attorney Finds FHA Race Policies Biased," *Atlanta Daily World*, December 12, 1948, 1. On the delay, see "Federal Delay and Red Tape Tie Up Project," *Chicago Daily Tribune*, May 7, 1948, SWA; "Negro Homes Project Will Start Soon," *Chicago Daily Tribune*, May 22, 1949, A10; and "Vets to Hold Program at Model Co-op," *Chicago Tribune*, July 24, 1949, S2. The cornerstone laying included educator and civil rights leader Mary McLeod Bethune, who presented the dedication address; Illinois governor Adlai Stevenson; Chicago mayor Martin H. Kennedy; Senator Paul H. Douglas (D-IL); Representative William L. Dawson (D-IL); and Senator Scott W. Lucas (D-IL). Lucas called the development a "great triumph of the cause of democracy and the American way of life." The community, which was to consist of thirty-five homes, a school, a clubhouse, a library, and indoor and outdoor recreational facilities, was in Lucas's estimation, "remarkable" in two respects. First, it was a pioneering example of self-help, and second, as the "only [such] undertaking in the country ever launched and carried through by a Negro group," it would show that "American Negroes have faith in the free way of life which offers more opportunities and more blessings to them." See Lucas quoted in "Lucas Praises Housing Project," *Atlanta Daily World*, October 5, 1950, 1.

96. Robert C. Weaver, "Housing in a Democracy," *Annals of the American Academy of Political and Social Science* 244 (March 1946): 102.

97. "Co-op Plan for Project Still Pushed," *Pittsburgh Post-Gazette*, January 3, 1953, 9, available at http://news.googlecom/newspapers?nid=1129&dat19530103&id=5kUNAAAAIBAJ&sjid accessed August 6, 2014.

98. On Wilner, see Kristin Szylvian Bailey, "The Federal Government and the Cooperative Housing Movement" (Ph.D. diss., Carnegie Mellon University, 1988), 132–133. The original interview with Rufus Simpson took place on April 3, 1987. See also Kristin Szylvian Bailey, "Defense Housing in Greater Pittsburgh, 1945–1955," *Pittsburgh History* 73, no. 1 (1990): 14–27.

99. "Munhall Homesteads," Historic American Engineering Record (HAER) PA-303, 19, available at http://www.lcweb2.loc.gov/pnp/habshaer/pa/pa2950/data/pa2950data.pdf, accessed July 22, 2014.

100. "U.S. Projects to Be Sold to Tenants," *Los Angeles Times*, November 10, 1948, 15. Normont Terrace was razed and in 1998–1999 replaced by a mixed-income development. See Julie Tamaki, "New Development Revitalizes Area of Harbor City," *Los Angeles Times*, February 7, 1999, 1.

101. Louis Stark, "Martin Battling Flint Union Reds," *New York Times*, November 28, 1937, 19.

102. Henry Kraus, *In the City Was a Garden: A Housing Project Chronicle* (New York: Renaissance, 1951), 119, 161.

103. Ibid., 170.

104. Kaufman (pseud.) quoted in ibid., 160.

105. Ibid., 163–164. The choice of pseudonym was unfortunate; Herbert Herman, the director of the FPHA New York field office, supported the sale of Lanham communities to mutual housing associations in the Mid-Atlantic region.

106. Colleen Doody, *Detroit's Cold War: The Origins of Postwar Conservatism, the Working Class in American History* (Urbana: University of Illinois Press, 2013); and Kraus, *In the City Was a Garden*, 164.

107. Kraus, *In the City Was a Garden*, 191. Only fifty people came to a rally for Burke. See "Mass Appeal Plan Fizzles," *Los Angeles Times*, October 29, 1946, A1.

108. "Rodney" quoted in Kraus, *In the City Was a Garden*, 195. See also ibid., 162–164.

109. Ibid., 170. See also Don Parson, "The Burke Incident: Political Belief in Los Angeles' Public Housing during the Domestic Cold War," *Southern California Quarterly* 84, no. 1 (2002): 53–74.

110. Don Parson, "The Decline of Public Housing and the Politics of the Red Scare: The Significance of the Los Angeles Public Housing War," *Journal of Urban History* 33, no. 3 (2007): 404. See also Don Parson, *Making a Better World: Public Housing, the Red Scare, and the Direction of Modern Los Angeles* (Minneapolis: University of Minnesota Press, 2005), 53–55.

111. Kraus, *In the City Was a Garden*, 247.

112. Ibid., 193, 248.

113. "Negro Housing Purchase by Tenants Due," *Washington Post*, November 16, 1948, 13; "Tenants' Offer Accepted for Carver Homes," *Washington Post*, December 1, 1948, 20; "Dunbar Homes Sold to Tenants at Half Cost," *Washington Post*, December 11, 1948, B1; "Housing Group Charted," *Washington Post*, February 1, 1948, M18; "Elder Michaux to Supervise Housing Co-op," *Washington Post*, June 11, 1949, B1; and "Deadline Eased for Purchase of Housing Projects," *Washington Post*, July 2, 1949, B1. In 1967 the cooperative planned to raze the original Dunbar Homes units and replace them.

See "Arlington Negroes Plan New Housing Cooperative," *Washington Post and Times Herald*, October 2, 1967, B1.

114. Lockwood quoted in "Attorney Finds FHA Race Policies Biased," *Atlanta Daily World*, December 12, 1948, 1.

115. "Loan Groups Pledge Aid on Housing," *Washington Post*, February 15, 1949, B1.

116. "U.S. Projects to Be Sold to Tenants," *Los Angeles Times*, November 10, 1948, 15.

117. Bureau of Labor Statistics, *Cooperative Housing*, 13.

118. Carr quoted in "See Housing Used to Socialize U.S.," *New York Times*, April 30, 1946, 16.

119. "Priorities on Homes Ended," *Chicago Daily Tribune*, December 15, 1946, 1. Postwar Congressional cooperative housing proponents included Wright Patman. See Nancy Beck Young, *Wright Patman: Populism, Liberalism, and the American Dream* (Dallas: Southern Methodist University Press, 2000), 145.

120. Eric Larrabee, "The Six Thousand Houses That Levitt Built," *Harper's* 197 (September 1948): 79–88.

121. Joint Committee of the National Association of Housing Officials and the National Public Housing Conference, *A Housing Program for Now and Later* (Washington, DC: National Public Housing Conference, 1948), 5, 33.

122. CIO Department of Education and Research, *Homes for People, Jobs for Prosperity, and Planes for Peace* (Washington, DC: CIO Department of Education, 1949), 26, 28.

123. "Success Village Saga: A Story of Courage," *Bridgeport Herald*, November 6, 1960, available at http://news.google.com/newspapers?nid=2229&dat=19601106&id=EJAyAAAAIBAJ&sjid accessed August 6, 2014.

124. House Subcommittee on Government Operations, *Third Intermediate Report*, 5.

125. Parker, "Cooperative Housing in the United States, Mid-1950," 259, table 1.

126. Housing and Home Financing Agency, *Ninth Annual Report*, Part III (Washington, DC: Government Printing Office), 321.

127. House Subcommittee on Government Operations, "Study of the War Housing Disposal Program," 44.

128. Alexander von Hoffman, "A Study in Contradictions: The Origins and Legacy of the Housing Act of 1949," *Housing Policy Debate* 11, no. 2 (2000): 299.

129. Robert C. Albright, "Busy '80th' Turned Clocks Back to the '20s," *Washington Post*, July 27, 1947, B1.

## CHAPTER 7

1. See the dust jacket on Elsie Danenberg, *Get Your Own Home the Co-operative Way* (New York: Greenberg, 1949).

2. "Ground-Breaking Set for 1st Coop in Area Today," *Washington Post*, January 15, 1949, B1.

3. Joel W. Schenker, "Cooperative Housing Projects Called Pattern of the Future," *New York Herald Tribune*, January 29, 1950, entered into the record of *Hearings Before the Committee on Banking and Currency, U.S. House of Representatives on H.R. 6618 and H.R. 6742*, 81st Cong., 2nd Sess. (Washington, DC: Government Printing Office, 1950) (hereafter *House Hearings*), 59.

4. "Low-Cost Homes Bill Agreement Reached," *Los Angeles Times*, November 13, 1945, A1; and "New Housing Bill Offered in Senate," *New York Times*, November 15, 1945, 38.

5. *Hearings Before the Senate Committee on Banking and Currency on S. 1592*, 81st Cong., 2nd Sess. (statement of James McEwan) (Washington, DC: Government Printing Office, 1949), 1103.

6. P.L. 901, 80th Cong., 2nd Sess., August 10, 1948; "Private Building Measure Passed for Uncertain Fate," *New York Times*, August 8, 1949, 1; Truman quoted in Richard O. Davies, *Housing Reform during the Truman Administration* (Columbia: University of Missouri Press, 1966), 83. In 1952 a distinction was drawn between 1948, when Congress empowered the FHA to underwrite a cooperative housing mortgage, and the period following the 1950 creation of the Section 213 program. See Department of Labor, Bureau of Labor Statistics, *Cooperative Housing in the United States, 1949 and 1950*, Bulletin 1093, Housing and Home Finance Agency, Housing Research Paper 24 (Washington, DC: Government Printing Office, 1952) (hereafter Bureau of Labor Statistics), 3.

7. Donald Monson and Astrid Monson, "Ideas from Sweden for an American Cooperative Housing Program," pt. 3, *American City* (May 1949): 141. Five mutual associations had FHA mortgage insurance, two mortgages had been purchased by the Federal National Mortgage Association, and one mortgage came with an additional "VA guarantee for $60,000 backed by individual notes of $1,200 per member." See Bureau of Labor Statistics, *Cooperative Housing*, 37–38, 75. The 1948 law might have contributed to the FHA's willingness to insure the mortgage granted to the Community Development Trust to develop the 694-unit, Parkway Gardens, an experiment in middle-income, mutually owned fair housing in Chicago. See Al Chase, "Negro Homes Project Will Start Soon," *Chicago Daily Tribune*, May 22, 1949, A10; and "Vets to Hold Program at Model Coop," *Chicago Daily Tribune*, July 24, 1949, S2.

8. "Realtors to Ask U.S. Aid for Cooperatives," *Washington Post*, December 19, 1948, R1.

9. Drew Pearson, "The Washington Merry-Go-Round: Truman Urged to Oust Generals," *Washington Post*, December 20, 1948, B15.

10. "Review Will Show Rent Control No Longer Justified, New President Tells Realtors," *Washington Post*, January 12, 1949, 10.

11. "Realtors to Offer New Housing Plan," *Christian Science Monitor*, January 6, 1949, 13. See also "Realty Boards to Urge a Cooperative Plan in Place of Public Housing," *Wall Street Journal*, December 20, 1948, 3.

12. P.L. 171, July 15, 1949, 81st Cong., 1st Sess. See also Davies, *Housing Reform during the Truman Administration*, 101; and Alexander von Hoffman, "A Study in Contradictions: The Origins and Legacy of the Housing Act of 1949," *Housing Policy Debate* 11, no. 2 (2000): 299–326.

13. *Report from the Committee on Banking and Currency to Accompany the Amendment in the Nature of a Substitute for S. 2246; A Bill to Amend the National Housing Act as Amended, and for Other Purposes*, 81st Cong., 2nd Sess. (Washington, DC: Government Printing Office, 1950), 49.

14. Catherine Bauer, "The Middle Class Needs Houses Too," *New Republic*, August 29, 1949, 19–20.

15. Ibid., 20. On the need for a body independent of the FHA to promote cooperative home ownership, see *House Hearings* (statement of Drayton S. Bryant), 115, 124–126; *House Hearings* (statement of Jerry Voorhis), 144–147; and *House Hearings* (statement of John C. Williamson), 128.

16. Bauer was chairman of the National Association of Housing Officials' Committee on Middle Income Housing. See NAHO, Committee on Middle Income

Housing, "Housing for the Middle Income Groups; A Report by the NAHO Committee on Middle Income Housing," typescript, n.d., 12, Catherine Bauer Papers, Bancroft Library, University of California, Berkeley (hereafter Bauer Papers), Box 14.

17. "AFL Urges Housing for Middle Groups," *New York Times*, February 1, 1949, 29.

18. Mary Spargo, "Housing Plan to Aid 'Little Man' Is Given," *Washington Post*, February 5, 1949, 12.

19. "Loan Groups Pledge Aid on Housing," *Washington Post*, February 15, 1 949, B1.

20. The CIO compiled the list of the nineteen bills: H.R. 4458, H.R. 4472, H.R. 4517, H.R. 4576, H.R. 4593, H.R. 4597, H.R. 4611, H.R. 4635, H.R. 4648, H.R. 4659, H.R. 4662, H.R. 4670, H.R. 4700, H.R. 4724, H.R. 4773, H.R. 4809, H.R. 4838, H.R. 4868, and H.R. 4982. See CIO National Housing Committee, "Summary of Middle Income Housing Bills," typescript, Bauer Papers, Box 14. On the Mitchell Bill, see Jack Carter, "Middle-Income Housing," letter to the editor, *Washington Post*, May 30, 1949, 6.

21. *Report from the Committee on Banking and Currency to Accompany the Amendment in the Nature of a Substitute for S. 2246*, 47.

22. Ibid., 49.

23. National Association of Real Estate Boards (NAREB) quoted in Robert S. Allen, "Lobbyists Hit New Bill on Housing," *Washington Post*, July 22, 1949, 23; and "Building Industry Nearing Stability," *New York Times*, August 14, 1949, R1. The House version of the bill sponsored by Representative Spence was passed in 1949 without the direct loan provision. See "Congress Gets Bill to Spur Housing for Middle Income Group," *Wall Street Journal*, January 7, 1950, 3.

24. "Anti-bias Rider Put in House Bill," *Washington Post*, August 25, 1949; "Middle Income Housing," *Washington Post*, August 26, 1949, 20; and Drew Pearson, "The Washington Merry-Go-Round: Bevin Is 'Ernie' at Hill Luncheon," *Washington Post*, September 20, 1949, B15.

25. "Cooperative Housing," *Washington Post*, August 14, 1949, B4; and Robert S. Allen, "The Washington Merry-Go-Round: Bevin Bringing India Bombshell," *Washington Post*, August 28, 1949, B5. See also Housing and Home Finance Agency, "Middle-Income Housing Program," typescript, December 9, 1949, Bauer Papers, Box 14.

26. Harry C. Bates, "Cooperative Housing for Medium Incomes," *Washington Post*, August 20, 1949, 5.

27. "American Legion Backs Bill for Direct GI Housing Loans," *Washington Post*, August 24, 1949, 11; and "AFL Renews Plea to CIO for Unity," *Washington Post*, October 7, 1949, 8.

28. John O'Grady, "Flaws in the Middle Income Housing Bill," *Washington Post*, September 1, 1949, 9.

29. *Middle-Income Housing Bill, S. 2246*, 81st Cong., 1st Sess. (statement of Senator Glen H. Taylor), *Congressional Record* 95:3267.

30. *Middle-Income Housing Bill, S. 2246* (statement of Senator Russell B. Long), 3297.

31. Ibid.

32. "Housing Co-ops," *Washington Post*, September 16, 1949, 20. The *Christian Science Monitor* praised Amalgamated union leaders because they expanded the 1926 development "without recourse to government and or other aids beyond their own initiative and enterprise." See "Union Builds Its Own Houses," *Christian Science Monitor*, November 30, 1951, 12.

33. Robert C. Albright, "Housing Bill Is Put on List of 'Musts,'" *Washington Post*, October 3, 1949, 2.

34. Senate Committee on Banking and Currency, Subcommittee Investigating and Studying European Housing Programs, *Cooperative Housing in Europe*, 81st Cong., 2nd Sess. (Washington, DC: Government Printing Office, 1950), 1.

35. The Monsons used what they had learned abroad to advise the UAW in planning the 500-unit Schoolcraft Gardens in Detroit. See Monson and Monson, "Ideas from Sweden for an American Cooperative Housing Program," 110; and *Hearings Before the Subcommittee of the Senate Committee on Banking and Currency on Amendments to S. 2246, to Amend the National Housing Act, as Amended, and for Other Purposes*, Part 1, 81st Cong., 2nd Sess. (Washington, DC: Government Printing Office, 1950), 5.

36. Charles Abrams, "Another String to the Bow," *The Survey* 85 (October 1949): 546.

37. Ibid.

38. *Report from the Committee on Banking and Currency to Accompany the Amendment in the Nature of a Substitute for S. 2246*, 51, 54.

39. "Scandinavian Housing Work Tops America's Senators Say," *Washington Post*, February 2, 1950, 2. See also *Final Report of the Subcommittee of the Senate Committee on Banking and Currency Pursuant to Res. 331*, 81st Cong., 2nd Sess. (Washington, DC: Government Printing Office, 1950); House Committee on Banking and Currency, Subcommittee No. 1, *Cooperative Housing Abroad*, 81st Cong., 2nd Sess. (Washington, DC: Government Printing Office, 1950); and Senate Committee, Subcommittee, *Cooperative Housing in Europe*.

40. "Sen. Sparkman Tells of Hope for Housing," *Washington Post*, December 15, 1949, B2.

41. Robert C. Albright, "Congress Fidgets through Opening Day; Legislative Program Shaping Up," *Washington Post*, January 4, 1950, 1.

42. *Report from the Committee on Banking and Currency to Accompany the Amendment in the Nature of a Substitute for S. 2246*, 5; and "Housing Coops," *Washington Post*, January 17, 1950, 8.

43. Sparkman quoted in Drew Pearson, "The Washington Merry-Go-Round: Hoover Does About-Face on Policy," *Washington Post*, January 10, 1950, B11.

44. Harry S. Truman, "Annual Message to Congress on the State of the Union," January 4, 1950, *The Public Papers of President Harry S. Truman* (Washington, DC: Government Printing Office, 1965).

45. Harry S. Truman, "Annual Budget Message to the Congress: Fiscal Year 1951," January 9, 1950, *The Public Papers of President Harry S. Truman* (Washington, DC: Government Printing Office, 1965).

46. *Report from the Committee on Banking and Currency to Accompany the Amendment in the Nature of a Substitute for S. 2246*, 49.

47. Alfred Friendly, "$2 Billion Increase for Welfare Asked," *Washington Post*, January 10, 1950, 4.

48. *Hearings Before the Subcommittee on Housing and Rents of the Banking and Currency Committee on Amendments to S. 2246*, 81st Cong., 2nd Sess. (statement of Raymond M. Foley) (Washington, DC: Government Printing Office, 1950), 23, Papers of Raymond Foley, Harry S. Truman Presidential Library, Independence, MO (hereafter Foley Papers), Box 4. Foley was slow to warm to cooperative housing. See J. E. Reeve to David Lloyd, interoffice memorandum, November 15, 1949, David D. Lloyd Files, Harry S. Truman Presidential Library, Independence, MO (hereafter Lloyd Files), Box 2; and *Hearings Before the Subcommittee on Housing and Rents of the Banking and Currency Committee on Amendments to S. 2246* (statement of Raymond M. Foley).

49. Russell and Sparkman quoted in "Witness Assails Housing Bill as 'Socialism,'" *Washington Post*, January 14, 1950, 2.

50. *Hearings Before the Subcommittee on Housing and Rents of the Banking and Currency Committee on Amendments to S. 2246* (statement of Thomas McCabe), Foley Papers, Box 4.

51. "Housing Coops," 8.

52. Chamber of Commerce of the United States, "Government Lending to Cooperative and Non-profit Housing Corporations," typescript, January 16, 1949, Bauer Papers, Box 14; and Chamber of Commerce of the United States, "Proposed National Mortgage Corporation for Housing Cooperatives; A Summary Analysis," typescript, February 1950, Bauer Papers, Box 14.

53. Reckman quoted in Mary Spargo, "Reuther Hits Realty Men on Housing," *Washington Post*, January 19, 1950, 22. Sparkman noted that the banking group had never endorsed the FHA.

54. Held quoted in Spargo, "Reuther Hits Realty Men on Housing," 2.

55. Daniel quoted in "Co-op Bill Would Ruin Rental, FHA Builder Says," *Washington Post*, January 22, 1950, R1.

56. "Cooperative Homes Face New Fight in Senate," *Washington Post*, February 12, 1950, R1. O'Grady quoted in Mary Spargo, "AFL Endorses Cooperative Housing Bill," *Washington Post*, February 15, 1950, 2.

57. Bricker quoted in "Bricker Hits Favoritism in Housing Plan," *Washington Post*, February 12, 1950, M8.

58. Daniel quoted in "Cooperative Homes Face New Fight in Senate," R1.

59. Ibid.

60. Ibid., R2.

61. Pearson quoted in "This Week in D.C. Real Estate," *Washington Post*, February 19, 1950, R6. See also National Association of Home Builders of the United States, "Washington Letter," no. 351, July 13, 1949, Bauer Papers, Box 14.

62. Mary Spargo, "Reserve Board Cool to Housing Bill Clauses," *Washington Post*, February 17, 1950, 4. See also Mary Spargo, "Reserve Board View on Housing Bill Due," *Washington Post*, February 16, 1950, 6.

63. *Report from the Committee on Banking and Currency to Accompany the Amendment in the Nature of a Substitute for S. 2246*, 85.

64. Spargo, "Reserve Board Cool to Housing Bill Clauses," 4.

65. McCabe quoted in Spargo, "Reserve Board Cool to Housing Bill Clauses," 4.

66. *Report from the Committee on Banking and Currency to Accompany the Amendment in the Nature of a Substitute for S. 2246*, 47.

67. Ibid., 48–49.

68. Ibid., 68–77. It was initially proposed that the National Mortgage Corporation for Housing Cooperatives be authorized to issue up to $2 billion in government-insured obligations to private investors. Cooperatives financed through the corporation were to purchase an amount of stock equal to 7.5 percent of the value of their twenty-year loan. See also Mary Spargo, "Medium-Cost Home Bill Is Introduced," *Washington Post*, January 7, 1950, 3; and "New Housing Bill Offered by Maybank," *Washington Post*, January 12, 1950, 10.

69. *Report from the Committee on Banking and Currency to Accompany the Amendment in the Nature of a Substitute for S. 2246* (statement of Senator William J. Fulbright), 102, 103. The Committee also reduced the amount of funds available to the

FHA for its Title I and Title II home mortgage insurance programs and those available to the VA for direct loans to veterans unable to obtain private financing. Loans were made available to educational institutions for the construction of faculty or student housing, and the RFC was authorized to lend $25 million to prefabricated housing producers. See Mary Spargo, "Senators Cut Housing Funds by 2 Billions," *Washington Post*, February 24, 1950, 1. See also "We've Been Asked: About Aid for Co-op Housing," *U.S. News and World Report*, January 27, 1950, 43–44; "To Meet the Housing Needs of Medium Income," *American City* 65 (February 1950): 84–85; "Dixie GOPs Delay Action on Co-op Housing," *CIO News*, February 13, 1950, 12; "Co-op Coup," *Business Week*, March 4, 1950, 24; and "Real Estaters Buck, but Housing Bill Is Cleared for Floor Action," *CIO News*, March 13, 1950, 7.

70. John Edelman closely tracked the bill. See John Edelman to All Textile Workers Union of America Officers, Representatives, Local Unions, Joint Boards and Legislative Committees, memorandum #40, August 2, 1949, The John Edelman Collection, Walter P. Reuther Library, Wayne State University, Detroit (hereafter Edelman Papers), Box 34; see also memorandum #6, February 2, 1950, memorandum #11, March 17, 1950, and memorandum #12, April 13, 1950, Edelman Papers, Box 34.

71. "Middle-Income Housing Bill Pressure Urged," *Washington Post*, March 12, 1950, M1.

72. Whitlock quoted in "Cooperative Housing Bill Called Unfair," *Washington Post*, March 12, 1950, R2.

73. Mary Spargo, "Lower-Priced Homes Here, FHA Reports," *Washington Post*, March 14, 1950, 5. On February 21, 1950, the House Banking and Currency Committee voted eleven to four in favor of approving the Spence middle-income housing bill with Title III intact. See "Builders See Huge Risk in Middle-Income Housing Cooperative," *Christian Science Monitor*, February 24, 1950, 13.

74. Mary Spargo, "House Group Backs Co-op Housing Bill," *Washington Post*, February 22, 1950, 8.

75. Ysabel Rennie and Robert Rennie, "Piecemeal-Plan Danger Shown in Housing Bill," *Washington Post*, March 15, 1950, 9.

76. "Co-op Housing Bill," *Washington Post*, March 15, 1950, 12. See also "FHA Insures Cooperative's $367,000 Loan," *Washington Post*, April 2, 1950, R7.

77. Lloyd kept careful account of who voted for and against the measure on behalf of the president. See David Lloyd to Charles R. Murphy, interoffice memorandum, March 16, 1950, Lloyd Files, Box 2.

78. "Senate Defeats Middle Income Housing Funds," *Washington Post*, March 16, 1950, 1.

79. "Today's Greater Washington Radio Programs," *Washington Post*, March 18, 1950, B11.

80. David Lloyd to Charles R. Murphy, interoffice memorandum, March 17, 1950, Lloyd Files, Box 2.

81. Truman quoted in "Housing Bill Killed in House; Truman Suffers Heavy Setback," *Los Angeles Times*, March 23, 1950, 6.

82. Truman quoted in Rockwell Clark, "Real Estate Lobby Hands People Another Licking," *CIO News*, March 27, 1950, 8.

83. Wolcott and Patman quoted in Mary Spargo, "Co-op Housing Faces House Battle Today," *Washington Post*, March 21, 1950, 16.

84. Clark, "Real Estate Lobby Hands People Another Licking," 8. See also Mary Spargo, "Plan to Aid Those in Middle Income Group Stricken Out by Vote of 218 to 155,"

*Washington Post*, March 23, 1950, 1; and "Aid Refused to Co-op Housing," *Commonweal* 51 (April 1950): 670.

85. "Co-op Plan Killed by House in Voting for 'Middle' Homes," *New York Times*, March 23, 1950, 1.

86. "Housing Bill Killed in House," 1. See also "Congress Defeats Co-op Plan," *Architectural Record* 107 (May 1950): 23–24; and C. P. Trussell, "Housing Bill Sent to Truman Shorn of Cooperative Aid," *New York Times*, April 11, 1950, 1.

87. "National Association of Housing Cooperatives Formed," *Journal of Housing* 7, no. 5 (1950): 249.

88. "Sen. Sparkman Renews Appeal for Middle-Income Housing Aid," *Washington Post*, June 13, 1950, B3. See also Howard Haygood to Senator John Sparkman, March 14, 1950, Papers of John Sparkman, Stanley Hoole Special Collections Library, University of Alabama, Tuscaloosa (hereafter Sparkman Papers), Box 137, FF 54; Ed W. Hile to John E. Horne, March 18, 1950, Sparkman Papers, Box 139, FF 54; John Sparkman to Leonel Weil, March 29, 1950, Sparkman Papers, Box 139, FF 54; and Robert C. Albright, "Fair Deal a Dim Memory as 'War Congress' Wanes," *Washington Post*, September 3, 1950, B1.

89. McKinney quoted in "Democrats Name Liaison Man with Party Members on the Hill," *Washington Post*, January 7, 1952, 1.

90. Westbrook quoted in "Demo Committeeman Loses Job in 5 Per Cent Probe," *Atlanta Daily World*, October 31, 1952, 1.

91. "Moral Vacuum," *Washington Post*, October 31, 1952, 24. See also "Probe Open in Westbrook Contract Deal," *Washington Post*, October 31, 1952, 1; "Demo Committeeman Loses Job in 5 Per Cent Probe," 1; "Portuguese Firm Official Calls Tungsten Dealings Legal," *Washington Post*, November 1, 1952, 4; "Westbrook, Ousted Democrat, Denies '5-Percenter' Charge," *Washington Post*, November 7, 1952, 27; and Hyman J. Cohen, "Five Percenters," letter to the editor, *Washington Post*, November 11, 1952, 12; "Fired Party Employee Praised by Mitchell for His Integrity," *Washington Post*, February 2, 1953, 1; and "Westbrook Cleared in Tungsten Deal That Raised Furor in 1952 Campaign," *Washington Post*, January 21, 1960, A24.

92. Bureau of Labor Statistics, *Cooperative Housing*, 64.

93. Wayne Phillips, "Title I Slum Clearance Proves Spur to Cooperative Housing in City," *New York Times*, July 2, 1959, 13; and Andrew S. Dolkart, *Morningside Heights: A History of Its Architecture and Development* (New York: Columbia University Press, 1998). On urban renewal in New York City and cooperatives, see Joel Schwartz, *The New York Approach: Robert Moses, Urban Liberals, and the Redevelopment of the Inner City* (Columbus: Ohio State University Press, 1993), 133–138; and Anthony Jackson, *A Place Called Home: A History of Low-Cost Housing in Manhattan* (Cambridge, MA: MIT Press, 1976).

94. Bureau of Labor Statistics, *Cooperative Housing*, 81.

95. Ibid., 65, 81.

96. Public Housing Administration, Mortgage Serving Branch, "Mortgages and Sales Contracts as of 3/31/53," AVMHA Historical Collection, 1; and Bellmawr Park Mutual Housing Corporation, untitled typescript, [1952], 3. Mayor Joseph Clark Jr. claimed the project was not a safety hazard and approved its exemption from city building and occupancy codes. See "Statement on Behalf of Pennypack Woods Home Ownership Association" and "Statement of Joseph S. Clark, Jr. Mayor," Pennypack Mutual Housing Corporation Historical File, Philadelphia.

97. Bureau of Labor Statistics, *Cooperative Housing*, 35, 37.

98. Housing and Home Finance Agency, *Ninth Annual Report*, pt. 3 (Washington, DC: Government Printing Office, 1955), 321; Housing and Home Finance Agency,

*Tenth Annual Report* (Washington, DC: Government Printing Office, 1956), 190; "Developments among Cooperatives in 1949," *Monthly Labor Review* 70 (March 1950): 286; and Florence E. Parker, "Cooperative Housing in the United States, Mid-1950," *Monthly Labor Review* 73 (September 1951): 261.

99. Bureau of Labor Statistics, "Cooperation in Ownership and Management—The 'Mutual' Projects," *Non-profit Housing Projects in the United States*, Bulletin 896 (Washington, DC: Government Printing Office, 1947), 32–39.

100. The mortgage was paid off in 1980. Ellen Pulver, "Temporary Houses, Lasting Homes," *Philadelphia Inquirer*, May 21, 1989, 4-DC.

101. George Damon quoted in Pulver, "Temporary Houses," 4-DC.

102. Ibid.

103. Bennett Karmin, "Housing Co-op Value Has Tripled," *Bridgeport Sunday Herald*, March 24, 1957, 17.

104. David J. Foster, "In the Northeast, F.D.R.'s New Deal Housing Project," *Northeast News Gleaner*, August 16, 1995, 7, 14.

105. "Agency Asks Haste in Success Park Quiz," *Bridgeport Herald*, August 14, 1955, 67, available at http://news.google.com/newspapers?nid=2475&dat=19550814&id=af4yAAAAIBAJ&sjid, accessed August 6, 2014; Karmin, "Housing Co-op Value," 17; and "Success Village Saga: A Story of Courage," *Bridgeport Herald*, November 6, 1960, 128, available at http://news.google.com/newspapers?nid=2229&dat=19601106&id=EJAyAAAAIBAJ&sjid, accessed August 6, 2014.

106. Eric Follo, "Kramer Homes: A Community Not a Complex," *Michigan History Magazine* 97, no. 3 (2013): 58.

107. Florence Kysor, "Operation Democracy," *American Home* 54 (October 1955): 52.

108. Pennypack Woods Home Ownership Association, "History and Background of MHO," Pennypack Woods Home Ownership Corporation Historical File, Philadelphia; and Foster, "In the Northeast," 7.

109. Mrs. Joseph H. Moore Jr. to Michael J. Galvin, June 25, 1952, National Archives and Records Administration, College Park, MD, RG 207, Box 483A; Pennypack Woods Civic Association to the Residents of Pennypack Woods, June 4, 1952; and Pennypack Woods Home Ownership Association, "History and Background of MHO," 4.

110. George Damon quoted in Pulver, "Temporary Houses," 4-DC.

111. James A. Maxwell, "Now That They're Landlords," *Saturday Evening Post*, August 13, 1960, 22–23. Among the temporary projects the PHA refused to sell under the Mutual Plan was Shanks Village, home to 350 veterans and their families. The deal soured because the residents did not want to purchase the entire 700-acre parcel in Rockland County, New York. See "U.S. Will Sell Shanks Village," *New York Times*, June 11, 1955, 15.

112. "Judge Recesses Housing Project Receivership Suit," *Dallas Morning News*, May 30, 1954, available at http://infoweb.newsbank.com/gbnl/newspaperes.doc/v2%/3A0F99DDB671832188%40GBL, accessed September 29, 2009; and Housing and Home Finance Agency, *Eighth Annual Report*, pt. 5 (Washington, DC: Government Printing Office, 1954), 373.

113. Louise Boggs quoted in "Aluminum City Terrace—In Successful Community," *Valley Daily News*, May 24, 1957, Aluminum City Terrace Housing Association Clipping File, New Kensington, PA.

114. "U.S. Completes Sale of Housing It Built for Wartime Emergency," *New York Times*, July 6, 1958, R1.

115. "It's Official! WWII Housing Program Ended June 30," *Journal of Housing* 15, no. 7 (1958): 222.

116. "Text of Report on Housing Endorsed by Kennedy," *New York Times*, October 20, 1960, 26.

117. Ibid. On Catherine Bauer, see "The Dreary Deadlock of Public Housing," *Architectural Forum* 106 (May 1957): 219.

118. Lawrence Westbrook to John F. Kennedy, November 25, 1960, 4, Lawrence Westbrook Papers, The Texas Collection, Carroll Library, Baylor University, Waco, TX, 2E444, FF 43.

119. Ibid.

120. Ibid.

121. "U.S. Loans Urged for Coop Housing," *Washington Post*, April 9, 1960, C19.

122. Peter Braestrup, "President Urges Vast Housing Aid to Combat Slump," *New York Times*, March 10, 1961, 1; and "Kennedy Proposes Housing Plan," *Christian Science Monitor*, March 10, 1961, 3.

123. "Remarks upon Signing Housing Act," June 30, 1961, available at http://www.presidency.ucsb.edu/ws/?pid=8216, accessed January 21, 2015.

124. David Clurman and Edna Hebard, *Condominiums and Cooperatives* (New York: Wiley-Interscience, 1970), 199–203. See also Matthew G. Lasner, *High Life: Condo Living in the Suburban Century* (New Haven, CT: Yale University Press, 2012).

125. "Lawrence Westbrook, 74, Dies; Roosevelt Administration Aide," *New York Times*, January 26, 1964, 81.

126. Leo Grebler, *Large Scale Housing and Real Estate Firms: Analysis of a New Business Enterprise*, UCLA Housing, Real Estate and Urban Land Studies Series (Los Angeles: Praeger Special Studies in U.S. Economic, Social and Political Issues, 1973), 33. See also Marian Dozier, "New Horizon Village Marks 15 Years," *Kalamazoo Gazette*, October 9, 1987, Kalamazoo Public Library Operation Breakthrough Vertical File, Kalamazoo, MI.

## EPILOGUE

1. Ruth Rejnis, "Old Barracks as Co-ops," *New York Times*, October 3, 1976, Winfield Park Mutual Housing Association Historical File, Winfield Park Mutual Housing Corporation, Winfield, NJ.

2. Bennett Karmin, "Housing Co-op Value Has Tripled," *Bridgeport Sunday Herald*, March 24, 1957, 17.

3. Zane L. Miller, *Suburb: Neighborhood and Community in Forest Park, Ohio, 1935–1976* (Knoxville: University of Tennessee Press, 1981), 227–241.

4. Oliveri quoted in Brian Louwers, "History Lives at Kramer Homes," June 25, 2014, available at http://www.candgnews.com/news/history-lives-kramer-homes, accessed July 21, 2014.

5. Joel A. Tarr, ed., *Devastation and Renewal: An Environmental History of Pittsburgh and Its Region* (Pittsburgh: University of Pittsburgh Press, 2003).

6. On the construction of defense housing outside of Pittsburgh, see Allegheny County Housing Authority, *Victory on the Homes Front; A Blueprint and Guide* (Pittsburgh: Allegheny County Housing Authority, 1945), unpaged.

7. Woodstock Homes in Alameda, California, also allows market sale of shares. For a realtor's perspective, see "Co-ops in Alameda? Yes!" *Marilyn Schumacher's The Second*

*Story!* available at http://www.marilynschumacher.com/2013/10/co-ops-in-alameda-yes.html, accessed October 17, 2013.

8. Bridgeport is the only city where there is mutually or cooperatively owned housing from both world wars. On Bridgeport Garden Apartments, see *Blackrockonline*, available at http:// blackrockonline.org/content/living-bridgeport-garden-apartments-black-rock, accessed July 25, 2014.

9. Author telephone interview, July 15, 2014.

10. Walnut Grove Mutual Housing Association, "About," available at http://walnutgrovemha.org/?page_id8, accessed July 20, 2014.

11. Bureau of Economic Research, Rutgers University, *An Economic Profile of Winfield Park, New Jersey; Including Alternatives for the Uses of Community Resources* (New Brunswick, NJ: Rutgers University, Bureau of Economic Research, 1965), 10-1.

12. Karmin, "Housing Co-op Value," 17.

13. James A. Maxwell, "Now That They're Landlords," *Saturday Evening Post*, August 13, 1960, 22–23.

14. "Pennypack, Where the Living Is Easy," undated clipping, Pennypack Woods Home Ownership Corporation Clipping File, Philadelphia.

15. Mock, Thompson, and Moucheron quoted in Meta McMillian, "Electric Heights: Making a Co-op Work," *Pittsburgh Press*, August 12, 1982, 45, available at http://www.news.google.com/newspapers/nid=1144&dat=19820812&id=E44cAAAAIBAJ&sjid=s14EAAAAIBAJ&pg=6608,6191635, accessed July 25, 2014.

16. Neil MacFarquhar, "Fire Burns Down School and Wakes Quiet Town," *New York Times*, April 5, 1995, available at http://www.nytimes.com/1995/04/05/nyregion/fire, accessed July 21, 2014.

17. Author interview with Alan Hartwick, August 23, 1997; and author interview with Steve Tyler, August 23, 1997.

18. Author interview with Ralph and Tommie McSpadden, July 7, 1994. The McSpaddens, like most residents, were unaware that Avion Village was one of eight model communities.

19. Purpura and Kennedy quoted in Mary Niederberger, "Aluminum City Lives On," *Pittsburgh Press* (Alle-Kiski Edition), May 15, 1983, A1.

20. McCreery quoted in Cece Lentini, "A Unique Method of 'Owning' Their Homes," *Philadelphia Inquirer*, March 22, 1998, R2. A similar observation was made about Pennypack Woods during the 1980s. See Lisa Ellis, "An Urban Village Built on Cooperation," *Philadelphia Inquirer*, September 17, 1987, 2NE.

21. Damon quoted in Ellen Pulver, "Temporary Houses, Lasting Homes," *Philadelphia Inquirer*, May 21, 1989, 5-DC.

22. "Chassobolak," *New Kensington—Other Opinions Please* (blog), May 14, 2007, available at http://www.city-data.com/forum/pennsylvania/69580-new-kensington-other-opinons-please, accessed July 21, 2014.

23. "Success Park Reflects Pride of Ownership," *Bridgeport Sunday Herald*, November 13, 1960, available at http://news.google.com/newspapers?nid=2229&dat19601113&id=EZAyAAAAIBAJ&sji, accessed July 31, 2014.

24. Headman quoted in Ellis, "Urban Village."

25. Barth quoted in Ellis, "Urban Village"; and Greig quoted in Rejnis, "Old Barracks as Co-ops."

26. "Bowling" quoted in "Greenmont as Garden Suburb," *Daytonology*, March 13, 2008, available at http://daytonology.blogspot.com/soo8/03/greenmont-as-garden-suburb.html, accessed July 22, 2014.

27. Isabel Bayley, "New Kensington Saga," *Task* 5 (1945): 30.

28. Author interview with Ben Fisher, December 8, 1986. One observer noted that the monthly fee to live at Aluminum City Terrace was lower than the cost of purchasing one of Breuer's famous chairs. See "Aluminum City Terrace," available at htpp://pittsburghplaces.org/accounts/view/Aluminum_City_Terrace, accessed July 21, 2014.

29. Resident quoted in "Aluminum City Terrace Housing," *Architectural Forum* 78 (April 1944): 76.

30. Department of Labor, Bureau of Labor Statistics, *Cooperative Housing in the United States, 1949 and 1950*, Bulletin 1093, Housing and Home Finance Agency, Housing Research Paper 24 (Washington, DC: Government Printing Office, 1952) (hereafter Bureau of Labor Statistics), 61.

31. "Avion Village, Taxpaying Mutual Cooperative One of Biggest Model Home Projects," n.d., Romie Stewart Clipping File, Avion Village, Grand Prairie, TX.

32. Stasulli quoted in Lentini, "A Unique Method of 'Owning' Their Homes."

33. Resident quoted in "Greenmont as Garden City," *Daytonology*, January 16, 2009.

34. "Mustangford," *Discuss Detroit: Centerline Kramer Homes* (blog), October 8, 2008, available at http://www.atdetroit.net/forum/messages/1481145/158229.html?1223866370, accessed July 21, 2014.

35. "Tenant Group Leases Ohio Project," *Reading Eagle*, October 12, 1943, 2, available at www.news.google.com/newspapers?nid=1955&dat=19431012&id, accessed July 21, 2014.

36. Meta McMillian, "Electric Heights: Making a Co-op Work," *Pittsburgh Press*, August 12, 1982, 45, available at http://www.news.google.com/newspapers?nid=, accessed July 21, 2014.

37. "Form Non-profit Housing Council in Delaware Valley," *Cooperative Housing* 3 (1965): 22; and "What State and Regional Associations Are Doing," *Cooperative Housing* 3 (1966): 10–11, 18.

38. Author telephone interview, July 8, 2014.

39. Author telephone interview, July 8, 2014.

40. Marcy Rein, "Atchison Village: A Cooperative in Richmond Changes with the Times," *Race, Poverty, and the Environment* 15, no. 1 (2008), available at http://reimagainerpe.org/node/1834, accessed July 19, 2014.

41. Author telephone interview, July 18, 2014.

42. Ken Hand, "'Mayor' Kept Busy by Unofficial City," *Dallas Morning News*, November 4, 1948, Romie Stewart Clipping File.

43. Author telephone interview, July 18, 2014.

44. Author telephone interview, July 9, 2014.

45. Author telephone interview, July 18, 2014; author telephone interview, August 9, 2014; and Bureau of Labor Statistics, *Cooperative Housing*, 54.

46. Bureau of Labor Statistics, *Cooperative Housing*, 15, 76.

47. Joseph I. Gradel to the Members of Pennypack Woods Home Ownership Association, October 25, 1950, Pennypack Mutual Housing Corporation Historical File, Philadelphia.

48. Don Parson, "The Decline of Public Housing and the Politics of the Red Scare: The Significance of the Los Angeles Public Housing War," *Journal of Urban History* 33, no. 3 (2007): 411–412. The original reads "localized but personalized" (p. 412).

49. Trinity Moses, "Dayton's Socialist Suburb," *Cyburbia*, May 7, 2005, 2, available at http://www.cyburbia.org/forums/showthread.php?t=17511, accessed July 21, 2014; and http://www.archive.org/stream/../investigationofc0104unit_djvu.txt, accessed July 21, 2014.

50. “Kim” quoted in *Baltimore City’s Past Present and Future* (blog), April 16, 2010, available at http://baltimorefutureblogspot.com/2008/07/could-armistead-gardens-experience-be.html, accessed July 25, 2014.

51. [Dorothy W. Partch], “History of Audubon Park,” typescript, [1964], 4, Camden County Historical Society Audubon Park Vertical File.

52. Louis R. Carlozo, “Town Is White Inside and Out,” *Philly.com*, March 10, 1991, available at http://articles.philly.com/1991-03-10/news/25791884_1_audubon-park-housing-municipal, accessed July 21, 2014.

53. Daniels and Rogers quoted in Carlozo, “Town Is White Inside and Out.” In 2010, Audubon Park was 97 percent white. See *Wikipedia.org*, http://en.wikipedia.org/wiki/Audubon_Park,_New_Jersey, accessed July 21, 2010.

54. According to Morris Milgram, the developer who built and became a resident of the adjoining Greenbelt Knoll, an integrated community of modernist detached dwellings, the “average black is frightened to be ‘the pioneer’ in a lily-white community.” Milgram quoted in Julie Liedman, “Pennypack Woods: ‘A Last Stronghold,’” *Evening Bulletin* (Philadelphia), n.d., Pennypack Woods Home Ownership Corporation Historical file, Philadelphia.

55. “Hearing Set on Housing Charge,” *Beaver County Times*, April 23, 1973, available at http://www.news.google.com/newspaper/nid=2002&dat=19730423&id, accessed August 11, 2014.

56. “Edict Is Handed to Housing Body,” *Beaver County Times*, November 19, 1973, available at http://www.news.google.com/newspaper/nid=2002&dat=19731119&id, accessed August 7, 2014; and Jane C. Musala, “Complaints Target Van Buren Homes,” *Beaver County Times*, April 1, 2001, available at http://www.news.google.com/newspaper/nid=2000&dat&-20010401&id, accessed August 7, 2014.

57. See, for example, John Wesley Alexander’s obituary in the *Allegheny Times*, February 14, 2001, available at http://news.google.com/newspapers?nid=2004&dat=20010214&id, accessed August 10, 2014.

58. Jonathan E. Zimmer, *From Rental to Cooperative: Improving Low and Moderate Income Housing*, Administrative and Policy Series 03-038 (Beverly Hills, CA: Sage, 1977), 27.

59. Author interview with Rufus Simpson, 1986, in Kristin Szylvian Bailey, “The Federal Government and the Cooperative Housing Movement, 1917–1950” (Ph.D. diss., Carnegie Mellon University, 1988), 131–134.

60. “Housing Unit Must Give Blacks Homes,” *Washington African-American*, November 22, 1977, 9, available at http://news.google.com/newspapers?nid=2238&dat=1971122&id=Q5glAAAIBA&sid, accessed July 21, 2014.

61. “Success Village Saga: A Story of Courage,” *Bridgeport Herald*, November 6, 1960, 18, available at http://news.google.com/newspapers?nid=2229&dat=19601106&id=EJAyAAAAIBAJ&sjid, accessed August 6, 2014; and “Success Park Reflects Pride of Ownership,” *Bridgeport Herald*, November 20, 1960, 17, available at http://news.google.com/newspapers?nid=2229&dat=19601113&id=EJAyAAAAIBAJ&sjid, accessed August 6, 2014.

62. Marilyn S. Johnson, “Urban Arsenals: War Housing and Social Change in Richmond and Oakland, California,” *Pacific Historical Review* 60, no. 3 (1991): 283–308.

63. Diaz quoted in Marcy Rein, “Atchison Village.”

64. “T.,” “Greenmont as Garden Suburb,” *Daytonology*, June 24, 2013.

65. Bruce Nelson “Utah” Phillips quoted in Moses, “Dayton’s Socialist Suburb.”

66. "Atchison Village, A Critical Part of Richmond's History," available at http://www.atchisonvillage.org/history_201207201623_0001.pdf, accessed July 18, 2014.

67. Author telephone interview, July 9, 2014.

68. David J. Foster, "In the Northeast, F.D.R.'s New Deal Housing Project," *Northeast News Gleaner*, August 16, 1995, 1.

69. "New Deal in Greenbelt," *Washington Post*, March 31, 1982, MD1.

70. "What the NAHC Convention Wanted Done," *Cooperative Housing* 5 (1967–1968): 3; and Rutgers Bureau of Economic Research, *Economic Profile*, 27, 49.

71. "Hornist9," *Discuss Detroit: Centerline Kramer Homes* (blog), October 12, 2008.

72. Bureau of Labor Statistics, *Cooperative Housing*, 79; and McConnaughey quoted in "Waiting List Staggering for Housing in Greenmont," *Nashua Telegraph*, February 20, 1975, 11, available at www.news.gooogle.com/newspapers?nid=2209, accessed July 21, 2014.

73. Pierre quoted in MacFarquhar, "Fire Burns Down School and Wakes Quiet Town."

74. Cullen quoted in Carlozo, "Town Is White Inside and Out."

75. "Greenmont Village Has Storied Past," *Dayton Daily News*, September 25, 2008, available at http://www.highbeam.com/doc/1P2-19120878.html, accessed July 22, 2014.

76. Author telephone interview, July 11, 2014.

77. Author telephone interview, July 18, 2014.

78. John Walker quoted in Ben Steelman, "What Is the History of the Housing Developments Surrounding Greenfield Lake" (blog), February 28, 2010, available at http://myreporter.com/2010/02/what-is-the-history, accessed July 20, 2014.

79. Winfield Cultural Heritage Commission, *History of Winfield* (Winfield Township, NJ: Winfield Cultural Heritage Commission, 1976). On the parade, see "Winfield Township, New Jersey," *Wikipedia.org*, available at http://en.wikipedia.org/wiki/Winfield_Township_New_Jersey, accessed July 21, 2014.

80. Edward G. Goetz, "The Transformation of Public Housing Policy," *Journal of the American Planning Association* 78, no. 4 (2012): 452–463; and Dawn Jourdan, "The Long View: Preserving Public Housing," *Journal of the American Planning Association* 78, no. 4 (2012): 482. On Techwood Homes, see "Atlanta Is Making Way for New Public Housing," *New York Times*, June 21, 2009, A16.

81. City of Greenbelt, Maryland, *Greenbelt Citylink*, available at http://www.greenbeltmd.gov/index.aspx?NID=333, accessed July 22, 2014; and http://greenbeltmuseum.org/history, accessed July 22, 2014.

82. The Historic American Engineering Record, "Aluminum City Terrace, East Hill Drive, New Kensington, Westmoreland County, PA" (HAER PA-302), erroneously identifies Aluminum City Terrace as the "first defense housing development sold under the federal government's Mutual Home Ownership Plan." It was the first Lanham project to be sold under the Mutual Plan with an FHA-insured mortgage. See HAER PA-302, available at http://www.lcweb2.loc.gov/pnp/habshaer/pa/pa2900/pa2949/data/pa2949data.pdf, accessed July 19, 2014. According to HAER PA-303, on Munhall Homesteads, the FHA granted mortgages to mutual housing associations; the agency insured mortgages made to mutual associations after 1948. See HAER PA-303, available at http://www.lcweb2.loc.gov/pnp/habshaer/pa/pa2900/data2950data.pdf, accessed July 21, 2014. On opposition to the project, see "War Changes Munhall View on Housing," *Pittsburgh Post-Gazette*, December 24, 1941, 11, available at http://news.google.com/newspapers?nid=1129&dat19411224&id=opRRAAAAIBAJ&sji, accessed July 31, 2014.

83. Ohio Historic Preservation Office, "Ohio Historic Inventory," MOT-05641-06, available at https://www.dot.state..oh.us/../Step, accessed July 19, 2014.

84. Author interview with Pat Levis and Barbara Schade, July 8, 2014. See also "I-295 Direct Connection Construction Report," available at http://njdirectconnection.com/contracts.html, accessed July 21, 2014.

85. "Wartime Housing: Atchison Village," *Rosie the Riveter Trust*, available at http://www.rosietheriveter.org/visit-discover/park-sites/item/51-wartime-housing-atchison-village, accessed July 24, 2014. The board of directors has discussed the possibility of restoring a dwelling unit to its original condition, furnishing it with period furniture and household items, and making it available for visitation or even a brief stay. No action has yet been taken on this proposal. Author telephone interview, July 12, 2014.

86. Marie Kochaver, "Mary Whitworth—Charter Member," *Atchison Riveter*, July 2012, available at http://www.atchisonvillage.org, accessed July 18, 2014.

87. Marie Kochaver, "History Corner," *Atchison Riveter*, August 2013, available at http://www.atchisonvillage.org, accessed July 18, 2014; and Marie Kochaver, "Missing!" *Atchison Riveter*, July 2014, available at http://www.atchisonvillage.org, accessed July 18, 2014.

88. Joseph Heathcott, "Curating the City: Challenges for Historic Preservation in the Twenty-First Century," *Journal of Planning History* 5, no. 1 (2006): 82–83.

89. Ned Kaufman, "Moving Forward: Futures for a Preservation Movement," in *Giving Preservation a History: Histories of Historic Preservation in the United States*, ed. Max Page and Randall Mason (New York: Routledge, 2004), 315.

90. During the past few years, bloggers writing about Baltimore's Armistead Gardens have offered the harshest assessments of any given to the mutual communities. Crime, drugs, and the "generational cycle of poverty and high school dropouts" were among the community characteristics that made one anonymous blogger write, "proud I ESCAPED!" Another indicated that living at Armistead Gardens was "very stressful and most of my childhood friends died of overdoses." See anonymous blogs on *baltimorefuture.blogspot*, available at http://baltimorefutureblogspot.com/2008/07/could-armistead-gardens-experience-be.html, accessed July 25, 2014.

91. Samuel Urick III, *221 Linmar Homes: Where My Love for the Elderly Began* (blog), December 8, 2013, http://doctorsamurick.com/2013/12/08/221-linmar-home-where-my-love-for-the-elderly-began-html, accessed July 24, 2014.

92. Editorial Staff, *The Story of Greenmont Village* (Greenmont Village, OH: Greenmont Mutual Housing Corporation, 1948), 2.

93. Girardi quoted in Niederberger, "Aluminum City Lives On."

94. Damon quoted in Pulver, "Temporary Houses."

95. Manuel quoted in Pulver, "Temporary Houses."

96. Chambers quoted in Tom Infield, "Influx of War Industry Workers Stretched City's Housing to the Limit," *Philadelphia Inquirer*, [1992], B4, Pennypack Woods Mutual Housing Corporation Historical File, Philadelphia.

97. "Jeffrey," "World War II Emergency Housing: Dayton/Fairborn," *DaytonOS*, November 11, 2008, available at http://daytonology.blogspot.com/2008/11/world-war-ii-housing-daytonfairborn.html, accessed July 21, 2014.

98. Mara Lee, "Greenmont Residents to Vote on Roof Pitch," *Dayton Daily News*, September 21, 2004, available at http://www.highbeam.com/doc/1P2-11927141.html/print, accessed July 21, 2014; and Bureau of Labor Statistics, *Cooperative Housing*, 81.

99. Brian Louwers, "History Lives at Kramer Homes," June 25, 2014, http://www.cangnes.com/news/history/-lives-kramer-homes, accessed July 21, 2014.

100. Author telephone interview, July 6, 2014.

101. Cullen quoted in Carlozo, "Town Is White Inside and Out."

102. "Pennypack, Where the Living Is Easy."

103. "Blueidone," *Discuss Detroit: Centerline Kramer Homes* (blog), October 12, 2008, available at http://www.atdetroit.net/forum/messages/1481145/158229.html?1223866370, accessed July 21, 2014.

104. Spence Lean, "Could the Armistead Gardens Experience Be Applied Today?" *Baltimore City's Past Present and Future* (blog), July 2008, available at http://baltimorefutureblogspot.com/2008/07/could-armistead-gardens-experience-be.html, accessed July 25, 2014.

# Index

**Kristin M. Szylvian** is Associate Professor of History and Library and Information Science at St. John's University in New York City.